WORKERS' COMPENSATION
AND WORK-RELATED
ILLNESSES AND DISEASES

WORKERS' COMPENSATION AND WORK-RELATED ILLNESSES AND DISEASES

Peter S. Barth
with
H. Allan Hunt

The MIT Press
Cambridge, Massachusetts, and London, England

First MIT Press paperback edition, September 1982
© 1980 by
The Massachusetts Institute of Technology

This book was set in IBM Composer Univers by To the Lighthouse Press and printed and bound by The Murray Printing Company, Inc., in the United States of America.

Library of Congress Cataloging in Publication Data

Barth, Peter S   1937–
  Workers' compensation and work-related illnesses and diseases.

  Includes bibliographical references and index.
  1. Occupational diseases.   2. Workmen's compensation.   I. Hunt, H. Allan, joint author.
II. Title.
RC964.B38   616.9'803   79–27254
ISBN   0-262-02141-2 (hard)
         0-262-52080-X (paper)

CONTENTS

PREFACE

Much of this work was initially prepared for the Interdepartmental Workers' Compensation Task Force, a federal interagency group created by President Nixon in 1974. In several respects, however, this book differs significantly from that earlier effort. In part, I hope that the present effort has benefited from the comments received on that report. Additionally, chapter 6 was written subsequent to that report and chapter 7 has also been very substantially altered.

Much of any credit that may attach to this book comes from others who helped at various stages of its development. The Task Force was consistently splendid in its support of this effort. The National Council on Compensation Insurance was especially generous in developing data for us. Ben Novicoff of Nebraska, Henry Howe of the American Medical Association, Thomas F. Mancuso of the University of Pittsburgh, John Noble of the Department of Health, Education, and Welfare, and Ronald Conley of the Task Force made significant comments on a previous draft. Extremely helpful comments were made by Nicholas Ashford of the Massachusetts Institute of Technology.

Special mention must be given to Muriel Scotta, who typed virtually the entire manuscript in each draft. She did so with skill and zest despite working under less than perfect circumstances for many nights and many weekends. Sheila Scepanski also provided her excellent typing skills. And the book would simply not have been written without the special care and handling it received from Nancy J. Barth. Along with the substantial moral support she provided, she edited and proofread each draft, usually facing the inhumane deadlines I imposed.

Chapter 6 could not have been prepared without the support provided by the German Marshall Fund of the United States. The fund's assistance allowed me to see how other systems cope with problems similar to those encountered in the United States. Many of the recommendations that appear in chapter 7 would have looked very different had I not had the benefit of visiting seven European countries and Ontario. So many persons there went to great lengths to edify me on how others deal with occupational disease that I could not begin to thank them by name. My debt, however, to them and to the German Marshall Fund is great.

All chapters but chapter 6 were prepared collaboratively with my colleague Allan Hunt. The primary responsibility for the latter half of chapter 5 was his, while mine covered the first half and all other chapters. The views expressed are solely our own and should not be construed to be those of any other person or organization.

I would like to use an author's license to make a dual dedication of this book. Looking toward the past, it is dedicated in the memory of my father, Lazarus Barth. His death robbed me of the opportunity to share the excitement of this subject with him and to benefit from his wisdom. Turning to the future, it seems unrealistic to suppose that workers' compensation will eventually become an anachronism because of the elimination of occupational sicknesses. As such, this entire effort has been inspired by the view that this form of social insurance — or one that may eventually replace it — can operate so as to deal fairly with those unfortunate enough to need it. There is no reason why this cannot be.

Peter S. Barth

WORKERS' COMPENSATION AND WORK-RELATED ILLNESSES AND DISEASES

1 INTRODUCTION

This book deals with occupational diseases and the compensation of workers who are disabled by them. In a very real sense the effort must involve the merger of two vastly disparate areas. On the one side is a burgeoning literature in the field of occupational health, developed by physicians, epidemiologists, public health specialists, hygienists, and others. In large part, though not exclusively, their purposes are to reduce the incidence of such disease, increase the likelihood of speedy and correct diagnoses, and improve the treatment of persons with such diseases. On the other side exists a small but growing body of knowledge regarding workers' compensation systems. Individuals who have contributed to this field are typically drawn from the fields of law, public administration, insurance, and economics. It is our purpose to provide bridges between those bodies of knowledge, thus permitting a better understanding of how workers' compensation deals with the problems of persons with occupational diseases.

In recent years the media have become interested in occupational disease cases. Consequently, outside of the technical literature, there is an almost inevitable tendency to discuss the issues in nonanalytical terms. The absence of good data reinforces this tendency and causes the field to be described primarily in terms of ad hoc examples or parables. Aside from the sensationalistic approach, a few have begun their examination of issues in the field with predetermined conceptions based on their professional affiliations. As a consequence their research has frequently generated more rancor than wisdom. Some strong views regarding this field have developed while preparing this book, most of which are found in the final chapter.

This work synthesizes much of what is known about occupational diseases and workers' compensation, but no attempt has been made to summarize the work done in the field of occupational health or in the area of workers' compensation. Instead, the intersection of these areas has been analyzed, but even in this more limited range the focus has been restricted. For example, the experience under the Coal Mine Health and Safety Act of 1969 has been excluded for two reasons. First, although the law is quite new, it has been changing substantially since first enacted. Second, it appeared that the subject was so large and complex that to cover it adequately here would swamp the remainder of this book. Another significant topic that is omitted is the way that federal employees are compensated for illnesses, which deserves considerable attention and, therefore, is not mentioned here.

The material in chapter 2 primarily examines the extent of the occupational disease problem and the medical and scientific issues that are particularly pertinent to workers' compensation. In chapter 3 particular attention is given to the problems of etiology since it is a central issue for a system that compensates persons whose disease is due to their work. Some problems of diagnosing occupational disease are also discussed in chapter 3. Chapter 4 contains a brief description of the legal and administrative milieu that provides the medical and income replacement remedies for workers disabled by disease. Chapter 5 presents some quantitative evidence, and chapter 6 describes workers' compensation for occupational disease in eight foreign jurisdictions. Chapter 7 contains a limited summary of our findings that bear directly on the recommendations concluding the report.

The Background of the Present Systems

The first country to protect workers from the consequences of occupational disease was Switzerland. In 1877 the Swiss Federal Council prepared a list of forty-five substances which, if used in industry, could cause specified occupational diseases. Germany in 1883 and Austria in 1897 compensated workers for work-related diseases, but the British workers' compensation statute of 1897 took no account of them. Less than a decade later, the British act was amended after the courts had demonstrated that the earlier law gave no coverage to workers with disease.

That the British quickly amended their law of 1897 to cover occupational disease might suggest that the American states, many of which shortly thereafter passed their own compensation laws, would specifically incorporate provisions for diseases. The states, however, excluded any mention of diseases in their earliest statutes; but there is evidence that the issue was not simply overlooked in their haste to pass these first laws. The Wainright Commission, which resulted from pressures to pass a workers' compensation statute in New York, reported that occupational disease probably fell outside its purview and that it would report later on the subject.[1] However, later reports made no mention of the issue.

Kelley argues that some of the drafters of the early statutes attempted to use language that would not alarm legislators but would allow the courts to extend the law's protection to persons with occupational disease.[2] Massachusetts was the first state to give compensation for occupational disease when the courts did expand the workers' compensation law in this way. In 1917 California incorporated specific provisions for disease in its statute. Wisconsin and Connecticut followed shortly thereafter. In 1920 New York amended its law and adopted the first schedule provision that followed the British practice of listing both specific diseases and the process in which an exposure might occur.

By the early part of the 1930s most states had passed workers' compensation laws.

Many of these provided little or no effective coverage of many of the occupational diseases that were being more frequently reported. Trasko describes how a wave of claims for a number of dust-induced diseases, particularly silicosis, occurred at this time due to the economic deprivation caused by the Depression.[3] Perhaps it was the compassion of the public, the efforts of early labor union activists, or understanding legislatures that caused the states to begin to cover these dust diseases under their statutes. But it may have been the threat of even costlier outcomes than those from a workers' compensation program that goaded employers and insurers to work for the inclusion of such diseases under the law. Trasko writes: "One writer estimates, in 1934 that damage suits amounting to over 300 million dollars had originated in that period. Other articles in the early 1930s tell of damage suits for silicosis for as much as 58 million dollars in one state, and against single companies for nine million dollars. Single awards by civil courts of $12,000 — which is the maximum compensation benefit in many states today — were common, and some were as high as $20,000 and $50,000."[4]

As coverage and claims expanded, insurance premiums skyrocketed in certain high-risk sectors. Fear of "insuring a burning house" also led to difficulty in finding carriers willing to underwrite policies for these industries. The majority of states responded by enacting special provisions for handling claims for dust diseases. In most instances these amounted to denying workers with silicosis the same level of benefits available to other disabled employees. Presumably these disparities were to be removed when the bulge of claims for silicosis moderated.

The experience in New York is highly revealing of prevailing conditions at the time.[5] In 1935 Governor Herbert Lehman and the legislature replaced New York's limited coverage law with a provision covering all occupational diseases. Several months after coverage of silicosis and other dust diseases began, the president of the New York State Federation of Labor wrote Governor Lehman urging that coverage for partial disability due to these diseases be dropped from the law. His letter indicated that a distressing situation had been created by the insurance industry which had set prohibitively high premiums and had required many employees to take physical examinations. If any condition appeared to exist in workers who had or would face exposures to dust, their employment opportunities were threatened. Consequently, Lehman reluctantly sent the legislature a bill in 1936 that deleted coverage of partially disabling silicosis or other dust diseases and provided limited benefits for total disability and death from these diseases.

The experience in other states differs somewhat from New York, however, occupational disease was a growing issue elsewhere. In Wisconsin there were 120 claims for disability due to silicosis from 1921 through 1930, but in 1933 and 1934 there were 190 and 321 claims filed for that disease.[6] As in New York State the factors that precipitated the sudden growth of claims were the workers' growing awareness of the disease plus an apparent effort to find some source of income by the unemployed, a number of whom had had the disease for some time but continued to work until economic conditions caused them to be laid off.

In other states in the 1930s coverage was expanded very slowly. Even where employers and workers agreed that such an expansion was desirable, certain trial lawyers were able to delay such changes. Keech persuasively demonstrates that a very small number of persons representing only this single interest group was able to delay expanding occupational disease coverage in North Carolina for several years out of concern for the anticipated reduction of tort actions.[7] Eventually all states provided some coverage for certain types of occupational disease.

The period of the 1930s is a watershed in workers' compensation and the handling of occupational diseases. During that decade many states developed an approach to occupational diseases that either remains largely unchanged or was not structurally altered until the current decade. Many of the apparent anomalies that exist today can be traced to changes and reforms in this earlier decade.

The Development of the Recognition of Occupational Disease as a Health Problem

In 1975 the United States was shocked by a revelation regarding the health conditions in a small Virginia plant manufacturing a pesticide known as Kepone®. The primary concern was the apparent disregard for the factory workers' health evidenced by the absence of precautions against the toxic effects of the chemical. Yet some of the alarm must also have reflected the public's surprise that such a hazardous environment existed at all, particularly since federal health and safety legislation had been enacted five years earlier. Workers exposed to Kepone® experienced loss of memory, tremors, general weakness and fatigue, impotency, and digestive disorders. Despite the absence of fatalities from exposures in this plant, the subject was given substantial attention in the national media, reminiscent of the vinyl chloride furor that had arisen less than two years earlier. In that instance, there appeared to be no general lack of concern about worker health. Rather it was the discovery that three vinyl chloride workers had died of a very rare form of liver cancer, angiosarcoma, that alerted the industry, the union, safety officials, and the public that vinyl chloride workers were being exposed to a potent carcinogenic agent.

The coverage by the media of the Kepone® and vinyl chloride cases suggests that the nation is on the verge of discovering a new problem, health conditions at the workplace. The two situations brought a number of significant issues to the national consciousness. What other health hazards exist at the workplace? Is there no way to assure that flagrantly unhealthy workplaces can be discovered and shut down quickly? What protective measures can workers take to assure that similar situations will not affect them or their families? What available recourse is there for workers or their survivors who have been damaged? This issue received limited public attention, but it must have been of some concern to persons familiar with workers' compensation laws. For these people the Kepone® and vinyl chloride affairs, placed alongside some recent revelations about asbestos, must have triggered some reflections on the viability of a system originally developed to deal with accidents and injuries. Would the public react to the recently uncovered problems by challenging the merits of the workers' compensation system as had happened in 1969? Was there a new public health problem being uncovered, or was it only the awareness of the problem that was changing? The passage of time should answer these questions. It appears evident that there has been a massive public disinterest regarding the problem of occupational disease for many years; this disinterest will occasionally be replaced by signs of concern, but the customary situation is one of apathy; and there is a serious health problem in industry, and although that condition has long prevailed, the characteristics of these problems have changed with the use of new substances, processes, and controls.

There are at least five reasons why the public has given so little attention in the past to matters of health at the workplace. The problem has not been easy to quantify and, therefore, periodic, isolated reports of occupational disease could be dismissed as rarities. Even now we are far from understanding either the extent or the depth of the problem. A second reason for the public's apparent inattention may be the nature of many occupational illnesses. Many of the classic occupational diseases, lead or mercury poisoning diseases, develop slowly and may seem part of the aging process. Additionally, fatalities from diseases escape public attention, unlike accidental workplace disasters that claim many lives at a single time. It would be incorrect, however, to suggest that industrial accidents and injuries have claimed much of the public's attention, as evidenced by the rather meager budgets of state safety agencies prior to the enactment of OSHA in 1970.[8]

A third reason for this disinterest might be a general lack of concern regarding environmental conditions. Surely this historical lack of concern could not have coexisted with a high level of interest in health conditions at the workplace. There was a generally passive or fatalistic attitude toward diseases in times when there were fewer preventive and curative measures available. Another factor may be the economic implications of seemingly excessive concern about such problems. Fearing loss of work or income, individual workers are reluctant to voice concerns about the conditions at the workplace. Workers who criticize employers might be dismissed, or employers could be forced out of business by efforts to eliminate existing health risks. It is likely that such fears on the part of workers, employers, and labor unions have muted possible sources of criticism and helped reduce the public's awareness of the problem.

The customary situation may have been apparent public disinterest, but it is incorrect to suppose that this has always been the case. Concern about safety conditions in the nation's coal mines finally resulted in the passage of the Coal Mine Health and Safety Act in 1969. Even though portions of the legislation deal with workers' health, it may have been enacted only because of the strong public reaction to an earlier mine explosion and disaster at Farmington, West Virginia, that resulted in large loss of life. Evidence exists of recurring if not maintained public interest in worker health. During the 1940s attention centered on the hazards to which luminescent dial painters were exposed. In the latter part of the 1930s considerable interest was aroused regarding various respiratory diseases, particularly silicosis. While tunneling on a construction project at Gauley Bridge, West Virginia, hundreds of workers were believed to have succumbed to fatal doses of silica dust. The stories of workers buried in shallow, group graves along the road being constructed led to well-publicized hearings by the U.S. Congress.[9] Concern regarding silicosis in the 1930s also led several states to pass special workers' compensation legislation dealing with this disease. Such interest in the United States even extends back to before the period when any workers' compensation laws existed. In 1906 the United States agreed at the Berne Convention to prohibit the manufacture and importation of white phosphorous matches, whose production exposed workers to a degenerative bone disease.

Such examples of public interest and governmental activity in the area of occupational disease are rare, however, it is not true that the medical-scientific community has only recently discovered the problem. Even without the usual reference to Ramazzini (1713), who may have been the first to catalog occupational diseases, there are many examples showing that knowledge of the problems is not recently acquired. Asbestosis cases were recorded as early as 1906, and in 1918 some American and Canadian companies ceased selling insurance to asbestos workers.[10] Liver damage and death were reported in 1894 in persons exposed to chloroform,[11], and in 1945 Eschenbrenner produced cancer in mice who were fed the substance for four months.[12]

Table 1.1
The timetable for the discovery of occupational cancers

Agent	Date	Target Organ
Organic chemicals		
coal soot	1775	skin
coal tar (lignite)	1876	skin
coal tar (bitumen)	1892	skin
coal tar (anthracite)	1910	skin
coal tar (fumes)	1936	lung
paraffin oil (shale)	1876	skin
parrafin oil (petroleum)	1910	skin
petroleum coke	1890	skin
anthracene oil	1908	skin
lubricating oil (shale)	1910	skin
lubricating oil (petroleum)	1930	skin
creosote	1920	skin
benzene	1928	bone marrow
isopropyl	1947	nasal sinus, larynx, lung
mustard gas	1959	larynx, lung
hydrogenated coal oil	1960	skin, mouth
Inorganic chemicals		
arsenic	1822	skin
arsenic	1930	lung
nickel	1932	nasal cavity, sinus, lung
asbestos	1935	lung
chromates	1935	lung
Radiations		
radioactive chemicals	1879	lung
ultraviolet rays	1894	skin
roentgen rays	1902	skin

Source: W. C. Hueper, *Recent Results in Cancer Research: Occupational and Environmental Cancers of the Respiratory System* (New York: Springer-Verlag, 1966), p. 8.

Benzene poisoning and deaths were recorded in 1909, and deaths from chronic benzene poisoning were acknowledged in 1920.[13] Leukemia and benzene were found to be linked in 1928 (see table 1.1). Byssinosis was known to afflict textile mill workers in the early 1800s, and references to the disease even appear in earlier literature.[14] Hueper, also, dispels any notions that occupational carcinogens have become known only recently.[15] Although proof regarding the carcinogenic nature of some of the substances listed in table 1.1 may have come at a later date, strong suspicions or evidence about a number of these hazards preceded the development of the first state workers' compensation law in the United States. When Pott first found scrotal cancer in English chimney sweeps in 1775, the United States was still under the leadership of George III. Thus it is abundantly evident that occupational disease is not a newly uncovered problem. It is certain that the difficulty has been to persuade all interested parties, workers, employers, and government officials, that the findings of the medical-scientific community had to be translated into ameliorative measures at the workplace.

Some Conceptual Issues in the Measurement of Occupational Diseases

The principal issue in the field of occupational disease and workers' compensation is the extent to which disabled employees or their survivors can count on being compensated. While many other questions of a legal, medical, economic, political, and social nature remain to be answered, overriding all of these is the matter of effective coverage. Effective coverage refers to the actual probability that compensation will be paid if a worker has been disabled due to an occupational disease. Thus, if data were available on both the extent to which occupational diseases of a disabling sort arise and the number of such illnesses that are being compensated by the states, the issue could readily be assessed. Unfortunately neither set of data is available. Despite the absence of the needed information from either the health side or the compensation side, some fairly strong judgments can be made about this issue.

From February 10 to 12, 1976, the Interdepartmental Task Force on Workers' Compensation conducted a conference on workers' compensation and occupational diseases. If any single matter frustrated the conferees and remained puzzling to them up to the end of the session, it was the identification of an acceptable definition of an occupational disease. For a number of the participants the issue became a puzzle only after the conference had begun. This newly developed uncertainty was the result of the variety of backgrounds that the conferees brought to the sessions. Those present included individuals from the fields of law, business, medicine, public administration at the state and federal levels, insurance, economics, and education. Although there were a number of problems involved in finding an acceptable definition, it was clear that the perspectives of legal practitioners and the health professionals were generally farthest apart in terms of their understanding of the concept. The tendency of the attorney is to consider an occupational disease in terms of the prevailing law, that is, to draw boundaries within which only certain classes of disablements will be covered. Individual attorneys can quarrel about where this delineation should take place, but their approach to defining such diseases is to categorize disablements as compensable or noncompensable. The perspective of the health professional leads to defining occupational diseases in a much broader context as an impairment whose etiology lies somewhere (and not necessarily fully) within the working environment.

The absence of a widely accepted definition of an occupational disease could be a significant handicap in assessing the quantitative dimensions of the problem. However, in the absence of solid data in this area and given the enormous amount of uncertainty regarding etiological questions, there is no need to dwell here on the variety of potential definitions of occupational diseases. Even if all observers could agree on a uniform definition, these other shortcomings prevent us from estimating the relevant magnitudes. What can be demonstrated, however, is that the choice of a definition will profoundly affect the size of the estimate and there are several reasons why so much difficulty exists in defining an occupational disease.

There are very few diseases or illnesses of mankind that occur only because of an activity or exposure at work. Certainly there may be some diseases that are typically contracted due to certain risks most often found at one's workplace. But even when certain industrial chemicals found only in a working environment may cause illness or disease, these ailments, for example, renal disorders, may originate from other sources and may also strike individuals who have never been exposed to that particular environment. Thus an occupational disease, typically, is occupational in its origin and not in the sense that it is unique to some kind of work. Almost any disease contracted at work could also occur as a consequence of some events entirely removed from the workplace, and there is no difficulty identifying the occupational origin of certain types of illnesses. Although any person may suffer from sunburn, a lifeguard who remains on duty during an entire day and is subsequently burned clearly has developed an occupational illness. Unfortunately, however, there are many diseases that are not readily identified as occupational. As a disease with this type of characteristic manifests itself, there is no way that a particular occupational exposure can be identified. Examples abound and Tepper has described this as follows:

The story of chronic benzene poisoning is a classic whether the response is leukemia or bone marrow failure, the fact is that leukemia and bone marrow failure are nonspecific diseases, and they cannot be distinguished against a background of naturally occurring leukemia and bone marrow failure. The response is entirely nonspecific. There may be a delay of years after a given individual stopped using, for example, rubber cement based on a benzene solvent.[1]

Now we don't have to stick to cancer. Cirrhosis produced by exposure to chlorinated hydrocarbons is probably indistinguishable from cirrhosis caused by chronic viral hepatitis, or by the over use of alcohol. . . . There is no way to distinguish the cause of hearing loss in a given individual with a hearing deficit.[2]

Dinman expands this point and explains that there is no difference between the biology of occupational and non-occupational cancers. Thus to discern an occupationally caused cancer depends on knowledge of the person's past association with well-known carcinogenic agents. Without such information and when less understood (or potent) carcinogens are the cause, the problem of identifying the disease as occupational is almost an impossible one based simply on the characteristics of the disease.[3]

Although most diseases do not have characteristics that are uniquely occupational, there are certain diseases that are so rare that they are almost certainly linked to specific hazards and may rarely if ever be encountered outside an industrial setting. Angiosarcoma of the liver is so rare a form of liver cancer that the mortality rate from it is less than 1:100,000 persons. When a number of workers from the same factory contract it, there is little doubt about its occupational origins, even if the precise etiology cannot be medically explained. Yet, although mesothelioma is also a very rare form of cancer, and it has been found in persons who have been exposed to asbestos, not all of its victims were workers. Cases exist of wives and children of workers or people living near an asbestos mine, who never worked there, contracting this form of cancer. The health community may be satisfied that it knows the causative agent, but the question remains whether it should be regarded as occupational in nature. If an individual lived his entire life in a home immediately adjacent to an asbestos mine and had worked in the mine for only one day of his life, the health professionals might find the question of work-relatedness uninteresting, but the legal professionals and the compensation board of administrators would not.

The primary difficulty in identifying diseases as occupational in origin occurs when the cause of disease is not known, as in mental illness. In 1970 over 800,000 persons had their activities limited to some degree due to mental and nervous conditions.[4] Even though psychological, chemical, physical injuries, heredity, or other causes of some mental disorders may be identified, we have no idea how the bulk of such illnesses originate. Because the cause of many such disturbances is not known, the contributing role of the workplace cannot readily be evaluated. Due to the large number of potential cases involved, however, the handling of such conditions would substantially affect the number of occupational disease cases estimated. The problem involves more than simply the absence of medical certainty about cause. Even if it were known that the stresses of life can cause such illnesses, what contributive role do job-related pressures play in the development of the disorder? If job loss began the process that led to an emotional disturbance, could this be termed an occupational disease? If so one probably should also consider as an occupational disease an illness resulting from the frustration of an unsuccessful job search even if the individual in question had never previously been employed.

If stress-induced emotional disabilities can be considered occupational diseases, so can similarly caused cardiovascular illnesses and alcoholism. Workers' compensation practitioners are aware that some heart disease cases are currently being compensated as job related, but few if any cases of alcoholism are being seen by the system. In either case, the incidence of both diseases is vast, with major cardiovascular diseases causing over 1 million fatalities in the United States in 1974,[5] and cardiovascular conditions causing over 4.5 million persons to limit their degree of activity in 1970.[6] Cirrhosis of the liver claimed 33,000 lives in 1974, but it is not known how many of these were associated with the excess use of alcohol, or how many non-fatal disabilities occurred in that year due to alcohol. There have been various estimates of the number of alcoholically disabled persons in the United States, all of them very large.[7] Surely by linking some significant fraction of these cases to the workplace, most estimates of the prevalence of occupational diseases would be greatly enlarged.

When a disease condition has multiple causes, if one of these is occupational, is it appropriate to consider it as an occupational disease? Selikoff has written that the effects of two or more contributive causes may not be additive but multiplicative.[8] When an interaction occurs between a hazard encountered on the job and one that is unrelated to work, how appropriate is it to term the condition an occupational disease? In some instances the matter is clear-cut. For example, "The interaction of carbon tetrachloride exposure and alcohol consumption is well known; fatal hepatic reactions to the solvent are much more likely to occur among individuals who have taken alcoholic beverages, sometimes in surprisingly small quantities."[9] The estimated 200,000 workers exposed to trichloroethylene also substantially increase their risks of liver and kidney damage if they also ingest alcoholic beverages.[10]

Perhaps Sagan has summarized the issue best: "Chronic disease among humans is almost certainly not the end-result of a single etiologic agent, but, rather, reflects the genetic and physiologic constitution and life experience of the individual. To evaluate the role of any one factor (such as occupational radiation exposure) to subsequent disease is to ignore the multiplicity of intertwined, still vaguely understood factors which operate to produce disease."[11]

Similarly, Selikoff concludes: "It is evident that little is yet known about such interactions, with many other probable causes still obscure; these may include physiological factors associated with age and nutrition. It may turn out that much occupational disease would not occur except with interaction of two or more agents including those in the work environment and those inherent in the individual."[12] In the same paper, Selikoff partially reviews the literature on the enormously potent interactive effects of cigarette smoking and a variety of substances including asbestos. He concludes that in all such cases in which disease results, the illness should be characterized as occupational, but it may be simpler to recognize this in a workers' compensation framework than in a medical one. It is not difficult to imagine circumstances where extraordinarily innocuous workplace exposures interact with potent substances encountered outside the workplace to cause disease.

Some uncertainty exists about the manner in which diseases resulting from multiple factors are categorized. There is at least as much question about whether to define diseases arising from the aggravation of a preexisting condition as occupational. The law in most states is relatively clear on the matter for purposes of adjudicating workers' compensation claims, however, there is room for considerable uncertainty in definitional terms and on the issue of how many occupational disease cases exist. No definitional problem exists where an occupational exposure exacerbates a condition that is also work related.

How should one classify a situation where a worker with non-occupationally induced emphysema is exposed at the workplace to dusts or fumes that are well below acceptable levels but are harmful to the employee in question because of his condition? A recent workers' compensation case can better illustrate the problem. In a 1974 Michigan case, a person who was a heavy drinker and in poor health was employed for less than two days with the Broad Crane Engineering Company.[13] Exposed to dusts in the work area, he was forced to leave when he began to choke, cough, and vomit. He was hospitalized and found to have an enlarged liver, presumably linked to his drinking problem. His condition worsened and he died shortly thereafter. The insurer's physician testified that the death was unrelated to his one and one-half days at work. Another physician claimed that the cause of death was pneumonia, which was aggravated by the employee's weakened condition due to his exposure to dust while at work. For reasons that will be discussed later, when compensation benefits were awarded and the decision upheld, the compensation system in Michigan was acting in a predictable and consistent manner. But it is doubtful that most persons would label this a fatality due to occupational disease.

Some ambiguity also occurs when a non-occupational exposure aggravates a condition that originally developed at the place of employment. A hypothetical example would be when a person suffers a heart attack brought on by jogging or by vigorous work in his garden, but the underlying weakness was caused by highly stressful or even sedentary employment. The compensation systems of virtually all states would handle this situation differently from one in which a worker, exposed to toluene or xylene, for example, becomes confused, lacking in muscular coordination and/or impaired in his visual perception, and is involved in an auto accident six hours after leaving work. This nonoccupational incident, the auto accident, may severely disable or kill a worker through the aggravation of a preexisting job-connected impairment. But is it appropriate to include the serious disability or death that results in such a case among those classified as occupational, much less as occupational disease?

There are many diseases whose etiology may be well understood, but they are problematic for purposes of categorizing them as occupational in nature. Generally these include all infectious diseases. Although several of them are virtually always considered occupational, others are almost never so considered. For example, when an animal handler or an employee in a stockyard contracts anthrax, psittacosis, or a variety of animal-borne illnesses, this is clearly an occupational illness and is generally considered as such by most observers. When an elementary school teacher contracts mumps or a department store clerk is exposed to many persons and develops a common cold or a mild case of flu, although the exposure very likely occurred at work, virtually no observers would count this as an occupational disease. Yet by considering that some proportion of cold and flu cases must occur due to contact at work with infected persons and because the number of such illnesses each year is enormous, the estimated aggregate incidence of disease could easily be raised or lowered by a factor of more than 100 percent.

Another area of dispute in terms of defining occupational disease that pits the health professionals against those associated with the law and the administration of workers' compensation programs involves occupationally induced impairments that are not disabling. Although exceptions exist, such as the treatment of permanent-partial hearing loss cases by workers' compensation laws in a small number of states, compensation is almost exclusively limited to instances where there is some economic disability. Yet one can conceive of a large number of cases in which a physical impairment occurs without any loss of earnings. For example, a recent National Institute for Occupational Safety and Health (NIOSH) study cited as examples of occupational disease, elevated levels of lead in blood or urine, permanent hearing loss and skin disorders, even when workers were unaware that a condition existed or lost no work time and wages as a consequence of the impairment.[14] Even more difficult to classify are circumstances where workers develop allergies or sensitivities to substances found at work, and are subsequently removed from contact with the agent on the job. In such a case the potential for a disorder is ever present, but contact would only occur outside of the working environment. Should the potential to become impaired be regarded as an occupational disease? If this person is impaired due to contact with the substance while away from work, should that be construed as an occupational disease?

The issue of physical impairment in the absence of economic disablement is not rare. One such set of injuries or diseases involves damage to the reproductive system of the worker. Although there is a disease per se if the employee loses the ability to reproduce, no explicit disease may occur in cases where genetic changes develop, but there is no fetus involved. Such problems were once thought to be rare and only found in the footnotes in legal textbooks, however, medical science is becoming more aware of a growing list of substances that can affect the human reproductive system.[15] There is no obvious way to classify such cases.

An issue related to medical impairment in the absence of disability is the category of diseases that are work-induced but affect nonworkers. Examples are asbestos-induced illnesses in family members who encounter the hazard through contact with a worker's clothing. Obviously, family members are also at risk when workers contract contagious occupational diseases. Hypothetically, if an employee relocates to be nearer to his place of employment at a copper smelter, the family could conceivably be put at as much risk as the worker from a variety of potent hazards including some powerful carcinogens. Yet depending on the individual who may develop the illness, an occupational disease may or may not be recorded as long as such diseases are defined only in terms of workers.

A final source of concern about categorizing occupational diseases in order to estimate their magnitude develops because of uncertainties regarding the handling of diseases resulting from accidental injuries. There is a conceptual issue regarding the classification of such disorders. If a laboratory worker is accidently splashed by a caustic substance and immediately develops some skin disorder, is this an occupational disease? If a worker's eye is injured because of an accidental blow to it, is this qualitatively different from a welder who suffers damage from an intense exposure to a welding operation in the absence of protective eye covering? Was it an occupational disease when a worker's lower lip was punctured in a work-related accident, and a carcinoma subsequently appeared at the site of the wound? The legal issues that arose in this actual case dealt with other matters, but it serves to illustrate the potential problems involved in attempting to rigidly categorize and count the incidence of occupational disease.[16] Although cancer caused by a single, sudden, unexpected event may be rare, the possibilities for such accidental injuries must be on the increase with the increased use of and access to radioactive substances.

Estimates of the Dimensions of the Occupational Disease Problem

For all the reasons already enumerated, it is not surprising that few persons have attempted to estimate the magnitude of the occupational disease problem. Aggregate measures have been made using the crudest kind of assumptions. Because of the way in which these estimates have been constructed, however, it cannot even be concluded that the estimates have either an upward or downward bias. Thus criticisms about these global estimates can as readily come from proponents of the view that they underestimate the "true" level as from those who argue that the dimension has been overstated. There can be little doubt about one thing: The extent of the problem as perceived by every commentator from the medical-scientific community vastly exceeds the number of claims made by employees or their survivors through state workers' compensation laws.

The most widely quoted and thus the most controversial estimate of the extent of the occupational disease problem appeared in the *President's Report on Occupational Safety and Health* in 1972. "The incidence of occupational disease is less well known, but recent estimates indicate at least 390,000 new cases of disabling occupational disease each year. Based on limited analysis of violent/non-violent mortality in several industries there may be as many as 100,000 deaths per year from occupationally caused diseases."[17]

The report provided neither the evidence with which to support this assertion nor any clue as to how the estimate was constructed. The format of these annual reports has been to have separate sections prepared by NIOSH and by the Occupational and Safety and Health Administration (OSHA). It is notable that the OSHA reports on work-related fatalities, published separately, are at considerable odds with the 100,000 person fatality estimate. NIOSH did not indicate what a reasonable minimum might be, and it left the reader hanging on the matter of whether the number of fatalities was expanding or declining over time. Subsequently, NIOSH has made available the following explanation of how a later estimate of 100,000 fatalities from occupational disease was developed.

"Method Utilized by the Office of Occupational Health Surveillance and Biometrics to Estimate the Annual Number of Deaths from Occupational Disease"

The approach taken to arrive at this estimate consisted of examining overall mortality rates for persons employed in a wide variety of occupations, and relating them to the mortality rate of the general population, taking into consideration age and relative socio-economic level. The data source utilized in the process was the 1951 Registrar-General's Occupational Mortality Report for England and Wales which is the only source currently available with sufficiently detailed information. From this compendium, occupational groups whose mortality rates were greater than the general population rate (after adjustment for age and social class) were counted as having an excess death rate attributable to the environment in which they worked. The number of deaths over and above those which would have been expected on the basis of age and social class were summed over all occupations and treated as occupational disease deaths. This figure was then divided by the total number of employed persons to form an occupational disease death rate. To estimate the number of occupational disease deaths that might be expected annually in this country, this rate was applied to a recent estimate of the number of employed persons in the United States. The result of this procedure yielded an estimate of 75,000. If one ignores social class in the calculations, the estimate would be 100,000.[18]

It would appear obvious that the NIOSH estimate represents a "quick and dirty" approach to the matter though the biases are not at all apparent. Clearly the British experience may have very limited relevance for that of the United States. Aside from differences in production techniques, health and safety conditions, nonworkplace environmental conditions, and hereditary factors, occupational definition discrepancies between the countries create potentially serious estimating difficulties. Additionally, there are myriad issues that one should raise with respect to a 1951 report on occupational mortality rates. For example, how was cause of death determined and how was occupation identified, particularly for persons who changed employment on several occasions? Although all of these raise formidable questions about the accuracy of the estimate of 100,000 fatalities per year, it would be inappropriate to dismiss the effort summarily. Although the effort suffers from a number of drawbacks, it does provide a possible technique for zeroing in on a fatality estimate by using U.S. excess mortality rates by occupation-industry affiliation.

Such an effort awaits the development of a death registry comparable in comprehensiveness to the British system, but an approximation could be made by resorting to data in the Social Security system. This enormously large file could be manipulated since individual records provide measures of age (at death or at time of permanent-total disability) and employment history for a large sample of persons. However, because persons tend not to be randomly distributed across industries by racial and ethnic background, industries are frequently geographically clustered by region, and the sex ratio as well as economic class varies substantially on an interindustry basis, differential mortality rates by industry would have to be estimated by a multivariate technique. Even this would not be free of problems of multicollinearity. Still, the effort would give us a better approximation than NIOSH has using possibly dated British mortality figures. It must be stressed that while the NIOSH estimate is crude, the net direction of the biases in the estimate and the extent of possible error are not clear.

Like the excess mortality technique described above, but cruder, is an approximation that has been prepared by estimating the environmental sources of some of the major causes of death in the United States (see table 2.1).[19]

Table 2.1
Environmental factors in major human health problems

Health Problems	%	Fatalities
Cardiovascular		
smoking	25	
food—nutrition	50	
occupational	5-10	50,500–101,000[a]
Cancer		
diet	35	
cigarettes	20	
occupational	15-25	54,000–90,100[a]
air pollution	0.2-2	
personal habits	5	
Accidents		(not applicable)
Pulmonary		
cigarettes	40	
occupational	10	2,700[b]
air pollution	2	
personal and home	3	
Total		107,200–193,800

a. Numbers are based on estimated proportions shown in the table and data on fatality by source in 1974. Thus in 1974 cardiovascular deaths were 1,010,926, cancer fatalities 360,472, and pulmonary deaths 27,630 (from United States Vital Statistics Report).
b. Pulmonary fatalities consist of those from acute bronchitis; bronchiolitis, bronchitis, emphysema, asthma, and excludes those caused by pneumonia and influenza.

Based on this approach, occupational disease fatalities from cardiovascular, cancer, and pulmonary conditions alone may range from 107,200 to 193,800. Obviously, the quality of this range estimate depends on the estimated proportions, the accuracy of the vital statistics in identifying cause of death, and the definition of "occupational." The margin of possible error here is large, principally due to our ignorance of the causes of cancer and cardiovascular diseases. Although there appears to be considerable agreement that "environmental factors" cause perhaps 85 to 90 percent of all cancer conditions,[20] there is much room for disagreement as to what parts of the environment are implicated. Even if by the most fortuitous circumstance these estimated proportions are correct, note that cancer due to occupational causes is much more likely to be implicated in certain types of the disease than in others. Given that there have been some dramatic changes in recent years in the proportions of cancer by site, as well as differential rates of successful treatments by site, the stability over time of these proportions is doubtful. If the scientists used the term occupational as synonymous with the term industrial, it would imply that this source of illness may include persons who are not employees of the establishment where the hazard originated. Thus, when firms pollute the environment in such a way as to increase the probability of disease (for example, an asbestos mine upwind from a community), would the scientists classify this as an occupational factor?

An unspecified technique was used by Peters to allow him to assert the following without qualification:

At least 24,000 Americans are killed each year because of their jobs. Some 14,000 die traumatically while another 10,000 deaths are directly traceable to occupational disease. This latter figure represents a conservative estimate based on known effects of occupational exposures, mostly physical or chemical in nature; there is a strong possibility that it would be substantially higher if we knew more about the subtle effects of various other exposures. Morbidity figures are more difficult to obtain but are nonetheless impressive; for example, seven million American workers are regularly exposed to hazardous noise levels.[21]

In personal correspondence with Peter Barth, Peters indicated that he did not know the source of this estimate.[22] He stated that he believed another estimate was actually closer to the truth. This estimate was essentially similar to the one indicated in table 2.1, although Peters estimated 100,000 persons died overall from pulmonary conditions and 10,000 of these were occupationally caused. Thus his estimates of deaths due to occupational disease range between 124,000 and 210,000.

In a recent paper Ashford argues that it may be more useful to focus on the total environmental impact of industry on health rather than to dwell on a component of that, that is, occupational diseases.[23] In so doing it would be observed that the broad variety of incidents suggests that a very serious problem exists. Ashford does not provide an aggregate estimate of fatalities for either occupational disease or the pooled category, but he believes that data from the OSHA surveys result in a serious underestimate of the magnitude of the problem. He appears to agree with those who believe the correct number may exceed 100,000 fatalities a year, simply from occupational causes.

A totally different approach to estimating the extent of occupational disease is based on the "Doctor's First Report of Occupational Injury or Illness" which California requires of the physician on first treatment of any injury or illness arising out of or in the course of employment. Obviously such a source can provide an excellent overview of the problem of acute diseases, however, there may be substantial underreporting because of some chronic conditions or illnesses of uncertain etiology (particularly when the latency period is lengthy). Further, physicians may inconsistently interpret the "arising out or in the course of" requirement for filing. Also, since the report is filed at the time of first treatment, subsequent contact with the patient may bring about a change in diagnosis but not a change in the report. Moreover, it is clear that the bulk of cardiovascular disease cases are not considered as occupational disease in California. But the primary problem is probably where the etiology is ambiguous or not known to the physician. This would tend to affect particularly those diseases that are due to nonacute exposures. Data from such first reports are available for 1973.

In 1973 California estimated that approximately 7.6 million employees were covered by the state's workers' compensation law and about 5.1 occupational disease cases occurred per 1,000 employees. Extrapolating to a labor force of roughly 90 million persons in the United States in 1973, this suggests that there were about 460,000 cases for the entire country, disregarding interstate differences in the industrial-occupational composition of the labor force and health and safety conditions. Again by crude extrapolation, these data would suggest that about 116,000 of these cases in the United States would have involved lost working time. Thus based on this set of data from the Doctors' First Reports, it appears that about 13 workers per 10,000 suffer from an occupational disease that results in some lost work time. These estimates are generally in line with those made by the Bureau of Labor Statistics for 1973, using OSHA data (see table 2.2).

A closely related source of data on occupational disease in California can be developed by using the *Employer's Report of Occupational Injury or Illness*.[24] These data

Table 2.2
Reports of occupational disease by estimated
time lost from work, California, 1973

No time lost	21,703	
Time lost	9,789	
1–7 days		6,965
8–14 days		1,001
15 days and over		1,215
indefinite		608
Not stated	7,103	

Source: *Occupational Disease in California,*
1973, California Department of Health, Occupational Health Section, p. 6.

are subject to the same limitations as are those from the Doctors' First Reports. However, unlike the latter, the tabulated report of the data provided by the employers is limited to injuries or illnesses in which the employee lost time for a full day or shift beyond the day of injury. Not surprisingly, the data correspond closely to those derived from the Doctors' First Reports. Data from these Employers' Reports are available for 1974 and indicate that there were 9,694 cases of such disabling work illnesses for workers covered under the state's workers' compensation law. Additionally, there are 55 cases recorded as fatalities from such occupational disease. Since the tabulation of these data indicate as a separate category "heart disease, injury or strain/vascular lesions affecting central nervous system," and this item had 93 fatalities and 1,625 cases for the year, we can pool these with "occupational disease" and thus find 148 fatalities and 11,319 cases. Assuming that 7.7 million workers were covered by workers' compensation in California in 1974,[25] there were approximately 2 fatalities per 100,000 employees and about 1.5 disabling illnesses per 1,000 employees in that year.

Several observations and generalizations should be made about both of these sources of data on California. First, the bulk of occupational diseases reported are not serious enough to cause a loss of worktime. Based on the Doctors' First Reports about 70 percent of the cases do not involve lost time from work. Perhaps an even stronger indication that most of the recorded cases are not serious is that 97.2 percent of cases in 1973 did not involve hospitalization. Thus it is clear that few if any diseases with long latencies are being found and included in these sources. A clear indication of the kinds of diseases that are reported can be found in tables 2.3 and 2.4 which are based, respectively, on the Doctors' First Reports, 1973, and the Employers' Reports for 1974.

Note that discrepancies between tables 2.3 and 2.4 occur for a variety of reasons. Not only do data in table 2.3 include disease where there was no lost worktime, the doctors' reports include instances where they found blood and urine levels exceeding acceptable amounts in tests for lead and other injurious substances. In such cases the physician may recommend that the employee be transferred or remain home. In some of these instances no employer report would be made.

Another useful source of data that can shed light on the magnitude of the occupational disease problem is based on reporting under the Occupational Safety and Health Act. A number of serious problems exist regarding the evaluation of the extent of the occupational disease problem, partly because the system of reporting is so new, and partly because the survey is based on employer record-keeping.[26] For example, the OSHA reporting system will miss diseases with long latency periods, or even relatively short ones, that may emerge only after a person ceases employment with the firm

Table 2.3

Reports of occupational disease by disease group, California, 1973

Disease Group	Number	%
Infective and parasitic diseases	432	1.1
Skin conditions	15,671	40.6
Chemical burns	3,898	10.1
Eye conditions	11,281	29.2
Respiratory conditions, mainly infectious	317	0.8
Respiratory conditions due to toxic materials	1,759	4.6
Pneumoconioses	13	a
Systemic effects of toxic materials	711	1.8
Digestive and other symptoms due to toxic materials	1,703	4.4
Loss of hearing	170	0.4
Other ear conditions	938	2.4
Effects of environmental conditions	408	1.1
Heart and other circulatory conditions	547	1.4
Other and unspecified	747	1.9
Total	39,595	100.0

Source: State of California, Division of Labor Statistics and Research, *Doctor's First Report of Work Injury,* statistics compiled by State of California, Department of Health.
a. Less than 1.0 percent.

Table 2.4

Disabling work injuries under workers' compensation, nature of injury (detailed), California, 1974

Nature of Injury	Fatal	(%)	Total	(%)
Occupational Diseases	55	(100)	9,694	(100)
Radiation effects (other than burns)	—		1	(0)
Tuberculosis	—		31	(0)
Effects of change in atmospheric pressure (except aerotitus)	—		—	
Coccidioidomycosis (valley fever)	—		25	(0)
Infectious or serum hepatitis	2	(4)	281	(3)
Anthrax, brucellosis, Q fever	—		7	(0)
Psittacosis	—		—	
Tetanus	—		1	(0)
Food poisoning	—		96	(1)
Other infective or parasitic diseases	3	(5)	394	(4)
Diseases of the nervous system (except vascular lesions affecting the central nervous system)	—		62	(1)
Skin diseases	—		3,170	(33)
Respiratory diseases	11	(20)	792	(8)
Circulatory diseases (except heart disease, hypertension, arteriosclerosis)	13	(24)	279	(3)
Ear diseases (including hearing loss due to noise and aerotitis)	—		578	(6)
Eye diseases (not due to trauma)	—		62	(1)
Diseases of the bones or organs of movement	—		1,508	(16)
Poisoning	17	(31)	1,436	(15)
Effects of general working conditions	1	(2)	295	(3)
Occupational diseases, n.e.c.[a]	8	(15)	676	(7)
Heart disease, injury or strain/vascular lesions affecting central nervous system	93		1,625	

Source: *California Work Injuries,* 1974, table 6.
[a]n.e.c.=not elsewhere classified.

where the hazard was contacted. When there is a dispute about etiology, the employer will probably not record it in his logs. It is not possible yet to estimate how much the OSHA data tend to underreport such diseases. Discher, Kleinman, and Foster found that the OSHA logs of certain employers very substantially understate the occupational disease problem in those establishments though it is impossible to extrapolate from that study to the entire nation.[27] Despite these shortcomings the OSHA data are the best source of information available, nationally and by state, particularly in the case of disease resulting from acute exposure. A clue that the data are becoming more representative, at least for acute cases, due to more complete reporting is that the number of fatalities from occupational disease jumped by about 133 percent, from about 300 in 1973 to 700 in 1974.[28] Over the same period work-related fatalities due to injuries actually declined.

The OSHA data are not entirely consistent with the two California sources noted above. Not only are there differences in the coverage of employments, there are definitional disparities also. For example, the OSHA logs would very probably record poisonings, chemical conjunctivitis, and chemical skin burns that result from a single incident as an injury, while the Doctors' Reports in California would record these as occupational illnesses; or a Doctor's Report would be filed if dangerous levels of lead are found in an employee's blood or urine, even without lost worktime, while there will probably not be a record kept in the employer's OSHA logs.

The data in table 2.5 provide a summary of the number of occupational diseases by category of illness in 1976 according to the OSHA data system. The data are quite consistent in several respects with data on occupational diseases from other sources, including California. The most common condition involves the skin. Of the more than 71,000 cases involving skin disorders reported in 1976, only 17,300 cases (28 percent) involved lost workdays. Conversely, disorders due to repeated trauma were 13.7 percent of all recorded illnesses, yet they accounted for 21.9 percent of all lost workday cases. Such disorders, which include noise-induced hearing loss, synovitis, conditions due to repeated motion, vibration, or noise, and the like, account for 47.0 percent of all lost workdays due to occupational disease. The absence from OSHA reports of diseases resulting from chronic exposures or where the latency period is long is abundantly evident. Only about 400 cases exist of dust diseases of the lungs where there have been lost workdays. Such diseases include silicosis, asbestosis, coal worker's pneumoconiosis (although coal mines per se are not covered under this reporting), byssinosis, and other pneumoconioses. Employers or the states may be reporting some of these cases

Table 2.5

Number (in thousands) and percent distribution of recordable occupational illnesses and lost workdays, private sector, United States, 1976

Category of Illness	Total Recordable Illnesses		Lost Workday Cases		Nonfatal Cases without Lost Workdays		Lost Workdays		Average Lost Workdays per Lost Workday Case
	No.	%	No.	%	No.	%	No.	%	
Occupational skin diseases and disorders	71.6	42.6	17.3	28.5	54.4	50.9	199.2	28.6	12
Dust diseases of the lungs	1.2	.7	.4	.7	.8	.7	16.5	2.4	45
Respiratory condition due to toxic agents	13.1	7.8	5.4	8.9	7.6	7.1	58.5	8.4	11
Poisoning	6.1	3.6	2.5	4.1	3.5	3.3	33.9	4.9	14
Disorders due to physical agents	24.2	14.4	6.6	10.9	17.6	16.5	60.3	8.7	9
Disorders due to repeated trauma	23.0	13.7	13.3	21.9	9.7	9.1	327.4	47.0	25
All other occupational illnesses	28.8	17.2	15.2	25.0	13.3	12.4	a	a	a
Total	167.9	100.0	60.7	100.0	106.9	100.0	1,490.5	100.0	25

Source: From *Chartbook on Occupational Injuries and Illnesses in 1976,* U.S. Bureau of Labor Statistics Report 535, 1978, table 8.
a. Indicates data do not meet publication guidelines.

Table 2.6

Number (in thousands) and percent distribution of recordable occupational illnesses and lost workdays, private sector, by extent of case and industry division, United States, 1977

Industry (private sector)	Total Recordable Illnesses		Lost Workday Cases		Nonfatal Cases without Lost Workdays		Lost Workdays	
	No.	%	No.	%	No.	%	No.	%
Agriculture, forestry, and fisheries	4.8	2.9	1.6	2.8	3.2	3.1	15.2	1.7
Contract construction	10.0	6.2	3.3	5.8	6.7	6.4	59.5	6.6
Manufacturing	96.3	59.4	33.6	59.2	62.6	59.8	555.6	61.3
Transportation and public utilities	9.1	5.6	4.0	7.0	5.1	4.9	43.2	4.8
Wholesale and retail trade	15.7	9.7	4.8	8.5	10.8	10.3	86.4	9.5
Finance, insurance, and real estate	2.3	1.4	.9	1.6	1.5	1.4	8.6	.9
Services	22.7	14.0	8.3	14.6	14.4	13.8	133.4	14.7
Mining	1.1	.7	.4	.7	.7	.7	4.1	.5
Total	161.9[a]	100.0	56.8	100.0	104.7	100.0	906.0	100.0

Source: From *Occupational Injuries and Illness for 1977,* U.S. Bureau of Labor Statistics Report 78-951, November 21, 1978, table 4.
a. Excludes farms with fewer than eleven employees.

incorrectly under the category "respiratory conditions due to toxic agents." These include such illnesses as pneumonitis, pharyngitis, rhinitis, or acute congestion due to chemicals, dusts, gases, or fumes, or farmer's lung.

Table 2.6 is based on later data than that of table 2.5. It indicates the substantial variation by industry in occupational disease. Industry groups where work is carried on outdoors seem to have a somewhat higher proportion of lost workday cases than their share of illnesses. This may reflect the severity of the occupational diseases found there or the difficulties of working under natural conditions with an illness.

Table 2.7 provides detail on the industries that show the highest incidence of lost workday occupational cases. The data were drawn from those industries in which the rate of lost workday cases per 100 full-time workers was 0.4 or more in 1974. The listing shows a tendency for rates to be at these relatively high levels in certain industries where exposures occur to chemicals, food products, and some metals. The exceptionally high rate in storage batteries (SIC 3691) may involve some lead poisoning, but it is likely that many more of the cases involve acid burns and dermatological disorders. Although a number of these industries also must account for many of the diseases due to long-term exposures and some of the diseases with long-latency periods, the cases recorded are primarily due to acute conditons and are the ones that may ultimately involve the workers' compensation system.

Unpublished data of the Bureau of Labor Statistics (BLS) provide some further insights into the characteristics of occupational diseases in the United States. Table 2.8 is based on OSHA reporting from the states for 1974 and indicates that substantial interstate variation exists in the reported magnitudes. The number of recordable illnesses in thirty-three states and the District of Columbia for 1974 was compared to levels of employment in those states according to the BLS-OSHA report for 1974. In twenty-seven states (with the District of Columbia) the range fell within two or three recordable illnesses per 1,000 employees, in seven states the ratio moved outside this range from well below one per 1,000 (New Mexico) to over five per 1,000 (in Wisconsin).

Disparities that are this large may be due to sampling errors in estimating the number of illness cases, differences in the occupational-industrial mix across the various states, or differences in employers' reporting practices. Interstate variation is somewhat lower in the proportion of all recordable illnesses that involve lost workdays but is still fairly large. Note that 49 percent of all recordable illnesses in North Dakota involve lost workdays, while only 19 percent of all occupational illnesses recorded in Wyoming involve lost workdays.

Table 2.7
Incidence rates of lost workday cases due to occupational illnesses, by select sector, 1974

Sector	SIC Code	Rate per 100 Full-time Workers
All private	—	.1
Horticultural services	073	.4
Fine earthenware food utensils	3263	.4
Concrete products, n.e.c.[a]	3272	.4
Primary nonferrous metals, n.e.c.	3339	.6
Secondary nonferrous metals	334	.8
Plating and polishing (metal services)	3471	.5
Refrigeration machinery	3585	.4
Electrical industrial apparatus, n.e.c.	3629	.5
Household appliances, n.e.c.	3639	.4
Noncurrent carrying wire devices	3644	.4
Telephone and telegraph apparatus	3661	.4
Cathode ray picture tubes	3672	.4
Storage batteries	3691	1.6
Engine electrical equipment	3694	.5
Electrical equipment, n.e.c.	3699	.4
Motor vehicles	3711	.4
Boat building and repairing	3732	.5
Sporting and athletic goods, n.e.c.	3949	.4
Meatpacking plants	2011	.8
Sausages and other prepared meats	2013	.4
Poultry dressing plants	2015	1.2
Canned and cured sea foods	2031	1.0
Canned fruits and vegetables	2033	.4
Fresh or frozen packaged fish	2036	.9
Beet sugar	2063	.6
Wines, brandy, and brandy spirits	2085	.5
Medicinals and botanicals	2833	.4
Soap and other detergents	2841	.4
Agricultural chemicals, n.e.c.	2879	.7
Adhesives and gelatin	2891	.4
Chemical preparations	2899	.5
Miscellaneous petroleum and coal products	299	.5
Tires and inner tubes	301	.4
Rubber footwear	302	.4
Leather tanning and finishing	311	.8
Sanitary services	495	.4

Source: *Occupational Injuries and Illnesses in the U.S. by Industry, 1974,* Bulletin No. 1932, U.S. Bureau of Labor Statistics, 1976, table 1.
[a]n.e.c. = not elsewhere classified

Table 2.8
Recordable occupational illnesses, 1974

State	All Recordable Illnesses	Column 1 ÷ 1974 Average Annual Employment	Lost Workday Cases	Column 3 ÷ All Recordable Illnesses (%)
Alaska	268	.003	98	37
Arizona	1,845	.003	468	25
Arkansas	1,389	.002	337	24
California	24,505	.004	8,227	34
Connecticut	3,565	.003	1,095	31
Delaware	671	.003	183	27
District of Columbia	626	.002	187	30
Hawaii	758	.003	336	44
Idaho	566	.003	195	34
Indiana	5,187	.003	1,604	31
Iowa	3,623	.004	1,234	34
Kansas	2,045	.003	695	34
Louisiana	2,704	.003	935	35
Maine	829	.003	301	36
Maryland	2,900	.003	932	32
Minnesota	5,404	.004	2,222	41
Missouri	2,842	.002	821	29
Montana	323	.002	111	34
Nebraska	1,450	.003	458	32
New Hampshire	692	.003	246	36
New Mexico	138	.001	62	45
North Carolina	3,224	.002	677	21
North Dakota	197	.001	97	49
Oklahoma	2,113	.003	670	32
Oregon	1,118	.002	346	31
Pennsylvania	11,762	.003	3.262	28
South Dakota	181	.001	74	41
Texas	9,801	.003	2,855	29
Utah	473	.002	113	24
Virginia	3,257	.002	842	26
Washington	3,119	.003	1,025	33
West Virginia	1,220	.003	312	26
Wisconsin	7,054	.005	2,158	31
Wyoming	199	.002	38	19

Source: Unpublished data made available by the United States Bureau of Labor Statistics. Relative standard errors by category of illness are not available for each state. However, judgments about the reliability of the state estimates can be inferred from the sampling errors that are generated for the national estimate of illnesses. The relative standard errors for the entire United States represent a probability level of one standard deviation. The standard error for total illnesses is 2 and for lost workday cases is 2.

Column 2 is based on data in column 1 and annual average employment in the private sector in 1974, used in state reporting for OSHA, 1974, from tables D-1 to D-40, U.S. Bureau of Labor Statistics Bulletin #1932.

Estimates of the Dimensions of Specific Occupational Diseases

The problems involved in estimating the quantitative impact of occupational diseases in toto are enormous. Some of the previous discussion has described the heroic assumptions that had to be made to arrive at some such estimate, typically only for fatalities. One can estimate the extent to which a hazardous substance, a productive process, or an industrial exposure causes occupational disease, but there are good reasons for the dearth of estimates of the numbers of workers suffering such a disease. This is not to suggest that there are no quantitative studies linking an exposure and a condition among a class of workers. While there are many such studies and the literature is virtually exploding, these findings are not readily converted into numerical estimates of workers involved.

There are several reasons why there are so few estimates of the numbers of workers with specified conditions in an occupation with a given occupational disease. First, much of the vast literature that has developed in the area of hazards and diseases is experimental in nature. Thus there may be an extraordinarily strong statistical inference that certain carcinomas and a given chemical (Kepone®, for example) are associated for a category of test animals, there necessarily will be an extended delay before the relationship is understood for man. Such experimental studies serve a number of crucial ends, but they shed no light at all on the quantitative relationship, if any, between the hazard in question and persons at the workplace.

A second group of studies takes a classical epidemiological form. The experience of a class of workers is traced, or examined retrospectively, and compared to some control group. In some instances the latter may be extremely large (the male, white population of the United States), or it may be no larger than the experimental group. Such experimental designs are common and have led to conclusive findings regarding particular hazards and specific disease conditions. But even in the presence of such findings it is rare that the scientist can generalize about the incidence of disease in the population at risk on the basis of a single experiment. First, conditions in the particular plants or establishments studied may be unlike those in the remainder of the industry where the hazard may be better or more poorly controlled and the average duration of exposure may vary. Second, in other establishments, exposures may be more or less hazardous in the presence of other substances that may interact in a synergistic way with the specified hazard. Third, turnover rates in the different establishments may vary, leading to differing kinds of exposure per employee. Moreover, the age, race, sex, and ethnic composition in differing establishments, as well as nonworkplace environment differences all might contribute to nonuniform levels of response to a hazardous exposure.

Another technical difficulty occurs in the cases of diseases with a long latency period between first exposure and the onset of the condition. If the epidemiological study is conducted before all of the disease cases that result from an exposure have been manifested, there will be a systematic undercounting of the incidence of that disease in the experimental group.[29] In addition, in observing a ratio of the incidence in the experimental group to that of the control group, the ratio will rise as the diseases in question manifest themselves, but it will peak and then decline as the control group, through the aging process perhaps, begins to manifest the condition also. Thus several researchers, working on establishing a possible link between a suspected carcinogen and a particular occupation and using different establishments for their case studies, may find strong statistical relationships, but their estimates of standardized mortality ratios may vary considerably. Under such circumstances substantially different estimates of the potential incidence of disease would emerge.

A third body of literature that does not involve test animals or very small sample sizes has been developed, exploiting the data of the Social Security Administration. The pathbreaking efforts by Mancuso and his colleagues have been most useful in identifying various hazards and occupational groups at risk.[30] But even these studies have limitations that undermine one's ability to add up the number of workers in an occupation or industry that have or will contract a specific (class of) disease(s). For example, even though these data provide detailed standard industrial classifications for an employer, they give no clue to how much exposure to particular substances any individual has had. The Social Security file will not identify the employee's occupation, where he worked in the establishment, hours of work, health and safety conditions of the work environment, cause of death, any illnesses suffered from which the individual recuperated, and so on. Obviously then, for certain types of studies supportive data must be found, and this involves returning to rather small sample sizes. Such samples may be sufficiently large to demonstrate conclusively that a hazard exists, but it will rarely allow one to generalize to all workers in that occupation or industry.

Another problem that yields similar conclusions is where the researcher must depend on registries or death certificates to estimate the number of workers affected by an occupational disease. Substantial evidence exists that such sources may be inadequate as guides to either the incidence of a disease or the cause of death. For example, in a study of over 58,000 steel workers in Allegheny County, Pennsylvania, who were employed in seven establishments in 1953, Redmond found that over 8,600 had died by the time of a 1975 report, but only 7,400 death certificates had been located.[31] Of these, 44 percent indicated only one cause of death, yet Mancuso and Coulter have noted the importance of having and using multiple causes of death for epidemiological research in order to overcome any errors of diagnosis at the time of death. Further, they describe the problems of classification, tabulation, differences in physician experience and training, and differing formats of death certificates.[32] Mancuso and El-Attar also report findings by Case et al., and Lieben where bladder cancers that were apparently occupationally caused did not appear on death certificates as the cause of death.[33] They report that of forty-two individuals in their study who had malignant neoplasms of the bladder and kidney, twenty-six had died, and eight had no mention of either form of cancer on their death certificates.

Data obtained from registries also have had significant inadequacies. One of the founders of the beryllium registry, Harriet Hardy, describes herself as "wildly disappointed" by the response to the registry, which currently holds approximately 870 records.[34] Such disappointment is not entirely surprising. Mancuso and El-Attar report finding a significant number of workers from a beryllium plant who died of beryllium disease, but whose names did not appear in the beryllium registry.[35] This study also found that some names appeared in the registry with no indication of beryllium disease on their death certificates. It may be concluded that while the epidemiologist may find statistically significant differential incidence or death rates, there are serious difficulties in attempting to generalize to some large population in an industry or occupation.

Another source of difficulty is the absence of reliable data on the numbers of workers exposed to particular hazards. The scientist must be inhibited from generalizing from research involving a small sample drawn from a population whose size is not known.[36] Most quantitative estimates involving single kinds of disease or of a category of worker are presented as standardized mortality ratios (SMRs). Such ratios are constructed by comparing death rates for a particular group to some overall population, holding constant as many demographic variables (age, race, sex, etc.) as are known to the scientist. For example, where ten deaths are observed and only five are expected, there is an SMR of 200. Once calculated, these ratios can be measured for levels of statistical significance. But for all of the reasons noted above, these SMRs are not readily translated into overall incidence levels for workers exposed to particular kinds of workplace hazards.

Despite the problems just noted there are a few scientifically based estimates of the number of cases of specific occupational diseases. In some instances these estimates have been made in part because the disease is relatively rare and as such, when *correctly* diagnosed, it receives some attention in the literature. In other instances, however, the estimates have emerged only through a combination of detective work and guesswork. Some illustrative findings of disease incidence may be helpful.

There are a number of studies that have focused on the problems of asbestos workers, and a variety of estimates of SMRs of workers at risk, morbidity rates, and so on. Based largely on such studies, asbestos union officials estimate that approximately 40 percent of the deaths of their members have been work-related.[37] Enterline and Henderson found SMRs that were quite high for asbestos workers from all cancers and respiratory diseases, while respiratory cancers were associated with an SMR of 267.[38]

Lloyd has reported that of 132 workers employed on the topside of a coke oven in 1953, by 1961, 15 had died of lung cancer. When this observed level is compared to an expected number of 1.5 deaths from this cause, it yields an SMR of 1,000.[39]

Mancuso has recently demonstrated the elevated lung cancer fatality rate for workers exposed to soluble and insoluble chromates.[40] He reported that 41 deaths occurred due to lung cancer out of 11,091 person years at risk. Interestingly, Mancuso's data showed how the particularly long latent period between the first exposure and the time of death probably accounted for some earlier, incorrect assessments that such chromates were not implicated in lung cancer.

Selikoff and Hammond have recently examined the mortality rates for workers exposed to vinyl chloride.[41] They found that for workers who had been exposed to vinyl chloride from ten to twenty-five years earlier, the observed fatality rate due to cancer was roughly twice the expected rate. This ratio was considerably greater than one reported for deaths due to cancer (at all body sites) of vinyl chloride workers by Tabershaw and Gaffey.[42] Milham found an SMR for cancer (at all body sites) of 127 for members of a New York City local union of carpenters and joiners.[43] For bladder cancer, however, he reported an SMR of approximately 217. Strikingly, though, for local union members in New York State but not in New York City, the SMR for bladder cancer was only 50. Since the sample sizes in the respective areas were small, the differences may be partially attributable to the limited number of observations, but they may be due to underlying factors such as medical reporting, different working environments, etc.

A study of white, male rubber workers indicates a very high rate of fatalities due to cancer.[44] Particularly alarming were the SMRs estimated for stomach cancer and lymphatic leukemia for persons from forty to sixty-four years of age. These ranged as high as 183 and 291 respectively.

Hueper has carefully examined the relationship between occupation and cancers of the urinary system, principally bladder cancer.[45] Based on his assessment of reported research findings, he reports large interindustry variation (3.6 to 9.6 percent) in the proportion of urinary cancers to cancer for all sites. This suggests that workers in certain industries may be three times more likely to incur bladder cancer than are others. Note also, that certain occupational groups in such high risk industries are exposed to even greater probabilities of contracting bladder cancer.

Hueper argues that

A reasonable estimate of the total number of cancers of the urinary system observed or indirectly placed on record from American plants making dye intermediates and antioxidants of aromatic amine type can be placed at well over 600. The actual number again, as in all other countries with such industrial activities is probably higher and may bring the total number of neoplasms to over 1,000 because there are several chemical plants in the United States that have not been heard from, other factories have reported partial figures, and none has so far made an attempt to determine the number of bladder cancers that have occurred among former workers. Mancuso and El-Attar (1967) noted, moreover, that in their experience bladder cancers are underreported on death certificates of dye workers.[46]

Based on Hueper's observation that former workers are apparently not incorporated in the sources of the estimates of urinary cancers among dye workers, and because the latency period may extend over four decades, the numerical estimates of urinary system cancers provided above must be much smaller than the actual number of cases. Moreover, some such cancers do not occur only because these occupational exposures may earlier cause cancers of the lungs, stomach, rectum, and prostate.

By 1975 there were approximately 870 cases listed in the beryllium registry. Hamilton and Hardy reported that 41 new cases of beryllium disease were documented in the registry in 1972 and of these 13 were fatalities at that point.[47] Some of the cases involved exposures prior to 1950, and they report that more than half of the newly registered ones involved first exposures to beryllium since 1950. This is noteworthy because the three U.S. manufacturers of fluorescent lamps agreed to cease using beryllium in 1949. This had been a primary source of exposure. However, the registry certainly underestimates the magnitude of the disease problem. Hueper constructs a number of estimates of the quantitative dimensions of the problem of occupationally caused respiratory cancer (see table 2.9).[48]

It should be said that Hueper has constructed table 2.9 from various fragments and sources, not all of which are based on large samples. Some of the carcinogens cited cause

Table 2.9
Attack rates of occupational respiratory carcinogens

| | | | Attack Rate | |
| | | | --- | --- |
Chemical	Site of Cancer	Incidence of Population at Risk	Morbidity rate per 100,000	Mortality rate per 100,000
Arsenic	Lung	—	—	145.7 (males)[a]
Asbestos	Lung	—	12 x Normal	13.2
Chromium	Lung	—	42 x Normal	146–338
Nickel	Nares	329:100,000	20 x Normal	
	Paranasal Sinuses	574:100,000		
Crude Isopropanol	Paranasal Sinuses Larynx	10:100	134.5[b]	—
Coal tar	Lung	500:100,000	—	—
Mineral oil	Lung	2,000:100,000		

Source: W. C. Hueper, *Recent Results in Cancer Research: Occupational and Environmental Cancers of the Respiratory System* (New York: Springer-Verlag, 1966), p. 24.
a. Expected rate is 10.9.
b. Expected rate is 6.5.

cancer outside the respiratory system, but their impact is only measured here in terms of respiratory cancers. The source is now becoming dated and the numbers probably could be revised in the light of later reported findings. Further, the table does not list a number of respiratory carcinogens, either because they were not known as such in 1966 or there were no data on the "attack rate" of such agents at that time.

Estimates of occupational disease rates for the United Kingdom have recently been summarized by Pochin (see table 2.10).[49] The rates are not fully comparable to those for U.S. workers, but they are indicative of similar kinds of findings to those reported for the United States. Pochin's table is particularly helpful because it does provide estimates of the standard errors for rates shown. Table 2.10 does include cadmium as a carcinogenic agent to exposed workers, a substance usually excluded from such lists in the United States. The large standard error of the rate may explain this.

Table 2.11 is based on another recent summary of the likelihood that workers will contract cancer. It differs from Pochin's in several ways: it is not limited to fatalities; it links risks to carcinogenic agents not to occupations; it appears to identify a wider list of substances.

The best source of information on the incidence of work-related respiratory illnesses is a little known study conducted by New York State in 1966.[50] The primary purpose was to evaluate the desirability of extending the coverage of New York's law to partially disabling dust diseases. A health survey of workers in high risk industries was undertaken. The state's workmen's compensation agency identified industries from data on earlier cases of dust-disease disablements. These industries were the source of 75 percent of all cases previously encountered by the state's board, and an estimated 33,000 persons worked in so-called dust occupations in New York State. In addition to a large mail survey of employers, 12,225 employees were surveyed. The employees were given X-rays, tests of pulmonary function, blood pressure, and other tests. Also, an interview was administered. Persons administering the test used no "computer formula" to evaluate disability: "On the contrary, the professional judgment of each consultant was an integral factor in such evaluation. There is no arithmetic or geometric formula to evaluate medical disability in dust disease."[51]

The sample allows generalizations to be made regarding the physical condition of all workers in dust occupations in New York State. According to the evidence, 88.5 percent of all such workers had no medical or industrial disability. About 8.1 percent (2,680 of the 33,000) had only minimal medical disability that was considered not industrially disabling for purposes of the study. There were 2.1 percent (700 workers) who had a mild medical disability, which was evaluated as 25 percent industrially

Table 2.10
Estimated rates of fatality (or incidence) of disease attributed to types of chemical or physical exposure

Occupation	Cause of fatality	Rate[a]	S.E.[b]
Shoe industry (press and finishing rooms)	Nasal cancer	130	35
Printing trade workers	Cancer of the lung and bronchus	≈200	40
Workers with cutting oils			
Birmingham	Cancer of the scrotum	60	—
Arve district	Cancer of the scrotum	400	50
Wood machinists	Nasal cancer	700	200
Uranium mining	Cancer of the lung	1500	
Coal carbonizers	Bronchitis and cancer of the bronchus	2800	650
Viscose spinners (ages 45 to 64)	Coronary heart disease (excess)	3000	1000
Asbestos workers (smokers)			
males	Cancer of the lung	2300	750
females	Cancer of the lung	4100	1150
Rubber mill workers	Cancer of the bladder	6500	3400
Mustard gas manufacturing (Japan 1929–1945)	Cancer of the bronchus	10,400	2200
Cadmium workers	Cancer of the prostate (incidence values)	14,000	8000
Amosite asbestos factory	Asbestosis	5300	1400
	Cancer of the lung/pleura	9200	1800
Nickel workers (employed before 1925)	Cancer of the nasal sinus	6600	1050
	Cancer of the lung	15,500	1500
β-Naphthylamine manufacuring	Cancer of the bladder	24,000	2700

Source: E. E. Pochin, "Occupational and Other Fatality Rates," *Community Health* 6, no. 2 (1974): 2–13.
a. Deaths per million per year that are in excess of the expected rate.
b. Standard errors are those estimated from the number of cases reported. Data are not necessarily for current levels of occupational exposure. Exposed populations estimated only indirectly in some cases. Rates are for death, except for the value for cadmium workers which records incidence.

Table 2.11
Risk ratios of occupational carcinogens

Agent	Organ	Risk Ratio[a]
Coal soot, coal tar, other products of coal combustion	Lung, larynx, skin, scrotum, bladder	2–6
Petroleum, petroleum coke, wax, creosote anthracene, paraffin, shale, mineral oils	Nasal cavity, larynx, lung, skin, scrotum	2–4
Benzene	Leukemia	2–3
Auramine, benzidine, alpha- and beta-naphthylamine, magenta 4-aminodiphenyl, 4-nitrodiphenyl	Bladder	2–90
Mustard Gas	Larynx, lung, trachea, bronchi	2–36
Isopropyl oil	Nasal cavity	21
Vinyl chloride	Angiosarcoma (liver), brain	200 (liver) 4 (brain)
Bis(chloromethyl) ether, chloromethyl methyl ether	Lung	7–45
Arsenic	Skin, lung, liver	3–8
Chromium	Nasal cavity, sinuses, lung, larynx	3–40
Iron oxide	Lung, larynx	2–5
Nickel	Nasal sinuses, lung	5–10 (lung) 100+ (nasal sinuses)
Asbestos	Lung, pleural and peritoneal mesothelioma	1.5–12
Wood	Nasal cavity and sinuses	—
Leather	Nasal cavity, sinuses, bladder	50 (nasal sinuses) 2.5 (bladder)
Ultraviolet rays	Skin	—
X-rays	Skin, leukemia .	3–9
Uranium, radon, radium, mesothorium	Skin, lung, bone leukemia	3–10
Hypoxia	Bone	—

Source: From Philip Cole and Marlene Goldman, "Occupation," in *Persons at High Risk of Cancer,* ed. Joseph F. Fraumeni, Jr. (New York: Academic Press, 1975) table 1, pp. 172–176.
a. Risk ratio represents the probability that has been determined of excess risk of contracting cancer for persons in occupations specified in the source table. Thus, a risk ratio of 5 implies that workers exposed to the carcinogen(s) are 5 times as likely to contract cancer, at the site(s) listed, as are other workers.

disabling. One percent of the workers (330 persons) were found to have a moderate medical disability — approximately 50 percent industrially disabling. About one-tenth of 1 percent of such workers (30 employees) had "marked" medical disability, which was equivalent in this study to 75 percent industrially disabling. Thus out of 33,000 employees in dust occupations in New York State, 1060 overall had a mild to a serious medical disability.

A minority of the study group, apparently representing the views of management, dissented from the recommendations presented in the report; the dissent and the majority's recommendations must be viewed as partisan. Several of the issues raised bear directly on the usefulness of the findings. The dissent correctly noted that only persons currently employed in dust occupations were included in the survey. Thus persons were excluded who no longer were employed but could conceivably contract a dust-caused occupational disability. Persons too disabled to remain in these occupations or who had died, possibly as a consequence of a dust-related disease, are also omitted, as are those who left the industry for reasons other than health. The dissent also noted that some individuals with medical disabilities may not have received lung damage from their current occupation but from a previous employment or even outside the workplace.

A far more damaging criticism of these findings was that the underlying population was seriously underestimated. The study group assumed that there were 33,000 persons in dust occupations in New York; the dissent noted that in 1964 there were 24,000 to 25,000 employees in the foundry industry alone in New York State. Finally, the business representatives assert that the survey systematically over-sampled younger workers, thereby minimizing the problem. This claim cannot be evaluated on the basis of the data shown in the report.

It is clear that the employers' dissent was based on a concern that partial disability claims would become an expensive aspect of the workers' compensation program. In seeking to undermine the findings, they argued that many more potential cases of disability would be forthcoming than was suggested by the study. The dissent, however, did not indicate the extent of the potential disease problem except to note, "in the event of a recession or depression, this cost (of expanded coverage) could run into many millions of dollars since it could be anticipated that practically everyone employed in a dust industry will file a claim."[52] This charge may contain more cynicism than fear, but the implications of the health status of workers in these occupations is obviously a matter for concern.

The study has two other major problems. Diseases not manifested for a number of years after contact with some of these dusts might be missed in a survey of this kind. The symptoms may not appear gradually but in a short time when the disease emerges fully. The industries identified as the sources of 75 percent of disabling dust diseases do not correspond with standard industrial classification codes. If they did, it would be simple to calculate the national total number of persons employed in such occupations to estimate how many workers in the United States are medically disabled, assuming the proportions found in New York apply across the country.

Data from the New York State study are presented on the age and experience distribution of workers in the dust occupations. Since length of employment in a dust occupation must be associated positively with the development of many chronic types of disorders, evidence of rapid turnover suggests that certain types of occupational illness might be minimized. Since some dust occupations are likely to be unpleasant due to the work environment, one might anticipate unusually high rates of labor turnover. Although no comparative data are presented on turnover, it is clear from table 2.12 that there are significant proportions of older workers employed in dust occupations for many years. For example, almost 40 percent of the workers in such occupations in New York State at the time of this survey were forty-five years of age or older. About 45 percent of all workers in these occupations were employed for ten years or more. Assuming that some workers may have been exposed to dust occupations in their prior jobs, the proportion of all workers exposed to such dusts for more than ten years must easily exceed 50 percent. Even if there are particularly high rates of labor turnover in these dust occupations, a very substantial proportion of workers spend most or all of their working lives subjected to such exposures. Although the length of exposure to such dusts may be less important than the type and volume of dust the worker encounters, the prolonged inhalation of substances such as the various ferrous and nonferrous metals, silica, and asbestos must be grounds for serious concern.

A second noteworthy finding emerged from a special survey of asbestos workers. The sample was small and limited to older workers who were being exposed to dust. The median age in the sample group was 47.5 years (compared with 36.4 years for all members of their local union), and they had been employed in dusty trades for twenty-two years (compared with eleven years for all workers in the local). The medical consultants reported the following: no medical disability, 40.5 percent; minimal medical disability, 32.5 percent; mild medical disability, 8.1 percent; moderate medical disability, 13.5 percent; marked medical disability, 5.4 percent. Thus even though the survey was limited to those persons still able to be employed in their trade, almost 60 percent had

Table 2.12
Duration of present employment and age of workers in dust occupations

Age	% of Workers	Years in Present Employment	% of Workers
Under 20	2.5	Under 1 year	15.8
20–29	19.2	1–2 years	16.4
30–39	25.0	3–4 years	9.4
40–44	14.3	5–9 years	13.9
45–49	13.6	10–14 years	16.8
50–54	10.7	15–19 years	11.2
55–59	7.6	20–24 years	6.9
60–64	5.3	25 and over	9.5
65 and over	1.8		
Median Age	41.1	Median duration	8.0

Source: From *Report and Recommendations on Occupational Dust Diseases Under Wormen's Compensation Laws,* Workmen's Compensation Board, New York (February 1, 1966), tables 8 and 9.

some medical disability (of a respiratory nature only) and more than one-quarter had more than a minimal medical disability. These findings are hardly surprising to persons familiar with the health threat posed by exposure to asbestos.

Estimates of the specific numbers of occupationally related diseases also have been made for some less publicized hazards. For example, sugar cane fiber can cause a pneumonitis in cane mill workers as well as in factory workers who use the fiber to manufacture paper, wallboard, insulating materials, cattle feed, explosives, and other products. This material, known as bagasse, was reported by Buechner to have caused sixty-two cases of bagassosis in the United States from 1937 to 1958.[53] Buechner added, "For every case reported, there must be ten or twenty other cases that never come to the attention of doctors who write papers."[54] He also noted that 60 percent of the workers who are involved with raising turkeys are said to develop respiratory illnesses, usually like asthma. But about 6 percent of the workers develop hypersensitivity pneumonias, and some then develop pulmonary fibrosis.[55] Unfortunately, Buechner gives no indication of the size of the population at risk from this exposure.

Another quantitative estimate of persons who become ill due to their occupational exposure also involves contact with animals. Hamilton and Hardy indicate that although there has been a substantial drop-off in cases of brucellosis, 262 new cases were reported in 1965.[56] They provide no estimate, however, of what the incidence of underreporting might be.

The extremely useful work of Discher and his associates has provided a basis for estimates for a variety of occupational diseases.[57] Unfortunately, some of the findings are being sensationalized and distorted.[58] Discher's report does not purport to provide national or representative estimates of the magnitude of all diseases, a single disease, or the risks associated with certain occupations, however, there are references to the study that neglect its obvious limitations. The Discher work was simply a pilot study conducted from July 1972 through August 1974 with two specific and clearly articulated goals. These were to determine the utility of a set of medical procedures designed for diagnostic purposes and see what types of useful data could be generated from the procedures used in the study. A survey was conducted of workers and work conditions in three nonrandomly selected urban areas. (Takoma and Seattle, Washington, and Portland, Oregon) and a convenient agricultural area (Yakima County, Washington). Only establishments of eight to 150 workers were included in the samples. A random sample of farms in Yakima County was drawn, but when these growers refused to participate, the local growers' associations helped provide volunteer participants from other farms.

The overall sample included 140 establishments and a medical survey of 1,400 employees therein, of which twenty establishments and 100 workers were drawn from the agricultural sector in Yakima County. The selection from the urban areas was purposely designed as follows: "To assure that the results would yield cases of occupational disease of special interest to NIOSH the sample was stratified according to target groups: lead using industries, chlorinated hydrocarbon solvent using industries, and agriculture. All other hazardous industrial categories in the sample formed the fourth stratum called other non-agricultural industries. Industries falling into the lead and chlorinated hydrocarbon solvents strata were oversampled compared to the fourth stratum—other nonagricultural industries."[59]

All of the 140 establishments were visited by an industrial hygienist in an environmental (walk-through) survey. Establishments were given ten to twenty days notice of the visit. Some firms that refused to participate in either the walk-through survey or the subsequent medical survey were allowed to drop out of the sample. The hygienist's environmental survey involved solely the use of his "subjective judgment" regarding the exposure of workers to all hazards. The sole exception to this was for the noise hazard, where test instruments were used. After the walk-through by the hygienist, a limited number of these establishments was selected, and only production workers in these establishments were asked to participate in a health survey. "The plants included in the medical survey were those in which workers were exposed to the target hazards and/or other hazards inadequately controlled as determined by the industrial hygienist. The lead and chlorinated hydrocarbon solvent strata were oversampled for the medical survey as well as the walk-through survey."[60]

The medical survey team consisted of a physician, nurse, and paramedical person, usually the field supervisor. Each medical examination took a total of thirty minutes, with approximately ten minutes spent with each member of the team. Aside from some tests given to all survey participants, in many of the examinations checks were made tailored to the worker's specific exposures. Such exposures were known from the environmental survey and detailed work histories that workers provided. Workers with lead exposures were given urine and blood tests, employees exposed to dusts received chest X-rays and spirometry tests, and persons exposed to noise were tested for permanent hearing loss after a minimum of sixteen hours since their last exposure to noise on the job.

With the sampling procedure described above, it is not surprising that significant exposures to hazardous substances and cases of occupationally related impairments were found. The hygienist found 11,873 exposures for 3,693 workers in 136 establishments, an average of 3.2 exposures per worker. The hygienist rated 72 percent of these exposures as "adequately" controlled and 5.2 as inadequate. The balance were rated either as unknown or marginal. Of the adequately controlled exposures, approximately half were adequate only because workers had limited contact with them.

Among those workers exposed to hazards that might create skin disorders, the medical examination found that 8.3 percent had some occupationally related skin condition. For workers exposed to known irritants, 12.2 percent were found to have some respiratory impairment. With this group the rate was as high as 16.3 percent among those whose exposure was only marginally or inadequately controlled.

The study by Discher and his associates provides a substantial amount of information, especially for a pilot study. It would be unfortunate if all the attention given to the study focused on the quantitative estimates of the occupational diseases that were found. Such estimates were based on a very small, nonrandom sample, and the procedures used to identify diseases were limited, thereby undermining the general applicability of the findings to all diseases found or counts of individual disease cases. Discher and his associates recognize the biases within their reported data because of the highly limited and one-time-only medical examination. "Omission of many procedures increased the possibility of missed information. As a result, bias in the study tends towards underrecognition of probable occupational disease, ranging from missed diagnoses to ascribing the relationship of the disease to the doubtful or nonoccupational instead of probable occupational because of missing data."[61]

No quantitative measures of the disease problem should be drawn from this limited pilot project, but several of the qualitative findings are quite significant. The authors conclude that "a vast reservoir of unreported occupational diseases"[62] exists in U.S. industry. Based on their immediate experience, such sobering conclusions should be seriously noted. Another very serious finding has significant policy implications; many workers do not know or cannot recall their past exposures to hazardous substances. Discher found that the response to the occupational exposure history in the medical questionnaire was poor. For seventeen out of twenty-seven questions relating to exposure, over 20 percent of the participants left blanks which were then classified by the researchers as unknown.[63] Even when workers recalled some exposures, they often did not indicate the number of years involved. Obviously such uncertainties have implications for the likelihood that problems can develop in compensating disabilities that could eventually result from such exposures. Such ignorance or uncertainty also may jeopardize the physician's opportunity to either correctly diagnose an illness or identify its etiology. At its worst such ignorance could mean that a sick worker continues to be exposed to a substance that is undermining his health.

Another rather firm finding pertaining to the identification of workplace hazards was that the hygienists found some rather unexpected conditions. In certain industries identified as sources of particular hazards, such hazards no longer exist. For example, of the thirty-three establishments where lead usage was anticipated, eleven were found not to have any lead hazard, such as in publishing and printing plants using photographic equipment instead of typesetting. Conversely, lead hazards were found in a number of industries where none was anticipated. Similarly, the walk-through surveys found significant disparities between expected and discovered hazards from halogenated hydrocarbon solvents. We are still a long way from identifying the number of workers who are currently being exposed to particular risks. As long as particular hazards are used in industries where they are not generally thought to be used, it raises issues similar to those of the physician's difficulty in diagnosing an illness and identifying its etiology. As questions of etiology are raised in connection with workers' compensation claims, the issues become significant for that system also.

Other Data Sources

It is not a simple matter to specify precisely what is an occupational disease. Even if an agreed definition were available, the difficult diagnostic and etiological problems would remain. Lacking both of these elements, there is little hope of arriving at a satisfactory overall estimate of the true magnitude of the problem. Those estimates that are limited in their scope — either by single hazard or industry — tend to contain serious biases. The staggering disparity between estimates of fatalities prepared by two agencies cooperating under a single piece of legislation, the Occupational Safety and Health Act of 1970, makes the problem evident. The gap derives from two separate approaches to the issue. Data from OSHA and states using Doctors' First Reports or other reporting systems depend primarily on self-reporting where the worker, his physician, or his employer are expected to acknowledge the presence of a work-related disease. Estimates by NIOSH and others, who believe that fatalities due to occupational disease could easily range between 100,000 and 200,000 per year, take an inferential approach. They assume that self-reporting badly underestimates those diseases where the etiology is complex and often unknown, where a number of diseases including cancer may remain latent for up to four to five decades, and where certain chronic diseases develop slowly as the worker is exposed to non-acute levels of a hazard for prolonged periods of time.

Those who estimate that the incidence of occupational disease is relatively low — in the range estimated by OSHA-BLS but correcting for uncovered sectors — argue that there are no other firm data to suggest that incidence is higher. Proponents of the higher estimates point to the problems of self-reporting techniques and the continually growing list of hazards to which workers are regularly exposed. There are bodies of data other than those already described that will shed light on this debate.

One source is the various registries, such as the beryllium registry, maintained by public and private groups attempting to catalog disease cases. One of the finer cancer registries is maintained by the Department of Health of the State of Connecticut. Other registries have been developed by labor organizations, often in conjunction with health personnel, to monitor the long-term health experience of their membership, sometimes even after retirement. A related source of data comes from the ten or so states that require physicians to report instances where they treat occupational diseases.

Very useful data emerges regularly from the National Center for Health Statistics mainly from annual samples in their Health Interview Survey. These surveys provide information on the kinds of illnesses and limitations persons report, often cross-classified by other variables such as occupation or industry of the person, age, sex, days lost due to condition, and so on.[64] Such data are interesting for several reasons. First, when evaluated comparatively, they can serve as an upper bound on estimates of persons who have either lost days of work due to illness or disease (this is limited to those persons currently employed), who have experienced some activity limitation due to a (chronic) condition, or who report having a chronic condition. Although many quantitative assessments of occupational disease have concentrated on fatalities, some boundaries on the magnitude of morbidity can be inferred from the Health Interview Survey. For example, in 1968 there were approximately 413 million working days lost due to illness or injury.[65] In recent years this rate has been very stable, but for the ten years 1959 to 1968 the rate ranged from 5.4 to 6.1 per employee. There is substantial interindustry and interoccupation variation within this range.[66] For professional and technical male workers an average of 4.0 days per year were lost; male service workers, except private household, lost an average of 7.2 days. Managers, officials, and proprietors lost only 3.2 days per year. Male workers employed in service industries (other than government) lost 3.9 days per year compared to highs of 6.4 days in the construction industry and 6.3 days per year in utilities.

It would be tempting and uncomplicated to assume that the interindustry or interoccupation differences are due solely to working conditions. By using the lowest rate found for any industry or occupation as a base, one could assume rates above this are due to working conditions. But such a simulation, even controlling for age and other demographic differences, is inappropriate. A major portion of interindustry or inter-occupation variation occurs because workers with a temporary or chronic illness will not be able to perform certain kinds of tasks, although precisely the same illness may allow workers in other employments to function adequately. Moreover, workers in certain lines of activity may exacerbate existing health conditions if they perform certain activities and not others.

Another explanation of differential rates is the opportunity to forego a day's work without neglecting responsibilities by rearranging one's work schedule. A final factor is the availability of fringe benefits such as "sick days allowed," or medical insurance. These two reasons may explain the somewhat surprising phenomenon that government employees lose 6.0 days of work due to illness and injury compared to a national overall rate of 5.4. Some portion of the differences by employments is due to accident and injury rates, which are known to vary systematically, as does occupational disease.

These data must be used with some care as is clear from an apparent error that was recently reported: "The costs of occupationally related disability and death are enormous: half a billion work loss days occur annually, resulting in human suffering as well as high social costs in terms of productivity losses for the U.S. economy, an estimated $9 billion annually. Investments in preventive and curative measures for disability associated with employment are not commensurate with the scope of the problem."[67] Yet the source of these estimates is clearly referring to time-loss due to injuries and illnesses from all causes, not simply from work-related ones. The passage neglects to note that productivity losses due to work-related disability should also include some estimate of time lost for persons who are not employed at all due to impairments incurred in previous years. Such an assessment would count, at a minimum, the product lost in the current year due to fatalities, total disabilities, and early retirement from work in previous years induced by such illnesses. It should also recognize losses due to the reduced level of productivity of employed persons with work-related permanent partial disabilities.

The time-lost data, even that correctly reported, may have limited value. Data from the Health Interview Survey on interindustry differences by condition are much more likely to lead to inferences about occupational disease incidence. For example, it is reported that the incidence of hypertensive disease conditions in 1972 was approximately 60 per 1,000 persons.[68] Based on unpublished data from the Health Interview Survey for 1972, the APHA reported the incidence for persons employed in service occupations was approximately 90 per 1,000 persons.[69] If these data are correct,[70] then if the national average of about 60 per 1,000 applies, approximately 660,000 persons in service occupations would have had chronic hypertensive disease, based on roughly 11 million such workers in 1972.[71] Given the reported incidence of about 90 per 1,000, the excess number of cases of hypertensive disease among persons in service occupations was about 330,000 cases. Some part of the difference across occupations may be due to self-selection; persons with hypertensive disease avoid certain kinds of occupations, retire earlier from certain employments after their disease occurs, or somehow become aware of their condition more rapidly. Still it is clear that so significant a variation is associated with some differential incidence caused occupationally.

Even more striking are the reported differences by occupation in chronic arthritic conditions. The national average incidence of this condition is 92.6 per 1,000, and the rate for persons in farm occupations is 162.4 per 1,000.[72] When this differential rate is applied to the number of persons in farm work in 1972 (about 3.1 million), 216,000 out of the roughly 503,000 farm workers with chronic arthritis represent the excess number of cases. It would be difficult to argue that self-selection is responsible for this difference in rates of chronic arthritis. Conceivably there may be some hereditary factor at work, but if there is, its contribution would be small.

Although the entire data base of the Health Interview Survey may suffer from some elements of self-diagnosis and the absence of detailed work histories, the available data are a sufficiently promising source to warrant specific analysis of the extent of occupational disease. Since the study of occupational disease morbidity has taken a back seat to the investigation of mortality rates, for which these data are unsuited, this source has been underutilized.

A different kind of inferential approach uses interregional variation in the incidence of disease to shed light on the role of certain causative agents. Hueper reports an early study that found that between 1940 and 1944, 10.3 percent of all cancer deaths in Salem County, New Jersey were caused by bladder cancer, while only 5.5 percent of cancer deaths for the state were the result of bladder cancer.[73] Salem County contained a concentration of dye factories. Air pollution might account for such regional discrepancies, but Hueper cites previous findings indicating that lung and bladder cancer rates did not generally show parallel differences across areas.

Scientists at the National Cancer Institute recently prepared a massive study of interregional differences of cancer incidence.[74] Maps were prepared for all counties and state economic areas in the United States showing death rates per 100,000 population

from sixteen common and nineteen other cancer sites. Some of the intercounty variation was enormous. The average rate of death from cancer of the bronchus, trachea,
and lung for males for 1950 to 1969 was 37.98 per 100,000 per year. In counties in the
lowest decile the age adjusted rate was 17.46 per 100,000 per year compared to 43.34
per 100,000 per year, age adjusted, for counties in the highest decile. The average rate
for females for the same time period was much lower, 6.29 per 100,000 per year; a
relative variation even larger than for males. Death rates were 2.34 per 100,000 per year
in the counties in the lowest decile compared to 8.02 per 100,000 per year for counties
in the highest 10 percent.

Interregional differences in cancer rates prove little regarding causality, but in certain
cases they are suggestive of a variety of etiological sources, including diet, heredity,
pollution, and climate. Death rates from skin cancer and melanoma, a rare form of the
disease, are significantly higher in southern than in the northern states where there is
less exposure to the sun.

According to the National Cancer Institute (NCI) report, occupational hazards are
implicated also.

High rates in the Northeast for cancers of the esophagus, larynx, mouth and throat, and
bladder were limited to males, suggesting the influence of occupational factors. In a
correlation study, the NCI scientists identified high rates of cancers of the lung, liver
and bladder in counties with significant employment in the chemical industry. Additional studies are needed to clarify any occupational risks.

It is nearly certain, the NCI scientists believe, that industrial exposures have produced the striking geographic concentrations of bladder cancer deaths in males in the
East. The NCI scientists also found above average lung cancer death rates in counties
where a significant percentage of the workforce is engaged in smelting and refining
of copper, lead, and zinc ores. Arsenic, a known human cancer-producing agent, is an
airborne by-product of the smelting operation for these ores. Above average rates
were found for females as well as males in these counties, suggesting spread of an
occupational risk to the surrounding community.[75]

These observations, while hardly incontrovertible evidence of a massive problem
of occupational disease, indict the workplace as a source of fatal cancers. Some of
this evidence suggests that carcinogenic substances originating at the workplace may
spread by air or other routes, thereby involving area residents who are not employees.
It is clear that the industrial environment serves as the launching ground for hazards
that are so carcinogenically potent that they yield statistically significant differences
in death rates by site of cancer. Further evidence may eventually develop that undermines this apparent linkage between industry and interregional death rates from cancer,

however, it is at least as likely that additional understanding of carcinogenesis will find an even stronger association between industry and cancer death rates.

The Changing Incidence of Occupational Disease

We have demonstrated that there are important conceptual issues that must be settled before wide agreement can be achieved on the aggregate incidence of occupational disease. Attempts to resolve some of these issues can await the development of the adequate definitions and necessary data to support such consensus. Thus in the absence of good data on the aggregate incidence of occupational disease and given the uncertainties involved in identifying the numbers of specific work-related illnesses, it may seem pointless to try to describe the changing character of the occupational disease problem. If we cannot measure the problem in the current year nor the magnitude of it in previous years, is it futile to concern ourselves with its changing incidence? We believe that while we cannot conclude that the incidence of occupational disease or fatalities from this cause have been increasing or declining, there are some significant changes occurring in the composition of the problem.

Some support exists for the contention that the occupational disease problem is growing worse. Ashford has argued that the striking increase in cancer rates over the past two or three decades and the similar rapid increase in new industrial chemicals may be more than coincidental.[76] The meaningfulness of this association remains to be tested, however, the rapid proliferation of new potential hazards is the correct basis for concern. Different estimates exist of the number of new chemicals developed and used in industry each year. Peters, for example, asserts that U.S. industry has about 5,000 chemical substances in common use and 500 new ones are added annually.[77] *The New York Times* cites an EPA estimate of 1,000 new chemicals being introduced, commercially, every year.[78] NIOSH is charged by section 20(a) (6) of the Occupational Safety and Health Act to prepare a list of toxic substances annually. The definition of such a substance was modified in 1973 and now is as follows:

A toxic substance is one that demonstrates the potential to induce cancer, tumors or neoplastic effects in man or experimental animals; to induce a permanent transmissible change in the characteristics of an offspring from those of its human or experimental animal parents; to cause the production of physical defects in the developing human or experimental animal embryo; to produce death in animals exposed via the respiratory tract, skin, eye, mouth or other routes in quantities which are reasonable for experimental or domestic animals; to produce irritation or sensitization of the skin, eyes or respiratory passages; to diminish mental alertness, reduce motivation or alter behavior of humans; to adversely affect the health of a normal or disabled person of any age or of either sex by producing reversible or irreversible bodily injury or by endangering life or causing death from exposure via the respiratory tract, skin, eye, mouth or any other route in any quantity, concentration, or dose reported for any length of time.[79]

Using this revised definition, in 1973 NIOSH listed over 25,000 entries, involving 11,000 different substances. The multiple entries for certain substances occur where there are different routes of exposure. The list is restricted to substances that were either reported or assumed to be pure chemicals. Unpurified extracts of natural substances, proprietary mixtures, and radioactive chemicals were not listed. A subset of these identified by NIOSH as "suspected carcinogens" numbers 2,415.[80] The enormity of this ever-growing list of chemicals alone suggests an increasing source of occupational disease. Many of the items listed were not known or did not exist only a few years ago. There also is a possibility that the list could be expanded by recognizing that even certain "safe" chemicals may become toxic under appropriate conditions. For instance, a researcher from the Institute of Industrial Hygiene and Occupational Diseases of the U.S.S.R. Academy of Medical Sciences has recently warned that in pyrolysis, the use of temperatures over 600°C can create carcinogenic by-products of hydrocarbons.[81] Thus persons exposed to normally nontoxic substances are placed at risk during such operations. As existing substances are mixed or processed in new ways, new potential risks are created. Such hazards would seem to be most alarming for employees of the chemical industry, but users of such industrial chemicals are also at risk. Those potentially jeopardized range from the scientists and chemists who develop and prepare these substances to production line employees and maintenance and service personnel in many areas of manufacturing.

Aside from the very rapid rate of growth of new substances and processes, the changing composition of the labor force is another source of concern. The dramatic increase of females in the labor force in the post–World War II years means a greater potential risk of reproductive abnormalities. In testimony John Finklea, former director of NIOSH, indicated that over one million women of child-bearing age are in jobs that could expose them to chemicals that might cause birth defects and miscarriages.[82] Twenty chemical agents were listed as the potential source of hazard.

There has also been a decline in agricultural-based employment and an increase in the industrial workforce. The effects of this trend may have been negated somewhat because the proportion of workers categorized as production workers has fallen off, relative to nonproduction workers, and the share of the labor force employed in manufacturing has been declining. In 1950 over one-third of all employees were in manufacturing compared to only one-quarter of all workers today. It is interesting that certain significant industries, like mining, have had precipitous declines in employment over the past one or two generations, and other key industries, such as chemical and allied industries, and clay, glass, and stone, employed precisely the same shares of the labor force in 1970 as they did in 1930.

There are several factors that may be causing the magnitude of the problem to decline. First, there is far more attention being given to the subject today than ever before. Such interest has generated, and in turn is fed by, scientific advances in identifying hazardous substances and employments. By simply identifying some of these risks, the likelihood that they will cause illness to the unwary or unwarned employee is reduced. Programs to inform workers of health risks have been developed at the University of California, Berkeley, and the University of Wisconsin. Such information also allows employers to seek alternative substances or processes that are not identified as hazards.

A second change that should reduce workers' exposure to health hazards is the increased role of regulatory authorities, particularly the Occupational Safety and Health Administration and the Environmental Protection Agency. In setting and monitoring effective health standards at the workplace and away from it, the risks of occupational illness are reduced. It is still premature to attempt to evaluate the impact that such protective agencies have had; it seems clear that they should have a net beneficial impact on the work environment.

The increasing importance of health and safety issues in collective bargaining is another improvement. Some of the larger industrial unions, in particular the Steelworkers, Oil, Chemical and Atomic Workers, United Auto Workers, United Mine Workers, and Rubber Workers have begun to show serious concern about such risks. Such change must have a long-run, beneficial impact on the incidence of disease, but many other unions have not yet shown concern in this area, and the large majority of the labor force in the United States is not represented by trade unions.

The recently developed technological improvements used to monitor and control hazards is also reducing the extent of work-induced illnesses. Some risks are now found only in entirely closed systems. Improved methods of cleaning and venting polluted air are other examples of such changes. More sensitive devices exist to monitor the presence of dangerous levels of substances at the workplace, and continued regulatory pressure can be expected to lead to continuing advances in this area.

A final possible basis for change has been workers' compensation laws. The Report of the National Commission on State Workmen's Compensation Laws took an agnostic position on the issue of incentives to safety provided by the experience rating of workers' compensation insurance. They found "the lack of clear evidence to support the theory that the present insurance pricing system reduces accident frequency."[83] For a variety of obvious reasons, if workers' compensation insurance premiums are not demonstrably effective in influencing accident frequency, they will be even less likely to significantly reduce occupational illnesses. Instances must exist where there has been such a relationship. A frequent example is the reduction in silicosis cases in Vermont during the 1930s after claims began to be paid; insurance premiums rose accordingly.[84] It is irrelevant whether the cases declined because employers changed their work practices, required the increased use of safety devices, altered their recruiting practices, or simply closed especially hazardous quarries. Any one or more of these changes could have reduced the number of workers contracting silicosis.

The above reasons why the numbers of occupational diseases have increased or declined have largely been speculative or theoretical, but there are some data and observations by experienced scientists regarding the changing quantity and composition of occupational diseases. These observations tend to be limited to specific diseases or hazards, but when a number of them are pieced together, a picture begins to emerge.

Hamilton and Hardy note at least four occupational diseases that have been substantially reduced or eliminated over time.[85] Exposure to beryllium has not been eliminated, but it has been reduced since the three major fluorescent lamp manufacturers in the United States agreed in 1949 to stop using it. The decision was made on the basis of health risks to workers exposed to this hazard. Beryllium, however, has not totally disappeared from industrial use. It has been estimated that in 1970 beryllium was employed in 8,000 plants in the United States, and this excludes both some very small establishments and those firms involved in producing beryllium.[86] But Hamilton and Hardy argue that even where exposure occurs, the level of beryllium is lower today than it was several decades ago. This seems to be confirmed by the observation of Woodward and Fondmiller that the acute disease has been largely eliminated.[87]

A second example cited by Hamilton and Hardy is that of "phossy jaw," a disease contracted primarily by match workers exposed to white phosphorous. The disease was brought under control in the United States by protective legislation, the Esch Act, and international agreement at the Berne Convention (1906) to cease the manufacture and importation of white phosphorous matches.

Hamilton and Hardy also deal with technological and scientific changes that have contributed to reducing the disease problem. At one time severe chronic bronchitis was a serious disability for some workers involved with handling paprika. Botanists have been able to develop a related plant that serves as an acceptable substitute but contains substantially less of the toxic substance capsaicin. There has also been a decline in asthma in cigarette cutters due to improved mechanical methods of handling tobacco.[88]

New uses of atomic energy have led to an increasing potential for exposures to radioactive materials, however, the greater knowledge about radiation hazards has caused far more caution to be exercised in recent years. Precautions taken in the production and use of radiation equipment have probably been the major forces in reducing the incidence of fatal diseases among radiologists in the United States. This group had formerly experienced exceptional rates of premature fatalities and statistically significant excesses in incidence of cancer. Hamilton and Hardy report that this phenomenon has apparently ended.[89] The increased knowledge about radiation hazards also has led to substantial reduction of the risks of lung cancer and leukemia in uranium mines.[90]

Increased knowledge and its dissemination can lead to a lower incidence of occupational disease, but this does not guarantee that improvements must occur. Benzene, or the commercial preparation benzol, has been used in the U.S. rubber industry since before World War I and is found today in many American industrial uses. NIOSH has estimated that 2 million workers have potential exposure to it.[91] Benzene poisoning and deaths have been reported since at least 1909. Chronic benzene poisoning was first reported in 1920 in England. The increasing awareness of the hazards of working with benzene has had some beneficial results: "The growing recognition of the hazard associated with the use of benzene led gradually to the substitution of other solvents and an accompanying decrease in the incidence of cases of benzene poisoning."[92] The "hazard," however, actually produces a number of unrelated medical problems including some dermatological ones and impairments of the blood forming system. NIOSH has reported that benzene (benzol) is linked to leukemia. In a recent article in the *Akron Beacon Journal,* the deaths from leukemia of six employees at Goodyear Tire and Rubber Company in a ten year period are reported.[93] Normally leukemia occurs about 2.3 times in 100,000 persons but at the Goodyear plant, it occurred at least 6 times in 1,100 workers. The connection of these deaths to benzene led Goodyear's vice president for manufacturing to say, "If I thought for one moment that there was any risk in the use of benzol, we would go out of that business."[94] Thus even in the presence of improved information about work-related risks, there is no guarantee that this will be communicated adequately or acted on.

Mercury has long been known to be dangerous to workers exposed to it. Prior to World War II it was found in many industries, but the major sources of occupational mercury poisoning were the fur and felt hat industries.[95] In the late 1930s a substitute for mercuric nitrate, used in the carroting of the fur, was introduced to these industries, eliminating exposure to mercury. Although this experience is gratifying, NIOSH estimates that "a minimum of 150,000 individuals are routinely exposed to mercury,"[96] and the demand for mercury is projected to grow significantly through the year 2000. Thus the likelihood that more hatters will be driven mad as in the days of Lewis Carroll is reduced; other kinds of workers are still being exposed in substantial numbers.

Knowledge of industrial-related hazards may not preclude workers, who feel that their only alternative is unemployment, loss of a skill, relocation or economic deprivation, from facing those risks. An extreme case is revealed in the situation in Anaconda, Montana, the setting for a huge copper smelting works. The National Cancer Institute has found that Deer Lodge County, where the Anaconda complex is located, has the ninth highest lung cancer rate of counties in the United States over a twenty-year period.[97] Though Hueper reports that arsenic has been a known occupational carcinogen since 1822 in causing skin cancer and since 1930 in causing lung cancer,[98] the Anaconda smelting complex releases twelve tons of arsenic through its smokestacks daily. This volume is twice as much as was being emitted in 1971 when the firm lost its sales market for arsenic and therefore stopped trapping and collecting it. Arsenic levels in Anaconda are 100 times higher than in Akron, Ohio, which has the highest arsenic concentration among cities in the United States. Despite the obvious danger, the risks are still as great as ever.

The commentaries of workers there are instructive. A local union president and truck driver at the smelter told a reporter, "What bothers me is not what happens twenty years from now, but how I feed my kids tomorrow." Another employee stated, "So the studies are right, what are my options? I'm forty-two years old, I've got six kids and a high school education. If the plant closes, what do I do?" A third worker, also a union official, was more picturesque, "Let's face it. Without the smelter this town couldn't support two cowboys and a saloon."[99]

The crucial variables are neither technological nor scientific, but the economic environment into which the information about risks is fed. Although the smelter employees in Anaconda, Montana, may be particularly vulnerable because of the lack of alternatives imposed by their geographic isolation, many urban workers feel similarly immobile. An obvious example is asbestos workers, virtually all of whom are now aware of their risks.[100]

Where a substance or a process is known to involve a serious risk and alternatives exist that are economically viable, as in the case of fluorescent lamps and beryllium, the incidence of disease is likely to be reduced. Dye manufacturers in most countries have voluntarily ceased to produce beta-naphthylamine, a known carcinogen, because they have a new method of making many chemicals without using it.[101] Yet Hueper reports that crude commercial alpha-naphthylamine still contains from 4 to 10 percent beta-naphthylamine. No chemical industries in any country, according to Hueper, have halted the production of benzidine, a powerful bladder carcinogen, because no satisfactory substitute for it has been found.[102]

Advances in medical science have been responsible for reducing the likelihood that certain occupational diseases result in serious disability or death. Hueper points out that while bladder cancer rates have been rising (not necessarily due to occupational causes), mortality rates from this disease have been declining.[103] Such reductions may be due to earlier and more accurate diagnoses and improved available treatments.

An improvement cannot be made of the observation of a German scientist who believes, "The incidence of many occupational diseases is decreasing as general hygienic conditions in industry are improved. Some previously well-known, widespread occupational diseases have disappeared almost completely. However, the permanent evolution in industry is the source of new health hazards which result from improved methods of production or from newly developed substances."[104] Some ancient scourges have already or are quickly disappearing from the workplace, but others remain, often to be found in industries where they previously were not known. The overall problem may be far more serious today than ever before as new hazards, some of which are carcinogenic, are quietly and widely spread into the industrial environment. Perhaps the positive and negative aspects of change can be illustrated best by an example that is only partially drawn from the workplace. A number of years ago, the Food and Drug Administration decided that codeine was too potent a narcotic to continue to be used in nonprescription cold medications widely sold over the counter. Many commercial producers at that time substituted chloroform in such preparations. Unfortunately a recent alert from NIOSH warns that chloroform has been shown to be carcinogenic when ingested by some laboratory animals.[105] The potential risk, obviously, is to users of such preparations, however, the workplace is implicated; NIOSH has estimated that 40,000 workers are exposed to chloroform in all of its industrial uses. Surely the lesson is not that hazardous substances should be eliminated from use only after safe alternatives have been found. Rather it is that hazards to workers and consumers will continue to be uncovered in an ever-wider variety of products and processes. It is imperative that we rapidly expand our knowledge about such hazards and act promptly in the presence of new evidence.

Estimates of Exposures to Hazards

Estimates of the extent of exposure to hazardous substances can provide some idea of the possible magnitude of various health and compensation problems that may occur. For example, beta-naphthylamine is a potent bladder carcinogen. It is believed that fewer than 100 workers in America are currently exposed to it. Such estimates can also provide important guidance for policy-makers in ranking priorities for research and monitoring activities and setting standards. Indeed NIOSH uses a formula, the product of a "severity rating" times the number of workers exposed, to determine priorities among hazards.[106] Such data could be used as inputs in the calculation of the extent of disease, where risk ratios or excess incidence rates are available for workers exposed to specified hazards.

Published estimates on the numbers of workers exposed to hazards are available only for a limited number of the 24,000 substances characterized as toxic by NIOSH. They do exist, however, for those substances NIOSH believes have highest priority. The NIOSH data on exposures are not the only ones available, but they are the most important. Other government agencies including OSHA appear to use the estimates prepared by NIOSH. Unfortunately it is difficult to evaluate the quality of the NIOSH figures since the agency cannot reconstruct how some of its earlier estimates were made. The estimation procedure used in recent years involves primarily the use of three sources of information. First, many occupations are linked to specific hazards on the basis of a 1964 Public Health Service volume by Gafefer.[107] Not only is the volume somewhat dated due to the ever-changing character of industry, the findings reported in it are based on even earlier work of the Public Health Service. Almost every NIOSH "Criteria Document" uses this volume as the basic source to identify occupations at risk, a basic step in estimating the number of persons exposed to a hazard. An updated version became available for use late in 1978.

Another source for identifying the occupations exposed to a specified hazard is the so-called Chicago Metropolitan study.[108] This 1970 study was based on an environmental survey of establishments where occupational hazards were anticipated. Many of the data from that study were not published, but they were utilized to establish relationships between industry, occupation, and the presence of hazards. In some recent instances these two sources, together with census data on industrial and/or occupational distributions, were used to estimate the number of workers exposed to a particular hazard. Since 1975 NIOSH has also made extensive use of telephone inquiries to persons familiar with the actual operating characteristics of an industry, hoping to better establish the number of workers at risk. The more recent method may appear haphazard, but it has decided advantages over using the Gafefer lists of occupations and hazards exclusively or in combination with the Chicago Metropolitan Survey findings.

To overcome some of these difficulties, NIOSH initiated a study (National Occupational Hazard Survey, NOHS) in 1972 that lasted for two years and involved sampling non-agricultural businesses.[109] Approximately 5,000 establishments in sixty-seven metropolitan areas were visited by a team of twenty engineers. On the basis of their findings, the data were extrapolated to a national population (38.3 million workers). The engineers evaluated the working environment and identified risks and hazards by a pass-through inspection of plants. This major effort is a highly laudable step, though the findings are far from definitive.

Some other concerns about exposure estimates should also be noted. A basic problem is the meaning of the term "exposure." The word has not been defined by NIOSH and the uncertainty that this causes is heightened by the occasional use of such expressions as "routinely exposed" or "potentially exposed." Is a worker exposed if his only contact is with a substance in a closed system? Are janitorial or service personnel in a chemical plant considered exposed? Does NIOSH consider the truck driver or airline pilot exposed if they simply transport the hazard? Is the employee exposed if his only contact with the substance occurs in the event of some accident or breakdown? Is a person exposed if he only deals with the hazard one shift per year or only while wearing some protective device? When NIOSH does develop a rigorous definition of exposure, it ought to take into account the dimensions of the exposure; the time exposed and the average dose of hazard per exposure. The level of workplace surveillance required for these determinations would be costly, however, the additional precision in calculating occupational diseases resulting from hazard exposure should yield considerable dividends.

Another concern about the meaning of these estimates deals with labor turnover. Even if NIOSH correctly estimates the number of workers exposed to a hazard, the number refers to a specific point in time. Holding aside questions of industry expansion or contraction, we know that labor turnover varies across occupations and industries. Even if employment in an industry is stable at 500,000 over the entire year, it may be that 600,000 persons have actually been employed there at one time or another during the period. In another industry with average employment of 500,000, the total number of persons employed there during the year may have been 700,000. In the case of certain hazards, for example those where illnesses can be contracted quickly with very short exposure, the overall number of persons employed may be more interesting than the average employment for the entire year.

Table 2.13 gives the NIOSH estimates of workers exposed to specific hazards, as of December 1973. For some of these substances, and others as well, estimates of the persons exposed have also appeared in NIOSH Alerts, Letters, or Criteria Documents that have been published since December 1973 and in NOHS. A number of these estimates are unchanged from those that appear in table 2.13, indicating that industrial or occupational employment changes in the interim have not been accounted for. Some later NIOSH estimates issued prior to NOHS are shown in table 2.14.

The estimates by NIOSH are subject to a number of criticisms aside from those already mentioned. A number of the recent estimates appearing in NIOSH Letters or Alerts give a totally unwarranted aura of precision. Recent public communications reporting new information on ethylene dibromide and trichloroethylene have estimated 9,111 and 282,653 exposed workers respectively.[110] NOHS estimated that 3,651,508 persons were exposed to trichloroethylene. The actual crudity of the NIOSH procedure is evident from an estimate made in 1974 of exposures to silica in 1970.[111] In a rare glimpse at the actual procedure employed at the time, NIOSH appears to have taken the six industries where most silica exposure occurs, totaled the numbers of workers there as reported in the 1970 *Statistical Abstracts*, and then added in a factor for all other industries. By this method 1.2 million were judged to be "exposed" to free silica. NOHS estimated the number at 3,212,836.

A more troublesome issue arises in the handling of asbestos. The asbestos *Criteria Document* of 1972 provides no overall estimate of exposure but indicates that about 1,000 people are employed in its mining and milling and about 40,000 field insulation workers are exposed to it when spraying it in construction, which in turn is responsible for the secondary exposures of 3 to 5 million building and shipyard employees.[112] Additionally, 50,000 are involved in the manufacture of asbestos-using products not including the secondary manufacture of products containing asbestos, such as electrical insulation. By 1973 NIOSH estimated that 200,000 workers were exposed (see table 2.13). In 1975 a NIOSH Letter reported that the workforce "potentially exposed" to asbestos in the manufacture and servicing of brake linings and clutches alone was 907,871. NOHS estimated the figure at 1,564,551. There is less detail about the exposures to chloroform in the NIOSH literature, but the estimates appearing in 1973, 1974, and 1976 were 75,000, 80,000, and 40,000 respectively.[113] No estimate is available from NOHS.

Table 2.13
Estimated number of workers exposed, December 1973 report

Hazard	Number	Hazard	Number
[a]2-acetylaminoflourene	<100	[a]Chloromethyl methyl ether	1,000
Acrolein	100,000	[a]Chromic acid	15,000
[a]Alpha-naphthylamine	1,000	[a]Chromium, hexavalent	75,000
[a]4-aminodiphenyl	1,000	Cold Stress	1,000,000
Ammonia	500,000	Cotton Dust	230,000
[a]Arsenic	1,500,000	[a]3,3'-dichlorobenzidine	2,500
[a]Asbestos	200,000	[a]Dieldrin	20,000
[a]Benzene	2,000,000	[a]4-Dimethylaminoazobenzene	1,000
[a]Benzidine	1,500	[a]Ethyleneimine	1,000
[a]Beryllium	28,000	Fibrous glass	200,000
[a]Beta-naphthylamine	<100	Flourides	350,000
[a]Beta-propiolactone	2,500	Hot environments	1,300,000
[a]Bis(chloromethyl) ether	1,000	[a]Industrial X-ray	10,000
[a]Cadmium	100,000	Laser (infrared)	10,000
Carboryl	100,000	Laser (ultraviolet)	20,000
Carbon monoxide	2,000,000	Lead (inorganic)	83,000
Carbon tetrachloride	160,000	Malathion	75,000
[a]Chloroform	75,000	Mercury (inorganic)	150,000
Methylene chloride	70,000	Silica	1,200,000
[a]4,4-Methylene-bis	25,000	Sodium hydroxide	150,000
[a]4-Nitrodiphenyl	1,000	Sulfur dioxide	500,000
[a]N-Nitrosodimethylamine	100	Sulfuric acid	200,000
Nitric oxide	350,000	Tetraethyl lead	35,000
Nitrogen dioxide	350,000	Tetramethyl lead	35,000
Noise	7,500,000	Toluene	100,000
Parathion	250,000	[a]Trichloroethylene	200,000
Polychlorinated biphenyls	10,000	[a]Ultraviolet (industry)	320,000
Selenium	3,300	[a]Ultraviolet (outdoors)	4,800,000

Source: *The President's Report on Occupational Safety and Health, December 1973* (Washington, D.C.: GPO, 1973), pp. 152–161.
a. Suspected or known carcinogens (not so noted in original source).

Table 2.14
Estimated number of workers exposed

Hazard	Number	Hazard	Number
Beryllium	30,000[a]	Hydrogen flouride	22,000[a]
Chloroform	80,000[a]	Methylene chloride	70,000[a]
Chloroform	40,000[b]	Nitric acid	27,000[a]
Chloroprene	2,500[b]	Polychlorinated biphenyls	12,000[b]
Chrystaline silica	1,060,000[a]	Toluene diisocyanate	40,000[a]
Coke oven emissions	10,000[a]	Trichloroethylene	282,653[b]
Cotton dust	800,000[a]	Ultraviolet xylene	140,000[a]
Ethylene dibromide	9,111[b]	Zinc oxide	50,000[a]

a. Source: NIOSH Criteria Document.
b. Source: NIOSH Alert, Bulletin, or Letter.

The estimates of exposures to lead reflect further problems in the estimates of exposed workers. In the *Criteria Document* on lead published in 1972 NIOSH pointed to a 1971 National Academy of Sciences report that concluded, "A reliable definition of the extent of risk of occupational lead exposure is unavailable."[114] NIOSH accepted this and did not offer an estimate of workers exposed: "Because of the changing usage of lead in industry and the widely varied trades where exposure occurs, the United States does not have a reporting system whereby the prevalence of occupational lead poisoning can be analyzed."[115] In the report to the president of 1973, however, occupational exposure is indicated as 83,000 (see table 2.13). NOHS later estimated lead exposure as 1,418,446 workers.

The *Criteria Document* for cotton dust does not estimate the number of workers exposed per se, but it reports that in 1973, 800,000 workers were involved in cotton fiber processing according to OSHA.[116] Yet the 1973 report of the president indicates that only 230,000 employees are exposed to the hazard of cotton dust. NOHS estimated that about 525,000 persons were occupationally exposed to cotton.

The most detailed and persuasive estimate of a population at risk emerges from the *Criteria Document* for coke oven emissions.[117] It uses data from earlier studies that found there were 13,218 coke ovens in the United States in 1970. Based on other research that reported that 1,327 persons were employed in two Pennsylvania plants containing 1,754 ovens, a ratio of coke workers to coke ovens was calculated, leading to an overall estimate of approximately 10,000 workers exposed.

For a variety of reasons NIOSH has become the primary source of data on the numbers of workers exposed to hazards. As such it has been forced by statute to provide estimates for many substances, even where data and research have been scarce or negligible. In its priority list of 1974, NIOSH listed quantitative exposure estimates for almost 400 substances.[118] NOHS allows for the provision of even more substances, but problems exist with many of these.

For example, a February 1978 *Criteria Document* specifies that about 11,000 workers are "occupationally exposed" to cresol. It is suggested that "this estimate is low, however, because it does not include workers who are intermittently exposed to a widely used commercial degreasing agent that contains cresol."[119] NOHS, strikingly, estimates that 1,913,823 workers are exposed to cresol.

It is imperative to try to develop a precise definition(s) of exposure, so that when better data do emerge they can readily be fitted into a framework of consistency and clarity of meaning. Only then will OSHA, NIOSH, workers' compensation administrators, and others have an idea of the size of working populations at risk. At that time also, it will be easier to estimate the potential number of illnesses in workers exposed to those substances where excessive risk or standardized mortality ratios are known with some certainty.

3

ETIOLOGICAL AND DIAGNOSTIC ISSUES

The purposes of workers' compensation systems have been widely accepted in principle, although their implementation has caused considerable controversy. In a brief and clear exposition the National Commission on State Workmen's Compensation Laws in 1972 enumerated these primary goals: the provision of adequate income maintenance for workers disabled by occurrences arising out of and in the course of employment; the assurance that such employees receive adequate health care and rehabilitation services; and structuring the system so that it encourages the maintenance of a safe and healthful workplace.[1] The commission also viewed broad coverage of injuries and diseases, wide coverage of workers, and an effective "delivery system" as important aims. Such goals create standards against which the entire system, or parts of it, can be evaluated. These goals, however, are interdependent. If the delivery system is inefficient, it could jeopardize the workers opportunity to begin rehabilitation at the most beneficial time. If an occupation or disease is not even covered, the adequacy of income maintenance to disabled employees or their survivors is not even an issue. There may be considerable disagreement about what is an acceptable level of income benefits, health services, safety impact, and coverages. The problems posed for the delivery system of benefits and services by issues of etiology and diagnosis will be analyzed. If the delivery system functions poorly, it jeopardizes all the other goals of workers' compensation. Subsequent chapters describe and evaluate many of the administrative aspects of current programs; however, here the particular problems of etiology are analyzed, and we conclude that it prevents the existing delivery system from adequately accomplishing its purposes.

To evaluate any aspect of the delivery system, it is important to recall the origins of compensation programs. The essential quid pro quo of these systems involved the abrogation of the injured employees' right to pursue a common-law action against their employer. In return they received an assurance of a speedy and certain award in amounts specified by law. A significant test of the delivery system, therefore, is the speed and certainty with which it receives and processes claims for compensation.

Many occupational diseases never enter the arena of workers' compensation, and for those that do, many are resolved neither with dispatch nor with certainty. It is important to emphasize strongly that the fault does not necessarily lie with the individuals involved with the program; attorneys, administrators, insurers, unions, and physicians. The fundamental problem is the need to determine etiology: What are the causes and conditions under which the disease was contracted? In the case of disability due to a disease an employee must prove that the disease arose out of and in the course of employment. In some jurisdictions the claimant may have the even harder task of demonstrating that the illness is peculiar to his occupation or industry. In either case a workers' compensation administrator or judge may be forced to decide whether the disease resulted from the workplace. All too often this places an intolerable burden on the decison maker. Since some of these questions cannot be resolved regularly with consistency and in conformity with the principles of the laws, their decisions appear capricious and inequitable.

The adversary process may work splendidly in other areas of the workers' compensation system, but it does not improve the handling of claims for occupational diseases. This process, which is designed to assure that all relevant information is fairly provided to the decision maker, may only obfuscate the issue of etiology, or it may allow the decision about compensability to rest on secondary issues. This problem does not exist for all cases of occupational disease nor do accidental injury cases always involve situations where the truth is clear and determinable. Occupational disease cases are far more likely to involve complex, if not fundamentally insoluble, questions of causation.

The Latency Period

In a routine accident and injury on the job, an employee and employer usually can quickly determine if a compensable injury has occurred. The opportunity for dispute is always present, but the vast majority of cases are settled without prolonged dispute or litigation. When differences do occur, they frequently involve the extent of disability not the question of compensability per se. The speedy resolution of most cases should be no surprise since the issues are typically straightforward: The employment relationship is known, the matter of fault is not at issue, the time and place of the accident-injury is generally supported by witnesses, the link between the accident and the injury may be apparent, and the wage is on record. Legal texts are filled with cases where one or more of these matters is disputed, but these are rare instances. For a significant group of occupational diseases one or more of these issues is probably not known and perhaps can never be determined. These involve diseases with long latency periods, that is, a significant period passes between the employee's first exposure to a hazard and the manifestation of a resulting disease.

The latency problem does exist in some accident-injury cases, but for certain occupational diseases the problem is substantially different for three reasons. For some of these diseases a long latency period always occurs between exposure and the manifestations of disease. The period of latency for many of these diseases is substantial. For many of these diseases with long latency the problem of the legal identification of the source is complicated by scientific ignorance regarding the causes of the disease.

Diseases with long latency cause two major types of problems for workers' compensation. First, because of the passage of time, the employee, the physician, and others may miss the link between the disease and a hazard encountered many years earlier. Even if the worker or the employer may have known that a particular substance was hazardous and the potential source of some disease, the employee may forget this contact occurred or that it might be responsible for an illness years later.[2] Thus there is little reason to suppose that a worker — or his survivor — will even be aware that the disease is work-related, let alone compensable.

The second major problem involving long latency periods is that of establishing sufficient proof to sustain a workers' compensation claim. The passage of time handicaps the employee and employer in their search for necessary evidence regarding the exposure to a hazard, the dose involved, the type of work being done, and so forth. Either side may face this difficulty; however, it is likely to be a far greater problem for the claimant because the burden of proof almost invariably falls on him or his survivor.

All of the known industrial carcinogens involve diseases with some latent period. The medical community is not unified regarding the average latency period for each carcinogen, but there is considerable agreement about the general ranges of the latency period. Table 3.1 provides a summary of some estimates of latency periods for cancer associated with a number of carcinogens. The very wide ranges for some of these hazards pose obvious difficulties for workers' compensation adjudicators. An additional complication is that the same hazard is often identified with different forms of cancer, which means that the latency period may vary considerably according to the site. In exposure to asbestos, Hueper estimates an average latency period of thirty to forty years for mesothelioma of the pleura compared to a range of fifteen to twenty-one years for lung cancer. Most of the hazards listed in table 3.1 have latency periods ranging up to three and four decades.

Jablon, in describing the Japanese experience with leukemia after the dropping of the atomic bombs in 1945, notes that there was a minimum latency period of about two years.[3] He compares this to the known minimum latency period of about five years for other types of cancer. While leukemia rates for survivors of the atomic bombs peaked in 1951 and 1952, excess rates continued into the early part of the 1970s.

The length of the lag may be due partly to the intensity of the exposure to a carcinogen. It may also be due to some predisposition or special receptivity of the individual. Inadequate information and insufficient cases make it difficult to explain these large

Table 3.1
Estimated latency periods for cancers due to hazards

Carcinogenic Substance	Range of Latent Period in Years	Average Latent Period in Years
[a]Asbestos	15–21	18
[a]Chromates	5–47	15
[a]Nickel	6–30	22
[a]Coal tar fumes	9–23	16
[a]Ionizing radiations	7–50	15–35
Petroleum, Petroleum coke, Wax, Creosote, Anthracene, Paraffin, Shale, Mineral Oils	12–30	
Benzene	6–14	
Auramine, Benzidine, Alpha- and Beta-Naphthylamine, Magenta, 4-Aminodiphenyl, 4-Nitrodiphenyl	13–30	
Mustard gas	10–25	
Isopropyl oil	10+	
Vinyl chloride	20–30	
Bis (chloromethyl) ether, Chloromethyl, Methyl ether	5+	
Arsenic	10+	
Chromium	15–25	
Nickel	3–30	
Asbestos	4–50	
Wood	30–40	
Leather	40–50	
Ultraviolet rays	Varies with skin pigment and texture 10–25	
X-rays	10–25	
Uranium, Radon, Radium, Mesothorium	10–15	

Source (except where a's appear): P. Cole and M. Goldman, "Occupation," in *Persons at High Risk of Cancer,* ed. Joseph F. Fraumeni, Jr. (New York: Academic Press), pp. 172–176.
a. Source (lung cancer only): W. C. Hueper, *Recent results in Cancer Research: Occupational and Environmental Cancers of the Respiratory System* (New York: Springer-Verlag, 1966), p. 27.

ranges. It is likely that as more data become available on specific cancer sites and particular carcinogens, the mean period between exposure and manifestation will be better known, but the increased number of observations will widen the range or the spread of the time period. This will increase the problem of identifying etiology for compensation adjudicators, for as the range widens it becomes increasingly difficult to determine when and where the causal agent may have been encountered. An example of this may be asbestos. In table 3.1, based on a 1966 source, the range of the latent period for lung cancer is shown as fifteen to twenty-one years. In 1972, however, NIOSH reported that a study had found that eighteen of fifty-nine lung cancer cases in asbestos workers occurred twenty-five years or more after first exposure to the hazard.[4]

The matter of proof in a workers' compensation claim for the specific case of radiation is spelled out in a paper by Sagan. The difficulty, according to Sagan, does not result from misunderstanding the problem: "On the contrary, of all environmental hazards to which workers are exposed, radiation is more clearly understood than most."[5] The central issue is establishing causality, and here the problems are immense. Sagan states that in the case of a long latent disease resulting from possible radiation exposure, establishing causality requires consideration of five criteria: (1) What was the extent of the exposure and its relationship to the development of disease? (2) Is the claimant's disease known to be related to radiation exposure? (3) Does the person have a biological predisposition or enhanced sensitivity to radiation's effects? (4) What are the synergistic effects of other materials or agents to which the claimant may have been exposed, either off or on the job? (5) Are there other sources of radiation outside his employment to which the claimant may have been exposed? (Sagan might have added a sixth consideration, the possibility of an exposure to radiation at a previous or subsequent job.)

Each of these criteria present problems when attempting to establish a causal relationship. First, there are difficulties in demonstrating how much exposure a worker may have had to radiation. Little is known about the relationship between the intensity of exposure and the risk of contracting disease. Second, there is little or no way of knowing if the claimant's illness was caused by exposure to radiation because the risk associated with exposure to radiation is small. Estimates exist that one case of leukemia per year would result from exposing 1 million persons to 1 rad.[6] The background rate of leukemia in the general population is seventy cases per million per year. Thus if a small number are exposed to occupational radiation, the impact probably will not show up against the incidence in the population at large. The third issue is certainly relevant since science has yet to identify many of the significant variables and the role they play in contracting the disease. The fourth consideration, that other agents may have acted in a synergistic way with the radiation to initiate the disease, is also plausible. These agents may not have been encountered in the workplace but may have been responsible for triggering the development of the disease. The fifth consideration is also significant since "occupational radiation exposures represent only a portion of the ionizing radiation to which an individual is exposed. Environmental exposures, both internal and external, as well as medical exposures for both diagnostic and therapeutic purposes may be as high or higher than the occupational exposure; yet these can rarely be quantitated."[7]

Even though the courts in some instances have relaxed their need for proof regarding causality and science may be better equipped today to help establish casuality than it was in 1969, compensation for disease due to radiation exposure is still an oddity. McCormick describes a case in Texas where a person who began work in 1961 in good health developed cancer of the lymph nodes by 1965 after constant exposure to radioactive materials.[8] A medical expert testified that the cause of cancer is not known, but the radiation to which the employee had been exposed for four years was a possibility. Although the claimant was awarded compensation by a jury, upon appeal the Court of Civil Appeals and then the Texas Supreme Court overturned the jury's verdict. The denial by the courts was based on a view that medical testimony indicating only a "possible" causal connection is inadequate. When the etiology is unclear, the claimant must prove a causal connection and in so doing offer evidence that other possible causes, such as natural radiation or viruses, are improbable. This Texas decision demonstrates that Sagan's concerns regarding the difficulty of establishing proof in radiation claims are fully warranted. A striking aspect of the Texas claim, reported by McCormick, was the fairly short latency period, which should have made it relatively easy to establish a causal connection.

Cancer is not the only type of disease with the problematic characteristic of long latency. The occupational health literature is filled with examples of diseases that are manifested a number of years after first exposure and, further, where there may have been no recent connection, occupational or other, with the hazard in question. For example, chronic benzene poisoning brought about the death of an artificial leather worker who had been exposed for four years but who had not had contact with benzene for the six years prior to death.[9] Various agents found at the workplace may begin to damage the lungs, kidneys, liver, and other organs so gradually that disabling disease is not observed until years later.

Mindful of these lags, the provisions found in a number of states that exclude compensation where there has been limited or no occupational contact with a hazard in some stipulated previous period seem patently inequitable. Such limits in states where they exist concentrate on certain dust diseases such as asbestosis and silicosis. Thus despite the fact that the asbestosis may develop years after a worker's last exposure to a hazard, a Texas court was forced to deny compensation when a long-term asbestos worker died of asbestosis.[10] His survivors were denied benefits on the grounds that the statute allowed compensation only when death or disability occurred within three years of the last exposure to asbestos. In this case the symptoms only began to appear four years after the person last worked in covered employment.

"The latent period for development of silicosis is usually four to twenty years or more."[11] The sheer vagueness implied by this observation attests to the problems inherent in statutes requiring some recent period of exposure before compensation will be paid. Numerous claims have been defeated and many more have never been filed because the disease did not appear until after the time limit had passed. Even where the courts might have stretched such statutes they have not always seen fit to do so. In Carr v. Homestake Mining Co., a claim was denied to an employee because South Dakota statute requires in silicosis claims that the employee has been injuriously exposed to silica dust for over five years in the ten years preceding the disablement.[12] Since acute silicosis can develop in a few months if workers have heavy exposure to dust containing silica,[13] the five-year minimum is clearly out of line with medical knowledge about the nature of the disease. But the Carr case reveals the legal inequity resulting from the lag in the development of the disease. While Carr did not meet the five years in the last ten years criterion, he clearly had substantial exposure (and most of that with the employer in question). Carr worked for Homestake Mining from September 1929 until February 1942, from September 1945 through February 1951, and from February 1952 until May 1962. Unfortunately for this employee of almost thirty years he did not become ill until April 1971, meaning that he only had slightly over one year of exposure to silica during the previous ten years and thus was denied compensation.

Colorado's statute not only included a five-year exposure out of the past ten years but required that the exposure occur in Colorado. In a recent decision a Colorado court has held this to be unconstitutional on the grounds that such limits are capricious and deny individuals due process.[14] The court indicated its displeasure with several aspects of the statute and correctly observed that the length of exposure is not the decisive factor in determining a causal connection. As the *Carr* case demonstrates, such statutes can cause claims to be barred even when there are almost thirty years of exposure if there is a lag between exposure to the hazard and the onset of the disease.

Although the problem of the long latent diseases may cause certain disease claims to be barred by statute or make proof difficult to establish, particularly for the claimant, perhaps the greatest effect on compensation systems is that numerous potential claims are not ever filed. The passage of time may understandably cause workers to forget that they ever were exposed to a hazard that would cause a disabling disease many years later. Such memory loss is an explanation for the absence of some potential claims only if two other conditions are met: first, the worker was aware of the nature of the substance or substances to which he was exposed (and not just by proprietary name); and, second, he knew that the substance represented a (nonacute) health risk. If both conditions are met, then the long latent disease may result in a claim if the worker recalls them when the disease begins to be manifested. It seems more likely that a claim will be filed if the worker is in the same line of work or same establishment as he was when first exposed to the hazard. Then at least he may know other workers with similar illnesses who have identified the source of the disease. The union, the employer in some cases, plant and/or local physicians may also be alerted to the linkage, making it more likely that the occupational origins of the disease will be perceived, causing a claim to be filed.

When the employee has changed his employer, his occupation, and/or his residence, there may be little reason to connect an illness and a much earlier workplace exposure. Thus a crucial issue with diseases of long latency, particularly when the disease does not differ from the "ordinary diseases of life," is labor turnover. The greater the extent of turnover, the better the chance that a long latent disease will not be recognized as occupational in origin. There are a variety of data available on labor turnover, but aside from the very limited New York State study of dust diseases,[15] they do not provide any special insight on turnover where various hazards exist. The U.S. labor force must be characterized as extremely mobile in terms of interfirm, interoccupational, interindustry, and interregional mobility. For men in the age group forty-five to fifty-nine, only 10 percent of white and 7 percent of black males have been with their present employer over their entire working careers.[16] Indeed 20 percent of the white and 25 percent of the black males in this age group have spent less than 10 percent of their working careers with their current employer. Fewer than one-quarter of these males are in the same broad occupational category as they were in their first regular job.

Over half of these males now reside in a different county or standard metropolitan statistical area than at the time of their first jobs, and about 30 percent of all males from forty-five to fifty-nine live in a different state than when they began work.

A false implication of labor turnover and diseases with long latencies is that increased labor mobility results in less extensive exposure to particular workplace hazards and, therefore, a reduction in the number of disease cases. One scientist confronts this issue directly:

. . . some (aromatic amine induced) cancers were found after an extraordinarily short exposure time, indicating the high potency of these substances. Apart from having a distinct medicolegal significance, this observation militates definitely against short-term employment for preventing the occurrence of occupational cancers in dye workers. Such a practice would in all probability aggravate the scope of this cancer hazard by creating a large number of individuals exposed. . . . Since similarly short exposure times have been observed with other occupational cancers (asbestos, arsenicals, ionizing radiation) this conclusion has general application.[17]

Such turnover serves to reduce the volume of diseases with long latency periods only if the limited exposures are below the threshold level that induces the disease. Minimum levels may exist for some of the carcinogens — and the matter is the subject of vigorous debate by scientists and others — but none have yet been specified.

Another implication of the interface between labor turnover and diseases with long latencies is that perhaps older workers should be allowed to handle those hazards where the disease would not be expected to occur until long after some other ailment has brought about the person's death. It is highly doubtful that society would opt for such a calculated policy. Moreover in the light of certain recent findings the policy might be highly unfortunate. The relationship between age at the time of first exposure to a carcinogen and the likelihood of developing cancer is unknown and inadequately studied, however, Cole and Goldman report on two recent papers suggesting that older persons may actually have greater susceptibility to cancer than do younger persons.[18] It is unlikely that the use of "industrial kamikazes" will develop in this nation in the foreseeable future. It is possible that the leading underwriter of workers' compensation insurance in America was considering the problem of long-latent disease when it recommended to its policy holders; "Do not expose young workers to certain industrial toxic substances as they are especially susceptible; older workers are apparently more immune."[19]

Diseases with long latency periods affect workers' compensation systems in other ways that undermine the basic purposes. Because new substances and processes are appearing rapidly and some resultant diseases will occur only years after initial exposures, there may be no restraints imposed on exposure until many persons have been placed at risk. Aside from the obvious implications about the delay in implementing safety and protective programs, the workers' compensation insurance premiums cannot possibly reflect the extent of the potential costs that may be incurred. By the time the hazard has been identified, the employer, the insurer, or the substance or process in question may no longer exist.

Multiple Factor Causality

With some significant exceptions, including cardiovascular diseases, the workers' compensation law is relatively straightforward and consistent with claims involving multiple causes. If an incident arising out of and in the course of employment disables a covered employee, the claim will be compensable, even if the impairment would not have resulted except for the presence of some other factor, including a preexisting condition. If the other factor or factors contribute not to the existence of the impairment but to the extent of disability, the matter is scarcely changed. The injury is still compensable. The rate of compensation or the source of the benefits (a second injury fund, perhaps) may be affected through an apportionment mechanism, which can vary substantially by state, but the compensability is usually not in doubt. (Some exceptions to the principle do exist; see chapter 4). The principle of compensation that accounts for this is drawn from the common law and is often summarized as "the employer takes the worker as he finds him." This principle is not explicitly undermined in the area of occupational disease, although such sources of disability create special difficulties because so little is known about multiple causes of disease.

This situation has been well summarized by Selikoff who, along with others, is aware of the issue.[20] He indicates that the traditional approach to identifying occupational diseases and the setting of standards for hazards has been based on the "one cause—one effect" concept. Research also has proceeded along this line. The technique is useful for a variety of reasons:

They (the one cause—one effect approaches) were practical, productive, orderly. With them, we have been able to sort out the biological potential of various metals, finding that some, as iron or tin, produced little pulmonary reaction while others, as beryllium, gave serious disease. Even today, it makes good sense to isolate a substance in the human environment, as far as possible, to study its effects, and this technique is almost universally used in animal investigations.

Nevertheless, however well this concept has served us to this point, there is now a growing realization that it is incomplete and restrictive and occasionally, even inappropriate or misleading.

Single agents in the workplace are the exception rather than the rule. Multiple exposures are much more common. When they occur, the effects can be varied and, often, unpredictable. Thus, when agents have the same toxic potential, summation of effects may be anticipated; this may be the case where neurotoxic solvents of like toxicity are used. On the other hand, the toxic effects may be distinct and related to the unique properties of the several agents. It is even possible that the effects may be multiplicative rather than additive, or even less than additive. We have comparatively little information on the effects of the various combinations, and it should be anticipated that in the next years much more will be known about this problem.[21]

The problem, then is to identify the cause of a disease that may begin to be manifested years after the contact. The source may have involved a factor (a substance or process) encountered at the workplace and another factor found either at work, at home, in one's food, water or air, or elsewhere. Ultimately the issue is not just that we do not know the cause of a disease (let alone have sufficient proof for purposes of compensation), but the etiological problem is much more complicated than imagined, and extremely limited progress in the identification of disease causes must be anticipated.

Several examples will better illustrate the problem. As reported in a 1926 paper by Turner and Thompson, guinea pigs were fed various amounts of a zinc oxide suspension in olive oil.[22] Using standard experimental techniques, one set of control animals was fed olive oil and another set was fed zinc oxide in chopped carrots. Of the sixteen experimental animals, eight died between days two and eleven of the experiment. It was found that their lungs, liver, and kidneys were involved. No such changes were observed in either set of control animals, indicating that while the zinc oxide by itself was innocuous, in combination with the olive oil it was extremely toxic. For the estimated 50,000 workers currently exposed to zinc oxide in the United States, there is no information about what other substances they may contact or ingest that will, in conjunction with zinc oxide, eventually be injurious.

Sulphur dioxide is not considered a carcinogenic agent, but it is suspected of enhancing the carcinogeneity of other substances found at the workplace, including arsenic.[23] Since NIOSH estimates that about 500,000 workers are exposed to sulphur dioxide, the problem is not a small one. The very widely found ferric oxide has been reported as a cofactor in the development of respiratory cancers in test animals in the presence of other substances such as diethylnitrosamine. This may be dwarfed by other potential areas of concern such as the possibility that many widely used chemicals like chlorine and ammonia may cause or interact with (preexisting) heart disease.[24]

A final example can be taken from the work of Mancuso, who examined the correlates of disease for cohorts of workers employed in two major firms in beryllium-extracting industries.[25] He found a much higher rate of lung cancer among the subgroup of workers who had had a prior respiratory illness due to beryllium exposure than among all workers in the sample. Apparently the prior illness was associated with a predisposition to lung cancer not found in other workers. He also found a higher lung cancer rate among those workers who had been employed from one to five calendar quarters than among those who worked six or more quarters. These striking findings lead Mancuso to suggest "that factors inherent among the short-term employees were contributing to the higher rates for the one- to five-quarter group," and "of importance, the findings of the present study as finally developed in contrast to the initial impression, provide support to the concept of the uniqueness of biological effects of beryllium host response. It may be safely speculated that beryllium is acting with other factors, rather than as a single etiology related to duration of employment."[26]

Such findings suggest that the common-law principle of taking the worker as the employer finds him involves two elements of chance for many diseases. On the one hand the employer has virtually no reliable basis for screening and so may hire a worker with a predisposition to a serious occupational disease. On the other hand the chances that any occupational disease that develops will be linked to the workplace are low. Thus although the employer is in a poor position to evaluate the worker as he finds him, the worker is in the unfortunate position of not knowing the (potentially) compensable conditions with which he may leave his employment.

Multiple Factor Causality: A Special Problem

A vexing problem for scientists, and therefore for workers' compensation adjudicators, involves multiple causality created by a claimant's history of smoking. Many of the diseases of the workplace involve a respiratory problem, and this category of illnesses may account for the largest share of difficult etiological issues currently in compensation proceedings. Because it is so widely accepted that cigarette smoking increases the likelihood of contracting a host of respiratory illnesses, it creates tremendous problems in adjudicating the compensation claims of smokers. Some view the problem as creating an escape hatch for employers:

It should be obvious that any wide acceptance of such scientifically unsound and socially irresponsible claims concerning the principal role of cigarette smoking in the causation of cancers, especially respiratory cancer, would paralyze not only a legitimate and urgently needed pursuit into the various environmental factors inducing such cancers, particularly the many industry-related pollutants of the urban air, but has provided already effective legal arguments before civil courts and compensation boards for denying justified claims for compensation of occupational respiratory cancers to the victims of such hazards as well as to their widows and orphans.[27]

The data suggest that cigarette smoking, itself carcinogenic, enhances the cancer-causing effects of some agents, and in other instances the interactive effects have not yet been sorted out. Selikoff has argued that asbestos causes lung cancer only in smokers (though it produces other forms of cancer in both smokers and nonsmokers).[28] Mancuso, however, using Selikoff's data concludes that asbestos induces lung cancer even in nonsmokers,[29] leaving the issue to be resolved as more data become available. Based on their own assessment of the state of scientific knowledge, the medical staff of the Ontario Workmen's Compensation Board has recently concluded that asbestos can cause lung cancer in nonsmokers, but smoking enhances the carcinogenic properties of asbestos.[30]

Ironically even though the employer takes the worker as he finds him, the worker (in the case of cigarette smoking) through his own disregard for his health may impose compensation costs on the employer or his insurer, even well after termination of employment. Cigarette smoking is also correlated with higher incidence rates and greater severity of byssinosis in textile workers.[31] For uranium miners with the highest levels of exposure to radioactivity, Jablon notes that lung cancer mortality increased to twenty-four times the expected rate. However, "most of the miners studied were cigarette smokers; the separate roles of smoking and radon exposure in the causation of lung cancers cannot be described explicitly nor can it be determined whether the two effects act independently or whether there is a synergism."[32]

This uncertainty on the part of the medical-scientific community is more than a technical issue that can be resolved eventually; there is as much controversy here as in any compensation dispute. Such contentiousness, which will hardly assure a rapid resolution of the pertinent scientific questions, can be seen in the following:

The recent allegation of Oettel that lung cancers in chromate workers were found only in individuals who smoked cigarettes thus appears to be an expedient subterfuge and skillful device helpful to industrial management for escaping their legal and moral obligations toward their employees and the human society. Such financial contentions have obviously no scientific basis in fact and belong to the pseudoscientific propaganda emanating during the last decade to an increasing degree from scientific guardians of commercial interests.[33]

While the scientists continue to seek out the truth, so too must compensation adjudicators. An Oregon court had to decide whether bronchitis in a heavy smoker was a work-related disability.[34] The employee had been exposed to dust from the sanding and grinding of metals and plastics and fumes from paints and fillers. Physicians testified on both sides of the issue; one side argued that the bronchitis was due to workplace hazards, and the other put the blame on the heavy smoking. The court was forced to choose its interpretation of etiology where multiple causality was a possibility. The claimant was awarded compensation in this case, apparently on the grounds that when he left work on his doctor's advice, his condition appeared to improve, even though he continued to smoke heavily.

Another state has resolved the issue of inadequate scientific knowledge regarding multiple causality and smoking through elaborate apportionment formulas. In a 1976 California decision, a person with thirty-two years of work experience with different employers was found to have lung damage, resulting in a 58 percent permanent disability.[35] The court held that half of the disability was industrially related, another one-quarter of the disability was due to nonindustrial causes, and the final one-quarter was due to cigarette smoking, one-third of which was incurred during on-the-job smoking. Since the latter was found to be compensable also, an award was ordered based on a net compensable disability of 33.75 percent (1/2 of 58%, plus 1/3 x 1/4 x 58%).

The compensation adjudicator is being asked to resolve issues in an area where considerable uncertainty exists, and continued contention between workers and employers is anticipated. As each side attempts to shift the responsibility either to cigarettes or the work environment, consider how far the compensation system has drifted from being a no-fault program.

Other Environmental Sources

A large number of substances that cause occupational disease are plentiful in our environment and can cause or contribute to illness and death of persons who are out of the labor force. Some of these substances are a consequence of an industrial operation; many others occur naturally. Some remaining potential hazards may not fit either of these classifications, as in the recently reported findings of chloroform and asbestos in the water supplies of some very large cities. A generality can be made that illnesses resulting from occupational exposure are compensable, and those due to an environmentally encountered hazard are not. Such a simple dichotomy rarely occurs, and the problem of etiology appears to be fundamentally insoluble for compensation purposes in many cases.

Birmingham, Key, Holaday, and Perone reported on the reopening of a gold mine where smelting operations produced about 40 tons of arsenic and 100 tons of sulphur dioxide to be burned off daily.[36] Children attending a local elementary school began developing skin lesions and ulcerations, as did nine of the eighteen workers on the day shift at the smelter. The source of the illness was traced by observing that youngsters who spent ten to twelve hours a day away from their community while attending a regional high school did not have any similar condition. Obviously some pollutant(s) from the smelter, arsenic, sulphur dioxide, or something else was at fault. Since workers, as well as others, suffered illness from residential exposure also, could it be argued that their dermatoses arose out of and in the course of employment? Clearly the industrial operation was involved, but exposure to the pollutant might have been negligible within certain sections of the factory, including offices, compared to potential exposure in the open air in the vicinity of the plant.

Individuals exposed to arsenic face an elevated probability of lung cancer. The National Cancer Institute has demonstrated this is not simply an occupational problem. Women (non-employees) had significantly excessive rates of mortality from lung cancer if they lived in a community where a significant share of the labor force was employed in the smelting and refining of copper, lead, and zinc. An airborne by-product of such operations is arsenic.[37] Arsenic is also found as a contaminant of water, food (including seafood), soil, and tobacco and can enter the human system through a variety of routes, though the degree of exposure may be small in some of these.

Arsenic is hardly unique, either in being so ubiquitous or diverse in route of entry. Mercury also occurs widely in nature. Besides being found in water and food (including fish), it is also ingested in air polluted by the burning of fossil fuels and the airborne discharges of mercury-using industries and is used in dental-medical treatment. Nickel is known to be carcinogenic to persons exposed at the workplace. It is the source of serious air pollution in certain communities where specific industries are located.[38] In addition to asbestos, certain carcinogens found at the workplace can be carried outside of the plant to the home, for example by the employees' clothing, thereby exposing family members. As mentioned earlier, residents in areas near dye-producing plants have been put at excessive risk of bladder-urinary system cancer.

Environmental hazards that occur at the workplace and are spread from there to persons not in the labor force are a serious and growing problem and not only for the workers' compensation system. Hueper observes, "It is apparent . . . that during recent decades technological developments have spread respiratory carcinogens originally mainly active among members of restricted occupational groups not only to ever larger and more general industrial worker groups, but also have disseminated such in part highly potent agents through industrial and industry-related wastes from occupational environments into local and general environments where they have contact with the population particularly its urban and industrialized components."[39] This comment was made prior to the expression of concern by the federal and state governments regarding clean air, and environmental protection safeguards. It is too early to assess either the long-term impact of such governmental policy on pollutant levels or the health problems that may appear resulting from the lack of such policy in the past.

Many workplace hazards also found in the environment are not transmitted from the former to the latter. As well as being a very significant workplace hazard, lead, a by-product of the internal combustion engine, is also an air pollutant. Lead exposure at the workplace has not been identified as carcinogenic, but lead ingested in the diet has been implicated in cancers of the stomach, small and large intestines, ovary, kidney, and in myelomas, all lymphomas, and all leukemia.[40]

It is difficult to conceive how the courts can sort their way in a consistent fashion through the tangle of possible etiological connections. The handling of the most ubiquitous of the carcinogens, radiation, is another knotty issue. Little doubt exists that excessive ultraviolet radiation from exposure to the sun causes cancer in certain persons. Jablon cites a National Academy of Sciences report that for Caucasians living at 40° latitude (Philadelphia), no less than 40 percent of the melanomas and 80 percent of the squamous and basal cell carcinomas are caused by ultraviolet radiation.[41] Further it has been demonstrated that mortality rates for melanoma in the band of states from South Carolina to Louisiana is 1.75 times greater than in the band of states from Washington to Minnesota. For skin cancer the corresponding ratio is 2.5. Persons placed at such elevated risks, aside from simply living in such areas, include those who spend considerable amounts of time working outdoors. Risky occupations include sailors, all agricultural workers, recreational personnel, service station attendants, sanitation workers, and construction workers. The workers' compensation systems could conceivably be called on to determine the compensability of claims for skin cancer or melanoma in persons who are or have ever been employed in these or similar kinds of exposed occupations. Some cases have already occurred, with little success for claimants. A 1965 Florida decision held that skin cancer in a worker exposed for a period of years to sunlight was not an occupational disease.[42]

Etiology and the Identification of Hazards

When a workers' compensation claim is filed for a disability due to an occupational disease, the adjudicator may have to decide if the impairment could have arisen out of and in the course of employment. The decision may hinge on a determination of whether a workplace exposure might have been sufficient to cause the disease. If the likelihood of contracting the disease is no greater for the employee than for any other person, the system may find this an ordinary disease of life and therefore not compensable. Thus the workers' compensation adjudicator has been and will increasingly be asked to evaluate the degree of risk that a worker has incurred. Such determinations can be made in a straightforward and consistent fashion for some diseases, however, they simply cannot be made for many others. When such decisions are made, they must necessarily appear capricious. This is one additional problem the system must bear due to ignorance regarding etiology.

Passage of the Occupational Safety and Health Act of 1970 has created an intense interest in setting standards. Because of the adversary-like process that generates OSHA's "maximum allowable exposure levels," substantial evidence is mustered by all interested parties to persuade the secretary of labor of the correctness of the various proposed levels. It is precisely this process that confirms the degree of uncertainty regarding the question of what is a "safe" level of exposure. Some scientists argue that no safe level of exposure to a carcinogenic agent exists, while others refute the generality of this contention. Congress seems to have spoken in favor of the former position since the 1958 Delaney Amendment to the Federal Food, Drug and Cosmetic Act stipulates that "no additive shall be deemed safe if it is found, after tests which are appropriate for the evaluation of the safety of food additives, to induce cancer in man or animals." Regardless of levels of exposure or dosage if a substance is carcinogenic, even in animals, it cannot be judged safe. Compensation claims can involve this type of matter, with medical judgments provided by attorneys on either side of the question. Since answers do not yet exist for many such questions, the workers' compensation adjudicator is in the difficult position of having to decide a fundamentally scientific issue.

An example of the complexity of the question of a safe level of exposure is shown in the technical paper by Holaday on the control of radon daughter hazards in uranium mines.[43] In the century since lung cancer was causally connected to uranium mined in the Erz Mountains, no substantial agreement has been reached on a "safe" level of exposure. Peters points out that over 50 percent of the threshold limit values used are based only on animal experiments or on chemical analogy.[44] He argues "Even assuming that animal data apply to man, which is a large assumption, most animal experiments on toxicity are either acute or subacute in nature and do not examine adequately the question of chronic effects."[45] The need for continued animal experimentation is obvious and so are the problems in identifying the quantitative extent to which a substance is hazardous in man.

Even where agreement exists regarding a minimal level of safety for a hazard, for the compensation system to function satisfactorily evidence is needed regarding the level of exposure, if any, encountered by the injured employee. If workers are unaware that they are exposed to a hazard, they will hardly be aware of the degree of exposure. Discher and associates found substantial numbers of workers who did not respond to a query regarding past levels or types of hazardous exposure. The point is strongly made by Woodward and Fondmiller:

It may be important to note that the starting point for all except a few cases was the knowledge of the claimant or his doctor that he had been exposed to potentially harmful material. Medical examination then led to a diagnosed beryllium or asbestos disease. Rarely did the doctor diagnose a possible asbestos or beryllium disease and then verify exposed employment to confirm it. Also, each of these diseases proved to have similarities to other lung diseases with which there is sometimes confusion. From these facts we might conclude that some workers may contract beryllium or asbestos diseases without connecting them to employment and not claim compensation.[46]

It is not surprising that employees may not know the substances to which they are or were exposed, but without this information the extent of the exposure is a moot question. Given the vast array of substances a specific worker may contact in a modern industrial setting and recognizing that many such hazards are difficult to identify because of proprietary names or because they appear as by-products in a process and so on, it is hardly shocking that even employers do not know to what substances their employees may be exposed. For example Schoenberg and Mitchell surveyed some Connecticut firms from September to December of 1972, on the heels of the June 1972 issuance of a highly controversial asbestos standard by OSHA.[47] They found that over one-third of the manufacturing firms sampled had no realization that their employees were being exposed to asbestos.

A decision in a workers' compensation case involving an occupational disease may involve some judgment about the extent to which a worker has been exposed and if it is sufficient to cause the disease in question. Many cases never enter workers' compensation proceedings because the worker is unaware he has been exposed to any hazard at all. Assuming the worker who develops an occupational disease is aware of the fact of his exposure, there is little chance that accurate estimates of the level of exposure can be obtained (beyond the simple question of how long a worker was in a place of employment on a specific job). Even if exposure levels were known and could be introduced as evidence, medical science in many instances could not demonstrate whether that level is sufficient to generate the disease. Occasionally the problem is dealt with legislatively, though even here the adjudicators may be called on to make such decisions. In 1974 in Arizona a coal miner died from cor pulmonale induced by the strain of a fibrotic lung condition.[48] For silicosis to be held compensable under Arizona's Occupational Disease Act, the employee must have had 1200 shifts of work during which he was exposed to harmful silicon dioxide dust. The decedent had worked only 832 shifts, so his survivor was ineligible for workers' compensation under the Occupational Disease Act. However, nothing precluded the survivor from bringing a workers' compensation claim under the state's Workers' Compensation Law, which requires that there be an injury that arose out of an accident in the course of employment. The court ruled in favor of the claimant on the grounds that each inhalation of silicon dioxide dust involved an impact on the lungs that was a miniature accident. An arbitrary and unidimensional standard (number of shifts of work exposed) does not remove the question of degree of exposure and thus causation from the discretion of workers' compensation boards and the courts.

Leukemia is a well-known consequence of exposure to radiation, but the specific exposure level is frequently unknown. An illustrative example is a 1969 Veteran's Administration case involving a former X-ray technician in the U.S. Army. There was no question that he had been exposed to radiation, but no measurement of levels was available, and the decedent had encountered no known exposure to radiation in the fifteen years since his discharge. The widow submitted testimony from two physicians, a radiologist, and a health physicist, all of whom agreed that this patient's leukemia was probably linked to the unquantified radiation exposure suffered earlier. The Veteran's Administration "held that it would be purely speculative to service connect cause of death in this case when no positive pathology has been shown between separation from service until just prior to veteran's death and it is not indicated from any source that the veteran received excessive doses of radiation during service."[49]

Very few hazards, perhaps none, are associated with only a single form of disease. A workers' compensation adjudicator may be forced to decide if a sufficient level of hazard existed during employment to cause the disease in question, but a safe level of exposure for one disease (for the same worker and the identical substance) may be above the threshold that will cause another illness. Because a given hazard may cause a number of different diseases, it complicates decisions on etiological questions. Although some boards now fully accept that asbestos causes cancer of the lung, pleura, and peritoneal mesothelioma, they may be forced to decide between the arguments of opposing physicians if the asbestos worker has cancer of the rectum. Not even the old scourges are always recognizable to the courts. Repko comments, "Lead poisoning in lead-related industries is usually chronic, rather than acute, in nature; under industrial exposure conditions, lead poisoning develops over a period of months or even years. The medical manifestations of chronic increase in body-burden of lead—usually directly observable—are as varied as the number of individuals who exhibit them."[50] One of the many suspected effects is that an excessive lead burden causes vascular lesions in the central nervous system. When a worker with lead poisoning dies from this cause, the issue will not be whether lead poisoning—induced by an occupational exposure—exists; instead the litigation will revolve around the ways in which the disease has been manifested. If Repko is correct in asserting that the manifestations are as varied as the individuals, it imposes an impossible burden on the courts and compensation boards, unless they choose to compensate every single disability found in the presence of excess lead levels in the body. Lead may be at one end of a continuum, however, there are other established hazards (for instance xylene, when uncontaminated by benzene, and hot environments), for which science has not even determined the kinds of illnesses they cause.

Etiological Problems of Diseases Induced by Psychological Stresses

Every year workers' compensation systems must make judgments regarding the causality of diseases that bring about disability. Criteria regarding legal cause may be clear, although often they are not, and questions of medical causality impose great burdens on the system. Among the most difficult questions of etiology are those involving work-related mental stress. This source has long been associated with a large variety of illnesses, but it has plagued the compensation system with regard to two main categories of disease, cardiovascular illnesses and mental impairments.

There is no doubt that work contributes to psychological and physiological responses by the human organism. Ironically it may often be the inability to find or retain work that is implicated in stress-induced outcomes. Kasl and Cobb have demonstrated on several occasions how such stresses can bring about significant physiological reactions. In a study of 162 married, blue-collar workers employed for at least three years prior to a plant closing, a significant correlation was found between job loss and blood pressure increases.[51] If one accepts that prolonged elevation of blood pressure increases the likelihood of developing hypertension, then unemployment and hypertension can be linked. Sleight and his associates summarized the literature: "The results indicate that severe occupational stress is indeed associated with a sudden and profound increase of serum cholesterol and a marked acceleration of blood coagulation time."[52] Contrary evidence is also cited: "Master (1960) in a study of 2600 cases of coronary occlusion, obtained data supporting his contention that coronary occlusion is not caused by modern stress and strain. He believes that the incidence has increased because of the increased age of the population, improved diagnostic skill of the physicians and changes in the classification of heart diseases."[53]

Caplan has approached the problem in a more analytical mode by evaluating the hypothesis that job stresses will produce "strains" in workers, and such strains will be correlated with higher rates of illnesses, absence from work, and so forth.[54] The study involved 2,100 men in twenty-three occupations, all of whom responded to a questionnaire that measured various occupational and demographic characteristics. Of these, 390 men in eight occupations provided physiological data based on six measures (blood pressure, heart rate, serum cholesterol, thyroid hormone, serum uric acid, and serum cortisol). Stress was defined as any characteristic of the job environment posing a threat to the individual. Strain, the hypothesized result of stress, was considered to be any deviation from normal responses in the person. Evidence of strain could be psychological (job-dissatisfaction anxiety, low self-esteem), and/or physiological (high blood pressure, elevated serum cholesterol). Substantial evidence was found that job stresses do produce measurable strains. Traits, needs, and ability of workers were shown not to be correlated with such strain. Most strikingly there was only limited support for the hypothesis that measured job-related strains induce higher rates of illness or absenteeism in workers. Since most compensation issues involve evidence of disability and not simply impairment, the finding suggests the limited relevance of the system for some of these stress-induced problems. The Caplan study shows how far we are from understanding the relationship between work stresses and disablility. As science proceeds to unravel such links, the compensation system is confronted with the task of equitably resolving controversy between the employee (or the survivor) and an insurer.

It is possible that job-related stresses represent simply a variant of the situation with long latent diseases. It is possible that such stresses, working in a number of ways, weaken or undermine the heart and the circulatory system and gradually bring about a disease condition. Although the deterioration may have begun years before on and/or off the job, disability may not manifest itself until much later. There are difficulties in distinguishing this situation from the so-called ordinary diseases of life. Workers' compensation boards and the courts have wrestled with so-called heart cases for many years, but the issue has almost never been to relate the underlying disease condition to the workplace. Instead attention is almost always directed to the proximate cause of the disabling event, that is, the circumstances preceding the myocardial infarction or the stroke. Rather than determining the basic source of the problem, the disease that is a necessary precondition to disablement, the law has chosen to deal only with the very last event in the chain of circumstances resulting in disability or death. It is true that knowledge regarding the basic sources of heart disease is still rudimentary, but it is no worse than the basis on which physicians must evaluate the cause of the final precipitating event before disability occurred. A distinguished committee of the American Heart Association with striking clarity reported, "The committee finds no method, either clinical or pathological, of determining the causative relationship between any given event and typical coronary thrombosis with infarct."[55]

Cardiovascular disease is the leading cause of death in the United States and millions more suffer varying degrees of disability. The causes of most forms of cardiovascular disease are not known nor are the factors that precipitate the manifestation of a disabling disease condition. Since work-related stresses may contribute to the development of the disease or events that precipitate disability, an immense problem for workers' compensation systems is being forestalled by expedient legislative and judicial decisions that may not withstand the weight of additional scientific evidence. Heart disease or its exacerbation may also enter the nexus of workers' compensation if more evidence is developed linking chemicals, heat, and other physical workplace hazards to it. (Plunkett has suggested a list of substances involved in the etiology or aggravation of heart disease.)

Stress has also been implicated in the development of or as a precipitating factor in the manifestation of disabling mental disorders. The etiology of many mental conditions, as with heart disease, is still unknown. Unlike heart cases, however, problems of diagnosis and evaluation of the extent of disability in mental cases may be equally as difficult as the issue of etiology.

Mental strains brought about by workplace stress are compensable in several states, although cases are less common than might be expected. A psychosis triggered by concern about being able to maintain the pace of an automobile production line was compensable.[56] A fire fighter in California who developed neurosis due to his anxieties over his demanding work was compensated.[57] Few such cases occur because etiology is so often unknown. The fear of or actual loss of work may be the most frequent source of mental impairment induced by the workplace. Brenner examined records of admissions to mental institutions in New York State and reported that short-term changes in the overall level of business activity seemed to be markedly associated with the level of admissions.[58]

There is no doubt that certain physical workplace hazards bring about mental disturbances, although very few ever enter the workers' compensation system. What is not understood, however, is how such agents and the resulting impairment interact with a preexisting mental condition or an underlying predisposition to such a condition. Intoxication, personality changes, nervousness, loss of memory, tremors, irritability, even psychoses all can result from contact with a large variety of widely used substances; lead, mercury, toluene, carbon monoxide, or xylene. Although suicide has never appeared on any list of occupational diseases, its exclusion must be considered an oversight in light of the effect of some of the aforementioned hazards on the human organism. Mancuso and Locke reported excess mortality from suicide among viscose rayon workers who were exposed to carbon disulfide.[59]

Mental disturbances are similar to heart cases in that the potential number of compensation claims is vast, the underlying cause is not known, and there may be a long latent period. The courts almost exclusively examine the last event that precipitated the disability and not the preceding occupational origins or aggravation. Physical agents, singly or in conjunction with other factors including stress may be responsible for a significant portion of the problem. Indeed, Ashford cites findings showing that some stressors can interact in a synergistic way with chemical toxins that intensify their toxicity.[60]

Etiological Problems of Cancer

Hundreds of thousands of persons each year die from or are disabled by cancer. Since the vast majority of those stricken are either currently employed or were at an earlier time, the problems posed by cancer for workers' compensation systems are potentially staggering. Some of these persons have been exposed to known carcinogens while at work, but many more have had no (or virtually no) known occupational exposure to cancer-causing substances. As the list of proven or suspected carcinogens expands, however, it may be discovered that a majority of all victims who have ever been employed have had an occupational exposure to such a substance. For a variety of reasons the cause of cancer in a specific person is rarely known, which creates problems that cannot be adequately handled by a system designed largely to cope with accidents and injuries.

The fundamental problem is that the various causes of the cancer process have not been identified and understood. A primary technique to gain better understanding has been to seek out and identify carcinogenic agents. The process is slow and expensive as evidenced by the National Cancer Institute's estimate of three years and $100,000 per agent in their bioassay program. Peters has indicated that the knowledge of hazards acquired in animal experiments at best may be of limited value. Obtaining persuasive evidence that a substance can be carcinogenic is difficult, particularly where economic interests are jeopardized by such a finding. In an adversary situation, the needed level of scientific proof may be unattainable. The entire history of establishing the health implications of cigarette smoking is instructive.

Even where economic interests are not at stake, the process of identifying and proving carcinogeneity is extremely slow. The cases of beryllium and chromates stand out as does the active debate about asbestos and lung cancer in nonsmokers. In the case of beryllium NIOSH shows no inclination to identify it as a carcinogen—but the U.S. Department of Labor does. A debate of almost three decades continues regarding the carcinogenic forms of chromates.

If a form of cancer is quite rare, for example, cancer of the scrotum or angiosarcoma, then a cluster of even a small number of cases will not be difficult to identify and then a search can begin for the causative agent. But when the type of cancer is not rare, for example, lung or skin cancer, it is difficult to identify a cluster of persons who were exposed to a common risk. Only where the carcinogen is quite strong can a disproportionate group of persons be identified as having been put at risk in the same environment. Even then the specific carcinogenic agent will have to be identified.[61]

Although scientists believe that 85 or 90 percent of all cancers are due to environmental phenomena and are aware that dramatic changes are occurring in the types of cancer being observed, the problem of isolating the important variables that explain cancer incidence has proved insurmountable. Yet compensation adjudicators must wrestle with such issues on an ad hoc basis. A Florida claims judge was overruled by a two to one decision of the state's Industrial Relations Commission, which in turn was overruled by the Florida Supreme Court (sustaining the claims judge), in a case where a cigarette smoker, working in a dusty environment, contracted lung cancer.[62] Although dust in the cement plant may not have been carcinogenic, the claimant argued that the tumor's growth was accelerated by the inhalation of the dust. This case also highlights the problem of etiology from the perspective of the employer or the insurer. Theoretically, workers' compensation should only award benefits where the excess risk of cancer, that is, the differential between the observed rate and the normal, U.S. age-adjusted rate has been due to a workplace exposure. If boards and courts begin to honor claims from workers who were employed in industries where excess numbers of cases have occurred, they will have to compensate all claims since there is no way to distinguish between the work-related cases and those that would have otherwise occurred.

Suppose that workers from a specific industry face a probability of contracting a certain type of cancer that is 50 percent higher than the U.S. age-adjusted rate. If seventy-five workers in the industry develop cancer, then fifty cases could have been expected to develop regardless of the exposure encountered at work. Statistics may allow us to judge approximately the number of cases due to work, but they cannot help to identify the persons whose tumors resulted from their employment relationship. How can the compensation system deal with this? Employers could be expected to object to compensating all seventy-five workers, although to compensate none of them would be equally objectionable to the workers. The case for employers or for workers can be made more compelling by altering the excess probability of contracting such a cancer due to this line of work. Assume the excess mortality rate is only 102 percent, or assume that it is 500 percent. The issue turns out to revolve not about a principle, but about an acceptable level of incidence for purposes of providing compensation. The controversy involves haggling over a number and not an ideological matter, yet precise quantitative notions about cancer and the workplace are exceedingly rare.

A related problem is that a number of carcinogens have been identified, but it is not understood how they trigger the disease. The issue is important for several reasons, including the handling of workers' compensation claims. Even if it is known that producers of the substance are at risk, little is known about the impact on employees who handle the product in later stages. Are automobile assemblers at more or less risk than automobile brake repair persons who handle asbestos, and what do the risks for both appear to be relative to an asbestos insulation worker?

As more workers' compensation cases develop, the courts will find, if they have not done so already, that a negligible degree of contact with a carcinogenic agent, either in terms of time or by some other measure of exposure, may be sufficient to trigger the disease years later. Threshold exposure levels can be used to screen unwarranted claims for a number of occupational diseases, however, it will be increasingly difficult to deny workers' compensation benefits solely on the grounds that the employee had only limited exposure to carcinogenic hazards. Evidence grows that brief, superficial kinds of exposure can be responsible for the later development of cancer.

Blair, in assessing the workers' compensation law of most states, summarizes them as not allowing benefits where there has been merely an exposure to an employment hazard like dust or chemicals.[63] For a recovery to be made, there must be proof that the exposure in question was the cause of the disease in question. The burden of such proof falls upon the employee. For most cases of cancer, no medical evidence, beyond the fact that contact with a carcinogen has occurred, is available to demonstrate this. Occasionally courts will recognize this, as in the case of the awarding of compensation to a survivor of a leukemia victim who had a very limited exposure to benzol.[64] The court acknowledged that since no minimal level of safe exposure to benzol is known, a highly sensitive individual could have been stricken due to the occupational exposure. Such decisions are not common, but they may become more so as additional cases are brought into the system. Developments will depend on future scientific evidence that can better persuade the courts to allow or reject such claims.

Diagnostic Issues of Occupational Diseases

A workers' compensation board or court must make a decision, explicit or otherwise, regarding etiology in cases involving occupational disease. If it cannot be demonstrated that the illness was caused by a hazard or condition encountered on the job, no compensation will be granted to the claimant. Throughout the section on etiology, it was assumed that the disease was correctly diagnosed and only its cause was in doubt or unknown. Of course in some cases the cause of the disease is the only thing that makes it an occupational disease. This is the case when one of the so-called "ordinary diseases of life" is induced by occupational exposure. In other situations diagnosis of the disease itself should be sufficient to indicate its occupational origins when the disease does not occur in the general population. Yet if the disease is incorrectly diagnosed, it will probably not be identified as work-induced, and very likely no claim will be filed (a Type I error). It is true that incorrect diagnoses can result in unwarranted claims (a Type II error), but it is more likely that the former effect is the dominant one for several reasons. Many occupational illnesses closely resemble but are different from other more common illnesses, and unless the physician suspects the workplace, he may assume that it is the more common sickness. It has been reported in numerous instances that many physicians tend not to inquire about working conditions or at least not in sufficient detail to uncover the source of the disorder and, hence, the disease itself.[65] According to Woodward and Fondmiller, physicians rarely correctly diagnose either beryllium or asbestos diseases unless the physician or the patient had prior knowledge of the employee's contact with the substance.[66]

Another problem is that very few physicians specialize in occupational medicine. In 1972 there were forty-six physicians with board certification in this branch of medicine.[67] Thus there may be a lack of familiarity with certain types of illnesses that are more likely to originate at the workplace.

Type II errors (attributing a non-work-related illness to one's employment) in diagnosis may occur, however, at least one factor tends to reduce their significance compared to Type I errors (not attributing a work-connected disease to one's employment). When an incorrect diagnosis initiates a claim, there is a good possibility that at least one other physician, employed by the insurer, the employer, or the compensation agency, will examine the patient. With this additional observation, the probabilities increase that a correct diagnosis will be made and the claim either dropped or undermined. A very large proportion of claims for occupational disease are controverted on the basic question of compensability (see chapter 5).

Many occupational diseases involve impairments of the respiratory system, which are difficult to diagnose correctly. This assertion is supported by experience since passage of the Coal Mine Health and Safety Act in 1969; problems in diagnosing coal workers' pneumoconiosis have hamstrung the law. Controversy continues regarding the ability of physicians to correctly and consistently diagnose emphysema, bronchitis, and other respiratory impairments in coal miners, and diagnostic problems are not unique to the coal worker.

Approximately 1.2 million workers are exposed to free silica, according to NIOSH.[68] Silicosis has been known as a cause of death in workers for centuries and received considerable public attention in this country in the 1930s. Yet there are no pulmonary function tests specific to silicosis.[69] Such tests are an objective indicator of respiratory dysfunction, however, they cannot be used to identify silicosis as the cause; at least forty other diseases resemble early silicosis. It has been reported that "X-ray findings alone cannot be the basis of diagnosis of silicosis, as many other diseases produce similar X-ray findings, but most workers' compensation insurance acts use X-ray criteria for compensation purposes."[70] In some states confirming X-ray diagnosis is a necessary condition for compensability, according to statute.

Silicosis can be easily diagnosed as another pneumoconiosis and is also mistaken for and undermines the diagnoses of other kinds of respiratory illnesses.

The difficulties not infrequently encountered in the clinical diagnosis of cancer of the lung, whenever chronic inflammatory conditions prevail in this organ, are common experience and are likely to be aggravated in the presence of a tuberculosilicosis. A definite diagnostic decision in some such cases may be possible only through an autopsy. The degree of diagnostic uncertainty which may be created under in vivo conditions may be judged by the fact that the diagnosis of cancer of the lung was found either to be incorrect or not justified by the clinical evidence presented in approximately 40 percent of several hundred cases in which cancer of the lung was listed on the death certificate as the cause of death.[71]

Beryllium disease also mimics a number of other diseases in its symptoms. Given the long latency period between a first exposure and onset of the disease, it is clear that the disease must be underreported. Bronchitis, a common illness for cotton textile workers—and a common disease generally—is very similar in its symptoms to byssinosis. Since bronchitis is not considered an occupational disease in certain states,[72] the nature of the diagnosis can cause a claim to be rejected.

There are a number of reasons why diagnostic problems are particularly severe in the case of respiratory diseases. X-rays cannot reveal a number of different conditions, and it is difficult to correctly read X-rays involving certain disorders.[73] Evidence of this was developed in the implementation of the Black Lung Law.[74] In addition, the variety of respiratory diseases is enormous, compounding the difficulties of diagnosis. Roshchin reports that there are at least sixty types of pneumoconioses.[75] Many of these can be mistaken for ordinary diseases of life and when incorrectly diagnosed as such, will almost certainly not be thought to be work related. Others are sufficiently rare as to be unfamiliar to most practicing physicians.

Diagnostic problems are not limited to respiratory diseases. NIOSH believes that more persons succumb each year to carbon monoxide than to any other toxic substance except alcohol.[76] Its prevalence is enormous; total emissions of carbon monoxide exceed those of all other atmospheric pollutants combined (except carbon dioxide). Ten percent of all such emissions are industrial. There are important chronic as well as the better known acute effects, but diagnosis of either is difficult. Even in acute cases, because the body can rid itself of the gas rapidly, by the time a worker has been moved from the plant to the hospital, all traces of the substance may have vanished. Under these circumstances a correct diagnosis, necessary for a successful compensation claim, may not be possible.

A relatively common occupational disease is chronic lead poisoning, developed over months or years. Symptoms of the illness are extremely varied. Blood tests reveal an indication of the levels of past exposure but not the effects of that exposure.[77] Some individuals have very high levels of blood lead but show no symptoms of disease, while other workers have symptoms in the presence of small levels of lead in the blood. Urine tests also provide a means to measure the body's level of lead, but there are difficulties similar to those encountered in the use of blood tests. Discher found substantial evidence of lead poisoning in his sample, although many of the workers apparently had no other symptoms aside from elevated levels of lead in the blood and/or urine.[78] When other symptoms are present, such as hearing loss, loss of endurance or muscular strength, hostility, aggression, or general dysphoria, they can easily be mistaken for other ailments.

One technique that can lead to better or at least less ambiguous diagnoses is autopsy. It can help uncover the presence of a potential public health hazard for purposes of workers' compensation proceedings and other ends. Autopsies have also demonstrated the weaknesses of death certificate reporting, thereby limiting the reliability of this epidemiological tool. But there are a number of problems. It may never be employed in situations where an occupational disease has been incorrectly diagnosed, and therefore no compensation claim is filed. The use of autopsy violates religious principles for certain groups and is unacceptable to others on ethical grounds. The technique can assist compensation cases only in claims involving fatalities. Thus it is of no benefit to a worker who may have sought compensation for disability prior to death. Even though the technique is of only limited value, it can be particularly helpful when the nature of the disease is at issue in a workers' compensation claim, and a large number of states provide for its mandatory use when the compensation commission orders it.

4

OCCUPATIONAL DISEASE
IN THE LAW

The legal treatment of occupational diseases will be briefly reviewed. The reader interested in the legalistic details should consult Arthur Larson's *Treatise*, an excellent source.[1] Specific listings of states according to characteristics of their statutes and administration can be found in the basic volumes and periodic supplements of Larson, Blair,[2] the U.S. Chamber of Commerce's annual *Analysis of Workmen's Compensation Laws*,[3] and in unpublished summaries prepared by the staffs of the U.S. Department of Labor and other government agencies.

Workers' compensation law in general and occupational disease provisions in particular have been undergoing very rapid change since 1972. To avoid the inevitable controversies regarding the legal handling of various issues, the present situation will not be quantified nor each state characterized.

It is possible that a workers' compensation law could be drafted that made no special reference to the issue of occupational disease. Such a statute would broadly define the terms (or find suitable replacements for) "accident" and "injury" and leave the "arising out of and in the course of" provisions untouched. In the overwhelming majority of current compensation cases, an injury caused by accident can be linked to the disability, and it can readily be observed whether the event arose out of and in the course of employment. It is the nature of disease that precisely this observation cannot be made. Even when medical science has identified the cause of an illness in the general case, it is rare that how and when a worker contracted an illness can be established with certainty. Because of this difficulty, and since all jurisdictions have opted not to use workers' compensation laws to provide medical and income maintenance insurance for all workers on a twenty-four-hour basis, states have introduced provisions designed to limit the extent of coverage. Thus rather than follow the hypothetical procedure in which no reference is made to occupational disease, the laws have all been written so that complete coverage for all diseases is not allowed. The complexity of the occupational disease provisions of these laws results from legislative and judicial attempts to set such limits while treating compensability as an entitlement in cases that appear to conform to the basic principles of workers' compensation.

The effort to reconcile such limits with most of the principles of workers' compensation poses no insurmountable difficulties, however, there is at least one problem area. The no fault concept underlies the quid pro quo of compensation. Although the matter of *who* is at fault has not crept back into the system through the provisions dealing with occupational disease, such aspects of the law raise questions about *what* is at fault. Was the disease caused by an exposure at the workplace? Could the disease have been contracted by another person who did not work? Was the stress of work sufficient to cause the manifestation of a disease whose cause is not even known? Is the source of illness the environment, one's heredity, or one's employment? Similar questions may occur in accidental injury cases since the incident must have arisen out of the employment. The difference is primarily one of degree. By making diseases compensable, but with significant limits on illnesses that can be successfully claimed, and given the uncertain etiology of many diseases, states have created a very large gap that is only dealt with by litigating the issue of what is at fault.

The first workers' compensation laws in the United States did not explicitly deal with occupational disease. This paralleled the British statute of 1897, and it might be supposed that the eventual English experience would alert American state legislatures to the issue. In 1905 a British appellate court denied compensation for a case of lead poisoning on the ground that such a disablement was not caused "by accident," a precondition stipulated in the British statute.[4] It was held that some identifiable event was needed for an accident to have taken place. Probably due to the 1905 decision, the law was amended in 1906, and employers were required to pay compensation for those specific occupational diseases listed in the statute. Despite this, occupational diseases were not mentioned in the early U.S. statutes, though the issue was not overlooked. Kelley speculates that in some of the earliest laws the term "injury" was substituted for "accident" to allow coverage to be extended judicially to occupational diseases and avoid alerting uninitiated legislators to their design.[5] The Federal Employees Compensation Act and a few states did require that compensation be paid in disease cases under these early "injury" provisions. Nevertheless in the first several years after Wisconsin passed the first (constitutionally upheld) state law, considerable confusion existed whether diseases were to be compensated. The status of the matter was summarized in 1917:

In this country "occupational diseases" are not, as a rule, included under the term "accident" in compensation acts, but in the administration of these acts an increasing tendency by administrative boards and by courts to include many forms of disease contracted during employment is evident. Thus, in one instance compensation was allowed for death from Bright's disease attributed to poisoning of the blood stream as a result of an infected heel blister; in another for death following an inflammation of a preexisting cancer due to an accidental blow; again for death from pneumonia where the power of resistance had been reduced by occupational strain.

The Supreme Court of the State of Massachusetts has specifically held that the term "personal injury" includes occupational disease. The Supreme Courts of Connecticut, Michigan and Ohio, on the other hand, have held that the compensation acts of their respective states do not include such disease, although all these acts employ the term "injury" and not 'accident."[6]

The uncertainty at the time of this 1917 report eventually disappeared, at least to the extent that some form of occupational disease is compensable now in every state of the union. Various techniques evolved to achieve this. A number of states began, as the British did in 1906, by explicitly extending coverage to certain scheduled diseases. In these states potential disease claims were limited by the restrictiveness of the schedule. In some states, including several that also used schedules, occupational disease was covered by specific provisions of the workers' compensation law or a new statute dealing only with occupational disease. When states did not use a restrictive schedule, the language of the statutes indicated what kinds of diseases were not to be covered, for example, "ordinary diseases of life" or chronic joint diseases. On numerous occasions a workers' compensation board or a court attempted to expand coverage to an occupational disease that was not listed in the schedule or did not meet all of the statutory conditions. Such cases generally treated the disease as an injury caused by accident resulting in disability that arose out of and in the course of employment. It is important to recognize that various state court decisions on whether a given disease was an injury caused by accident customarily reflect attempts to exceed the specific limits on occupational diseases.

While most states began to cover occupational disease via schedules or special language statutes, other states expanded coverage by gradually widening their definition of accidents and injuries. In these states legislatures eventually attempted to specify the limits on coverage by the language used to describe an occupational disease. In many instances the statutes were a reaction to the way boards and courts were developing their own notions of appropriate coverage. Some laws were meant to ease restrictive practices by adjudicators, and other statutes reflected a fear that coverage was being extended far beyond any reasonable limit.

What Is an Occupational Disease?

Where statutes did not specify the limits of coverage for occupational diseases, the courts found it necessary to provide them. Virtually every state statute now contains language defining the term "occupational disease"; many were guided by the language that emanated from the courts in earlier years. One of the earliest efforts to provide a definition or clarification came in a 1925 decision in Maryland:

An occupation or industry disease is one which arises from causes incident to the profession or labor of the party's occupation or calling. It has its origin in the inherent nature or mode of work of the profession or industry, and it is the usual result or concomitant. If, therefore, a disease is not a customary or natural result of the profession or industry, per se, but is the consequence of some extrinsic condition or independent agency, the disease cannot be imputed to the occupation or industry, and is in no accurate sense an occupation or industry disease.[7]

A New York decision that is also frequently cited, explained:

An occupational disease is one which results from the nature of employment, and by nature is meant not those conditions brought about by the failure of the employer to furnish a safe place to work, but conditions to which all employees of a class are subject, and which produce the disease as a natural incident of a particular occupation, and attach to that occupation a hazard which distinguishes it from the usual run of occupations and is in excess of the hazard attending employment in general. Thus compensation is restricted to disease resulting from the ordinary and generally recognized risks attendant to a particular employment, and usually from working therein over a somewhat extended period. Such disease is not the equivalent of a disease resulting from the general risks and hazards common to every individual regardless of the employment in which he is engaged.[8]

Even though a number of decisions and statutes have extended the concept of occupational disease since these findings, they illustrate an early and still commonly found view. First, as much attention is given to what is not an occupational disease as to what is, reflecting the very serious fear of excessively widening the scope of coverage. Second, even where a particular incident that generated a disablement occurred in the process of work, that is, it arose out of and in the course of employment, it need not be compensable, for example, many infectious diseases. The New York decision introduces issues in occupational disease cases that are well beyond those occurring in an accident-injury case. Questions that must be answered are: To what conditions are employees as a class subjected? What illnesses are a natural concomitant of a particular occupation? Of these, which occur in excess of the probability of occurring in employment "in general"? How long is a "somewhat extended period"? If a disease is common to every individual regardless of employment, is it impossible to be compensated for disability due to that disease no matter how it was caused?

Answers to each of these questions vary by state, and all states have not yet clarified some of them. However, legislatures have tried to put their stamp on these issues and have provided boards and courts with some direction. A clear and fairly typical definition can be found in Missouri's statute:

... the term "occupational disease" is hereby defined to mean a disease arising out of and in the course of the employment. Ordinary diseases of life to which the general public is exposed outside of the employment shall not be compensable, except where the said diseases follow as an incident of an occupational disease as defined in this section. A disease shall be deemed to arise out of the employment only if there is apparent to the rational mind upon the consideration of all the circumstances a direct causal connection between the conditions under which the work is performed and the occupational disease, and which can be seen to have followed as a natural incident of the work as a result of the exposure occasioned by the nature of the employment and which can be fairly traced to the employment as the proximate cause and which does not come from a hazard to which workmen would have been equally exposed outside of the employment. The disease must be incidental to the character of the business and not independent of the relation of employer and employee. The disease need not to have been foreseen or expected but after its contraction it must appear to have had its origin in a risk connected with the employment and to have flowed from that source as a rational consequence.[9]

Even when a claimant's disabling disease does not meet all of the conditions stipulated in the statute, a workers' compensation board or a court could conceivably award benefits on grounds that the injury was caused by accident and not by an occupational disease. Some legislatures (for example, Iowa and Louisiana) have attempted to bar such potential avenues for expansion by stipulating that an injury must be caused by accident, it must involve violence to the physical structure of the body, and it cannot be construed to include an occupational disease. Further, since an accident is defined to mean an unexpected, undesigned, and unlooked for mishap, or an untoward event that can be reasonably located as to the time when or the place where it occurred, most disease cases will not be compensated under such provisions.

Even though considerable variation in the interpretation and application of "occupational disease" exists, several elements of the law are rather consistent across all states. Where there is a disabling injury involving an accident that arises out of and in the course of covered employment, if a disabling illness or disease develops due to the injury, it is compensable. An example is an infection that develops in a wound that occurred in a work-related injury.

Second, if an accident (a sudden, unforeseen event occurring at a definite place and time) injures a worker, and the injury involves a disease, it is compensable. An eye disease from a welder's flash burn, a laboratory assistant's dermatosis from being splashed with a caustic substance, sudden hypoxia in an underwater occupation due to a mechanical failure all would be straightforward cases.

A third common element across states is to deny claims based on disability due to ordinary diseases of life and compensate, where other conditions permit, diseases that are peculiar or particular to some line of work. Workers' compensation boards in some states have interpreted this to mean that particular diseases could not be compensated (except, perhaps, as accident-injury cases). Other boards have directed their attention to the degree to which a hazard existed at the workplace. The former is exemplified by a seemingly harsh decision in a Pennsylvania case brought under the state's Occupational Disease Act. The court denied compensation for disability due to lung cancer resulting from past exposure to asbestos.[10] Had the claim been for asbestosis, which is not considered to be an ordinary disease of life, the claim would have been found compensable. Pennsylvania's position has recently been reversed, and compensation was awarded to a survivor of another employee whose contact with asbestos at the same firm resulted in a fatality due to lung cancer.[11]

Some states exclude ordinary diseases of life in part by stipulating that the toxic materials or working conditions that cause a disease must be responsible independent of any other cause. In a 1974 case Wyoming denied compensation to a maintenance worker disabled by chronic bronchitis, although for twenty years he had been exposed to very dusty working conditions and subjected to extreme, temporary temperature changes at his employment.[12] This decision is clearly consistent with an earlier Kentucky decision denying compensation on the grounds that chronic bronchitis is an ordinary disease of life,[13] but not with an Oregon case in which a heavy smoker with bronchitis did receive compensation,[14] nor with a variety of cases found compensable involving diseases brought on by temperature changes or extremes. For example, a butcher who contracted pulmonary emphysema from a long-term exposure to refrigerated air did receive compensation.[15]

An extreme case by current standards occurred in Idaho. Compensation was denied because pleurisy was held to be an ordinary disease of life.[16] The town fire chief contracted the noncompensated disease as a result of battling a fire for three hours in below zero temperature, while exposed to smoke and moisture. Since the court found the exposure in this case to be routine to the work, the resultant disease was not compensable since it was an ordinary disease of life. In a much later decision in Missouri, a worker claimed that his exposure at close quarters to paint and dust from sanding work contributed to the contraction or aggravation of a tubercular condition.[17] Compensation for an occupational disease was denied on grounds that tuberculosis is an ordinary disease of life, nor could it be compensated as an injury due to accident since it did not result from an unexpected or unforeseen event. A North Dakota taxi driver did receive compensation for pneumonia contracted after a brief exposure while attempting to push his cab out of the mud.[18]

Some differences in the views of courts seem difficult to explain if one seeks some underlying consistency. For example, the Ohio Supreme Court recently upheld the state's Industrial Commission in granting workers' compensation to a telephone installer and repairman who contracted histoplasmosis of the right eye as a result of his frequent contact with pigeon droppings and dead pigeons.[19] Although the decision seems reasonable, it is out of line with a position taken only three years earlier. Phillips, a crane operator, developed viremia with resulting ataxia of lower limbs.[20] It developed after working forty-four feet above ground in the cabin of a crane that had several windows missing and a defective heater. He was exposed to severe winds blowing through the cabin and temperatures ranging from eight degrees below zero to eight or nine degrees above zero. The court found the claimant's argument that he was subjected to a hazard greater than that to which the public was generally exposed was without merit. The issue then became: Was this disability due to a compensable injury caused by accident? Since the injury was judged to be neither unusual nor unexpected, it was not accidental and compensation was denied.

A similarly striking disparity appears in the handling of the same disease in two different jurisdictions. In one a claimant performed a manual task for one hour per weekday and six to eight hours on Saturday for two weeks.[21] Pain developed in her arms and fingers and was diagnosed as carpal tunnel syndrome. The insurer argued that this was an ordinary disease of life with many possible causes outside the workplace, including ordinary functioning as a housewife. Beyond that, the insurer argued, there was no peculiar hazard of employment that brought about this disorder. The court awarded compensation on the grounds that the work required a constant repetitive movement, and this exposed the claimant to a greater risk of contracting the syndrome than if she had worked only as a housewife. The court found that "what is distinctively occupational in a particular employment is the peculiar risk or hazard which inheres in the work conditions, and a disease which follows as a natural result of exposure to such occupational risks, an exposure which is greater or different than affects the public generally is an occupational disease, not an ordinary disease of life." According to this decision, whether a disease is occupational does not depend on its being literally peculiar to the claimant's occupation, but rather, whether there is a recognizable link between some distinctive characteristic of the work — common to all such jobs — and the disease. Mayes points to Illinois and Indiana decisions (states with occupational disease statutes that are the same as Missouri's) that are consistent with this.[22] What constitutes an occupational disease for such states appears not to depend on what is common to the public, but instead on the special or inherent conditions of the claimant's work that may constitute a hazard.

This must be contrasted with a more recent decision in Delaware also involving carpal tunnel syndrome.[23] An automobile production worker suffered a wrist injury — diagnosed as carpal tunnel syndrome — allegedly incurred from the continual use of a nine to ten pound vibrating air gun. The court denied compensation on the grounds that a predisposition to the syndrome existed (the employer was not told that it took the worker as it found him) and because the disease was not a "natural incident" of his occupation. The finding on the latter issue was based on evidence from the employer that for over 2,000 employees, only three or four recorded cases of carpal tunnel syndrome were reported in the previous four years.

Similar disparities in evaluating whether a disease is an ordinary one of life abound, for example, cases involving viral hepatitis. In *Esposito,* the New York Supreme Court granted compensation to an employee of a state school where viral hepatitis was alleged to be endemic.[24] The claimant did not present evidence to demonstrate close contact with a sick patient at the school; such direct contact is not necessary to contract the illness. Medical opinion on the etiology was split, and compensation was awarded. Comparably the survivor of a photographer for a public relations firm was awarded compensation after the photographer contracted viral hepatitis in Bolivia.[25] The court held that in traveling in Bolivia the photographer was necessarily exposed to deplorable sanitary conditions. Yet a plumber, who alleged that he contracted viral hepatitis when he repaired an overflowing commode in a hospital, was denied compensation in North Carolina. Though the claimant argued that this work constituted a routine exposure to sources and carriers of hepatitis, the court did not find the evidence sufficient to allow that this was an occupational disease, arising out of and in the course of employment.[26]

Some of these decisions seem to suggest that the courts are gradually widening the limits of coverage under occupational disease provisions or statutes. While it is not likely that workers' compensation will eventually be a source of medical benefits and wage replacement for all sick workers (or former workers), some tendency toward widening seems evident. Recent awards of compensation for a foot condition to a meter maid whose work involved walking on hard pavements,[27] a bakery's porter who developed asthma,[28] and to a person who regularly drove an automobile in her work and developed phlebitis,[29] all suggest a loosening of the limits that disallow benefits for ordinary diseases of life. If courts and workers' compensation boards find that any illness is compensable so long as a recognizable link exists between the disease and some aspect of the occupation, for example, an exposure to a hazard, it may follow in the future that a very large number of cases of cancer and cardiovascular disease will be dealt with by the workers' compensation system. That this is not destined to occur immediately can be seen in the decisions limiting the expansion of coverage that continue to be handed down.

The Role of Scheduled Diseases

The explicit legislative move to cover occupational disease in England took the form of a precise listing of diseases to be covered. The manner in which coverage was broadened attests to the reluctance to include many such disablements. Thus rather than leave the matter of whether a disease arose out of and in the course of employment to the compensation adjudicators, very clear boundaries of coverage were delineated.

In the United States, schedules of diseases developed for similar reasons. By providing that diseases could be compensated, the states have broadened the overall coverage of workers' compensation, but by limiting claims only to those diseases enumerated on the schedule, they have served to preclude wholesale expansion of the system. Because such schedules have no obvious analog in the handling of accident-injury claims, however, confusion exists about the role that such schedules play.

Many states at one time depended heavily on schedules to determine compensability for disease, but very few do so today. Only Alabama, Arkansas, Louisiana, Oklahoma, Tennessee, and Wyoming still use schedules to limit the coverage of the compensation system. Where schedules still exist outside these six states, the schedule is either a historical vestige, or it serves as a form of presumption that a disease (or a listed hazard) is not an ordinary disease of life. Thus where a schedule coexists with a provision that diseases are "broadly covered," the schedule actually can enlarge the number of successful claims by easing the burden of proof for a claimant. Even where the scheduling of a disease may be a necessary condition in order to be awarded compensation benefits, it is not a sufficient condition. In *Butler* v. *National Lead Co.*[30] even though lead poisoning was listed as an occupational disease, the claim was denied when it was not proven that the disease was contracted through the person's employment.

There are several advantages in having a schedule of covered diseases. They eliminate some of the uncertainty about whether a disease is to be considered occupational or an ordinary disease of life. By limiting uncertainty they tend to reduce litigation and allow a larger number of worthy claims to be filed and compensated. They can provide a clear legislative direction to the courts and workers' compensation boards regarding the extent of coverage of diseases. These are the reasons the countries of Western Europe use schedules as the principal determinant in the matter of compensability of occupational diseases.

The primary problem of schedules, where not supplemented by broad disease coverage, is their restrictiveness. This means of limiting coverage often appears harsh, inflexible, and contrary to the nature of the compensation system. Limiting compensable diseases to a few dozen specified ailments seems an anachronism when viewed in terms of the myriad diseases medical science has conclusively shown are caused by occupational exposures. Such inflexibility is illustrated by a case where compensation was denied to an employee suffering from tardy ulnar neuritis, a disease resulting from repeated pressure on the claimant's elbow and ulnar nerve, which arose out of and in the course of her employment.[31] Although the disease was not listed on the exclusive schedule prevailing in Arkansas, the claimant argued it was caused in essentially the same way as synovitis, tenosynovitis, and bursitis, all of which appeared on the schedule. The court held that the schedule is exclusive, and it is not in the court's prerogative to add additional items. Similarly, an Oklahoma court would not allow compensation to a packing house worker because brucellosis was not a scheduled occupational disease.[32]

Strictly exclusive schedules can also appear so capricious as to warrant some suspicions about the motivation behind the entire statute. When Colorado used an exclusive schedule, the state's Industrial Commission would not award benefits to a worker disabled from dermatitis caused by exposure to metal.[33] In order for dermatitis to be compensable (at that time), the causative agent had to be part of an oil, cutting compound, lubricant, solvent, synthetic cleaning compound, or detergent. Since the substance was a metal, it was not compensable. Although the schedule allowed compensation for "poisoning" due to contact with metal, the disease in question was dermatitis and not poisoning. Had the dermatitis resulted from contact with a detergent, it would have been compensable, but if the detergent had caused a poisoning, it would not have been compensable. One can only marvel at how such provisions evolved. It is not surprising that in 1975 Colorado broadened disease coverage by eliminating the schedule.

Where the exclusive schedules exist, workers' compensation boards and courts have occasionally found opportunities to widen coverage beyond the very narrowest of limits. When South Dakota still used such a schedule, compensation was awarded to a painter disabled by bronchitis and bronchiolitis, although the condition was not enumerated in the prevailing schedule.[34] Since the illness was allegedly brought about in part through the inhalation of zinc chromate fumes while painting, and since chrome ulceration and poisoning appeared in the South Dakota schedule, compensation was upheld.

Tennessee's approach to coverage is unique in that it has an exclusive schedule of covered diseases, but it also allows employers to elect broad coverage. According to state officials, most large employers have elected to so so.[35] Even when an employer's coverage is limited to the schedule, the law allows for compensation of unlisted diseases that are related or similar to those on the schedule. Thus considerable flexibility can be exercised, depending on the willingness of the courts. In one case the evidence did not support the claimant's argument that his bronchitis was closely related to one of the specified compensable occupational diseases.[36] In a later decision compensation was denied to a claimant disabled by rhinitis and sinusitis when he did not show how these illnesses were related to any scheduled disease.[37] But compensation was allowed recently to a disabled miner who claimed that his chronic lung disease was closely related to some other diseases enumerated in Tennessee's statute.[38]

Some latitude in dealing with a list of scheduled diseases also exists in Louisiana. Where a worker's employment allegedly aggravated his bronchial asthma and disabled him, the court denied compensation on the grounds that the disease was not on the schedule.[39] However, where the preponderance of evidence was held to support the claimant's contention that he contracted bullous emphysema due to exposure to toxic substances while in the course of employment, compensation was granted.[40] This disease, also, does not appear on Louisiana's schedule. The willingness to expand compensation might be due to restrictions elsewhere in the law. Louisiana's statute explicitly disallows occupational diseases to be compensated as injuries caused by accident.

Where schedules of diseases exist, it would seem desirable that the list be expanded: first, as medical science (and the law) discovers new links between work and the disease and, second, as the work environment is modified through the use of new processes or substances, or as new kinds of industry locate in a state. Unless a schedule becomes totally vestigial, one should expect to see it expanded frequently. An extreme example of inflexibility in this regard was North Carolina before it moved to broad coverage. Fashbaugh related in 1971 that only two diseases, undulant fever and parrot fever, had been added to the state's original schedule of diseases since it was first established in 1935.[41] Such legislative lethargy was particularly troublesome in this major textile-producing state, which did not list byssinosis on its schedule.

When a state does not allow workers' compensation benefits for certain diseases, the worker generally has the right to seek common-law damages from a negligent employer.[42] An apparent exception to this principle occurred in North Carolina where common-law relief was not allowed in cases involving diseases not enumerated in the schedule.[43] It has not been unusual to find employers seeking to prove that a claim resulting from disability due to occupational disease was in fact compensable, thereby putting a limit on their potential liability. For example, when a claimant sought a tort remedy against his employer for exposing him to dust and heat that resulted in disabling pulmonary emphysema, the court supported the worker's contention that this was not an occupational disease on the grounds that the disease was not peculiar to the plaintiff's industry or occupation and was common to the general population.[44]

Infectious Disease Cases and the By-Accident Provision

The occupational diseases referred to in most statutes do not include most infectious diseases.[45] Workers' compensation laws have been written and interpreted to exclude coverage of ordinary diseases of life, which include most infectious illnesses. Although legislators, courts, and workers' compensation board personnel within the same state may differ substantially in their views regarding what constitutes an ordinary disease of life, most include infectious diseases.

This treatment of infectious diseases may seem curious since some of the earliest successful claims for compensation for disease in this country involved such illnesses. It occurred when disease was a consequence of an accidental injury that arose out of and in the course of employment. If a worker suffered a wound that became infected, the disease was a natural consequence of the original disability and compensable. Even in the absence of explicit coverage of occupational diseases, such claims could be successful.

Eventually, successful claims for diseases could be made even when the disease was the only disabling injury caused by an accident, so long as the disability could be traced to an accidental occurrence. Claims were often litigated over the meaning of "by accident" and "injury." The former was not easy to demonstrate for claimants with illnesses since "by accident" required the presence of a number of conditions. First, an accident involved an unexpected happening or occurrence and, second, the event had to occur at a definite time and place. Thus if a disease developed gradually and not as a consequence of a particular event, no accident was involved. Classical occupational diseases were not covered by these injury-by-accident provisions since such illnesses were treated as an inherent hazard of the occupation and were not unexpected. Infectious diseases that could be compensated involved a specific, unexpected event such as a scratch that resulted in infection or illness. In that case the scratch was considered to be an unexpected event that occurred at a definite time and place. Injuries due to insect stings were often compensated for such reasons also. Where the courts showed a willingness to expand such extremely limited coverage, it involved compensating such diseases developed from an infectious contact at the workplace to a wound that had occurred previously away from work. Other attempts to widen coverage involved decisions about the source of the accident. If the illness, infectious or otherwise, resulted from conditions that were normal or customary in the industry or occupation and if science had not learned how to eliminate these conditions, no accident was judged to have occurred and such a claim was denied. If the condition, however, was capable of being controlled or eliminated, but an employer had failed to do so, the case was held to be an accident and as such compensable. Larson observes that such clear efforts to identify fault were totally antithetical to the principles of compensation systems.[46]

Virtually all the states eventually moved in the direction of explicitly covering occupational disease by schedules and/or specific provisions for such coverage. Yet the fear of excessively broadening coverage caused the states to limit the kinds of diseases that were considered occupational. State laws still force many infectious disease cases to be evaluated as injuries caused by accident. Consequently a most haphazard approach currently characterizes the handling of infectious disease and other disease claims based on the accidental nature of the injury. Messina has characterized the entire situation as a "Serbonian bog."[47] Examples of such haphazardness are not difficult to find.

In *Mason* v. *YMCA* a telephone operator contracted tuberculosis after taking over the headset and mouthpiece of another operator who had the disease.[48] She was granted compensation since this was presumably a particular hazard of being a telephone operator. In another, more recent New York case a driver shared a truck cab for several months with another driver who had tuberculosis; when he too contracted the disease, compensation was denied to him.[49] In this case the court found that the hazard was not peculiar to being a truck driver but simply of being in that particular truck. Comparing this New York case to a more recent one from Michigan illustrates the perplexing status of the law. There, the court granted benefits to a tool and die worker who contracted tuberculosis at his workplace.[50] The disease allegedly was contracted from a fellow employee. Because of the noisy conditions in the shop, the two workers were required to put their heads together and shout in order to be heard above the din. Under such forced proximity, the disease was assumed to be transmitted. Although conditions (not noise, but the presence of tuberculosis) that caused the disease were not peculiar to the business, they were peculiar to the claimant's work and hence, in this case found to be compensable.

The inconsistency of the compensation system in handling claims is obvious when comparing two decisions made less than one month apart by the same judicial body in the same state. In *Herdick* v. *New York Zoological Society* the Appellate Division, New York Supreme Court, awarded compensation to an animal keeper who had contracted tuberculosis.[51] The claimant alleged that the disease was the result of contact with infected animals and the court allowed that such exposure is a natural incident of a particular occupation and attaches to that occupation a greater hazard than that attending employment in general. The same court then overturned a decision awarding compensation for disability due to tuberculosis to Middleton, a correction officer in a state facility.[52] The court held that because the disease was not a natural and unavoidable result of the occupation, the claimant must establish that the inception of the disease is assignable to a determinate or single act, identified in space and time, and assignable to something extraordinary or catastrophic. Unlike *Herdick*, tuberculosis was not an occupational disease in this case and the claimant's burden was therefore to prove that this was an injury caused by accident. Since the mere exposure of the officer to a tubercular inmate was neither catastrophic nor extraordinary, the claim was denied.

The *Middleton* decision on its own may seem harsh, but coming immediately on the heels of *Herdick*, it also appears capricious. If one works with animals behind bars, tuberculosis is an occupational disease, but if one works with humans behind bars, it is not. The court of appeals later overturned *Middleton*, but it did not do so on the grounds that this was an occupational disease. Instead, the court of appeals noted that the corrections officer was exposed through head to head contact with a tubercular inmate for three to four months prior to developing the disease.[53] According to the court of appeals, this was an accident as judged by the commonsense viewpoint of the average man. The time definiteness requirement was well satisfied according to the court — repeated coughing by the inmate represented repeated trauma that caused the injury.

The issue here is not the fairness of the eventual outcome of *Middleton*, but that the grounds on which the decision was based seem tortuous and distinctly arbitrary. It is surprising that a state as progressive as New York must still use the injury-by-accident route in 1975 to compensate a worker with a serious disability that so clearly appears to have arisen out of and in the course of employment. The resulting climate of uncertainty may keep workers and their attorneys from filing claims in spite of their worthiness, or it may lead to much more litigation until the rules are understood by all concerned parties. Consistency in the treatment by law of such claims is a significant criterion to use to evaluate the system. It can be achieved in a negative way as in Arkansas, which allows no compensation for any infectious disease except for employees in a hospital or sanitorium. This approach characterizes how the western European countries and Ontario have dealt with this issue.

The fortunate claimant (eventually) in *Middleton* can be compared to his less successful counterpart in Illinois.[54] A welder had begun work in good health six years earlier. The welding work caused a dense smoke to rise and hang in the air around him. The claimant did not allege that his disablement from emphysema was caused by these fumes; he argued that his condition was aggravated by exposure to the noxious agents involved in the welding work. The cause of emphysema is unknown, however, it is clear that it can progress more rapidly among persons exposed to respiratory irritants. Since emphysema is a general disease of life, it is not compensable under Illinois's occupational disease statute and must be evaluated in terms of an injury caused by accident. The circuit court awarded compensation on the grounds that such an injury need not be limited to a single event that occurs at a specific time or place. Each movement or exposure contributed slightly to the ultimate disability. However, the Illinois Supreme Court flatly rejected this line of argument in denying compensation. It held that the disability could not be traced to a definite time or place nor was there a requisite sudden disability. Thus there was no accident and the disability was not compensable. In recent years other states have also used such grounds for continuing to deny claims even where the disease clearly arose out of and in the course of employment.[55]

The Handling of Heart Cases and the By-Accident Provision

In certain respects workers' compensation systems treat cardiovascular diseases (heart disease or heart cases) similarly to infectious diseases. Workers' compensation laws have largely considered heart disease as an ordinary disease of life and, if compensation has been sought, it was for an injury caused by accident, not an occupational disease. However, unlike infectious diseases, the cause of heart disease is not known. As a result a special body of law has grown up in each state to cover such claims.

It is particularly important in analyzing heart cases to recall that the compensation laws are characterized by a concern with protecting the system from unworthy claims. With over 1 million fatalities alone each year from cardiovascular diseases in the United States, an "open-door policy" would totally reshape, even swamp, the existing system. The states have moved very slowly and haltingly to cover such diseases and at any sign of an upsurge in claims have managed to create impediments, statutory or judicial, to expanded coverage. A major bulwark in defending the system from such an onslaught has been the use of the "injury-by-accident" requirement for compensability. The accident provision could—or perhaps should—have been interpreted to refer to the result of an event. Instead United States laws tended to seek out the accident in the cause of the precipitating event. Larson does not equivocate about the reasons for this:

Holmes' statement that the life of the law has not been logic but experience is probably truer in compensation law than in any other field. For while most of the law built up around the "accident" requirement, for example, has been based on false premises and embroidered with irrelevant distinctions, there has been a utilitarian purpose behind it all which cannot be disregarded when all the logical criticisms have been exhausted. That practical consideration is the fear that the heart cases and related types of injury and death will get out of control unless some kind of arbitrary boundaries are set, and will become compensable whenever they take place within the time and space limits of employment. Most states have chosen to press the "accident" concept into service as one kind of arbitrary boundary, but with a few exceptions, one gets the impression that what is behind it all is not so much an insistence on accidental quality for its own sake as the provision of an added assurance that compensation will not be awarded for deaths not really caused in any substantial degree by the employment.[56]

Had the British precedents in such cases been adopted, the situation would have developed differently. Even before any state had successfully passed a workers' compensation law, the British, whose system we otherwise largely copied, resolved the matter in two cases. The British statute of 1897 required that compensation be paid when an employee sustained a personal injury by accident that arose out of and in the course of employment. In *Fenton* v. *Thorley* compensation was granted to Fenton, who sustained a hernia while attempting to operate a jammed press.[57] Thorley's defense was based on the view that no accident had occurred. It was rejected by the House of Lords who found that an accident did not require the occurrence of an "unusual external event." An accidental injury merely meant the experiencing of some unexpected result. This decision was then applied to a heart case in 1910 in *Clover, Clayton & Co.* v. *Hughes.*[58] A boilermaker in a shipyard, immediately after lunch, screwed together only two nuts and bolts, each requiring only six turns of a wrench, before he collapsed and died of an aneurysm of the aorta. A medical witness testified that the walls of the man's aorta were extremely weak and he might as easily have died in his sleep. The House of Lords, using *Fenton* v. *Thorley*, granted compensation on the grounds that the injury resulted from an accident, that is, the worker had not expected this to happen. The "strain," though not itself unusual, triggered an unusual incident. According to Larson, the controversies surrounding heart cases in the United States need not have occurred if the courts had followed the well-established doctrine that when a legislature adopts a statute that has already been authoritatively construed, it has adopted the construction.[59] The British had clearly decided by 1910 that the by-accident provision could refer to a catastrophic or unexpected outcome, thus allowing compensation to be paid even where the cause was a routine one.

In rejecting the by-accident construction used in England, American courts sought the accident in the cause. The presence of an accident in heart cases implied, or was found to mean, that some "unusual exertion" was a necessary preconditon. The need to demonstrate unusual exertion has created problems for workers' compensation boards. The courts have had to decide in many cases whether a particular exertion or stress was unusual. Is an unusual exertion for a minister the same as one for a construction worker? If the latter is accustomed to lifting and carrying hundreds of pounds in the course of an hour, is it an unusual exertion if he collapses while engaged in such work? Is it unusual if a sedentary minister develops a coronary occlusion after picking up a ten pound box containing hymnals? Such issues have been the basis for numerous and protracted disputes.

Cohen and Klein argue that the unusual exertion rule is simply a throwback to the common-law defense of assumption of risk, a defense that was supposedly rendered obsolete under the quid pro quo of workers' compensation.[60] Although their reasoning differs somewhat from Larson's, they agree that this means of limiting compensation in heart cases has been inappropriate. States are moving away from the unusual exertion rule; about two-thirds have already eliminated such a precondition. It is not always apparent how rigidly, if at all, a state applies the unusual exertion doctrine. New York relaxed its unusual cause requirement a number of years ago after the courts were able to find something unusual in most events that precipitated a disabling injury. The doctrine was not entirely dropped out of fear that many more cases would enter the workers' compensation system, but it was loosened up by the use of a "wear-and-tear" provison. Although New York did retain the unusual exertion rule, an unusual event could be measured against the employee's usual work effort, the usual effort of other employees, or the usual wear and tear of nonemployment activity. Stress or exertion exceeding any of these criteria is held to be unusual. It is most important to recognize that even where an exertion test, usual or unusual, is met, the claimant still has the burden to prove that the activity was responsible for the ensuing disability.

By eliminating or relaxing the unusual exertion test, states have risked opening the system to many more claims. Some persons have warned that this would be too expensive and unsound in view of the medical knowledge regarding heart disease. Hellmuth warns:

If the courts accept claims for compensation for natural, untraumatic, nonoccupational disease, they open the way for Workmen's Compensation to become an all-encompassing health insurance program. For medical knowledge shows that the problem of heart disease is a good deal more complicated. A man with a perfectly healthy heart will never have an attack, no matter how great the exertion. Preexisting heart disease must be present to produce a heart attack. In fact, it is unrelated to employment, since, medically speaking, the etiology of arteriosclerotic heart disease is unknown.[61]

The precise source of such disease in individual cases is still unknown, however, there is little doubt that the working environment can enhance the probability of the disease or exacerbate a condition.

In analyzing the states' compensation practices regarding occupational diseases, their efforts to avoid overburdening the system have been stressed. Few areas pose so grave a threat of doing this as heart cases. This fear, evidenced by the cautious movements of states and the considerable controversy surrounding the problem, exists for two reasons. First, the sheer volume of cases that could emerge each year is enormous. The potential for a greatly expanded volume of cases is aggravated by the fact that neither the underlying cause of the disease condition nor the physiological source of the disability when it is manifested is known. Second, heart cases are expensive by the standards of workers' compensation. They easily can be expected to involve longer, costlier, more serious disabilities—and more death claims—than most other diseases or injuries due to accident. (Evidence of this is presented in ch. 5.) It is not surprising, therefore, that the area has been the source of considerable concern, even though relatively few cases seem to be compensated each year.

The administration of heart cases is uneven across states, with some evidence that the etiological issues are overwhelming the system's ability to provide fair and consistent treatment. At one extreme is Nevada, which will not compensate heart cases except under particular conditions in a narrowly specified group of public-sector, protective occupations. At the extreme are the states that allegedly have made it relatively easy to receive compensation. Dalenberg argues that Illinois is such a state.[62] In Illinois, the claimant must demonstrate the asserted pathology, prove that there was some (any) exertive activity, show that no more than a relatively brief period transpired between the exertion and the onset of clinical symptoms, and obtain a medical opinion that the exertion might or could have triggered the attack. According to Dalenberg, since the first three criteria are clear-cut, a claimant's success depends on finding a credible medical witness to testify that the exertion might or could have been the proximate cause of the injury, apparently a simple matter since the cause of heart disease is not known. As a consequence, according to Dalenberg, claimants in heart cases in Illinois no longer face serious obstacles to winning compensation, and most cases are largely decided on the basis of the relative skills of the attorneys. If his observation is correct, it seriously indicts a system whose no-fault character was designed initially to eliminate precisely this source of delay and uncertainty.

Although Dalenberg may be correct for Illinois, it is surely not true that the issue of the time period between exertion and the onset of clinical symptoms is straightforward. States use the time lag between an exertion, usual or unusual, and the onset of symptoms as the basic mechanism to limit claims. Wyoming has not only elected the protective barrier of an unusual exertion rule, it further requires that the acute symptoms of the cardiac condition in question are clearly manifested not later than thirty minutes after the alleged causative exertion. From a medical perspective the Wyoming rule makes no more sense than one that allows up to twelve or twenty-four hours or twenty-four days to pass. On the one hand, work is clearly implicated in the underlying disease condition for many persons with heart disease, though the manner of involvement is not known. It is virtually impossible for workers with such conditions to be compensated where no clinical symptoms or manifestation of the disease occur, or the symptoms occur at a time or place well removed from the workplace, for instance, after the employee has retired from work. On the other hand, any exertion can trigger the onset of symptoms if the worker's cardiovascular system is badly deteriorated. Since this might occur at almost any point after a causative stress has occurred, an arbitrary time limitation, regardless of its duration, makes little sense. It can be defended only on the economic grounds that it prevents excessive opening-up of the compensation system.

In the administrative survey, states were asked if any persons in the past year had been compensated in heart cases in which the attack occurred while the employee was away from the workplace. Of the forty-two states that responded, twenty-five responded affirmatively, fourteen said no, and three did not know. A number of states indicated that such cases were very rare; Delaware had one such case in the past eight years.

In evaluating how workers' compensation has dealt with the medical issue of causality in heart cases, studies for Wisconsin and California suggest serious difficulties. Hellmuth, in examining Wisconsin's record, evaluated cardiac cases found in the state's workers' compensation agency's files.[63] Using the medical criteria for compensability established earlier by the American Heart Association (AHA), he found that half of the successful claims could not be justified medically. He then submitted some workers' compensation case histories to a panel of seven physicians and asked them to evaluate the issue of compensability for each claim, using the AHA criteria. The three physicians with a broad range of experience in treating heart disease generally agreed with each other. The other four physicians with less experience differed greatly in their assessment of claims. In an earlier, comparable study in California conducted by the California Heart Association,[64] five cardiologists examined the files of 319 cases. In only forty-seven of the cases did the entire panel agree on issues of causality (and thus on compensability). In 48 other cases not even three of the five physicians could agree, and in 215 cases three physicians only could agree. Far more troublesome, however, was the finding that when 101 of the records were later reviewed again by the panel, without their knowing that the records were the same, in 30 percent of the cases the cardiologists reversed themselves. This finding is consistent with a hypothesis that to ask anyone, either a compensation administrator or a physician, to evaluate the cause of a disease whose etiology is almost always unknown for the purpose of satisfying a legal proceeding, results in arbitrary, capricious, and inconsistent determinations that are ultimately based on secondary or tertiary considerations.

The "problem" of heart cases lies as much with the unsettling concern about the future as it does with the morass that currently prevails. A number of writers and groups have suggested ways to deal with the problem.

1. The Committee on the Effect of Strain and Trauma of the American Heart Association reported in 1962 that no method existed for determining the causative relationship between any given event and typical coronary thrombosis with infarct. It concluded "that in view of the current absence of acceptable scientific confirmation, heart disease, except in the rare instances mentioned, shall not be considered as arising out of employment and that presumptive legislation affirming causal relationship of heart disease to any time of employment is unjustified by present scientific evidence."[65]

A legal subcommittee of the committee made five recommendations for improving the administrative and judicial processes in the handling of heart cases. They urged: encouragement for the interpretation and publication by authoritative medical groups of evidence on causative factors related to cardiac disease; dissemination of more medical information on cardiac disease to the general practitioner; education of the medical witness as to his role; lessening of emphasis by commissions and courts on the language in which medical testimony is couched; and the wider use of autopsies. These recommendations are ameliorative measures that appear quite bland when contrasted with the overall committee's view that heart cases be removed from the system.

2. As a follow-up of his study of heart cases in Wisconsin, Hellmuth conducted a survey of attorney's attitudes (N = 344) toward such claims.[66] The survey was structured

to draw equally from attorneys that normally represent either respondent or claimant and a random sample of other attorneys in Wisconsin. The response rate of 38 percent was reasonable for a mail survey, but a disproportionate share of the respondents were from the group that usually represented the plaintiff. The attorneys generally liked the existing system; under 20 percent responded to a question asking for feasible alternatives to supplement or replace the existing law, and some of those who answered endorsed the current system. The attorneys soundly rejected the use of impartial medical witnesses (available but rarely used under Wisconsin law). They indicated that physicians tend to be partial and favor their own (sometimes disparate) theories. A majority also rejected the suggestion that a panel of impartial medical witnesses be used by the Industrial Commission. Only 9 percent approved of a suggestion that a determination by such a panel be final, at least on medical questions, compared to 72 percent opposed. Even the suggestion that the findings of a panel of physicians be made available on request to a claims examiner was rejected by 42 percent of the respondents, compared to 41 percent who would accept this technique. Frequent comments were made that if such a system were used, the panelists should be made available for cross-examination and their evidence should carry no greater weight than that of other witnesses.

A large majority of respondents reported a difference between cardiac specialists and general practitioners. The former were reported to less commonly find a causal connection between an activity and the onset of the disability. The vast majority of respondents did not want heart cases removed from the workers' compensation system nor have the system adopt medically developed criteria for compensation. In summary, the responding attorneys consistently rejected any systematic changes that would reduce the role of litigation and the adversary approach in the handling of such cases. Not surprisingly, since they may have had some part in its shaping, the respondents found the system to their liking.

3. Hellmuth, in an earlier paper, endorses the AHA position that except in rare instances, such as cor pulmonale, heart cases should be removed from the system.[67] He concurs that if such cases are not removed, compensation should be paid only if physical or emotional exertion occurs that is clearly unusual for the individual, and heart failure takes place during the actual exertion. He also pleads for greater reliance on state-appointed experts and the increased use of postmortems. In his view, the fault has been the use of inexperienced nonspecialists.

4. A different position has been taken by J. Goshkin: "That an acceptable solution can only arise from arbitrary action and not from developments in the science of

medicine or the art of case law. . . .''[68] Goshkin favors the AHA approach of legislatively removing heart cases from the compensation system but believes this is currently un-feasible for political reasons. As a compromise he urges that benefits be denied in cases based on alleged mental or emotional strains; claims based on allegations of ''continuous trauma,'' the cumulative effects of the daily work routine over a period of time, should be denied; claims be permitted that are based on specific incidents of physical exertion where the onset of the symptom occurs within twenty-four hours of the exertion and there is medical evidence that a causal relationship exists; and apportionment of indem-nity benefits (but not the medical benefits) in cases involving death and permanent disability and provision of a second-injury fund to finance the nonindustrial portion of such benefits. This would lead to lower costs by reducing the number of litigated cases.

The striking characteristic of Goshkin's proposal is that it is based on neither medical nor legal theory. He aims for a feasible solution that would be imposed by statute. It would, presumably, reduce the uncertainties of the current system and limit the poten-tial growth in the volume of claims.

5. Arthur Larson's suggested solution for heart cases begins with a recognition that causality must be separated into a legal and a medical concept.[69] The law must define what level of exertion meets the ''arising out of'' test; a physician must show that the exertion could (or did) cause the collapse. The legal test proposed would depend on the claimant's condition prior to the event that triggered the illness. If there is some ''personal causal contribution''—in this case implying a previously weakened or diseased cardiovascular condition—the employment contribution must take the form of an exertion greater than that of nonemployment life. (This is akin to New York's wear-and-tear rule.) The exertion would not be compared with this employee's usual exertion but with the exertions encountered in nonemployment life by an ordinary person.

Where no ''personal causal contribution'' exists—implying no prior weakness or preexisting disease—any exertion would satisfy the legal test of causality. In either case the exertion must be shown to be causally connected to the manifestation of the disease. Larson is aware that some medical scientists hold that heart attacks cannot occur in persons without preexisting disease and replies that this only means that most cases will involve personal causal contribution.

According to Larson, if the views of the American Heart Association are correct, that is, a heart attack only occurs where some underlying disease condition exists, then virtually all cases will have to be evaluated in terms of a wear-and-tear rule. The obvious virtue of such an approach is that a body of case law would develop, eventually creating a clear measure of routine exertion. Larson believes that the maintenance of the medical test linking the exertion to the attack will keep the floodgates from being swamped by such an approach. Larson agrees that very few cases may involve no "personal causal contribution," however, he still advocates using different legal tests depending on the employee's previous health condition, opening the way to arguments that a very small or "insignificant" prior weakness should be judged in a particular case against that less rigorous standard. At what point would a court decide to apply that easier standard instead of the one in which the exertion must be evaluated against the exertions of ordinary nonemployment life? Would it apply the more rigorous test even when the claimant's cardiac history involved only some minor elevation in blood pressure? If the preexisting disability was not a cardiovascular one but, for example, a pulmonary disorder, which test would apply? Larson's approach obviously creates a variety of snags. It may be desirable to cope with such difficulties by adhering to certain legal principles, and it is probably true that heart cases can only occur in the presence of an underlying weakness, but it is more reasonable to avoid such controversy altogether. This would lead, in the Larson solution, to the use of a wear-and-tear rule in every case. The physician still must testify as to whether an exertion is causally connected to an attack.

6. The proposal put forward by Cohen and Klein largely builds on the Larson suggestions.[70] There are two significant differences, however, based on a recognition that the etiology of most heart disease is unknown. So long as medical science cannot establish causality in such cases, the only test for compensability would be based on legal criteria and not on any medical ones involving etiology. Thus, unlike Larson's suggestions, every case would involve the use of the exertion exceeding that found in ordinary nonworking life criterion, and no distinction would be made that depends on the preexisting condition of the claimant. The medical test of causality would be dropped under this approach. Physicians would only attest to the resulting pathology and on the degree of physical impairment. Although Larson sees this medical causality criterion as a necessary one, applied in each case, Cohen and Klein advocate dropping it on the grounds that medical science cannot yet provide the answer. Since Larson sees this medical test as the potential bar to an onslaught of claims, either the prospect does not trouble Cohen and Klein or they believe that the eventual construction of the wear-and-tear rule by the courts will provide the necessary barrier.

7. Roberts has reviewed a number of approaches to heart cases, including the personal risk approach (Larson), increased use of waivers and apportionment, coverage of such cases as occupational diseases and not as injuries caused by accident, and wider use

Table 4.1

Source of Ultimate Disability	Source of Preexisting Condition	
	Work-connected	Non-work-connected
Work-connected	Case A	Case B
Non-Work-connected	Case C	

of second injury funds.[71] Although sympathetic to each of these proposed remedies, he prefers a medical approach to the problem. He suggests that minimum medical criteria be established by law with specific provisions to cover the time when symptoms appear, the necessary degree of exertion, and so on. Ideally, according to Roberts, an impartial medical panel would be selected to evaluate the merit of claims (disputed or possibly initially denied) on the basis of these criteria. The panel's finding would not be binding on the board, but would be treated as conclusive in the absence of appeal. This approach is consistent with some of Hellmuth's views and a procedure already used in Utah.

Aggravation, Acceleration, and Preexisting Conditions

In worker's compensation the aggravation of a preexisting condition is not unique to occupational disease, but it arises relatively more often in those cases than in cases of injury caused by accident. The aging process itself can increase the likelihood that a preexisting condition will worsen or become more susceptible to the various health hazards to which one may be exposed. There are many disease conditions that may not be compensable but in conjunction with other diseases may accelerate disability or death. Either the precondition or the eventual sickness may be due to the workplace. It is also likely that certain occupational exposures become much more likely to result in disease or death if the person is a cigarette smoker. The possible ways diseases and preexisting conditions arise are categorized and summarized in table 4.1.

Case A In this situation a worker develops an initial condition as a consequence of his work. This condition may range from a predisposition to become disabled in the presence of some subsequent occurrence or exposure to the actual manifestation of a disease or illness that is nondisabling and/or noncompensable. The situation becomes a matter for the compensation authorities if and when the worker becomes disabled as a consequence of a later workplace occurrence or exposure, or if the preexisting condition exacerbates the disablement caused by the later workplace occurrence. A related situation occurs where the preexisting condition accelerates the disablement process caused by the subsequent occurrence.

Case B This situation differs from the case A only in one respect; the original source of the preexisting weakness or condition is not work connected. As in case A, however, the disability ultimately occurs because of some incident related to the workplace.

Case C In this group as in case A, a preexisting condition is due to the workplace but unlike cases A and B, the disablement that either aggravates or is accelerated by the underlying condition is not caused by events occurring at work.

There is little debate about the compensability issue in case A, although there are differences across states in how the costs of providing compensation are assessed. So long as the resulting disability is considered by the state to be an occupational disease or an injury due to an accident, this case is not at all complex. The states were asked in the survey of administrative practices whether such cases are compensable (see table 4.2, column 1).

The situation in case B, however, is not clear (see table 4.2, column 2). In most states the general rule is that the employer takes the worker as he finds him. Whether the source of the preexisting condition is work connected is often considered irrelevant where the rule is rigorously applied. In such instances there are obvious implications for preemployment screening programs, safety and health programs at the workplace, and second injury funds and other measures to encourage the employment of the handicapped. In practice the states do not always apply the rule rigidly. For example, in *Warren* v. *General Motors Corp.* compensation was denied an employee who contracted carpal tunnel syndrome.[72] The claimant contended that damage to his wrist was due to the vibrations of a nine- to ten-pound air gun. The court found persuasive the evidence that only three or four recorded cases of the disease had occurred over the previous four years among the 2,000 employees using air guns. This, combined with the evidence suggesting that Warren had a "predisposition" to the disease, caused the court to deny compensation.

This kind of decision points up the dilemma that workers' compensation authorities face when two major operational principles of the system conflict. With only three or four cases of the disorder recorded among such employees over a four-year period, carpal tunnel syndrome may be simply an "ordinary disease of life" and, hence, not likely to be compensated. Without hard data on a disease incidence rate for the population at large, one cannot conclude that a seemingly small number of cases in a plant is extraordinary or not. (Very few cases of angiosarcoma were found in vinyl chloride workers.) Even when there are very few cases of a disease among workers exposed to a given hazard, it is clear that something predisposes certain persons to contract some disorders while the majority of the work force is not affected. This tendency for certain persons to react to specific toxic substances may stem from many sources including diet, the nature of other substances the person is exposed to at home or at work, previous illnesses, or heredity. The importance of such predisposition should not be overemphasized, particularly as to do so may imply the lack of urgency in assuring healthful work environments. But workers' compensation claims have often hung on this issue.

Given an excessive risk of contracting certain illnesses and the principle that the

Table 4.2
Aggravation of preexisting conditions

| | Aggravation of Preexisting Condition, Compensable if | | Compensable if Occupational Disease Aggravates Fatal Non-Work Connected Cause |
	Preexisting condition work related	Preexisting condition not work related	
Alabama	N.A.	N.A.	N.A.
Alaska	Yes	Yes	1
Arizona	Yes	Yes	Yes
Arkansas	N.A.	N.A.	N.A.
California	Yes	Yes	Yes
Colorado	Yes	Yes	Yes
Connecticut	Yes	Yes	Yes
Delaware	Yes	Probably	1
Florida	Yes	Yes	Yes
Georgia	N.R.	N.R.	Yes
Hawaii	Yes	Yes	Yes
Idaho	Yes	Yes	Yes
Illinois	Yes	Yes	Yes
Indiana	Yes	Yes	2
Iowa	Yes	Yes	No
Kansas	Yes	Yes	Yes
Kentucky	Yes	Yes	2
Louisiana	N.A.	N.A.	N.A.
Maine	N.A.	N.A.	N.A.
Maryland	N.A.	N.A.	N.A.
Massachusetts	Yes	Yes	Yes
Michigan	Yes	Yes	No
Minnesota	Yes	Yes	Yes
Mississippi	Yes	Yes	Yes
Missouri	Yes	No	No
Montana	N.R.	N.R.	Yes
Nebraska	Yes	Yes	Yes
Nevada	Yes	Yes	N.R.
New Hampshire	Yes	Yes	Yes
New Jersey	Yes	Yes	Yes
New Mexico	Yes	Yes	Yes
New York	Yes	Yes	Yes
North Carolina	Yes	Yes	Yes
North Dakota	Yes	Yes	Yes
Ohio	Yes	No	Yes
Oklahoma	2	2	N.R.
Oregon	Yes	Yes	Maybe
Pennsylvania	N.A.	N.A.	N.A.
Rhode Island	Yes	Yes	Yes
South Carolina	Yes	Yes	Yes
South Dakota	N.A.	N.A.	N.A.
Tennessee	2	2	2
Texas	Yes	Yes	N.R.
Utah	Yes	Yes	2
Vermont	Yes	Yes	1
Virginia	Yes	Yes	Yes
Washington	Yes	Yes	Yes
West Virginia	Yes	No	No
Wisconsin	Yes	Yes	Yes
Wyoming	N.A.	N.A.	N.A.

Source: Survey of State Administrative Practices.
N.A. No response to the questionnaire.
N.R. No response to this question.
1. No experience on this yet.
2. Don't know.

employer takes the worker as he finds him, a basic contradiction occurs. The claimant must demonstrate that the employment contributed in some way to the development of the disability, and the predisposition to the disability can hardly be considered detrimental to the claimant. There are instances where other courts have ruled as in the Warren case,[73] however, in many others the decision has favored the claimant. In Oregon in *Baudry* v. *Winchester Plywood Co.,* a work-induced aggravation of a preexisting condition of bursitis of the hip was held to be a compensable occupational disease.[74] In *Hammond* v. *Albina Engine & Machine Works, Inc.,* a claimant was found to be permanently and totally disabled and granted compensation when dust at the workplace aggravated an underlying asthmatic-bronchitis condition and accelerated its deterioration.[75] In *Jenkins* v. *Ogletree Farm Supply,* the court held that prolonged exposure to caustic sprays and dust aggravated a preexisting condition of emphysema and asthma and gave rise to a compensable disability.[76] Despite the gradual nature of the deterioration in the claimant's health, the award was made on the basis of an injury. Compensation benefits, however, were reduced by the proportion of the disability that resulted from the preexisting condition.

An extreme example in which case B was found to be compensable is the recent Michigan decision, *Riddle* v. *Broad Crane Engineering Co.*[77] A person employed less than two days was hospitalized due to coughing and choking from working in a dusty environment. The employee was found to have an enlarged liver due to excessive drinking and died of pneumonia shortly thereafter. Medical testimony was contradictory with the claimant's physician testifying that the dust exposure so weakened the employee that he could not recover. The insurer's doctor testified that the exposure to dust on the job did not cause the employee's illness or death. In granting compensation the court of appeals reversed the board partially on the grounds that it was improper to question the effects that the work environment would have had on a healthy individual. The board should have limited its inquiry to the effects the workplace had on this employee. If the employment aggravated, accelerated, or combined with a preexisting disease or infirmity so as to cause the person to become disabled, the disability has arisen out of the employment.

The most complex and difficult area occurs in case C. Permitting compensation in cases in which disability is enhanced or its onset accelerated by a preexisting work-connected condition but the event that ultimately causes the disability is not work-connected, creates an enormous potential for widening the system. To systematically close the door on all such claims would demonstrate a lack of recognition that the aging process or a seemingly innocuous illness can seriously disable or even kill a previously nondisabled person whose health has been pushed to the edge of soundness by a work-connected event. Examples of this abound, particularly in cases of respiratory or pulmonary diseases. The question will surely grow in importance as it is shown that certain diseases occur or are accelerated only if the employee smokes cigarettes.

In some instances the justice of certain decisions is difficult to question. Where persons are disabled or die from heart disease that is aggravated by a pulmonary condition, such as work-connected silicosis, compensation would be warranted without question in most states[78] (see table 4.2, column 3). A more difficult case occurred in North Carolina. Benefits were awarded a worker who died from a malignant brain tumor that was unrelated to his preexisting condition of asbestosis.[79] Clearly the underlying condition could be expected to weaken the employee and hasten his death but one wonders whether any preexisting condition would not have contributed to the weakening of the human organism when confronted with such a malignancy. Would the court have awarded benefits if the underlying condition had not been asbestosis but a work-connected but previously nondisabling case of bronchitis? It does not seem unreasonable to suppose that almost any underlying disease condition can hasten or accelerate the disabling or fatal effects of serious diseases. Decision making in this area by workers' compensation authorities involves a combination of difficult technical-scientific matters and some philosophical questions about the purpose of the program.

For a number of diseases the worker may not be disabled at all at the time he ceases to have contact with a hazard, but his health may deteriorate solely through the passage of time. For example, a person with nondisabling silicosis can expect his condition to worsen as he ages even when he is no longer exposed to harmful dusts. The progressive nature of the disease implies that even after the employee's condition is diagnosed and evaluated for compensation purposes, the extent of disability will increase. This has obvious implications for rules on time limits in which to file claims, the advisability of compromise and release awards where certain diseases are involved, and the need for periodic reevaluations of the extent of disability. Age is an important ingredient, but it is not clear how the aging process interacts with preexisting or underlying conditions that were formed at the workplace. The average male employee in the age group forty-five to sixty-four loses 50 percent more time from work due to a chronic condition than does a male twenty-five to forty-four, but there is no way of knowing what share of this difference stems from work-connected preexisting conditions.[80]

Cigarette smoking also creates difficult scientific and philosophical problems for the compensation adjudicator. Selikoff and others argue that asbestos causes lung cancer only when workers are also cigarette smokers, (although others have vigorously disputed this).[81] Jablon suggests that the highly elevated rates of lung cancer in uranium miners may be related to a synergism between the work and cigarette smoking.[82] In *Dillow* v. *Florida Portland Cement Plant* an employee was awarded compensation when his lung was removed due to cancer.[83] It was not claimed that his work caused the cancer but the exposure to dust at work, together with his cigarette smoking, accelerated the growth of the malignancy. Since either alone could have hastened the development of the cancer, compensation was awarded.

Several states, including California, Florida, Maryland, and Mississippi, currently will allow benefits to be apportioned so that the portion of disability due to a non-work-connected condition is not the insurer's responsibility.[84] In a 1970 decision in West Virginia, it was held that the claimant was entitled to recover only for that portion of his disability due to silicosis.[85] No compensation was awarded for that portion of the disability due to the combination of silicosis and the preexisting conditions of asthma and emphysema that were not caused by the work. In the Fuentes case in California, apportionment was carried to the refined extreme where even the contribution of on-the-job and off-the-job smoking determined the size of the benefit awarded.[86] Such apportionment rules mitigate the harshness of the doctrine that the employer takes the worker as he finds him. They may contribute marginally to programs to hire the handicapped, although the same can be accomplished by second injury funds. Such apportionment rules also create the need for precise quantitative evaluations regarding contributive shares of responsibility for disability that are frequently impossible to substantiate on scientific grounds except in the broadest terms. Although the use of apportionment creates extremely difficult judgments for compensation administrators, the approach can make it easier by allowing non-categorical decisions. Instead of all or nothing opinions, it allows for partial victories for both the plaintiff and the defense.

Larson estimates that in approximately half of the states the provisions of second injury funds are broad enough to cover preexisting occupational diseases.[87] In a few states, including Colorado, Kansas, Kentucky, and Ohio, occupational diseases are specifically placed under the second injury funds. But such provisions largely deal with situations corresponding to case A. As the scientific and medical problems of occupational diseases become better understood, most of the difficulties will involve problems from the other kinds of situations, particularly case C.

Time Limitations in Occupational Diseases

One of the crucial differences between injuries caused by accident and occupational diseases is the role of time. Some diseases are of long latency and others develop gradually over a prolonged period of time. Under workers' compensation the routine type of injury case occurs at a discrete point in time. The laws of all states recognize this aspect of occupational diseases in some way. The successful lobbying efforts in state legislatures of the Atomic Energy Commission, which sought to assure compensation for workers who became disabled due to past exposures to ionizing radiation, reflects this recognition. Some states protected these workers if they developed long latent diseases, however, the time aspect of many other diseases has not been incorporated into the law.

The time aspect of occupational disease cases involves a number of factors, particularly statutes of limitation, which are found in most areas of civil and criminal law. Similar rules had existed for many years before they were incorporated into England's first Workers' Compensation Act in 1897. As the states passed their compensation laws, they included statutes of limitations that had the time period for filing a claim begin either at the time of the accident or at the time of injury. Many states became dissatisfied with this arrangement and reversed their positions, some more than once. The issue is still not entirely resolved in all states. Kelley notes at the time of his writing (1974) that the courts of at least six states still have not determined the precise definition of when the claims period begins for purposes of these limits.[88]

Statutes of limitations are supposed to serve at least three purposes. The evidentiary purpose is to reduce the likelihood of error or fraud that may occur when deciding factual issues long after the incident has occurred. Personal certainty is meant to assure a potential defendant that he will not be liable under law indefinitely. The diligence purpose is to discourage prospective claimants from "sleeping on their rights." The statutes of limitations were created to protect potential defendants and force claimants to act within a reasonably prompt period, if they are to act at all. At one time they served as an effective barrier against workers with certain types of occupational diseases, but in recent years the states have been converting their statutes to make the laws less harsh.[89]

Time limitation rules on workers' compensation claims take a number of different forms.

Minimum Exposure Rule A significant number of states have time limitation rules that bar workers' compensation claims for occupational diseases (usually specified) unless the claimant can prove that his exposure to a hazard at the workplace occurred over a specified minimum period of time. Idaho and Maine bar occupational disease claims unless the claimant has been employed at least sixty days with the firm where he contracted the disease. Louisiana law presumes that a disease is noncompensable when contracted during the first year of working for a particular employer, unless the evidence overwhelmingly demonstrates otherwise. (This is directly at odds with the frequent assertion that workers' compensation protects employees from the first day they begin on the job.) Many states (for example, Georgia, Iowa, Kansas, and Utah) require that claimants with silicosis and/or asbestosis prove that they have been exposed to the hazard in question for a substantial period of time, typically five years. These rules disregard relevant issues such as the person's age and condition prior to being employed, the concentration of the hazardous substance to which the worker was exposed, and the nature of the working environment, including the use of protective equipment. A few states still create minimum exposure rules in terms of the number of shifts worked (see table 4.3, column 1).

Recent Exposure Rule Many states, including most of those using a minimum exposure rule, also have legislative requirements barring claims for diseases caused by hazards encountered on the job more than a specified number of years earlier. Many of these rules are specifically aimed at claims for silicosis and/or asbestosis, but occasionally they are applied to other diseases. With silicosis and asbestosis many statutes require a combination of a minimum and a recent exposure rule; a minimum exposure of at least five years out of the past ten years.

Such arbitrary and broad recent exposure rules have undermined many actual and probably many more potential claims. In *Yocum* v. *Jones,* Kentucky's former, extremely harsh rules disallowed a claim for silicosis to a permanently and totally disabled worker.[90] The claimant had spent twenty-five years in the coal mines until 1958 when he left that line of work. Then from May 1968 to February 1970 he returned to the mines of his former employer and was again exposed to mine dusts. In February 1970 he was forced by poor health to cease work. Since Kentucky required two years of continuous exposure to the hazard prior to the onset of disability, his claim was denied. A number of other Kentucky decisions made at this time highlight the strictness of their statute.[91] Pennsylvania barred compensation on comparable grounds in *Bethlehem Steel* v. *Gray*.[92] A long-term employee at Bethlehem Steel was employed until February 11, 1963, when he became disabled with lung cancer. From then until his retirement on August 30, 1963, he received sickness and accident benefits under a company plan. Although the person was diagnosed as having silicosis in February 1963, he did not

Table 4.3
Time limitation rules

State	Minimum Exposure Rule	Recent Exposure Rule	Statute of Limitations Rule[a]	Hearing Loss Time Delay Rule
Alabama	N.A.	N.A.	N.A.	N.A.
Alaska	No	No	2 years[a]	No
Arizona	No	No	1 year	No
Arkansas	N.A.	N.A.	N.A.	N.A.
California	No	No	1 year[a]	No
Colorado	Yes	Yes	6 years[a]	No
Connecticut	No	No	1 year[a]	No
Delaware	No	No	1 year[a]	No
Florida	No	No	2 years	No
Georgia	Yes	Yes	1 year	6 months
Hawaii	No	Yes	1 or 2 years[a]	No
Idaho	Yes	Yes	1 year	No
Illinois	No	Yes	3 years[a]	No
Indiana	Yes	Yes	2 or 3 years	No[b]
Iowa	Yes	Yes	2 years	No
Kansas	Yes	Yes	1 year	No
Kentucky	No	Yes	1 or 3 years	90 days[b]
Louisiana	N.A.	N.A.	N.A.	N.A.
Maine	N.A.	N.A.	N.A.	N.A.
Maryland	N.A.	N.A.	N.A.	N.A.
Massachusetts	No	No	1 year[a]	No
Michigan	No	No	N.R.	No
Minnesota	No	No	2 years[a]	No
Mississippi	No	No	2 years[a]	No
Missouri	Yes	No	1 year[a]	6 months
Montana	Yes	No	30 days[a]	6 months
Nebraska	No	No	6 months[a]	No
Nevada	Yes	Yes	90 days[a]	No
New Hampshire	No	No	2 years[a]	No
New Jersey	No	Yes	1 or 2 years[a]	No
New Mexico	Yes	Yes	1 year and 30 days	No[b]
New York	Yes	Yes	90 days or 2 years[a]	6 months
North Carolina	Yes	Yes	2 years[a]	Yes
North Dakota	No	No	1 year[a]	No
Ohio	Yes	Yes	6 months or 2 years[a]	No
Oklahoma	No	No	3 or 18 months	No
Oregon	No	Yes	180 days[a]	No
Pennsylvania	N.A.	N.A.	N.A.	N.A.
Rhode Island	No	No	2 years	6 months
South Carolina	N.R.	N.R.	N.R.	No
South Dakota	N.A.	N.A.	N.A.	N.A.
Tennessee	No	No	1 or 3 years	No
Texas	No	No	6 months	No
Utah	Yes	Yes	1 year[a]	6 months
Vermont	No	Yes	1 year[a]	No[b]
Virginia	No	Yes	2 years[a]	No
Washington	No	No	1 year[a]	No
West Virginia	Yes	N.R.	2 or 3 years[a]	No
Wisconsin	No	No	2 years[a]	2 months
Wyoming	N.A.	N.A.	N.A.	N.A.

Source: Survey of State Administrative Practices.
N.A. Did not return questionnaire.
N.R. No response to question.
a. Indicates some form of discovery rule is used.
b. No benefits are paid for chronic hearing loss.

become disabled by silicosis until July 6, 1967. Thus the worker's disability from silicosis did not develop until more than four years after his last exposure to the hazard, but less than four years after his employment in the firm. Based on a four-year recent exposure rule, Pennsylvania denied benefits to the decedent's survivor. In *Carr* v. *Homestake Mining Co.* the claimant had been employed by Homestake Mining from September 1929 to February 1942, from September 1945 until February 1951, and from February 1952 to May 1962; more than twenty-eight years.[93] He became totally disabled in April 1971. Since he had only worked for one year and forty-seven days in the preceding ten years and South Dakota law required that injurious exposure to silica must occur for at least five years during the ten years preceding disability, the claim was barred. At least nineteen states currently employ such a rule (see table 4.3, column 2).

Exposure in the State Several of the states have minimum time requirements regarding the state in which the exposure occurred. Some of these are attached to the silicosis/asbestosis provisions, creating at least three different time requirements for filing claims; the worker has been exposed to the hazard for at least five years out of the past ten years, and at least two of these five years must have occurred in the state in which the claim is filed. Utah requires that persons with silicosis claims have worked at least five years in the state. The presence of such rules can readily create situations where disabled workers or their survivors become locked out of the compensation system and have no opportunity to file a claim anywhere. These provisions protect employers from being liable for compensation when previously exposed persons move into states for the purpose of drawing higher compensation benefits. A more positive approach, however, by employers and these states would make use of stiffer preemployment screening, second injury funds, and interstate compacts.

Notification of Employer Regardless of what type of statute of limitation rule applies, states typically require that workers notify employers of claims filed within some time period. Failure to do so in a timely fashion can undermine a workers' compensation claim, but cases of this sort are rare. It is also unclear why the claimant's compensation can be denied on these grounds when the state compensation agency has the claim (on time) and could notify the employer directly.

The Discovery Rule Most states have shown a considerable willingness in recent years to acknowledge the special problems created by cases of occupational diseases for standard statutes of limitations. The vast majority have developed special time limitation rules for these claims, requiring that they be filed within some time period after the claimant knows or should have known that he had a probably compensable disability. "Discovery rules" are often written exclusively for cases involving occupational diseases. Even where there is a discovery rule, a timely claim may not be compensable if it does not meet other existing time rules, such as a minimum or recent exposure rule.

The discovery rule, Kelley finds, is inconsistent with both the evidentiary and the personal certainty purposes of statutes of limitation. The justification for such rules must be considered a matter of equity: it is more desirable to protect ignorant plaintiffs from rigid limitations than to seek the traditional purposes of such laws. The discovery rule does not end the use of such statutes but simply shifts the time period for filing, usually until ninety days to two years after the employee is aware of the nature of his disability. Of the forty states reporting statute of limitation rules, twenty-six use some type of discovery rule (see table 4.3, column 3).

The application of the discovery rule provides more opportunity for claiming compensation, however, it creates a whole set of new issues. What if the worker is advised by a company's physician that his hearing loss problem could not have been due to his work, but learns eight years after retirement from another doctor that the first physician was wrong?[94] What if the worker knows that he has a work-related impairment but does not realize that the disease has also disabled him until several years later? Should rules regarding "reasonableness" be applied in the same way to disabled employees as to their surviving spouses? Should discovery rules be interpreted liberally? The answers to many such questions will need to be settled in the future.

Hearing Loss Rule Another form of time limitation, applied in cases of chronic hearing loss, requires that the claimant delay filing until he has been away from the allegedly noisy work environment for some time, usually six months. Ostensibly this time limit rule allows persons to have their hearing tested after it has returned from a "temporary threshold shift" (TTS). Any damage beyond the normal loss of hearing associated with age will presumably represent permanent hearing loss, and the worker must then demonstrate that his work environment contributed to his condition in order to receive compensation. Nine states use such a rule (see table 4.2, column 4).

The time limitation rule reduces claims for hearing loss since many workers cannot absent themselves from their working environment until death or retirement. Workers may fear asking their employer for a transfer to a quieter area of the establishment for purposes of filing a claim. A full six months in a quiet environment is not needed in order to return from temporary threshold shifts. Ginnold and others claim that TTS can be greatly reduced or eliminated in one or two days;[95] Ontario uses forty-eight hours.

The time limitation rule for hearing loss as it relates to the statute of limitations was tested in New York in 1975.[96] In *Kopp* v. *Delco Products Division, General Motors Corp.*

the last day of the six months separation from noise was June 30, 1972. This date was held to be the date of disablement, and since the claim was filed within two years of that, it was found timely. A puzzling decision occurred when a worker left a noisy establishment in New York but during the ensuing six months was exposed to considerable noise in a New Jersey establishment.[97] Although the spirit of the six months rule was clearly violated, the statute was construed to mean that a six-months separation from noise in employment in New York was all that was required, and the rule was met.

Among the various time limitation rules in cases of occupational disease, the one used in hearing loss cases limits more claims than all of the others together. Some see this as a boon in reducing the number of relatively nonserious disability cases handled by the states, but the goal of workers' compensation is not to minimize the number of cases flowing into the system.

Compensation Benefits

Assume that a worker suffers some type of work-related disease, there is no dispute about its etiology or the timeliness of its being reported, and it occurs in a state where there is no limited or exclusive schedule. If the case goes to a workers' compensation board, it would be expected that the claimant receives compensation. Three issues still must be determined. Did the disease create or contribute to a disablement? How much should the claimant be compensated? Who is responsible for paying the claimant? The answers generally do not depend on whether the case involves an accident by injury or is an occupational disease, however, there are certain aspects of these questions that are important in dealing with work-connected illnesses.

As a general rule compensation is paid only when employees suffer from some disability. In its report the National Commission helped clarify the issue by delineating the terms "impairment," a strictly medical concept referring to some physical (or emotional, presumably) damage to the human organism, and "disability," a socioeconomic consequence. In workers' compensation it is not impairment nor its side effects of pain and suffering that are compensated. Larson writes, "In compensation, unlike tort, the only injuries compensated for are those which produce disability and thereby presumably effect earning power. . . . impairment or destruction of sexual potency is not in inself a basis for an award, and, presumably the same result would apply to such an injury as destruction of child-bearing capacity in a woman."[98] The National Commission's report reiterates Larson's view.[99] Since it is disability and not impairment that is compensated, uniform benefits in the case of scheduled impairments, such as the loss of a thumb, are anomalous unless one assumes that such an averaging scheme benefits most injured workers by reducing the legal-administrative costs involved in estimating loss of earnings on a case by case basis. As a consequence of exposures to certain workplace hazards, there are many workers who suffer various kinds of impairments, some of which may eventually worsen but not be disabling, that is, cause loss of time from work (or not enough time to pass the minimum waiting period for benefits to be paid). Thus workers suffering from impairments such as headaches, digestive disorders, coughing, shortness of breath, and elevated blood lead levels are usually not sick enough to be disabled and, hence, compensated. It is not surprising that Discher, Kleinman, and Foster found such a high incidence of occupational disease (impairment) in the absence of compensation.[100]

In other instances it is difficult to gauge the extent, if any, of actual or potential loss of earnings with various types of disease. In *Stepnowski* v. *Specific Pharmaceuticals* a male employee had inhaled dust with female hormones that caused effemination and impotency.[101] Stepnowski sought common-law relief on the grounds that he did not suffer an occupational disease and, therefore, workers' compensation did not apply. The court, however, held that this was an occupational disease, granting that it was difficult, but not impossible, to assess earnings loss. Even in the absence of earnings loss it would have awarded compensation. It held that a permanent injury involving loss of physical function and detracting from the efficiency of the body or its members in the ordinary pursuits of life is compensable even if there were no loss in earning power. Conceivably such views of occupational disease will become more widespread as related cases are more widely experienced. Though effemination may be extremely rare, increasing concern is developing as science identifies hazards that contribute to miscarriages, deformed and defective infants, and sterility. If workers' compensation does not extend into these areas, damaged persons will increasingly seek relief through tort action. Recently the director of NIOSH reported that at least one million women of child-bearing age are being exposed to hazards at their workplace that can damage fetuses or jeopardize pregnancies.[102] As information about such health problems becomes more widely disseminated and more tort actions occur, it is likely that employers' groups will seek to have such cases handled under workers' compensation laws.

A significant exception to the compensation for wage-loss principle involves retired persons. If a person is exposed to a hazard at the workplace that does not cause disease to manifest itself until after the worker retires, the former employee is generally eligible for compensation.[103] Similarly, if a retired employee dies of a long-latent disease that has not manifested itself until his retirement, his survivor can claim death benefits under workers' compensation law (subject, of course, to time limitation rules). In most states (Michigan is an important exception) few new claims for compensation involve retired employees, but as in the case of women of child-bearing ages, such cases may grow rapidly as new information about the disease process is disseminated to unions and to workers. Some unions currently notify their members on retirement of their rights to workers' compensation benefits if they believe eventual illness (or impaired hearing) is a result of their former employment.[104]

An area of growing concern involving compensation for non-wage loss is hearing loss. Ginnold argues (and Larson concurs) that until 1948 in *Slawinski* v. *J. H. Williams Co.* employers were able to limit claims for hearing loss to those cases where some wage loss had occurred.[105] Following this a number of states opened up compensation to hearing-loss claims by allowing partial disability benefits for gradual hearing loss, in the absence of any wage loss, by making it a scheduled disability. This liberalized approach created a concern about a deluge of cases, but the available data do not suggest that the system has been swamped. Even so there is potential for vastly greater numbers of persons to claim an occupational disease, particularly on retirement. On the other hand, many states have not yet awarded compensation for chronic hearing loss in the absence of wage loss. In *Hinkle* v. *Heinz* a worker with twenty years of exposure to noise in a body shop was denied compensation because partial hearing loss was not an occupational disease and was not unexpected—it was a very noisy establishment—and there was no "accident" that brought about the injury.[106] This attitude stands in marked contrast with the recent California award to a retired steel worker.[107] After twenty-six years employment with a single firm the worker retired in 1963 and retired from all work in 1965. In 1971 he filed a successful claim against his long-term employer for partial disability due to hearing loss.

Few areas of the law are more likely to undergo careful scrutiny and change than this one. If the principle holds that non-wage-loss cases can be compensated in instances of occupational disease, there are areas far removed from hearing loss that will be affected also.

Employees disabled with occupational diseases are almost always compensated in the same way as workers with similar degrees of disability resulting from accidental injuries. There are instances, as Lloyd Larsen has indicated, where "some states do not pay benefits for partial disability resulting from occupational diseases, some pay lower medical benefits than for industrial accidents, and a few pay lower benefits for other types of disability and for death." He also reports that in a small number of states benefits for silicosis and asbestosis are subject to limitations not placed on other occupational diseases.[108] Ginnold points out that in Wisconsin, scheduled benefits for traumatically induced hearing loss are greater than for the same degree of loss due to chronic workplace exposure to noise.[109] Such anachronistic differentials reflect the initial caution and fear regarding disease coverage dating from the spurt in claims in the 1930s. As states review their laws with a view to reform, these differentials will disappear.

One of the special problems of occupational diseases is the calculation of the employee's lost wages. Some diseases are manifested years after the worker has been exposed to the hazard that disables him, and involve a retired worker who has no wages at all. Since some sicknesses occur gradually and over an extended period, the situation is unlike the bulk of injury-by-accident cases in which the time of injury and disability are unambiguous.

Stoeckle and others shed some light on this in a study of workers suffering from beryllium disease.[110] They reported instances where claimants received compensation for this long-latent disease on the basis of rates and maxima prevailing at the time of exposure and employment, not when the disease became manifest. A woman employed from 1941 to 1942 was diagnosed as having beryllium disease in 1962 and after a prolonged dispute received total disability benefits. Since the benefit was based on her wage during 1941 and 1942, this meant a weekly award of $13.33. Moreover she had no dependents at the time of the exposure, so she was ineligible for any dependents' allowances, despite the fact that she had minor children at the time she became totally disabled.

This approach is not the most common one used by the states. Recently the California Court of Appeal granted compensation at the allowable level prevailing in 1960 to a mechanic who developed a lung condition in that year even though he had been exposed to the injurious dusts from grinding in 1954.[111] A comparable decision in Minnesota in 1975 specified that the level of wages to be replaced was based on earnings at the time the disability occurred and not at the time the disease developed.[112] Although the persistent inflation of the past four decades generally means that the later the base of earnings is calculated, the better off the worker will be, the issue is not always so obvious. In Van Voorhis v. Workmen's Compensation Appeals Board a worker in California ceased work with his long-term employer in 1963, retired from work in 1965, and filed a claim for partial hearing loss due to chronic exposure to noise at his employment until 1963.[113] The board set his earnings loss on the basis of his retirement income of approximately $1,000 per year. This was reversed on the grounds that compensation should be based on the employee's earning capacity as of the time he incurred the compensable disability, which the court found was at approximately the time the employee retired and not at the time of filing.

The appropriate wage base in diseases of long latency presents no special problems for insurers despite the uncertainties about future levels of wages. Insurers already cope with many analagous uncertainties including the cost of health care for long-term disabled persons and cost-of-living formulas that are provided in certain cases to recipients of compensation.

There are many cases in the history of workers' compensation dealing with the question of who is the responsible employer or insurer. Generally such disputes are rare since most compensation cases involve injuries due to accident, and the timing of the triggering incident is known, as is the employment relationship at that time. In occupational diseases, however, where a disease has been long latent or has developed gradually until it disables an employee, there may be room for considerable doubt over where and when the responsible hazardous exposure occurred, at what point the disability began to be manifested, and who bears any financial responsibility. Some states have placed the burden entirely on the last employer where the hazard was encountered, and others have developed rules for apportioning financial responsibility over more than a single firm. There is no reason to suppose that in the long run the costs to individual firms will average out so that a typical employer will pay out the same amount of compensation over all using either system. Since different firms have different policies regarding preemployment screening efforts, hiring of the handicapped, method of insurance, and so on it does matter to employers which technique of settling responsibility is used.

As a public policy issue the matter is not clear-cut. When the last employer is fully responsible, there must be a tendency for firms to use more rigorous health screening in the hiring of new employees as well as to favor, where possible, hiring younger, less experienced persons. An employer (or insurer) may be more likely to dispute a potentially large claim when its entire burden falls on him. Finally, there is the issue of the administrative or frictional costs to the system where an apportionment formula is used, due to having to identify the various sources of past exposures and assure that each firm is assessed and then pays its appropriate share.

The survey of administrative practices of the states contained two questions regarding apportionment policy. They were asked if apportionment among previous employers was possible in cases involving hearing loss due to long-term exposure to noise. The majority of states indicated that such apportionment is not allowed or it is legally permitted but not practiced. Several states reported that they could not answer since the issue had never arisen (see table 4.4, column 1). States were also asked if previous employers might be liable for benefits under an apportionment rule in the case of cardiovascular disease where long-term work activities contributed to the disability. The vast majority of states that do compensate such disability would not apportion responsibility among employers (see table 4.4, column 2).

The policy on apportionment among employers is clear, but an examination of individual cases reveals some uncertainty. A Michigan court found that an employee's disability due to emphysema, byssinosis, and bronchitis was partly due to his prior employment.[114] It held that the last employer was entitled to some apportionment of the compensation costs. This 1973 decision was unlike that in *Aseltine* v. *Leto Construction Co.* (1972) in which a brick mason developed "tennis elbow."[115] The disease developed gradually over a number of years while the claimant was employed by many employers in the construction industry. The last place of employment where Aseltine had been exposed to the hazard of lifting and setting bricks was fully liable.

An extreme case of apportionment occurred in *Yocom* v. *Eastern Coal Corporation*. The employee spent all but two days of his thirty-six years in the coal mines with the same firm.[116] On the basis of those two days, however, the Kentucky Court of Appeals found that it could not be conclusively proven that the miner's pneumoconiosis was solely attributable to his thirty-six years exposure in that mining company's employ. Liability was apportioned, with the bulk of the costs made the responsibility of the state's special fund created for such cases.

A recent Texas decision held the last employer responsible for compensation even when the asbestosis of an installer was due to a hazard he had been exposed to over a long period of time.[117] Yet even where no apportionment is allowed, previous employers may be held liable for compensation costs when a disease contracted at that firm "recurs" in an employee at another place of employment. In *Fields Plastics of Tennessee, Inc.* v. *Ownby* an employee contracted dermatitis in the plastics factory.[118] On a physician's recommendation, the person left this employment but in his next two jobs again contracted dermatitis. The Tennessee Supreme Court acknowledged that the state adheres to the "last injurious exposure rule," but indicated that since subsequent disability resulted from a recurrence of a disease contracted in the original employment, the first firm was fully liable for compensation. It is increasingly difficult, however, to separate cases involving the aggravation of preexisting or underlying conditions from those that are simply a recurrence of an earlier illness.

Table 4.4
Apportionment in hearing loss and heart cases

State	Chronic Hearing Loss Cases	Heart Cases with Long-Term Causes
Alabama	N.A.	N.A.
Alaska	In practice, no	No
Arizona	No	No
Arkansas	N.A.	N.A.
California	Yes, 1	Yes, 1
Colorado	No	2
Connecticut	Yes	Unlikely
Delaware	No	No
Florida	No	No
Georgia	No	No
Hawaii	3	No
Idaho	Yes, but not done	Yes, but not done
Illinois	No	No
Indiana	4	2
Iowa	Yes	N.R.
Kansas	Yes, but not done	No
Kentucky	5	5
Louisiana	N.A.	N.A.
Maine	N.A.	N.A.
Maryland	N.A.	N.A.
Massachusetts	No	No
Michigan	No	No
Minnesota	Yes, but not done	Yes
Mississippi	No	No
Missouri	No	2
Montana	Yes, but not done	2
Nebraska	No	No
Nevada	No	No
New Hampshire	4	No
New Jersey	Yes	6
New Mexico	2	2
New York	Yes	No
North Carolina	No	2
North Dakota	No	No
Ohio	Yes	2
Oklahoma	Yes	No
Oregon	No	No
Pennsylvania	N.A.	N.A.
Rhode Island	No	4
South Carolina	No	No
South Dakota	N.A.	N.A.
Tennessee	No	No
Texas	3	No
Utah	No	2
Vermont	No	2
Virginia	No	2
Washington	Yes	2
West Virginia	No	4
Wisconsin	Yes	No
Wyoming	N.A.	N.A.

Source: Survey of State Administrative Practices.
N.A. No response to questionnaire.
N.R. No response to this question.
1 Only for the last five years.
2 Not applicable since no benefits provided in such cases.
3 Last employer unless medical records substantiate prior loss.
4 No experience on this question.
5 Only through second injury fund.
6 By case law no, in practice yes.

Workers' Compensation and Worker Health

Workers' compensation agencies in a number of states can and occasionally do play a role in affecting the extent of the problem of occupational disease. In some instances the role is the negative one of encouraging sick persons to further expose themselves to an occupational hazard that may eventually kill or totally disable them. In other instances the role is positive in that the agency provides incentives to the worker with impaired health to leave harmful work surroundings.

The device that allows the workers' compensation agency to play such a negative role is the waiver, an agreement between the employee and his employer that relieves the latter of responsibility for compensation in the event that the former becomes disabled. The waiver is not unique to occupational disease, but it is harmful primarily where disease is involved. The rationale for waivers is pragmatic. Employers who are subject to experience rating of their compensation insurance premium may avoid hiring or retaining persons with health impairments that, if aggravated by a work-related event, could exacerbate their existing conditions and result in a costly claim. To prevent employers from not hiring persons with such impairments, some states allow the worker and the employer to agree to waive the latter's responsibility in the event the worker becomes disabled at a later date. Sometimes the employee has nothing to lose in such an agreement, for in the event of further damage, compensation can be awarded from a second injury fund. Most states have such second injury funds. Usually waivers must be approved in advance by the workers' compensation agency. The use of second injury funds to remove the deterrents that the compensation scheme imposes on hiring impaired persons is generally acceptable to most of the involved parties. The principal criticism of this approach is that it is rarely used, and many employers are unaware of its existence. Obviously when employers waive responsibility and no second injury fund exists, the situation is unacceptable.

When an employee has developed a chronic disorder from past exposure to a toxic substance, continued exposure can only increase the likelihood that he will develop a more serious disability. By sanctioning a waiver agreement between an employer and a worker with an existing health problem the worker's compensation agency effectively may be encouraging a further deterioration of the latter's condition. The problem is most common in the case of dust diseases, where the condition develops gradually and the worker may have few symptoms of ill health except some indication by X-ray. It is particularly bad in mining where the location of the mines and the educational and employment backgrounds of the miner imply that few employment alternatives exist outside the mines. Under such conditions the worker is reluctant to forego the relatively high pay and the favorable fringe benefits available to him, and an employer is reluctant to hire a miner with symptoms of disease in the absence of a waiver. Yet when the compensation agency condones such a waiver, it is sanctioning the further exposure of an already sick worker. At the worst, employers might even prefer such miners on the grounds that this will assure reduced future compensation costs.

The problem, though involving workers' compensation, is fundamentally an employment and training problem. It is doubtful that knowledgeable workers with a disease condition willingly continue to expose themselves, much less agree to forego compensation claims, as waivers imply in some states, unless they believe that no acceptable employment alternatives exist for them. In some states, however, this "economic reality" forces the compensation system to allow the worker to incur a potentially fatal risk.

While the waiver may protect the employer from responsibility for disability due to specific diseases, there is of course room for some uncertainty, as indicated by a recent Virginia case.[119] Williams, who had a mild case of silicosis, applied for work with Clinchfield Coal. He agreed to waive his right to workers' compensation in the event that the work aggravated his silicotic condition. He did become disabled but from pneumoconiosis and not from silicosis. Virginia's Supreme Court held against Williams on the grounds that the waiver was intended to rule out worker's compensation for aggravation of an existing lung condition, regardless of its technical name. According to the court, pneumoconiosis and silicosis are so closely related that the waiver applied to either, and presumably to a host of other lung diseases that might have disabled the worker. Although the willingness of the court to be flexible enough to deny benefits to a disabled worker may be troublesome, the issue is the initial approval of the waiver by the state to a person with existing silicosis.

Aside from the matter of waivers the state compensation agency can directly affect a worker's exposure to a hazard in two other ways. When a worker is partially disabled by a disease and receiving workers' compensation benefits, the state agency may compel the worker to transfer to employment where he will not continue to be injuriously exposed. But statutes that enable the state boards to do this customarily allow it only where it is reasonable to conclude that the employee has the actual or potential competency to work with substantial regularity in the new employment.[120] If the worker has no other apparent job opportunities, the board will allow compensation for partial disability from a disease to be paid even though the worker continues to be exposed to the hazard at the workplace.

The workers' compensation agency may also encourage workers with early cases of nondisabling dust diseases to change employment. Larson indicates that a small number of states provide benefits to such workers in an effort to reduce the ultimate severity of their illnesses.[121] In either case state compensation agencies give very limited attention to the kinds of programs that can improve or help to maintain the health of workers. This contrasts sharply with the programs that exist in western Europe or in Ontario. Ontario has recently developed a program to assist miners to leave such work, even before any sign of disease is present, simply on the basis of small changes in a worker's periodic X-rays that may be an indicator of eventual illness. This approach can be described as preventive rehabilitation.

QUANTITATIVE FINDINGS ON OCCUPATIONAL DISEASES AND WORKERS' COMPENSATION

The Volume of Occupational Disease Cases

It is not known how many disease incidents occur annually nor even the number of fatalities from occupational diseases each year, so there is no basis for judging precisely the adequacy of the system's coverage. If we had a good idea of the overall extent of the disease problem, we might be able to evaluate the systems at least in those few states that compile data on disease claims filed and upheld. Data from those states might shed sufficient light on conditions to allow some generalizations for the whole nation.

The deplorable lack of data on workers' compensation systems has stymied most efforts to analyze and evaluate the state programs. An early evaluation (1917) of these laws by the National Industrial Conference Board led to the first recommendation for data: "The states should promptly undertake, under expert guidance, the establishment of a permanent, scientific, uniform system of compensation statistics."[1] Unfortunately this recommendation was not implemented and six decades later there is still only fragmentary information.

The data that do exist on occupational disease are not uniform in meaning. Caution must be exercised in making any type of interstate comparison from the tables in this chapter. The first caveat is that the term "occupational disease" has a somewhat different meaning is each state. Hernias are considered an occupational disease in New York. Almost 3 percent of all occupational disease cases in Hawaii are due to "blisters," which are not considered a disease in most states. Some states consider heart attacks and cardiovascular illnesses as diseases. California equivocates by considering "circulatory diseases (except heart disease, hypertension, arteriosclerosis)" as occupational diseases but not "heart disease, injury or strain/vascular lesions affecting the central nervous system." California does not consider welders' conjunctivitis to be an occupational disease, however, retinitis-conjunctivitis is the leading source of occupational disease in Hawaii.

Aside from questions of definition, states report their data differently. The variations in reporting can be categorized in three ways:

Cases Reported   Information from various sources indicates the occurrence of a disability due to disease. These sources may be tied to OSHA reporting requirements, or taken from employers' "first reports" of injuries or similar reports of physicians or insurers. Some of them may lead to claims being filed. In other cases, however, insurers may make payment until the employee returns to work, but in some states there is no assurance that a claim passes through the workers' compensation system. Also, when a case is reported, no claim may result if the worker is not disabled long enough to fulfill the waiting period. If a case is reported and a claim results, the claimant may not be awarded any compensation. For example, from July 1, 1974 to June 30, 1975 in Nebraska, 2,939 occupational disease cases were reported (excluding heart cases), but for the same twelve months only 141 claimants were awarded indemnity benefits. It is unclear how many others received only medical benefits.[2]

Claims These data may provide a good approximation of the number of cases entering the compensation system. It is not always clear, however, whether a claim actually occurs when an insurer agrees to make payments to the worker without any direction from the state agency. Even if the workers' compensation board is involved, if an informal hearing before a referee or claims examiner brings about agreement, in every state this may not represent a claim. In some instances, claims are filed but agreements are reached before a hearing occurs. For all of these reasons the number of claims processed is not an accurate indicator of the activity in the system.

Cases Closed Some data are reported only for cases that the agency considers settled during the reporting period. New York regularly publishes statistics on cases closed. The data for New York, however, refer only to cases where indemnity payments are to be made. Wisconsin follows a similar practice, but their compensated cases are usually divided into those closed by compromise settlements and those closed otherwise. Data on closed cases are useful in evaluating the number of workers actually receiving benefits for occupational diseases, however, they usually do not reflect the number of workers who unsuccessfully sought relief.

Mindful of the difficulties, five separate sources of data on workers' compensation claims for occupational diseases were examined. Each is fragmentary and suffers from one shortcoming or another but taken in toto a picture emerges of how the disease problem is handled. The data sources are the following:

Telephone Survey On January 22 to 23, 1976, staff of the Interdepartmental Workers' Compensation Task Force undertook a telephone survey of all states except Alaska, covering seventeen issues pertaining to occupational disease claims. Question 2 of the survey was: "For the most recent available annual period, how many OD claims were filed in your state?" The vast majority of states could not answer the question.

Administrative Survey A consultant to the Interdepartmental Task Force undertook a mail survey (followed by telephone calls and some visits) of administrative practices in each state. The instrument contained the following questions: "For the most recent calendar year or similar period for which data are available (a) In how many cases were occupational disease benefits claimed? and (b) In how many cases were occupational disease benefits awarded?" Only ten of forty-two states could answer either part; only Kansas, Montana (by approximation), and Wisconsin could answer both questions.

Annual Reports A number of states publish annual reports containing summaries of the case load of the state workers' compensation agency. Some of these provide information of one sort or another on occupational disease claims.

The National Council on Compensation Insurance assists insurance carriers in setting premiums. As the major repository for information on claims for workers' compensation, they have detailed interstate and interindustry data based on the experience of member carriers. Since data from the council are originally generated by the carriers, no information is available about the experience of self-insurers, certain state funds, and those carriers who use other rate-making bureaus. The council went through its data bank on a state by state basis to prepare compilations on occupational disease claims that had been filed with them for the previous year. The paucity of cases reported suggests that the member carriers are not differentiating many of their occupational disease cases from all other claims they submit to the council.

The Task Force commissioned Cooper and Co. to undertake a survey of cases closed during sample periods in the fall of 1975. Data came from the files of participating insurers.

Data in table 5.1 are drawn from the telephone survey, the administrative survey, and the available annual reports. Whenever an annual report provided data on disease and non-disease cases, the former was calculated as a proportion of all cases. Disease cases are approximately 1 or 2 percent of all cases, though the proportion is higher in Nebraska and is only 0.5 percent in Oklahoma. Certain disparities appear, depending on the source of the information (for example, Mississippi). The data mean quite different things across states; California includes cases reported by employers even when no compensable claim may result, and New York includes only cases that have been indemnified and closed.

Table 5.2 indicates the kinds of diseases involved. Detailed data are currently available from only seven states, but their size suggests that they may be fairly representative of most, if not all, states. The most common occupational disease case, accounting for at least one-third of all cases, involves some type of dermatological disorder. Diseases of the joints, muscles, organs of movement, for example, bursitis, are relatively common ailments, as are respiratory problems and poisoning. Lung diseases were the most common occupational disease in Ohio in 1973, which is quite out of line with other states.

Table 5.1
Occupational disease cases by state for most recent year

	Telephone Survey	Administrative Survey	Annual Reports	
Arizona	885	472		
Arkansas	170[b,c]			
California	9,694		9,694[j]	(3.6%)[a]
Delaware	2[b]			
Florida			1,600[k]	(1.7%)
Hawaii	1,422		1,611[g]	(4.4%)
Idaho			971[b,d]	(1.5%)
Indiana	137			
Iowa	85[c]			
Kansas	535	536	535	(1.3%)
Kentucky	1,200	1,560[e]		
Maryland	213		346	(1.2%)
Mississippi	300[c,d]	85[d]	42[h]	(0.6%)
Missouri	3,500			
Montana	31		22[g]	(0.1%)
Nebraska		188	3,008[l]	(5.5%)
Nevada	200[c]			
New Mexico	304[c]			
New York	1,605		1,605[i]	(1.4%)
Ohio	3,194		3,950	(1.1%)
Oklahoma			21[f]	(0.5%)
Virginia	688			
West Virginia	3,500[c]			
Wisconsin	1,689	1,574	1,574	
Wyoming	846			

Source: Interdepartmental Workers' Compensation Task Force surveys, states' annual reports, and the National Council on Compensation Insurance.
a. Occupational disease cases as a proportion of all cases reported.
b. For a two-year period.
c. Estimate.
d. Cases closed.
e. 370 were denied.
f. Excludes 213 "heart cases."
g. Cases reported.
h. Compensable cases.
i. Excludes 649 "heart cases;" case closed where indemnity payments involved.
j. Excludes 1625 "heart cases;" California data are not claims but employers' reports of injuries.
k. Excludes 100 heart cases, 1972.
l. Injuries reported.

Table 5.2
Occupational disease cases (%), selected states

Wisconsin[a]	N = 1,574
Dermatitis	36.7
Inflammation or irritation of joints, tendons, muscles	22.3
Contagious disease	7.3
Loss of hearing	5.6
Systemic poisoning	4.7
Radiation effects (includes sunburn)	4.6
Other	18.8
Hawaii[b]	N = 1,611
Retinitis-conjunctivitis	28.3
Respiratory	5.5
Cardiovascular	3.4
Blisters	2.9
Bursitis	2.8
Virus	2.2
Other	3.7
Nebraska[c]	N = 2,783
Skin disease or disorder	58.0
Disorders due to physical agents	14.8
Disorders due to repeated trauma	9.3
Respiratory conditions due to toxic substances	5.4
Other	12.5
Ohio[d]	N = 3,950
Lung diseases: silicosis, T.B.	46
Skin diseases: dust, fumes, liquids, etc.	29
Specific conditions: bursitis, ganglion, tenosynovitis, etc.	20
Chemical poisonings	5
California[e]	N = 9,694
Skin diseases	32.8
Diseases of the bones, organs, or movement	15.6
Poisoning	14.8
Respiratory	8.2
Ear diseases	6.0
Other infective or parasitic diseases	4.1
Infectious or serum hepatitis	2.9
All other	15.6
New York[f]	N = 1,605
Dermatitis	33.5
Loss of hearing	14.1
Occupational hernia	11.5
Contagious diseases	8.8
Silicosis and other dust diseases	6.4
Occupational strains, n.e.c.[h]	6.2
All other	19.5
Florida[g]	N = 1,600
Diseases of the skin	67.8
Poisoning	20.9
Respiratory diseases	4.4
All other	6.9

Source: Selected annual reports of states.
a. Cases reported, 1973.
b. Reported injuries, 1973.
c. Court cases, 1974-1975.
d. Claims, 1973.

e. Disabling injuries reported, 1974.
f. Compensated cases closed, 1973.
g. Disabling work injuries, 1972.
h. n.e.c. = not elsewhere classified.

This may represent claims filed by miners for coal workers pneumoconiosis. Since the federal Black Lung Law of 1969, state workers' compensation claims filed for this disease have jumped in states with coal mining industries.

Data on occupational disease fatalities, and on the controversial areas of heart cases and hearing-loss cases are presented in table 5.3. Unlike table 5.1, which excludes heart cases, where the data are available fatalities due to heart disease are included with other causes of death. Although the overall volume of heart cases is small, if considered as occupational disease they would account for the majority of deaths recorded. All deaths in Nebraska classified as due to occupational disease are from heart cases, 205 of the 269 deaths in New York involve heart cases, and 94 of the 148 deaths reported in California are due to heart disease. Of these 94 fatalities, 51 involved police officers, firefighters, correction officers, sheriff's deputies, and other public sector employees whose deaths are presumed work connected under section 3212 of the state code.[3] Although there is no assurance that all of these will be compensated, the significance of this presumption is striking.

The concerns regarding hearing loss in workers' compensation are well out of line with the volume of cases reported (see table 5.3). Not only is the number small, but some of the cases involve damage to hearing from traumatic causes or the presence of an acute and not a chronic condition. In addition many of the cases reported will not be compensated, as evidenced by Nebraska's experience. Although thirty-three hearing-loss cases were reported in 1974 and 1975, no successful claims for indemnity benefits were made that year. A few cases are entering the system, but very few are receiving indemnity benefits. Data for Michigan, a state reputed to have a large volume of hearing-loss cases, were not available.

Occupational disease data listed by the extent of disability involved rounds out the picture (see table 5.4). There are very few cases of occupational disease in the compensation system, and the overwhelming proportion of these cases are relatively minor disabilities entailing compensation only for medical benefits or temporary total benefits. This is particularly true when heart cases are excluded as in most states. Mississippi best exemplifies both observations. Mississippi reports data on a cumulative basis since January 1, 1949. It indicates that in almost two and one-half decades, only two deaths from occupational disease have been compensated, and there have been no compensated cases for permanent total disability involving occupational disease.

Because the number of cases by extent of disability according to the National Council on Compensation Insurance is so small for each state, only their aggregated figures

Table 5.3
Death cases, heart cases, and hearing-loss cases, selected states

	Deaths	Heart Cases	Hearing-Loss Cases
California[a]	148	1904	578
New York[b]	269	649	227
Wisconsin[c]	1		82
Nebraska[d]	18	69	33
Kansas[e]		52	4
Oklahoma[f]		213	
Montana[g]		58	
Hawaii[h]		56	
West Virginia[i]	11		
Maryland[j]	3		
Oregon[k]	4		
Idaho[l]	2		
Florida[m]		100	17
Pennsylvania[n]		213	30

a. Includes 94 fatalities due to "heart cases," injuries reported, 1974.
b. Includes 205 fatalities due to "heart cases," compensated cases closed, 1973.
c. Includes cases closed and cases compromised, 1973.
d. All fatalities are due to "heart cases," reported injuries, 1974–1975.
e. Cases reported, 1975.
f. Compensation awarded and settled for, 1973.
g. Work injuries reported, 1973–1974.
h. Work injuries reported, 1973.
i. All 11 fatalities from pneumoconioses, 1973–1974.
j. Claims, 1973–1974.
k. 3 fatalities are "heart cases," the other due to bee sting, 1974.
l. Closed claims, biennium, 1972–1974.
m. Disabling work injuries, 1972.
n. Compensation awarded and settled for, 1973.

Table 5.4
Occupational disease by extent of disability, selected states

	Death	Permanent Total	Permanent Partial	Temporary	Medical Only	Total
Wisconsin[a]	1 (0)	7 (1)	165 (14)	975 (85)		1148
Idaho[b]	2 (0)	0	13 (1)	147 (16)	734 (82)	896
Mississippi[c]	2 (1)	0	5 (2)	254 (86)		297
Maryland[d]	4 (1)	2 (1)	19 (5)	333 (93)		358
New York[e]	64 (4)	45 (3)	482 (30)	1014 (63)		1605
National Council[f]	16 (1)	16 (1)	328 (10)	453 (14)	2351 (74)	3164

Source: Annual reports of states and the National Council on Compensation Insurance.
Note: Parentheses are percents of the total column.
a. Cases "settled" and cases compromised 1973.
b. Biennium, 1972–1974, closed claims.
c. Grand total all compensable cases, January 1949–December 1972. 36 cases undetermined.
d. Claims, 1973–1974, for "heart cases," contact with "poisonous and corrosive substances," and occupational and infectious diseases.
e. Compensated cases closed, 1973.
f. National Council on Compensation Insurance, see text.

are reported. These data suggest that few cases are being compensated, and it is possible that insurance carriers are underreporting disease cases to the council.

While most disease cases involve relatively minor disabilities, it is likely that occupational disease cases involve death and permanent total disability more than workers' compensation cases in general. In a 1975 report of most states for all disablements, the National Council calculated the number of cases by extent of disability.[4] Comparing the number of temporary total disability cases to deaths and permanent total disability cases, these data indicate respective ratios of 143.1 and 528.8. The proportion of very serious claims is significantly higher in occupational disease cases (see table 5.4). In occupational disease cases there was one death and one permanent total case for every 28.3 temporary total cases. In New York there was one death case for every 15.8 temporary total cases, and one permanent total case for every 22.5 temporary total cases. So in terms of severity occupational diseases are bimodally distributed. A large number of cases involve relatively minor ailments, including many temporary skin disorders, and a small number of cases involve very serious disorders. Nevertheless these serious disorders are proportionately more important than in cases involving injuries due to accidents. If heart cases are included among occupational diseases, the proportion of very serious cases due to disease would rise even more sharply.

An alternative evaluation of the quantitative extent of the occupational disease problem is an examination of the costs of such cases. Based on the bimodal distribution of cases by severity, it is not clear, a priori, how average costs for compensated occupational disease claims will compare to those for all workers' compensation claims. Scattered evidence on costs is available from various states and the National Council on Compensation Insurance (see table 5.5; figures in parentheses refer to numbers of cases). Although the data are not directly comparable on an interstate basis, they further substantiate the thesis that disease cases tend to be distributed on a bimodal basis; some cases are quite inexpensive or about comparable to the average for accident-injury cases, and others are extremely costly. Where not specified, the costs per case only involve indemnity payments. Data for Vermont, however, also include claims where no indemnity payments were made. Most parts of table 5.5 list only serious disabilities. Indemnity costs per case for dermatitis in New York exceeded the average for all workers' compensation cases because only serious cases meriting indemnity were included. The many dermatoses resulting in a claim for medical benefits alone are excluded.

The data in table 5.5 represent both indemnity and medical costs estimated by insurance carriers for the National Council on Compensation Insurance. They only include cases involving medical benefits and more serious cases. Unfortunately the sample size is quite small for the occupational disease cases. Occupational disease cases are more expensive than others except in the few cases involving death and permanent total disability. If any heart cases are included in the data, they are probably not considered as occupational disease. These data are based on insurers' "first reports," the earliest estimates of the projected costs of the cases. The insurers subsequently file updated estimates for each claim with the National Council as more information develops, however, the data on occupational disease claims are available only from first reports.

Using the National Council's data and their categories of extent of disability by state but omitting medical only provides a perspective of disease and other cases (table 5.6). Any cell with less than ten observations was eliminated to avoid distortions, reducing the number of states from thirty-eight to ten. This means that no estimates were made for costs of permanent total disability cases and an estimate of costs for death due to disease was made only in Michigan. The eleven fatalities there from occupational disease were expected to cost (both medical and indemnity) $18,686 compared to $32,991 for those not caused by disease.

These data from the National Council are an incomplete representation of the actual volume of occupational disease cases entering the state workers' compensation systems, even after taking into account the council's limited scope of coverage. When seen with the other data on claims, it suggests that the volume of disease claims is very small and not remotely related to the numbers discussed by NIOSH and others who have estimated the extent of the disease problem in the United States. If one focuses simply on fatalities caused by occupational disease, less than 500 cases a year are compensated through the state systems, excluding heart cases. Although New York compensated 205 fatalities due to heart cases in 1973, this is clearly out of line with the national picture. In California, which has a larger population than New York, only ninety-four heart cases were reported in 1974 and over one-half of these arose because of California's special presumption covering certain public employees. Further, not all ninety-four will be compensated. Thus there are well under 1,000 compensated claims annually for fatalities in heart cases. About 225,000 persons between the ages of twenty-five and sixty-four died of a cardiovascular disease in 1974, and most of them were in the labor force prior to the time of their attack. Claims for cancer, either in fatality cases or otherwise, are extremely rare and probably nonexistent in the majority of states. The volume of disease cases is small and most involve some acute rather than chronic disease.

Based on data on claims volume from the 1960s, occupational disease claims in the

Table 5.5

a. Average cost per case, Florida, 1972

All compensated work injuries	$ 933	(95,183)
All compensated occupational diseases	428	(1,600)
diseases of the skin	254	(1,085)
poisoning	493	(334)
respiratory diseases	990	(71)
Heart cases compensated	7,133	(100)

Source: State Annual Report.

b. Average cost per case processed, Hawaii, 1973

All compensated workers' compensation cases	$ 426	(45,915)
All compensated occupational diseases	378	(1,872)

Source: State Annual Report.

c. Average cost per case where compensation ordered, Kansas, 1975[1]

	Indemnity	Medical	Total
All compensated workers' compensation cases	$5,212	$1,139	$6,351 (2391)
All compensated occupational disease cases	2,882	1,093	3,975 (20)
compensated hearing loss cases	1,172	420	1,592 (3)
compensated heart cases	4,435	1,203	4,638 (19)

Source: State Annual Report.
1. Last three quarters of fiscal year.

d. Average cost per compensated case closed, Minnesota, 1966–1968

	Indemnity	Medical	Total
All workers' compensation	$ 972	$ 430	$1,402 (32,828)
All occupational disease	1,091	399	1,490 (1,228)

Source: State Biennial Report.

e. Average cost per compensated case closed, Mississippi, 1949–1972

All workers' compensation cases	$ 859	(206,388)
All occupational disease cases	680	(297)

Source: State Annual Report.

f. Average cost per compensated case closed, Nebraska, 1974–1975

Skin diseases	$ 483	(60)
Dust diseases of the lungs	421	(3)
Respiratory conditions due to toxic agents	805	(6)
Poisoning	1,915	(18)
Disorders due to physical agents	93	(7)
Disorders due to repeated trauma[1]	615	(40)
Infectious diseases	604	(6)

Sources: Total indemnity received in year from annual report of the state. Number of persons receiving indemnity payments per disorder provided by private correspondence with Ben Novicoff.
1. Excludes hearing-loss cases.

g. Average cost per compensated case closed, New York, 1973

All workers, compensation cases	$ 2,092	(117,337)
All occupational disease cases	5,179	(1,605)
dermatitis	2,273	(538)
hernia	1,326	(184)
loss of hearing	2,395	(227)
silicosis and other dust diseases	28,005	(103)
bronchitis, laryngitis, asthma, rhinitis, etc.	13,884	(91)
Infectious diseases	2,792	(147)
Cancer	12,010	(4)
Heart cases	24,501	(649)

Source: Unpublished material to be used in the 1973 Report of *Compensated Cases Closed.*

h. Average benefits awarded per case, Vermont, 1973–1974

	Indemnity	Medical	Total	
All workers' compensation cases	$ 177	$ 107	$284	(14,431)
Dermatitis	85	27	112	(166)
Silicosis	5,161	72	5,233	(15)
Poison ivy, oak, etc.	291	46	337	(55)

Source: State Annual Report.

i. Reserves set aside per case, West Virginia, 1973–1974

	Permanent Partial	Total Disability	Fatalities
Pneumoconiosis	$7,896 (2030)	$63,471 (184)	$21,260 (11)
Other occupational disease	2,740 (33)	44,925 (8)	

Source: State Annual Report.

j. Average cost per compensated case closed, Wisconsin, 1973

All occupational disease cases	$ 928	(1046)
permanent total	44,746	(4)
permanent partial	4,891	(90)
temporary total	477	(952)
Hearing loss (closed)	$ 2,801	(54)
Hearing loss (compromised)	2,419	(28)
Asbestosis (closed)	42,337	(1)
Asbestosis (compromised)	20,475	(1)
Silicosis (closed)	16,847	(10)
Silicosis (compromised)	15,878	(3)

k. Average estimated cost per case, National Council on Compensation Insurance Coverage[1]

	Occupational Disease Cases		All Workers' Compensation Cases	
Death	$21,123	(16)	$23,676	(2,934)
Permanent total	28,542	(16)	56,067	(870)
Major partial	17,988	(59)	15,564	(24,674)
Minor partial	5,621	(269)	3,400	(84,014)
Temporary total	875	(453)	803	(420,434)
Medical only	44	(2,351)	41	(2,631,628)

1. Based on different dates by thirty-eight states, typically covering 1972.

Table 5.6
Average estimated cost per case, National Council on Compensation Insurance

State	Death	Permanent Total	Major Partial	Minor Partial	Temporary Total
Connecticut					$ 909 (46) 640
Florida					455 (21) 765
Illinois				$3,077 (14) 2,367	403 (19) 947
Indiana				521 (15) 3,835	
Michigan	$18,686 (11) 32,991		$17,731 (46) 21,305	6,198 (183) 4,460	1,572 (454) 1,136
Minnesota					635 (47) 988
New Hampshire					512 (14) 664
Rhode Island					743 (13) 663
Tennessee					458 (14) 839
Wisconsin				7,276 (13) 3,271	556 (87) 583

Note: Numbers in parentheses are the number of occupational disease cases in the cell. Since the sample is substantially larger for non-disease cases, no cell size is reported. The first line for each state is average cost for occupational disease cases; the second line is for non-disease cases.

1970s are not growing any more rapidly than other types of workers' compensation claims. In some cases the more serious disability claims entering the system are not expanding at an equal rate with the labor force. In 1954, 128 compensated cases for silicosis and other dust diseases were closed in New York compared to 103 cases in 1973. The overall volume of closed compensated cases due to occupational disease was 20 percent lower in 1973 than in 1967 in New York. In Wisconsin there were more compensated disease cases closed in every single year from 1942 to 1956 than there were in any year from 1957 through 1973. There were more cases compensated for silicosis in 1929, the last year before the Depression began (and claims began to rise steeply) than in 1973. There were sixteen compensated fatality cases due to occupational disease closed in 1936 in Wisconsin and none in 1973. Claims data are not available from California, however, the volume of disease cases reported by physicians from 1964 to 1973 has grown at about the same rate as the number of employed persons covered by workers' compensation.

Few occupational disease cases are being compensated by the workers' compensation system. Discher, Kleinman, and Foster reported that only 3 percent of the cases of occupational disease they found involved a workers' compensation claim.[5] O'Toole's detailed study of claims for radiation injury in state files led him to report:

The volume of claims for delayed consequences of radiation exposure is surprisingly small. There appear to be fewer claims filed than would be expected, considering (a) present medical knowledge of biological effects and (b) the number of serious accidental exposures known to have taken place. . . . Although the examined claims cover a wide variety of alleged diseases there is a noticeable absence of claims for some diseases which have been demonstrated through medical research to be among the consequences."[6]

Giammattei compared diseases reported to be occupational in California with the types of disability known from the Social Security System to exist in the population at large.[7] Although her data sources are far from ideal, she concludes that the workers' compensation system is not handling many cases of occupational disease.

The Closed Case Survey

In the fall of 1975 the Interdepartmental Workers' Compensation Task Force commissioned Cooper and Co. to undertake a survey of "closed" workers' compensation cases.[8] The survey was designed to secure a large national sample of current workers' compensation cases to examine the administration of the workers' compensation systems in all jurisdictions. The intent was to gather information on those cases for which a firm idea of ultimate disposition was available and do so on a "real time" basis, that is, as the decisions were being reached. This suggested a "slice in time" design, where the sampling occurs through the choice of the particular time period. All workers' compensation cases "closed" during the sample period (slice in time) were to be included. This is an easy design to administer and leads to problems only if there is a strong seasonal component in the "closure" of workers' compensation cases.

Substantial preparatory work was done by both Cooper and Co. and the Task Force, with the help of the National Council on Compensation Insurance (NCCI), American Mutual Insurance Alliance, American Insurance Association, National Council of Self-Insurers' Associations, and American Association of State Compensation Insurance Funds. These organizations assisted in varying degrees with the development of the questionnaire, the sampling frame, and sanctioning the survey itself.

The sampling frame consisted of 600 carriers who were members of the NCCI, 120 other carriers who were not NCCI members, the 20 state funds, and 800 self-insurers with more than 1,000 employees. Given the omission of the smaller self-insurers, this represented Cooper and Co.'s best estimate of the universe of workers' compensation insurers. Letters were sent to the chief executives of all these units requesting participation in the survey and seeking an immediate response in the form of the name of an individual to be used as the contact for the survey and an estimate of the number of cases that would be reported.

Approximately 150,000 questionnaires were distributed to about 280 insurers who responded to the letter. Follow-up contacts were made to large insurers if they did not respond to the letter. Data on 40,066 cases closed in the fall of 1975 were gathered from workers' compensation insurers (the term insurer includes workers' compensation insurance carriers, state workers' compensation funds, and self-insurers). These 40,066 cases constitute slightly over half the workers' compensation cases actually closed during the sample periods, September 29 through October 10, 1975 for temporary disability cases, and September 29 through November 7, 1975 for permanent disability and fatality cases. Information was collected on claimant characteristics, the nature of the injury or illness, the way the case was "handled" by the workers' compensation system, and the settlement. The 908 closed cases in the sample, identified as occupational disease cases, are of greatest interest.

Representativeness

The initial difficulty that arises in discussing the response rate to the closed case survey derives from ignorance about the universe. The Task Force prepared an estimate of the workers' compensation lost-time cases that could be expected to be closed during the sample periods. This was based on a number of factors, all of which were estimates. The total number of closed cases was estimated for the years 1970 through 1975. Then the aggregate number of cases was spread over the different disability levels according to the following proportions (in percent): fatality cases, 0.60; permanent total cases, 0.15; permanent partial cases, 27.00; temporary total cases, 72.25. Estimated closure rates, specific to the vintage of the case and to level of disability, then were applied to the estimated number of cases. For example, for 1970, it was estimated that one million cases were initiated; applying the above ratio it was estimated that 0.60 percent of these (6,000 cases) were fatality cases. The Task Force guessed that 10 percent of the fatality cases initiated in 1970 (600 of the 6,000) would be closed in 1975, the sample year.

The last step was to estimate what proportion of the cases closed in 1975 would be closed during the sample period; two weeks for temporary cases and six weeks for permanent disability and death cases. Thus, for the death cases originating in 1970, the 600 closures expected in all of 1975 are reduced to 69 case closures expected during the six-week sample period (600 $\times$ 6/52). Similar estimates were made for each of the twenty-four levels of disability and case vintage combinations (4 levels of disability $\times$ 6 vintages).

The final outcome of this process was an estimate of 77,539 cases as the universe, that is, the number of cases that could be expected to be closed during the sample periods.

Cooper and Co. made two supplementary estimates utilizing rate-making data provided by the NCCI. They adjusted for non-NCCI cases, self-insurers and some state funds, according to the proportion of responses to the closed case survey. About 20 percent of the closed case survey sample came from non-NCCI respondents, so Cooper inflated the case numbers shown in the NCCI July 1975 summary by 20 percent and then applied the sampling proportions by type of case (2/52 for temporary disability cases and 6/52 for permanent disability and death cases). The result was an estimate of 72,995 as the potential sample size.

Their second estimate was based on the volume of workers' compensation benefit payments as reported by the Social Security Administration. Assuming that the number of cases is proportional to the volume of benefit payments and applying the resulting

Table 5.7
Responses to the closed case survey by insurer type

	Number of Cases	Proportion of Cases (%)	Number of Responding Units
Carriers	28,499	72.2	77
State Funds	7,745	19.6	17
Self-Insurers	3,234	8.2	98
Total	39,478	100.0	192
Missing[a]	588		
	40,066		

a. The number of missing cases in this table results from the fact that it was constructed from a source table that had an additional criterion variable, the state. Some of the 588 missing cases did not respond on the insurer, some did not respond on state.

estimated balance of NCCI and non-NCCI cases (18.5 percent non-NCCI) to the same basic case data mentioned previously results in a potential sample estimate of 71,665. Unfortunately this is the best information available about the universe.

Table 5.7 shows the actual response in numbers of cases and responding units by type of insurer. The completed sample of 40,066 cases apparently includes over half of the cases closed during the sample period. Seventy-two percent of the sample cases were reported by carriers (49 percent from stock, 23 percent non-stock insurance companies). An additional 19.6 percent of the sample comes from state funds and the remaining 8.2 percent from self-insurers.

Response rates based on the sampling frame are not as attractive as those on the number of cases. Only ninety-eight of 800 self-insurers responded to the survey. It is not known how many non-respondents had no closed cases during the sample periods. Seventeen out of twenty state funds participated (those in Oregon, West Virginia, and Pennsylvania did not), but Ohio chose only to report a sample of cases closed during the sample period. Only seventy-seven of the 720 carriers in the sampling frame responded.

Roughly half of the estimated potential cases were reported and only about 10 percent of insurers responded (except for the category of state funds), which obviously means that small insurers are underrepresented in the closed case sample. It is not known to what extent the special follow-up efforts of Cooper and Co. account for the higher response rate among large insurers. Table 5.8 shows the number of responding units by number of cases reported. Again, it is difficult to assess the degree of bias in the sample due to lack of information about the universe of closed cases.

Examination of the distribution of cases in the sample by extent of disability could reveal bias. Table 5.9 shows the comparison Cooper and Co. has made between the proportion of cases by level of disability in the NCCI case reports and the actual responses to the closed case survey. The NCCI numbers represent the application of the sampling ratios (2/52 or 6/52 for temporary or permanent and death cases respectively) to the number of cases by level of disability in the 1975 NCCI list.

There are some remarkable discrepancies in the most serious cases. The closed case survey sample shows about one-half the incidence of death cases but over six times as many permanent total disability cases as the NCCI. We have no idea what accounts for this discrepancy. Temporary disabilities are slightly overrepresented in the closed case survey sample. Those cases counted as missing in the closed case survey sample are predominantly cases that were not compensated (excluded from NCCI statistics).

Table 5.10 gives the number and percent of cases by jurisdiction for the closed case sample. For comparison purposes the percent of nonagricultural employment in 1974

Table 5.8
Number of insurers responding by number of
cases reported

Number of Cases Reported	Number of Insurers
More than 4000	1
2001 to 4000	4
1001 to 2000	11
501 to 1000	5
251 to 500	7
101 to 250	20
100 or less	144
Total insurers	192

Table 5.9
Distribution of cases by level of disability,
NCCI and closed case survey

Level of Disability	NCCI Cases (%)	Closed Case Survey (%)
Temporary total	50.9	54.9
Permanent partial	47.8	43.1
Permanent total	0.2	1.3
Death	1.1	0.6
Total	100.0	100.0
Missing		(3.6)

is also presented. The effect of the missing state funds is apparent in the ranking of West Virginia, Pennsylvania, and Ohio, which rank markedly lower than would be expected given their levels of employment. On the other hand, Oregon shows a similar proportion of cases in the closed case sample and employment even without the state fund. California and Washington have markedly higher case levels in the closed case sample than would be predicted. New York, New Jersey, Texas, Arizona, and Colorado also show up on the plus side. Aside from the states that are underrepresented due to the nonparticipation of state funds, deficits are apparent for Indiana, Virginia, Georgia, and Iowa.

There are a number of influences at work here. The coverage of responding insurers by state is probably the largest factor. If a large insurer who did respond did not do equal amounts of compensation business in all jurisdictions, biases in the distribution of cases by jurisdiction must arise. Even in the absence of these biases, the workers' compensation cases closed by state should also vary according to the type of industry in a state and the nature of the state's workers' compensation law.

Problems

The primary focus of the closed case survey was on securing a large sample, making it possible to examine the operation of the workers' compensation systems on cases at all levels of disability and in all jurisdictions. This emphasis on number of cases rather than their representativeness is demonstrated by the fact that no resources were allocated to follow up the initial survey contacts or checking for non-response bias. All known insurers were contacted and invited to participate in the survey, and those who did respond were taken to be an adequate representative sample. The only follow-ups done were of the very largest insurers. Personal contacts were made to assure cooperation by the large potential respondents because their participation was essential if the desired number of cases was to be obtained.

This sample design was not optimal for a study of occupational disease cases. When concentrating on a relatively small subsample of cases, the law of large numbers offers no refuge. It is necessary to design a survey with great precision to insure, to the maximum extent feasible, that the population is truly represented by the sample. There are only 908 occupational disease cases in the closed case survey sample; confidence in the results hinges on the degree to which the sample is representative of the underlying population of cases. Non-response biases or even anomalous responses threaten the entire effort.

The closed case survey is biased. Unbiased results for this population are not now and never have been available, so the degree of bias cannot be evaluated. Correcting the

Table 5.10
Distribution of cases by jurisdiction in the closed case sample

	Number of Cases	Percent of Cases	Percent of Nonagricultural Employment, 1974
California	5931	14.9	10.0
New York	4225	10.6	9.0
Texas	2635	6.6	5.5
Washington	2601	6.5	1.5
Illinois	2320	5.8	5.6
New Jersey	1977	5.0	3.5
Michigan	1446	3.6	4.2
Florida	1304	3.3	3.7
Pennsylvania	1229	3.1	5.8
Massachusetts	1037	2.6	3.0
Wisconsin	996	2.5	2.2
North Carolina	808	2.0	2.6
Missouri	804	2.0	2.3
Colorado	737	1.9	1.2
Maryland	724	1.8	1.8
Indiana	642	1.6	2.6
Arizona	639	1.6	0.9
Georgia	627	1.6	2.3
Connecticut	616	1.6	1.6
Oklahoma	612	1.5	1.1
Minnesota	593	1.5	1.9
Tennessee	575	1.4	2.0
Alabama	567	1.4	1.5
Virginia	501	1.3	2.3
Oregon	480	1.2	1.1
Ohio	434	1.1	5.3
Louisiana	418	1.1	1.5
Kentucky	377	0.9	1.4
Federal Acts	328	0.8	n.a.
South Carolina	302	0.8	1.3
Idaho	301	0.8	0.3
Arkansas	294	0.7	0.8
Utah	291	0.7	0.6
Mississippi	284	0.7	0.9
Nevada	264	0.7	0.3
Iowa	233	0.6	1.3
Kansas	232	0.6	1.0
Maine	228	0.6	0.5
New Mexico	167	0.4	0.5
Montana	164	0.4	0.3
New Hampshire	160	0.4	0.4
North Dakota	157	0.4	0.2
Hawaii	128	0.3	0.4
Rhode Island	113	0.3	0.5
Alaska	107	0.3	0.2
District of Columbia	103	0.3	0.9
Nebraska	100	0.3	0.7
Delaware	83	0.2	0.3
Wyoming	65	0.2	0.2
Vermont	61	0.2	0.2
South Dakota	28	0.1	0.3
West Virginia	4	—	0.7
Total	39,733	100.0	100.0
Missing	333		
Sample n	40,066		

unknown errors and biases rests on a future, more adequate investigation into the occupational disease case population. Meanwhile the closed case survey sample is the best source of information currently available on occupational disease cases in workers' compensation.

The definition of "closed" case is one of the keys to interpretation of the survey, especially when one is aware of some of the inconsistencies in use of this term across various jurisdictions and insurers. Because of the interest in current cases, closed cases could not be those on which all payments had been completed. Such a definition would mean that for death and permanent disability cases involving lifetime payments, the claims were necessarily initiated many years ago and bear little resemblance to current practice. Thus closed cases were defined as those where payments had ceased (in temporary disability cases) or a specific determination of the ultimate indemnity payment had been made (in permanent disability and fatality cases) during the respective sample periods (see figure 5.1).

This definition gives rise to a rather peculiar sample of workers' compensation cases that cannot be directly compared to other information available on workers' compensation cases. No "medical only" cases are included in the closed case survey, which makes it impossible to compare sample statistics with other data sources that do include medical only cases.

Another problem is that the closed case survey sample consists mostly but not entirely of compensated cases. Controverted cases in which the judgment went against the worker are included. Thus the closed case survey sample is not representative either of all claims or of all compensated claims but something in between. This sample, therefore, cannot help to close the gap between estimates of the incidence of occupational disease and the number of occupational disease cases being compensated.

Problems also arise because the sample cases were gathered in clusters from insurers rather than individual claimants. This is the least expensive and perhaps the only feasible way to gather data on large numbers of cases. Since there are a smaller number of surveyed units, the distortions introduced by differential response rates are more dramatic. For example, when the West Virginia state fund chose not to participate, there was a sudden deficit in the sample of cases from West Virginia that cannot be remedied. Moreover, since this is a survey of insurers, there is a possibility that insurers have "selected" the cases they reported, introducing a source of bias that could not be evaluated.

INTERDEPARTMENTAL WORKERS' COMPENSATION TASK FORCE —
CLAIM SURVEY

DETAILED INSTRUCTIONS AND INFORMATION

Definition of Cases to be Covered

The objective of the Task Force is to collect data on the most recent closed cases. The definitions of *closed cases* for purpose of this survey are:

(1) *All* temporary total or temporary partial cases only, on which payments are terminated during the survey period, for any reason, and there is *no* reasonable expectation that they will be resumed; or, all temporary cases which you have closed during the survey period, based on your own company's definition of "closed". You may use either definition as long as you use it consistently on all cases.

(2) *All* permanent partial, permanent total and fatal cases, no older than 5 years (i.e., cases for which a claim was filed after September 1, 1970), on which a specific determination of the probable ultimate indemnity payment was made during the survey period. Such determination must have been as a result of (1) an award, or review, or directed settlement by a court, board, commission, hearing or referee; or (2) a voluntary agreement or acceptance, compromise and release settlement, redemption, stipulation, or wash-out.

Note that in some of these cases payments to the claimant(s) may not be complete, but there should *be no doubt about what they are expected to be,* (excepting a change in circumstances).

The object of the above definition is to capture relatively current cases at a point when there is some kind of firm decision about expected liability. You should also include as "closed cases" those cases over four years old (but still less than five years) in which your Claims Department has made an *internal formal annual review* of the case during the survey period in question and decided to continue payments even though these may not have been directed by an outside party or arrived at by a formal agreement.

The survey periods are:
(1) For temporary cases Sept. 29 — Oct. 10, inclusive.
(2) For other cases Sept. 29 — Nov. 7, inclusive.

The study is nationwide covering all states, all carriers, all state funds, and all large self-insurers. *All* cases which meet the above criteria are to be included.

Figure 5.1

The Subsamples

To analyze the occupational disease cases in the closed case survey, it is necessary at least to divide the sample into occupational disease cases and other cases. The heart cases have been kept separate also. This is a compromise between the feeling that most heart cases are actually occupational diseases and the general practice of treating heart cases as injuries by accident.

The occupational disease subsample was selected according to the answer to question 43 on the instrument (see Appendix A for the questionnaire). Questions 40 to 43 were to be completed for occupational disease cases only and question 43 called for identification of the specific type of disease involved:

1. Occupational skin diseases and disorders, for example, dermatitis, eczema.
2. Dust diseases of the lungs (pneumoconioses), for example, silicosis, asbestosis.
3. Respiratory condition due to toxic agents, for example, pneumonitis, pharyngitis, rhinitis.
4. Poisoning, systematic effects of toxic agents, for example, metals, gases, organic solvents.
5. Disorders due to physical agents (other than toxic materials), for example, heat stroke, frost bite, effects of radiation.
6. Disorders due to repeated trauma, for example, noise induced hearing loss, synovitis, bursitis.
7. Occupational cancers and tumors, for example, lung, liver.
8. Other.

This is the only means of identifying the occupational disease cases in the closed case sample, and the identification of the occupational disease cases was left entirely to the respondent. No guidance was offered beyond that implicit in these response categories. No doubt there were some occupational disease cases that did not get reported as such; there also must have been some accident cases for which a careless respondent filled out question 43, suggesting the case was an occupational disease case.

A total of 908 occupational disease cases (respondents to question 43) were found among the total sample of 40,066 cases. Forty-nine of these 908 cases were removed because it was indicated in response to question 15 that the part of the body injured was the heart; this left 859 occupational disease cases for analysis.

The largest segment of the heart case subsample came from those cases that indicated in response to question 15b that the nature of the injury was a heart attack. There were

290 heart attack cases among the 40,066 cases in the closed case survey. The forty-nine heart cases from the occupational disease subsample were added to this number. Thus the heart case subsample contains an unweighted total of 339 cases.

From the 38,868 injury-by-accident cases in the closed case sample, a random subsample of 3,950 cases was drawn to keep costs of computation within reasonable bounds. The work reported is based on 859 non-heart occupational disease cases, 339 heart cases (some acknowledged as occupational disease cases, most not), and 3,950 injury-by-accident (hereafter referred to as accident) cases. This means that the occupational disease subsample is 2.1 percent of all closed cases (859/40,066) and the heart subsample is 0.8 percent (339/40,066) of closed cases.

Table 5.11 shows the distribution of cases by jurisdiction for both the occupational disease and heart case subsamples. The last column is the percentage of nonagricultural employment accounted for by the state in 1974. Over three-fourths of the occupational disease cases come from just three states: California, Michigan, and New Jersey. These states also account for over 40 percent of the heart case subsample. This cannot be representative of the total population of closed occupational disease cases or heart cases, but in the absence of other information about the case populations, exactly how much distortion exists in the subsamples cannot be determined.

If a state is underrepresented in the overall sample, it will also tend to be underrepresented in these subsamples. This is not certain because further distortions are introduced by the particulars of the state's occupational disease law and the incidence of occupational disease in the state. California only accounted for 10 percent of nonagricultural employment in 1974, however, almost 15 percent of the workers' compensation cases in the closed case survey sample were California cases. Nearly 30 percent of occupational disease cases in the sample are California cases (see table 5.11). The apparent discrepancy could reflect that California's occupational disease coverage was twice as liberal as the average (in terms of the probability of compensation), or the incidence of disease cases was twice as great as the average. The specific number of occupational disease cases in the sample for a given state is the product of the number of workers' compensation cases closed in the state, closed case survey response rates by state (reflecting insurer coverage), the incidence of occupational diseases, the liberality of occupational disease coverage in workers' compensation laws, and sampling variability.

Occupational disease cases are reported in a total of forty-one jurisdictions, heart cases in forty-two jurisdictions. No cases of either type were reported in Hawaii, Idaho, Maine, or South Dakota.

Table 5.11
Distribution of occupational disease and heart cases by jurisdiction

	Occupational Disease Cases	Percent	Heart Cases	Percent	Percent of Non-agricultural Employment, 1974
California	254	29.7	81	23.9	10.0
Michigan	227	26.5	39	11.5	4.2
New Jersey	180	21.0	29	8.6	3.5
New York	54	6.3	23	6.8	9.0
Texas	12	1.4	16	4.7	5.5
Oregon	11	1.3	2	0.6	1.1
Washington	10	1.2	1	0.3	1.5
Kansas	8	0.9	3	0.9	1.0
Pennsylvania	8	0.9	5	1.5	5.8
Virginia	8	0.9	0	—	2.3
Florida	7	0.8	10	2.9	3.7
Wisconsin	6	0.7	2	0.6	2.2
Federal Acts	6	0.7	4	1.2	—
Arizona	5	0.6	4	1.2	0.9
Colorado	5	0.6	1	0.3	1.2
Minnesota	5	0.6	4	1.2	1.9
Nevada	5	0.6	1	0.3	0.3
Illinois	4	0.5	18	5.3	5.6
Kentucky	4	0.5	4	1.2	1.9
Maryland	4	0.5	2	0.6	1.8
Massachusetts	3	0.4	12	3.5	3.0
Rhode Island	3	0.4	0	—	0.5
Arkansas	2	0.2	1	0.3	0.8
Indiana	2	0.2	2	0.6	2.6
Mississippi	2	0.2	8	2.4	0.3
New Hampshire	2	0.2	1	0.3	0.4
Ohio	2	0.2	2	0.6	5.3
Tennessee	2	0.2	6	1.8	2.0
West Virginia	2	0.2	0	—	0.7
Alaska	2	0.2	0	—	0.2
Alabama	1	0.1	1	0.3	1.5
Connecticut	1	0.1	9	2.7	1.6
District of Columbia	1	0.1	0	—	0.9
Iowa	1	0.1	4	1.2	1.3
Louisiana	1	0.1	5	1.5	1.5
Missouri	1	0.1	2	0.6	2.3
Montana	1	0.1	3	0.9	0.3
North Dakota	1	0.1	1	0.3	0.2
Oklahoma	1	0.1	19	5.6	1.1
South Carolina	1	0.1	1	0.3	1.3
Vermont	1	0.1	0	—	0.2
Delaware	0	—	1	0.3	0.3
Georgia	0	—	5	1.5	2.3
Nebraska	0	—	1	0.3	0.7
New Mexico	0	—	2	0.6	0.5
North Carolina	0	—	2	0.6	2.6
Utah	0	—	1	0.3	0.6
Wyoming	0	—	1	0.3	0.2
Total	856	100.0	339	100.0	
Missing	3		0		
Subsample total	859		339		

To check for possible systematic classification errors that would affect the occupational disease subsample, the part of the body involved for all occupational diseases cases was investigated (table 5.12). Table 5.12 checks for two possible problems: accident cases with responses to question 43 (leading to inclusion of the case in the occupational disease subsample), and simple errors or scrambled responses. For example, there are two cases classified as dust diseases of the lungs that have affected the head and the foot of the claimant, respectively. These are clear anomalies; either these are not lung disease cases or the responses on the part of the body are in error. The same is probably true of the four dust disease cases reported as affecting the back. Similar isolated observations can be made for the cases identified as respiratory conditions due to toxic agents.

Most lung diseases were assigned to chest, multiple parts of the body, or "other" parts of the body. Multiple parts of the body and "other" parts of the body contain a majority of all occupational disease cases in the subsample. Given the choices for parts of the body, they are clearly accident oriented. A hearing-loss case, for example, would be a disorder due to repeated trauma (assuming it was a chronic condition), but since there is no "ear" response for parts of the body, these cases would appear primarily as "other" parts of the body. There are 182 such cases in the occupational disease subsample, it is assumed they are primarily hearing-loss cases. Other repeated trauma diseases (mostly diseases of the joints) and skin diseases are spread throughout the categories on parts of the body.

Classification errors cannot be shown to be a large problem. There are a few obvious anomalies, but they involve a very small number of cases. The information is not as complete as would be desirable, but there is no evidence that a large number of accident cases have been mistakenly included in the occupational disease subsample.

The Weighting Procedure

To make meaningful comparisons among the occupational disease, heart, and accident subsamples, the cases must be weighted to offset the different sampling ratios for temporary disability cases (two weeks) and permanent disability and fatality cases (six weeks). Otherwise, if any of the three subsamples differed substantially by severity of case, the sample statistics would be seriously distorted. Since heart cases are more likely than accident cases to be permanent disabilities, this difference will be exaggerated in the closed case sample where permanent disability cases were sampled at three times the rate of temporary disability cases. Comparisons between the average heart case and the average accident case will not be accurate unless the cases are weighted

Table 5.12
Part of body affected by category of occupational disease

	Skin Diseases	Dust Diseases	Respiratory Conditions due to Toxic Agents	Poisoning	Disorders due to Physical Agents	Disorders due to Repeated Trauma	Cancers and Tumors	Other	Total
Head	2	1	1			7			11
Back		4	3	1	1	60	1	10	80
Chest		47	21	3		2	4	4	81
Abdomen				2	1	1		1	5
Hip						1			1
Groin			1			1			2
Leg/Knee	1					5		2	8
Ankle						1			1
Foot	2	1				2		1	6
Arm/Wrist	3			1		13		2	19
Hand	40				1	8		5	54
Face	4								4
Eye	1				1	1		2	5
Multiple	18	44	46	5	2	39	2	19	185
Other	28	39	31	6	1	182	1	16	294
NA	5	13	7	2	1	17		5	50
Total	104	149	110	20	8	340	8	67	806
Missing									53
n subsample									859

Table 5.13
Subsample sizes, raw and weighted

	Occupational Disease	Heart	Accident
Unweighted cases	859	339	3950
Weighted cases	1127	461	8242
Ratio weighted/unweighted	1.31	1.36	2.09

to offset this bias. For the closed case sample, it is necessary to weight temporary disability cases by a factor of three to return to the true population distribution of case severity. There are problems in weighting the sample, however.

Information about the level of disability comes from question 34 of the instrument. It asked the respondent to indicate under which of the standard disability categories indemnity payments were made, what were the weekly payments, and the number of weeks. The level of disability is gathered in combination with data on weekly benefits. When weekly benefits are paid under multiple categories, the most serious disability category is taken to represent the level of disability for that case. In the event a compensation claim is settled by formal compromise without any weekly benefits ever having been paid (a lump-sum payment), there is no appropriate response to question 34. Weekly indemnity payments were not made under any disability category, so there is no response for level of disability. These cases are almost certainly permanent disability cases and are so classified for this analysis.

Another problem arises in the cases that received weekly benefits as temporary disabilities but were eventually closed by compromise. Using question 34 as a guide, these cases would be deemed temporary disability cases since weekly benefit payments were made under that disability category. However, the compromise settlement indicates a permanent disability, so these cases would be misclassified as temporary disability. For this analysis these cases too are considered permanent disability cases.

When the temporary disability cases are weighted by a factor of three to offset the sampling ratio, the accident subsample increases from 3,950 cases to 8,242 (2.09 times its former size) (table 5.13). The same 3,950 cases are being analyzed, but the apparent size of the sample is inflated by the weighting process. The weighting has a larger effect on the accident subsample than on either the occupational disease or the heart subsamples. Although the accident subsample more than doubles when weighted, the occupational disease subsample increases by 31 percent and the heart subsample by 36 percent. The average accident case is revealed to be substantially less "serious" in terms of level of disability. The weighting procedure is superior to using unweighted (unrepresentative) data. From this point only the weighted data are used.

The Handling of Closed Cases

Findings
The first element of analysis is the proportion of closed cases that were compensated. Uncompensated cases are not a large proportion of the closed case survey sample

Table 5.14
Compensation of closed cases by case type

	Occupational Disease	Heart	Accident
Compensated	1052	434	8146
Not compensated	75	27	96
Proportion not compensated	6.7%	5.9%	1.2%

(table 5.14). There is a substantially higher incidence of uncompensated cases among the occupational disease and heart subsamples. This results primarily from the greater likelihood of controversion in these cases rather than from differences in the outcome of the controversion process itself.

The proportion of cases uncompensated in this sample does not reflect the typical claim experience. The proportions in table 5.14 represent the relationship between uncompensated cases that were controverted (went to a formal hearing) and the total number of compensated cases (whether controverted or not). There is no particular interpretation of this datum. It does not move us closer to understanding what proportion of claims are compensated among occupational disease and heart cases since there is no information about the number of uncompensated claims that did not reach the formal hearing stage. Combining these reservations with the possibility of respondent error, especially taking "closed" case to mean compensated case, it is preferable to focus on compensated cases.

There is a substantial discrepancy in the insurer origin of the cases in the subsamples (table 5.15). Twenty-five percent of the occupational disease cases were reported by self-insurers while the corresponding figure for accident and heart cases is only about 8 percent. This finding is the result of an anomaly in the closed case survey. About two-thirds of these self-insured occupational disease cases come from Michigan, and the bulk of those from one large self-insurer. That the only self-insurer reporting more than 250 closed cases (between 1,000 and 2,000 closed cases) was one who reported a fairly large number of occupational disease cases has distorted the sample statistic, reflecting a sample design problem. Throughout the empirical examination of closed cases, it is important to keep the sample limitation in mind.

For the purposes of the closed case survey, contested or controverted was defined as "a claim for which a formal or informal hearing was held to resolve any issues in question." Over 60 percent of compensated occupational disease cases and over half of compensated heart cases are contested (table 5.16). This is in marked contrast with accident cases, only about one-tenth of which are contested.

There is a substantial tendency for these cases to be controverted (table 5.17). In nearly 67 percent of occupational disease and 60 percent of heart cases, the claimant had formal representation, but only about 15 percent of accident claimants had such representation.

Question 21 of the survey was, "If claim was contested or controverted, or hearing held, what was the most important reason(s)?" The dominant reason for controversion in both occupational disease and heart cases is the issue of compensability (table 5.18).

Table 5.15
Distribution of cases in the subsamples by type of insurer

Type of Insurer	Occupational Disease (%)	Heart (%)	Accident (%)
Stock	43.2	57.0	48.3
Nonstock	19.1	14.8	23.5
State fund	13.4	19.2	20.6
Self-Insurer	24.3	9.0	7.6
Missing	6	1	38
n subsample	1052	434	8146

Table 5.16
Proportion of cases controverted by case type

Was Case Contested or Controverted?	Occupational Disease (%)	Heart (%)	Accident (%)
Yes	62.7	55.2	9.8
No	37.3	44.8	90.2
Missing	14	14	225
n subsample	1052	434	8146

Table 5.17
Representation of claimant by case type

Representative	Occupational Disease (%)	Heart (%)	Accident (%)
Attorney	65.5	58.8	14.6
Fee Paid Specialist	0.7	1.4	0.5
Union Official	0.4	0.2	0.4
Other	--	--	0.4
None	33.5	39.6	84.1
Missing	6	7	387
n subsample	1052	434	8146

The proportion of cases contested and the primary reason for controversion can be combined. Since 72 percent of controverted occupational disease cases were contested on the issue of compensability, and 62 percent of all occupational disease cases closed are contested, apparently 45 percent (72 percent × 62 percent) of all compensated occupational disease claims were thought not compensable by the insurer. The corresponding figure for heart cases is 42 percent (55 percent contested, 76 percent on issue of compensability). The contrast with accident cases is very sharp. Only 2 percent of accident victims have to fight the issue of compensability (10 percent contested, 20 percent on issue of compensability).

The figures have not involved controversion for any of the systemic reasons; jurisdiction, doubtful diagnosis, multiple liability, coverage questions (see table 5.18). Although 7.5 percent of all compensated occupational disease claims are controverted on degree of impairment (62 percent contested, 12 percent on degree of impairment), only 5.5 percent of all compensated accident cases (10 percent contested, 56 percent on degree of impairment) are controverted on degree of impairment. The degree of impairment is the dominant reason for controversion in accident cases, however, the proportion of all compensated occupational disease claims controverted on degree of impairment is actually higher. Only about 6 percent of heart cases (55 percent contested, 11 percent on degree of impairment) involve controversion on the degree of impairment.

Table 5.19 shows the responses to question 22, "If the claim was contested or controverted was the employee's position: sustained, denied, modified by decision, settled by agreement, dismissed, or other?" Most controverted cases resulting in benefits paid are settled by agreement with the proportion ranging from 55 percent for accidents to 67 percent for occupational disease cases. Perhaps the most interesting thing is the proportion of cases that were denied or dismissed (see table 5.19). Since only compensated cases are included, it is apparent that some portion of the claim was denied or dismissed rather than the overall claim. Temporary benefits may be paid, but the claim for a permanent partial award is found unworthy. This is much less likely for occupational disease claims, apparently because occupational disease cases do not typically start as temporary disability claims.

For all closed cases (including the uncompensated, controverted cases), 8.3 percent of occupational disease, 9.9 percent of heart, and 9.4 percent of accident cases were denied or dismissed. Although the occupational disease cases still show a slight deficit relative to the others, the reduction in the gap suggests that denied or dismissed is more likely to mean that there is no compensation at all.

Table 5.18
Primary reason for controversion by case type

Reason	Occupational Disease (%)	Heart (%)	Accident (%,
Hearing by law	7.8	2.7	12.0
Compensability	72.5	76.0	20.6
Jurisdiction	0.8	0.9	0.9
Degree impairment	12.0	11.6	55.8
Doubt diagnosis	1.6	0.4	3.8
Disability length	0.2	2.2	3.1
Multiple liability	4.2	4.4	1.0
Coverage	0.6	0.4	0.4
Other	0.5	1.3	2.3
n	644	225	781
Missing	408	209	7365
n subsample	1052	434	8146

Table 5.19
Outcome of controversion by case type

Employees Position	Occupational Disease (%)	Heart (%)	Accident (%)
Sustained	15.1	16.4	13.6
Modified	16.6	13.1	20.2
Settled Agreement	66.7	63.5	55.4
Denied or Dismissed	1.5	5.7	7.4
Other	0.2	1.2	3.5
n	657	244	778
Missing	395	190	7368
n subsample	1052	434	8146

Over half the compensated occupational disease cases and the heart cases are settled by a formal compromise agreement (compromise and release, redemption, stipulation), compared to slightly over 15 percent of accident cases (table 5.20). If the system involves compromise arrangements in this proportion, the automatic nature of compensation is a conspicuous feature of the workers' compensation system in these areas.

Another significant dimension of handling claims is their timing. Striking differences exist in timing between the occupational disease and heart cases and accident cases. In part they result from the contrasts in the way the cases enter the system, in part from the length of the controversion process. They reflect the seriousness of the cases and sample problems that are not apparent.

There are substantial differences in the average of the three types of cases (table 5.21). The questionnaire asked for the date lost time began. The difference between this date and October 1, 1975, was the days since lost time began. At closure, even given the attempt to keep the survey current in case coverage, the average heart case is more than twice as old as the average accident case. The occupational disease cases occupy a middle ground but still are nearly 200 days older on average than accident cases. (Both these differences are statistically significant at the 99 percent level.) In terms of absolute values, the average occupational disease case compensated is closed in about thirteen months, and heart cases and accident cases take about eighteen and eight months respectively. It does not take thirteen months for payments to begin in the average occupational disease case, but thirteen months elapse before payments are completed, or a firm definition of benefits is reached.

The non-response situation on this variable is equally interesting. Nearly half (47 percent) of occupational disease cases did not give a date that lost time began. A fairly large proportion of these cases must involve no lost time. The non-response rate for heart cases was 21 percent and for accident cases only 6 percent. What proportion of these cases might be hearing-loss and other "injury without lost time" cases is unknown. Once again the results must be tempered with the uncertainties of the sample.

Table 5.22 shows the number of days between the beginning of lost time and the date notice of injury or illness was received by the insurer. The contrasts among the three types of cases are even greater than in table 5.21. Only nineteen days elapse between the beginning of lost time and receipt of notice for the average accident case. However, the average occupational disease case involving lost time is already 111 days old before the insurer even hears of it. The corresponding figure for heart cases is 101 days. These differences highlight the lack of similarity in the compensation experience of the typical occupational disease or heart case compared to accident cases.

Table 5.20
Proportion of cases settled by formal compromise by case type

Case Settled by Formal Compromise?	Occupational Disease (%)	Heart (%)	Accident (%)
Yes	55.3	55.0	15.8
No	44.7	45.0	84.2
Missing	20	16	361
n subsample	1052	434	8146

Table 5.21
Days from beginning of lost time to date of closure by case type

	Occupational Disease	Heart	Accident
Mean	404	554	233
Standard deviation	408.0	512.8	310.8
n	559	341	7626
Missing	493	93	520
n subsample	1052	434	8146

Table 5.22
Days from beginning of lost time to receipt of notification of injury or illness by insurer by case type

	Occupational Disease	Heart	Accident
Mean	111.9	101.2	19.1
Standard deviation	203.4	211.0	62.7
n	504	282	6259
Missing	548	152	1617
n subsample	1052	434	8146

Table 5.23
Days from notification of insurer to issuance of first check by case type

	Occupational Disease	Heart	Accident
Mean	255.6	210.1	43.2
Standard deviation	287.9	301.5	125.9
n	816	342	7373
Missing	236	92	773
n subsample	1052	434	8146

Another element of timing is the "system delay," that is, how long it took the workers' compensation system to respond once notice of injury or illness was finally received. The number of days from receipt of notice of injury or illness by the insurer to the date of the first check to a claimant in accident, occupational disease, and heart cases is shown in table 5.23. On the average it takes six times as long for the sytem to respond in compensated occupational disease cases as it does in accident cases. This reflects the disproportionate incidence of controversion.

The non-response problem is much reduced, but still substantial. There is no response for about one-fourth of the occupational disease cases on either the date of the first check or date of notice. Since all of these cases are compensated, it is likely that the date of notice caused the problem. It is likely though not certain that all these differences are linked somehow to the claims administration in the various jurisdictions, possibly in the handling of formal compromise cases.

The relevant time delay between injury or illness and commencement of benefit payments from the claimant's viewpoint is the time from beginning of lost time to the issuance of first check. The average accident case claimant begins receiving benefits in 62 days, the average heart claimant waits 311 days, and the occupational disease claimant waits 367 days. Whatever the reason for these delays, it is clear that benefits for occupational disease and heart claimants are neither automatic nor timely.

Levels of Compensation
Two elements of the severity of closed cases are the level of disability and the amount of compensation. Table 5.24 shows the highest level of disability for the occupational disease, heart, and accident subsamples. Closed occupational disease cases are nearly three times as likely as accident cases to be permanent partial disabilities. They are four times as likely to be fatalities (although the number of cases is much too small to be confident of this; there are eleven fatalities among the occupational disease cases and twenty-two among the accident cases). Over 6 percent of compensated occupational disease cases are permanent total, and only one-half of 1 percent of accident cases fall in this category. In this respect heart cases generally fall between the occupational disease and accident cases, except for fatalities. Almost 9 percent of compensated heart cases are fatalities. The "typical" accident case is a temporary disability, but these cases are a minority of heart and occupational disease case populations. Occupational disease and heart cases are substantially more serious on the average.

There are differences in the status of benefit payments among the closed cases. In 92 percent of the occupational disease cases, all benefit payments have been completed

Table 5.24
Highest level of disability by case type

	Occupational Disease (%)	Heart (%)	Accident (%)
Temporary partial	4.1	5.7	7.9
Temporary total	35.0	37.5	71.9
Permanent partial	53.8	45.0	19.5
Permanent total	6.1	3.1	0.5
Death	1.1	8.7	0.3
n	1030	424	8035
Missing	22	10	111
n subsample	1052	434	8156

at the time of closure (table 5.25). At the other extreme are the heart cases, of which only 80 percent are no longer drawing benefits. Keeping in mind the survey's definition of closed case, cases in which benefits are not yet completed must be permanent or fatality cases, unless the insurer used his own definition of closed for the temporary cases (see figure 5.1). Since closed occupational disease cases are usually more serious than accident cases, that is, more likely to involve permanent disability or death, why do a lower proportion of occupational disease cases show continuing benefits, even when we know that these cases are also "older" on the average? The answer lies in the cases settled by formal compromise.

Table 5.26 shows that over 40 percent of occupational disease cases and heart cases received lump-sum payments compared to only 11 percent of accident cases. Since the payment of the directed or compromise lump sum usually closes the case, the lower percentage of occupational disease cases with continuing payments falls into place. Even though these cases tend to be older and more serious, a large proportion are settled by formal compromise and do not involve continuing indemnity payments over time. This argument is not true for heart cases because of the much higher incidence of fatality cases.

Fifty-five percent of compensated occupational disease cases were settled by formal compromise (see table 5.20). The data in table 5.26 deal with the size of payments in such cases. In this instance data are available only on the 44 percent of the sample reporting lump-sum payments by size of award. It is not clear why this difference is so large. Possibly it represents non-response to the question of the amount of the lump sum.

There are also substantial differences in the size of the compromise lump-sum payments by type of case. Not only do nearly three times as many occupational disease closed cases receive compromise lump-sum payments as do accident cases, but the average benefit is about 50 percent larger. The difference between the mean lump-sum payments in these two types of cases is not statistically significant due to the large variance, but this demonstrates that the compromised occupational disease cases are not all "trivial" cases involving some "nuisance payments." These lump-sum-payment averages are not out of line with the overall average compensation levels by type of case.

Question 33 of the instrument asked for the amount that had actually been paid on the case as of the date of closure by the categories of medical and indemnity. Respondents were to record "aggregate payments to claimant, claimant's attorneys, and dependents including penalties and interest, but not payments to second injury or

Table 5.25
Status of benefit payments at time of closure by case type

Have All Expected Benefits Been Paid?	Occupational Disease (%)	Heart (%)	Accident (%)
Yes	92.0	79.9	86.7
No	8.0	20.1	13.3
Missing	19	16	204
n subsample	1052	434	8146

Table 5.26
Directed or compromise lump sum payments by case type

	Occupational Disease	Heart	Accident
Mean	$ 5,232	$ 9,236	$3,440
Standard deviation	36,462	33,811	6,491
n	458	181	869
Subsample (%)	43.5	41.7	10.7

Table 5.27
Medical payments as of date of closure by case type

	Occupational Disease	Heart	Accident
Mean	$ 501	$2,849	$ 816
Standard deviation	1,064	5,463	2,372
n	697	305	7,026
Subsample (%)	66.3	70.3	86.2

Table 5.28
Indemnity payments as of date of closure by case type

	Occupational Disease	Heart	Accident
Mean	$ 3,520	$ 7,190	$1,799
Standard deviation	28,546	26,776	9,313
n	1,035	420	8,032
Subsample (%)	98.4	96.8	98.6

other special funds, or other case expenses which are not benefits." This sample suggests that medical costs in occupational disease claims are not relatively large (table 5.27). The average level of payments is less than one-fifth the level of heart cases and is 40 percent less than the average medical costs in accident cases. (These differences are significant at the 99 percent level.) Furthermore, medical payments are made in a lower proportion of all closed cases for occupational disease cases. Some of the difference is due to the incidence of compromised cases where separate dollar amounts for medical and indemnity are not given. There could be other non-response influences at work since the proportion of the subsamples receiving benefits is not extremely high, but there is no reason to be concerned in this case. Occupational disease cases are less likely to receive medical payments, and when they do the average cost is significantly lower. Heart cases, on the other hand, show significantly higher levels of average medical cost, probably reflecting the greater likelihood of hospitalization.

The average indemnity paid by date of closure is about 95 percent greater for occupational disease than for accident cases (table 5.28). (This difference is not quite significant at the 95 percent level, a consequence of the large variance within the occupational disease subsample.) The greater incidence of uncompleted payments among accident cases accounts for a portion of this differential (see table 5.25), but it is not responsible for much of it.

Heart cases are twice as expensive on the average as occupational disease cases by this measure. This makes them about four times as costly in indemnity as accident cases (a significant difference at the 99 percent level).

The high average indemnity payment for occupational disease cases results entirely from the higher average severity of the occupational disease cases since in most disability categories the mean indemnity payment is higher for accident cases (table 5.29). The differences between heart cases and accident cases tend to hold up across disability categories although the differences are much less marked than before. There is no explanation for the high mean indemnity in temporary partial accident cases nor for the low mean in fatal occupational disease cases.

The instrument provided amounts of future lump-sum payments that are expected or agreed to, as well as information about continuing weekly payments to make an estimate of future payments possible. Future lump-sum payments are the largest within the heart cases and are least prevalent among occupational disease cases, where only 1.5 percent of closed cases are expected to receive such payments (table 5.30). In neither case is the difference from the mean of the accident cases statistically significant, even though the average for heart cases is more than twice that for accidents.

Table 5.29
Indemnity payments as of date of closure by highest level of disability by case type

	Occupational Disease	Heart	Accident
Temporary Partial			
Mean	$ 812	$ 764	$ 2047
Standard Deviation	1408	562	10849
n	42	24	630
Temporary Total			
Mean	$ 1385	$ 3238	$ 948
Standard Deviation	3190	4180	4061
n	360	159	5763
Permanent Partial			
Mean	$ 4792	$10110	$ 4219
Standard Deviation	38992	39371	12251
n	546	184	1549
Permanent Total			
Mean	$ 5863	$ 9930	$ 7489
Standard Deviation	8533	6640	8982
n	63	13	37
Death			
Mean	$ 3376	$13335	$15836
Standard Deviation	3962	14010	12919
n	11	36	21
Missing	30	18	146

Table 5.30
Expected future payments by case type

	Occupational Disease	Heart	Accident
Lump Sums			
Mean	$ 4,234	$ 8,545	$ 3,656
Standard deviation	6,450	13,873	7,225
n	16	18	154
Subsample (%)	1.5	4.1	1.9
Weekly Payments			
Mean	$22,446	$24,025	$11,260
Standard deviation	32,710	33,157	37,932
n	17	45	199
Subsample (%)	1.6	10.4	2.4

Table 5.30 also gives the other dimension of future payments, the expected sum of weekly benefits before payments are terminated. This sum is calculated as follows: If a fixed term of weeks remaining was specified, then the expected future weekly payments are simply the weekly payment times the remaining weeks of benefits. If lifetime benefit payments were indicated, the aggregate future weekly payments were estimated as the product of the weekly payment times the expected weeks of life remaining (assuming a life expectancy of seventy-eight years for female and seventy-three years for male beneficiaries, respectively).

The incidence of these future payments varies widely. The occupational disease and accident subsamples show about the same incidence as with future lump-sum payments (it is not known whether these are substantially the same cases), but over 10 percent of the heart cases indicate continuing weekly payments. Those occupational disease and heart cases that receive benefits can anticipate about twice the benefits paid in accident cases. (Only the heart difference is statistically significant due to the small number of observations in the occupational disease category.) That future payments will be made in a smaller proportion of all closed occupational disease cases than in accident cases, even though the proportion of serious cases is much higher among occupational disease cases, reflects the impact of formal compromise. Insurers are much more likely to settle occupational disease cases with a lump-sum payment.

Total compensation is the sum of medical payments and indemnity payments already made as of the date of closure plus anticipated future payments, both weekly benefits and future lump sums. In this sense the average occupational disease case is 50 percent more expensive than the average accident case. When controlling for level of disability, however, it is apparent that occupational disease cases are not expensive, especially for permanent total and fatality cases. Heart cases are four times more expensive than accident cases on the average (table 5.31). Only temporary total and permanent partial heart cases are more costly than equivalent accident cases, so the seriousness of the average case is the main influence on total compensation per case.

Compensated Occupational Disease Cases

The closed case survey produced an unexpected distribution of occupational disease cases (table 5.32). There is no previous tabulation of closed cases by type of disease; a comparison of these results with the distribution of lost workday cases (see table 2.5) is suggestive, however.

Marked differences would be expected between the distribution of OSHA employer

Table 5.31
Total compensation (paid and expected) by highest level of disability by case type

	Occupational Disease	Heart	Accident
Temporary Partial			
Mean	$ 1,174	$ 1,234	$ 2,827
Standard deviation	1,428	767	13,025
n	42	24	633
Temporary Total			
Mean	$ 1,780	$ 7,713	$ 1,627
Standard deviation	3,662	12,007	5,819
n	360	159	5,778
Permanent Partial			
Mean	$ 5,429	$12,899	$ 5,832
Standard deviation	38,992	41,733	14,766
n	554	191	1,566
Permanent Total			
Mean	$ 9,676	$19,320	$23,352
Standard deviation	19,538	21,226	45,603
n	63	13	37
Death			
Mean	$ 3,511	$29,014	$57,474
Standard deviation	3,990	57,258	89,262
n	11	37	21
Missing	22	10	111
Total			
Mean	$ 4,222	$11,805	$ 2,822
Standard deviation	28,889	33,846	12,384
n	1,052	434	8,146

Table 5.32
Compensated occupational disease cases by category of disease

	Number of Cases	Percent
Skin diseases	243	23.1
Dust diseases	170	16.2
Respiratory conditions due to toxic agents	122	11.6
Poisoning	49	4.7
Disorders due to physical agents	10	1.0
Disorders due to repeated trauma	347	33.0
Cancer and tumors	11	1.0
Other	100	9.5
Total	1052	100.0

reported diseases and compensated cases as measured here. The OSHA figures would probably include very few if any long latency diseases. Yet these would make up a larger proportion of the compensated case population since many minor OSHA recorded disease events would not involve indemnity payments. It was therefore anticipated that the OSHA data would reveal more cases involving skin diseases than would the closed case survey. OSHA reported that 33 percent of all recordable illnesses in 1973 were skin diseases, and 23 percent of the cases in the closed case sample are skin diseases.

The relatively small discrepancies between OSHA statistics and the closed case sample results for poisoning cases (OSHA 3.9 percent, closed case sample 4.7 percent) or for respiratory conditions due to toxic agents (OSHA 7.0 percent, closed case sample 11.6 percent) are also unproblematic. But the discrepancy for dust diseases is substantial. OSHA reported that 0.9 percent of lost workday cases involved dust diseases of the lungs, the closed case sample shows 16.2 percent of occupational disease cases are in the dust disease category. For the reasons suggested, dust diseases would be expected to loom larger in the population of compensated cases but the extent of the discrepancy was surprising. Table 5.2, which showed the distribution of disease cases for various states that compiled such statistics (on varying bases), generally indicated that respiratory diseases constituted 4 percent to 8 percent of all occupational disease cases. An exception was Ohio, which indicated that 46 percent of claims were for lung diseases (this is not the same as dust diseases of the lungs). Only the New York figures are directly comparable to these data since they too represent compensated cases closed. In 1973, 6.4 percent of the closed compensated occupational disease cases in New York were silicosis and other dust diseases. The closed case sample contains more than two and one-half times this proportion of dust disease cases.

An unusually high proportion of dust disease, respiratory conditons due to toxic agents, and "other" cases were reported in the survey by self-insurers (33 percent, 46 percent, and 34 percent respectively; no other category of occupational disease exceeds 22 percent for self-insurers). One and probably several large self-insurers with numerous respiratory disease claims have biased the sample. It might be a seasonal component in the "closure" of dust disease cases that has biased the sample. It is also possible that insurer respondents more readily recognized certain types of cases as occupational disease cases. Therefore they may have reported a higher proportion of these cases. This result is not a product of the weighting process. On an unweighted basis the closed case sample actually contained more dust disease cases than skin disease cases (173 to 104).

No other discrepancy between the closed case sample and the OSHA lost workday case distribution is so significant. The closed case sample shows a marked deficit in disorders due to physical agents (OSHA, 12.1 percent; closed case sample, 1.0 percent) and a marked excess in disorders due to repeated trauma (OSHA, 18.8 percent; closed case sample, 33.0 percent). This is illustrative of the relative biases in the two underlying data sources. The OSHA log will pick up the "routine" accidentlike occupational disease cases (disorders due to physical agents include heat stroke, frost bite, and effects of radiation), while missing completely those diseases characterized either by long latency or a gradual onset, unaccompanied by any dramatic incident or symptoms (disorders due to repeated trauma include hearing loss, synovitis, and bursitis). It also reflects the heavy weight of California in the sample, a state experiencing a proliferation of such claims. The remaining discrepancy is in the "other" category. Lumping the cancer and tumors category (not specifically identified in the OSHA reports) with the "other" yields 10.5 percent of the closed cases; OSHA reports 23.9 percent of lost workday disease cases are "other."

The distribution of level of disability within each disease category is presented in table 5.33. The heart and accident subsample figures are also shown for comparison. The skin disease and poisoning cases within the occupational disease case subsample are very much like accident cases in the balance between temporary and permanent disability cases. Skin disease and poisoning cases, like accident cases, are mostly temporary disability cases. There are, however, substantial differences in the balance between permanent partial, permanent total, and death cases among these groups. In the typical indemnified skin disease or poisoning case, the workers' compensation system functions much like it does in the typical accident case. Neither of these areas is dominated by the tough etiological issues that set serious occupational disease cases apart from serious accident cases.

Dust diseases of the lung and respiratory conditions due to toxic agents tend to be more serious and, therefore, indicative of the larger stakes involved in these cases. A minority of these cases are temporary disability cases. The situation is almost the reverse of that in accident cases in that over 75 percent of these cases involve permanent disability or death. The average occupational disease case closed in these categories then appears even more serious than the average heart case closed (about 40 percent temporary disability).

The occupational disease cases in the trauma category exhibit another pattern. Nearly 90 percent of these cases are permanent partial disability cases, and many are hearing-loss cases. Due to the high incidence of compromise settlements among these case categories, the distribution of the level of disability depends heavily on the

Table 5.33
Percentage distribution of occupational disease cases by level of disability

	Temp. Partial (%)	Temp. Total (%)	Perm. Partial (%)	Perm. Total (%)	Death (%)	n
Skin diseases	5.0	82.8	10.9	1.3	—	239
Dust diseases	—	12.8	69.5	15.2	2.5	164
Respiratory conditions due to toxic agents	2.5	20.0	62.5	14.2	0.8	120
Poisoning	6.1	73.5	14.3	2.0	4.1	49
Disorders due to physical agents	60.0	30.0	10.0	—	—	10
Disorders due to repeated trauma	1.8	8.9	87.5	1.8	—	337
Cancers and tumors	—	54.5	36.4	9.1	—	11
Other	12.0	42.0	32.0	10.0	4.0	100
Total	4.1	35.0	53.8	6.1	1.1	1030
Heart	5.7	37.5	45.0	3.1	8.7	424
Accident	7.9	71.9	19.5	0.5	0.3	8035

Table 5.34
Degree of controversion by category of disease

	Cases Controverted	Category (%)
Skin diseases	33	14.2
Dust diseases	149	88.2
Respiratory conditions due to toxic agents	95	78.5
Poisoning	18	36.7
Disorders due to physical agents	1	10.0
Disorders due to repeated trauma	297	85.8
Cancers and tumors	5	45.5
Other	53	53.5
Total	651	62.7
Heart	232	55.2
Accident	776	9.8

inference that compromised cases should be regarded as permanent partial disability cases. These allocations range up to 40 percent of some disease categories, and among repeated trauma cases one-third showed no response on level of disability.

The "other" occupational disease cases are typically somewhat more serious than accident cases. This sample shows a particularly high incidence of death cases in this category. (This is only an observation of four cases.) The remaining categories, disorders due to physical agents and cancers and tumors, contain too few observations to make discussion of them meaningful. It is strange, however, that the bulk of the cancer cases are recorded as temporary total disabilities.

The conclusions drawn from examining occupational disease cases by level of disability confirm that occupational disease cases are distributed bimodally. There is a subset of occupational disease cases that, because they involve an identifiable event at the onset of disability, are handled very much like injuries due to accident. There are other occupational disease cases that do not fit the accident mold and are not readily accommodated by the workers' compensation systems.

Examining the issue of controversion further confirms this observation. The number and percentage of cases contested is given in table 5.34, with heart and accident statistics for comparisons. The proportion of controverted cases is lowest for accident cases (9.8 percent), but the incidence of controversion among skin diseases is close to that level (14.2 percent). At the other end of the distribution 88.2 percent of compensated dust disease cases were contested. Disorders due to repeated trauma also reveal a very high controversion rate (many of these are hearing-loss cases). Among the poisoning, cancer, and disorders due to physical agents categories less than half the compensated occupational disease cases are controverted, but in other occupational disease categories a majority of those claimants who are compensated must go through the controversion process. In four of the eight occupational disease categories, a higher proportion of compensated claims have been contested than among heart cases.

Table 5.35 reinforces the judgments made earlier about controversion among occupational disease cases. The foremost issue in these cases is compensability itself. Although only about 20 percent of contested accident cases are contested on compensability, over 60 percent of every category among occupational disease cases is contested on this question. It is possible to combine these two proportions: Among compensated dust disease cases, 73 percent (88.2 percent controverted × 83.2 percent contested on compensability) of these cases were denied compensation in the first instance because the insurer did not think the case compensable. One wonders what the "success" rate

Table 5.35
Reason for controversion by category of disease

	Compensability (%)	Degree of Impairment (%)	Other Issues (%)
Skin diseases	62.2	24.3	13.5
Dust diseases	83.2	9.8	7.0
Respiratory conditions due to toxic agents	84.2	6.3	9.5
Poisoning	66.7	5.6	27.7
Disorders due to physical agents	100.0	0	0
Disorders due to repeated trauma	62.5	15.1	22.4
Cancers and tumors	80.0	20.0	0
Other	85.2	3.7	11.1
Total	72.5	12.0	15.5
Heart	76.0	11.6	12.4
Accident	20.6	55.8	23.6

Table 5.36
Cases settled by formal compromise by category of disease

	Cases	Category (%)
Skin diseases	33	14.1
Dust diseases	137	82.0
Respiratory conditions due to toxic agents	78	64.5
Poisoning	14	28.6
Disorders due to physical agents	3	42.9
Disorders due to repeated trauma	236	68.6
Cancers and tumors	10	90.9
Other	60	60.6
Total	571	55.3
Heart	230	55.0
Accident	1230	15.8

among these cases must be. How many claims are there for every compensated case? And how many persons are discouraged from ever filing because of the seeming inevitability of delay and contention?

The number and percent of compensated occupational disease cases settled by formal compromise are shown in table 5.36. Only in skin diseases is the proportion compromised (14 percent) similar to the experience in accident cases. Poisoning cases and disorders due to physical agents are compromised often, but not usually. In all other occupational disease categories a majority of cases are closed by formal compromise agreement. The compromise proportions are extremely high for dust diseases and cancers and tumors. The workers' compensation system for disease cases works quite differently from both the theoretical ideal and the practice in accident cases. *Controversion and formal compromise are the rule and not the exception.*

The process of controversion and the settlement by formal compromise are related (table 5.37). Three-fourths of the closed occupational disease cases contested are eventually settled by compromise. On the other hand, less than 20 percent of uncontested cases are settled by compromise. The connection between controversion and formal compromise is strong, although it is by no means absolute. Forty-nine percent of all compensated occupational disease cases involve both controversion and settlement by compromise (503 of 1020). Furthermore, of the 311 cases (30 percent) that were neither contested nor settled by compromise, 179 or 57 percent are skin disease cases. If skin desease cases are deleted from table 5.37, about 60 percent of all compensated occupational disease cases (503 of 841) would involve a compromise of a controverted claim.

The statistics on the time dimensions of the handling of occupational disease cases are presented on length of time from beginning of lost time to date of closure, from beginning of lost time to notice to insurer, and from notice to insurer to issuance of first check (table 5.38). In all these dimensions the skin diseases and disorders due to physical agents remain similar to accident cases. Poisoning cases take significantly longer to close, presumably because they are more serious, and weekly payments extend over a longer period of time. The other categories are all over one year old when closed, and the average dust disease involves nearly two years from the beginning of lost time to closure.

The statistics for beginning of lost time to notification of insurer are difficult to explain. There is a tremendous range from a low of 22 days average for skin disease cases to 315 days for cancers and tumors. Most of the category means are greater than that for heart cases. There are two factors at work. The first is delayed recognition

Table 5.37
Formal compromise by controversion for occupational disease cases

	Settled by Formal Compromise?		
	Yes	No	Total
Case Controverted?			
Yes	503	141	644
	(78.1%)	(21.9%)	
No	65	311	376
	(17.3%)	(82.7%)	

and diagnosis of occupational diseases. The work-related nature of many occupational diseases only gradually becomes apparent even to the worker, so claims are not filed immediately. Second, understanding in a general way the difficulty of his position (perhaps no such disease condition has been compensated before in the worker's experience), the decision to seek benefits could be delayed while more information is gathered from medical, legal, or other sources. Whatever the reason, dust disease, cancer and trauma cases (probably not including hearing loss) are more than six months old by the time the insurer is notified of the claim. The hearing-loss cases are not included, and the number of trauma cases reported has dropped to 67 out of the original 297; many of these cases would not involve lost time.

To better evaluate how much of the substantial delay from the onset of lost time to closure is due to the systematic differences in the time the insurer was first notified, examine the time from notice to the insurer to issuance of the first check in table 5.38. This period directly reflects the controversion experience. The preponderance of controverted cases in the occupational disease experience is reflected in long delays between notice and benefits. The longest delay is in the case of dust diseases, followed closely by respiratory conditions due to toxic agents and disorders due to repeated trauma. These are also the three categories with the highest proportion of cases controverted (see table 5.34). The lower controversion rates for skin disease cases, disorders due to physical agents, and poisoning cases have shorter average periods from notification of insurer to issuance of the first benefit check.

To approximate the average gap from the onset of lost time until the commencement of benefits, add the time from beginning of lost time to notification of insurer and the time from notification to issuance of the first check. This is not strictly appropriate when the coverage of cases is not identical, but a rough approximation can be made. The average dust disease case takes about two years from onset of lost time (where there is lost time) to receipt of the first benefit check (if any benefits are forthcoming). The influence of compromise settlements is apparent in the similarity of this figure to that for the start of lost time to closure. They are the same because there are few cases with periodic payments. By contrast, skin disease cases begin receiving benefits in about eighty-one days (compared to about sixty-two days for accident cases), and the difference between this figure and the average age of the case at closure represents the benefit period. The bimodal character of occupational disease cases is apparent.

To determine what the possible relationship is between occupational disease and retirement, the average age of claimants for the closed occupational disease cases was investigated. The oldest claimants on the average are in the categories of dust diseases,

Table 5.38
Time elements in the handling of occupational disease cases

	Skin Diseases	Dust Diseases	Respiratory Conditions due to Toxic Agents	Poisoning	Disorders due to Physical Agents	Disorders due to Repeated Trauma	Cancers and Tumors	Other	Heart	Accident
Days from Beginning of Lost Time to Closure										
Mean	225	665	583	377	221	530	583	445	554	233
Standard deviation	266.3	419.7	593.2	416.7	128.5	413.2	30.4	389.2	512.8	310.8
n	219	77	44	46	9	81	5	78	341	7626
Days from Beginning of Lost Time to Notice to Insurer										
Mean	22	286	85	35	32	224	315	135	101	19
Standard deviation	36.4	277.1	148.9	67.5	38.0	269.7	168.5	237.1	211.0	62.7
n	196	74	42	45	9	67	5	66	282	6259
Days from Notice to Insurer to First Check										
Mean	59	390	389	111	79	362	260	186	210	43
Standard deviation	117.9	290.3	383.9	179.7	89.9	256.0	122.5	283.3	301.5	125.0
n	212	105	104	46	10	256	9	74	342	7373

cancers and tumors, and disorders due to repeated trauma (table 5.39). Generally the diseases in these categories develop gradually, so the higher average age of claimants is not surprising. In addition the trauma category is not filled with retired workers with hearing-loss claims. Although these cases cannot be examined directly, if they were a large group, the mean age of the trauma category would be higher.

Not every closed case will have received medical payments and the means given in table 5.40 are based on the number of cases actually reporting benefits. The payments range from an average of $199 for skin disease cases to $2,066 for the few cancer cases in the sample. Only one-sixth of the cancer cases received medical payments although over 80 percent of skin disease cases did. In addition to skin disease cases, a high proportion of poisoning cases and "other" cases showed some medical payments. The proportion of cases receiving medical payments varies as the nature of the injury requires medical treatment and inversely to the likelihood of a compromise settlement. The highly controverted areas (dust diseases, respiratory conditions due to toxic agents, and disorders due to repeated trauma) show lower incidence of medical payments because the cases were settled with a lump-sum payment covering indemnity and medical benefits.

Average indemnity payments in dust diseases and cancer cases are in the $8,000 to $10,000 range, substantially above even the average for heart cases (table 5.41). Respiratory conditions due to toxic agents and "other" cases have mean indemnity payments close to the average for all occupational disease cases. Benefits in poisoning and trauma cases fall below the overall average, though still slightly above the average for accident cases. Disorders due to physical agents and skin disease cases have lower indemnity costs than accident cases.

Table 5.42 sums all benefit payments that have been paid as of the date of closure (medical payments and indemnity) and expected future payments to derive total benefits by disease category. Among the occupational disease cases there were only sixteen cases where the insurer expected to make future lump-sum payments and seventeen cases that had continuing weekly benefit payments. Average total benefits for skin disease cases are less than half the average for accident cases. Poisoning cases, repeated trauma cases, and disorders due to physical agents have average benefit levels roughly equal to accident cases. Respiratory conditions due to toxic agents and "other" occupational disease cases cost slightly more on the average than accident cases, and dust disease and cancer cases are more expensive, with total benefits comparable to heart cases.

Table 5.39
Average age of claimant in closed occupational disease cases by category of disease

	Claimant's Mean Age (years)	Standard deviation	n
Skin diseases	41.0	14.0	242
Dust diseases	52.5	10.6	168
Respiratory conditions due to toxic agents	48.0	12.8	119
Poisoning	38.7	13.7	49
Disorders due to physical agents	34.7	11.7	10
Disorders due to repeated trauma	50.7	10.8	339
Cancers and tumors	51.3	11.3	10
Other	39.0	14.0	97
Total	46.6	13.4	1034
Missing			18
n subsample			1052

Table 5.40
Medical payments as of date of closure, by disease category

	Medical Payments			Cases Receiving Payments (%)
	Mean ($)	Standard deviation	n	
Skin diseases	199	266.8	205	82.0
Dust diseases	484	975.2	94	49.7
Respiratory conditions due to toxic agents	902	1285.1	56	43.4
Poisoning	867	1237.1	42	85.7
Disorders due to physical agents	874	414.9	9	60.0
Disorders due to repeated trauma	430	1087.1	213	56.2
Cancers and tumors	2066	2259.9	2	16.7
Other	948	1706.1	76	71.7
Total	501	1063.8	697	61.8
Heart	2849	5463.5	305	66.2
Accident	816	2371.7	7026	85.2

Table 5.41
Indemnity payments as of date of closure, by disease category

	Indemnity Payments			Cases Receiving Payments (%)
	Mean ($)	Standard deviation	n	
Skin diseases	684	1732.0	239	96.3
Dust diseases	9,762	70032.9	167	88.4
Respiratory conditions due to toxic agents	3,500	6435.4	121	93.8
Poisoning	2,574	6569.5	49	100.0
Disorders due to physical agents	1,414	1194.8	10	66.7
Disorders due to repeated trauma	2,619	5297.4	338	89.2
Cancers and tumors	8,316	6125.1	11	91.7
Other	3,091	4175.6	100	94.3
Total	3,520	28545.6	1035	91.8
Heart	7,190	26776.2	420	91.1
Accident	1,799	9313.5	8032	97.4

Table 5.42
Total compensation paid as of date of closure plus expected future payments, by disease category

	n	Total Expected Benefits ($)
Skin diseases	243	1,217
Dust diseases	170	11,462
Respiratory conditions due to toxic agents	122	4,090
Poisoning	49	3,317
Disorders due to physical agents	10	2,201
Disorders due to repeated trauma	347	2,989
Cancers and tumors	11	8,692
Other	100	3,811
Total	1052	4,222
Heart	434	11,805
Accident	8146	2,822

Summary: Closed Case Survey

All the results are subject to a number of qualifications. The representativeness of the closed case survey sample is in doubt. There are biases present in the distribution of occupational disease cases by jurisdiction, type of insurer, and size of insurer. There are probably biases introduced by the respondents' selection of occupational disease cases from among all closed cases. Other biases exist due to the lack of direction or guidance in assigning those closed cases perceived as occupational disease cases to the appropriate occupational disease category. There may have been biases introduced by the differential sampling rates for temporary disability and permanent disability and death cases. These might have been further complicated by the uncertainties of the weighting process, which reflects the basic limitation that the occupational disease cases do not fit well into the accident-oriented closed case survey instrument. This sample was not expressly designed to examine the issues related to occupational diseases, but it is the best currently available.

Given these serious limitations, the observations are as follows. The occupational disease cases break down into three basic groups. First, and perhaps most numerous, are the cases that are not much more complicated than accident cases. These include the skin disease cases, poisoning cases, and the cases arising from disorders due to physical agents. This subgroup of occupational disease cases is characterized by an identifiable event or series of events leading to disabling consequences not unlike those in accident cases; lost time from work, necessity for medical treatment, and so forth. They are sufficiently similar to accident cases so that conceptually they do not constitute a separate population of cases.

There is another group of cases, typified by the hearing-loss and other trauma cases, that occupy a middle ground. Etiology may be a complicating issue, but it is usually a problem only for evidentiary matters. Can the exposure be demonstrated or proven to be excessive? These cases present problems for the workers' compensation system to the degree that they resemble the third category of cases in which the cause of the disability is the fundamental issue. The high level of controversion of these cases follows in the wake of questions of causation.

The third category consists of an unknown number of very serious and/or very difficult cases which are handled very differently from the first group. Evidence from this closed case sample indicates that these cases constitute a majority of compensated occupational disease cases. This is uncertain, but there are large numbers of these cases.

As the frontiers of compensation of occupational diseases are pushed back by medical advances and administrative decisions, these cases will grow in importance. For this group of occupational disease cases, given the level of controversion and incidence of compromise settlements, it would be fair to question whether the workers' compensation system is "handling" these cases at all. It is difficult to justify use of the term "no-fault" to apply to a group of cases that have, in the overwhelming majority, been controverted on the question of compensability. These claimants' typical experience with the workers' compensation system bears little resemblance to the theoretical or textbook description of the operation of the system.

England

The Workers' Compensation System

The workers' compensation system that began in England under the Act of 1897 re-placed a liability system for industrial injuries. It was based on the no-fault principle that was emulated eventually by the various American states. This approach linked compensation benefits to wages lost and provided the exclusive remedy for injured workers or survivors. The direct costs were borne by employers. In 1942 a committee headed by Lord Beveridge issued a report recommending very substantial changes in England's approach to social insurance, and from 1946 through 1948 England adopted many of the committee's suggestions. The present-day approach to compensating work-related injuries largely reflects changes that were first put into effect in July 1948.

The current industrial injuries scheme only faintly resembles the approach used in England prior to 1948 or currently in the United States. The British workers' compen-sation system is no longer the exclusive remedy and common-law actions by disabled workers against employers are now commonplace. The system is financed as a part of the overall social insurance system and as such is supported by taxes levied on em-ployees as well as employers. A third major difference is that the basic benefits provided are not tied to a worker's wage. Instead they are paid, typically, on a flat-rate basis with some adjustments for the extent of physical impairment.

Although the system has been substantially altered, it is still a workers' compensation system. First, compensability hinges on meeting the "arising out of and in the course of" test. Further, as is common in workers' compensation programs in Europe and the United States, coverage begins on the first day of employment, unlike most social security programs that only go into effect when more substantial tests of eligibility are met, such as time in covered employment and an earnings test. Also, England has a number of social insurance schemes that parallel workers' compensation, but benefit levels are set somewhat higher for injuries due to the workplace, attesting to the separa-bility of the programs.

Financing and Benefits

For persons injured, made ill, or killed in a situation arising out of and in the course of employment, there are an extraordinary number of benefits available. The complexity occurs not because of the myriad qualifications and exceptions that the law provides — although this is the case — but due to the variety of existing programs. A brief sketch of the benefits available to an injured worker for either a work-related or non-work-related injury or sickness follows. Because workers' compensation provides benefits that in many respects are only slightly above those available to others, it is important to place the former in perspective with the latter.

Non–Workers' Compensation   Sickness Benefits are provided until return to work or up to twenty-eight weeks. Weekly benefits, beginning in November 1975, are paid at a fixed level:

single person	£11.10/week
insured married woman	7.80
plus allowance for	
dependent adult	6.90
dependent first child	3.50
dependent subsequent children	2.00

From the thirteenth day of sickness, persons with wages of over £500 per year receive an Earnings Related Supplement. These benefits, which supplement Sickness Benefits, can be paid for up to six months (expiring when Sickness Benefits do in long-term disability). Benefits are paid on one-third of the worker's (previous) income over £10 and up to £30 plus 15 percent of income over £30 up to a maximum of £54. The maximum benefit under this program is £12.27 per week.

If the individual has not returned to work after twenty-eight weeks, he is eligible for an Invalidity Pension. Like the Sickness Benefit, this weekly pension is not related to the worker's lost wage. It is, however, related to any earnings of the spouse:

single person	£13.30/week
plus allowance for	
adult dependent	7.90
dependent first child	6.50
dependent subsequent children	5.00

(Allowance is reduced with
dependent's earnings above £20.09/week)

The Invalidity Allowance supplements the Invalidity Pension for persons with a significant working lifetime ahead of them. It is payable, after the first twenty-eight weeks of incapacity, as follows:

incapacity beginning before age 35	£2.80/week
incapacity beginning before age 45	1.70
incapacity beginning ages 45 to 60 (males)	0.85
incapacity beginning ages 45 to 55 (females)	0.85

In the event of an insured person's death, there is a Widow's Allowance paid for twenty-six weeks at fixed levels:

widow	£18.60/week
plus allowance for	
dependent first child	6.50
dependent subsequent children	5.00

During this period, the widow may also receive the Earnings Related Supplement, depending on her own level of earnings.

After the twenty-six weeks passes the widow is entitled to the Widowed Mother's Allowance, which provides a flat rate of £13.30 week plus £6.50 for each child.

If a widow ceases to be eligible for the Widowed Mother's Allowance and is over forty years of age, or if her Widow's Allowance ends and she is not qualified for the Widowed Mother's Allowance and was over forty when her husband died, she is entitled to a Widow's Pension. The benefits depend on the woman's age at the time her husband died or her Widowed Mother's Allowance ends and range from £3.99 (age forty) to £13.30 (over fifty).

Workers' Benefits for Industrial Injuries or Occupational Diseases A workers' compensation case first involves the payment of an Industrial Injury Benefit payable up to a maximum of twenty-six weeks. Payments are made after the third day from the accident or onset of the disease and are at the weekly flat rate of £13.85, except for persons under eighteen (paid £11.10). Persons cannot receive simultaneously an Industrial Injury Benefit and a Sickness Benefit or an Invalidity Pension, but if the worker was eligible for the Sickness Benefit, he is entitled to the Earnings Related Supplement.

When the Industrial Injury Benefit ceases, even if the worker returns to work he is entitled to a Disablement Benefit. This benefit is paid for any remaining loss of physical or mental faculty once the Industrial Injury Benefit ceases. The award, unlike most others in Europe, is not affected by the nature of one's occupation or the lost earning capacity and continues to be paid even after the individual returns to employment.

Even if there is no handicap per se, awards are made for disfigurement. Disability is rated in multiples of ten from 100 down to 20 percent and in units below this level. A schedule is used for clearly defined impairments (the loss of one hand is 60 percent, an index finger is 14 percent). When it is unscheduled, the disability is evaluated by comparing the victim's condition with that of a normal, healthy person of the same age and sex. For persons who are 100 percent disabled, the Disability Benefit is £21.80 per week and is scaled down to £4.36 per week for persons with a 20 percent disability rating. Below 20 percent, a lump-sum payment is made. Persons below the age of eighteen receive reduced benefits.

In addition to the Disability Benefit, injured or sick workers can receive the following supplements:

Special Hardship Allowance is payable up to £8.72 per week but together with the Disability Benefit cannot exceed £21.80 per week. It is for persons who cannot return to their regular job and must take a job at a lower level of earnings.

An Unemployability Supplement of £13.30 per week with dependents' allowances at the same level as the Invalidity Pension is available for anyone who is permanently unfit for work. An allowance of precisely the same size as the Invalidity Allowance is available for younger workers.

The Constant Attendance Allowance of up to £8.70 is available if the disabled worker needs a person to attend him.

An Exceptionally Severe Disablement Allowance of £8.70 is paid to anyone receiving a Constant Attendance Allowance and whose need for such attendance appears to be permanent.

The Hospital Treatment Allowance raises the worker's Disability Benefit to the level of 100 percent disability while the claimant is hospitalized for the industrial injury or occupational disease.

The Industrial Death Benefit closely parallels the allowances and benefits for widows in non-workers' compensation cases. This benefit provides £18.60 per week for twenty-six weeks, and the survivor may be eligible for the Earnings Related Supplement for the same time. Thereafter an Industrial Widow's Pension (or other pensions for other survivors) will be paid weekly, £13.85 or £3.99 (depending on the presence of children, the widow's age at the time of the worker's death, and so on). Special allowances are also paid based on the number of dependent children in the household.

Aside from the various programs just described, there is a large number of additional programs that are not a part of the social insurance system and designed to assist families or individuals with low incomes. When viewed in conjunction with the social insurance benefits, the following conclusions can be drawn. Aside from the disablement benefits there are only very minor differences for workers between benefits for work and non-work-related injuries, sicknesses, or death. The British system provides much less of a link to the worker's level of income, prior to disablement or sickness, than any other system in Western Europe or the United States. Flat levels of benefits, unrelated to previous earnings, characterize most benefits, and even Disablement Benefits are tied to the extent of impairment (physical loss) rather than to disability (socioeconomic concept). Although the benefits involve a variety of programs, many workers (or survivors), especially those who are higher paid, are compensated badly in relation to their lost earnings. The system is extraordinarily complex, and it is doubtful that many workers know or can anticipate what their entitlements are if they become injured or ill. The British system's inadequacies are very likely to be related to the alternative sources of income available to disabled workers. Specifically, the availability and levels of tort damages and sick pay (usually through collective bargaining agreements) may be caused by or may be a contributing factor in keeping the level of workers' compensation benefits relatively low.

Coverage of persons by the British system of social insurance is very broad, extending not only to the entire labor force but also to the nonemployed, on a voluntary basis. Self-employed individuals are required to participate in the scheme. As complex and varied as the benefits are, the financing is a model of simplicity. For wage earners there is no assessment on employer or employee when the wage is below £11 per week. For others there is a tax on earnings up to £69 per week; 5.5 percent on the employee and 8.5 percent on the employer. The government provides subsidies to the fund through direct supplements. Since April 1975 the fund to support industrial injuries and diseases has been fully integrated with all other social insurance funds.

Occupational Diseases
In order for a person to receive benefits for an occupational disease, the condition must be covered by the schedule of diseases that includes specific occupations and/or exposures. The only reason for qualifying this is that in certain instances employees have been successful in pursuing claims for diseases not on the schedule by terming them injuries due to accident. Thus the British experience is parallel to that of several of the American states. The British have adopted a rule, however, such that if the unscheduled disease cannot be traced to a specific incident but instead was caused by prolonged continuous exposure to a hazard (set at three months), then the

disablement is considered an "injury by process" and is not compensable. Since diseases such as Reynaud's Phenomenon, for example, are not on the schedule and usually occur after more than three months of continuing exposure, workers disabled by it cannot be compensated for it either as a disease or under the injury by accident provision. Such gaps in the system are an obvious though not a large-scale problem in the British law.

The British schedule as of January 1976 contained a listing of forty-nine sets of diseases. For each disease listed there is a description of the occupations associated with such diseases. Most listings tend to be quite broad, for example, for the disease of cadmium poisoning, the associated "occupation" is "exposure to cadmium fumes." In some instances, however, such as for the disease of occupational deafness, the covered occupations are extremely precise and narrow: "Any occupation involving (a) the use of pneumatic percussive tools or high speed grinding tools in the cleaning, dressing or finishing of cast metal or ingots, billets or blooms; or (b) the use of pneumatic percussive tools on metal in the shipbuilding and ship repairing industries; or (c) work wholly or mainly in the immediate vicinity of drop-forging plant or forging press plant engaged in the shaping of hot metal."

The British schedule lists only two infectious diseases (aside from those associated with contact with animals), tuberculosis and viral hepatitis (only added as of February 1976), and the associated occupations for each are specific. Several carcinogens are indicated on the schedule but frequently are associated with only a partially complete list of potential diseases. Mesotheliomas resulting from exposure to asbestos are on the schedule, but lung cancer resulting from asbestos is not. Squamous cell carcinoma of the skin is compensable for persons exposed to arsenic, but lung cancer due to arsenic exposure at the workplace is not. Beryllium is on the list but is not considered a carcinogen. Vinyl chloride is not yet on the schedule.

If a worker or survivor believes that an illness is a covered occupational disease, he files a claim with the local Social Security office, and the case falls under the management of an insurance officer. The insurance officer is statutorily independent of the ministry and is the only person able to decide whether benefits are to be paid. Three conditions must be met for the claim to be compensated: the disease must be on the list, the individual must have been in insurable employment in one of the specified occupations, and the disease must be due to the nature of the work. If the first two conditions are met, the third only rarely becomes an issue. Since the latter could be an issue, however, the schedule provides a rebuttable presumption in favor of the claimant. There are no minimum or recent exposure rules that must be met in England except in a few circumstances. In the case of occupational deafness, the worker must have been exposed to noise in a covered occupation for at least twenty years, and the claim must be made no more than one year beyond leaving such employment. Another special rule limits industrial injuries benefits for byssinosis to persons exposed in specified occupations for at least ten years and only when the person is permanently disabled.

The insurance officer usually asks the claimant to be examined by a "special doctor" who makes a report to him. The report essentially contains a diagnosis of the condition with a view toward establishing whether the illness is one on the schedule. If the medical evidence is not conclusive, the worker will be examined by a Medical Board, consisting of two physicians, at least one of whom is likely to be a specialist in the area of the condition in question. These physicians represent the Ministry of Social Security and report their findings to the insurance officer, but they are not government employees. They have their own medical practice and provide such services to the ministry for perhaps one morning a week. Their primary responsibility is to provide a diagnosis to determine whether the disease is prescribed, and they do not attempt to ascertain etiology except in cases of dermatitis. It is the Medical Board's task, also, to evaluate the extent of the disability.

Should the claimant be dissatisfied with the decisions of the insurance officer based on the findings of the Medical Board, an appeal must be made within three months to a Medical Appeal Tribunal that consists of two physicians and an attorney. (Appeals by claimants based on nonmedical issues may be appealed beyond the level of the insurance officer to a local tribunal within twenty-one days of the decision. The tribunal consists of an employer representative, a union representative, and a local attorney.) If the claimant wishes to appeal the decision of the Medical Appeal Tribunal, he may do so, and the case is heard by a National Insurance commissioner, who is appointed by the Crown. The commissioner is a full-time judge who hears only cases involving the Social Security System. The commissioner has discretion to hear a case or not, but the only issues that can be appealed to this level are matters of law and not of fact.

An exception occurs in cases involving pneumoconioses. The insurance officer usually directs a case to a physician drawn from a panel of specialists. If X-ray evidence is negative, the claim will be denied, but the matter can be heard on appeal by a two-member pneumoconiosis board. If there is some X-ray evidence of disease, the case also goes to such a board for evaluation. Unlike other disease cases, however, the decision of the board is conclusive and cannot be appealed—on medical grounds—to a Medical Appeal Tribunal. The reason for the bifurcated handling of disease claims is the special problems of pneumoconiosis, that is, a large number of claimants, a small number of medical specialists in the area, and the complicated nature of the disease and its diagnosis.

Very few cases ever hinge on the question of etiology because the schedule creates a strong, though rebuttable, presumption that covered diseases of those in listed employments are compensable. Medical issues are primarily determined by physicians and their judgment is final at the level of the Medical Appeal Tribunal.

The British Trades Union Congress (TUC) has a number of objections to this basic system. They object to the finality of medical questions at the Medical Appeal Tribunal level and that decisions at this level are frequently not fully explained or clarified. They also object to the lack of published decisions made in cases heard by the National Insurance commissioner. In 1972, for example, 2,106 appeals were decided at this level (not simply occupational diseases) and only twenty-three decisions were published. The TUC claims there are no known criteria for publishing such decisions.

Diseases are compensated only when it is determined that there is a loss of "physical or mental faculty," which the British construe as some impairment of the power to enjoy a "normal life." It is assessed by comparing the claimant's condition — as a consequence of the injury or disease — with that of a normal healthy person of the same age and sex. Thus disablement is not an economic concept but entirely a medical one. There are no benefits where the loss of faculty is below 1 percent; if an employee has elevated blood lead levels, but no loss of faculty, there is no compensation. There are exceptions to these practices. An individual diagnosed as having pneumoconiosis is assumed to have a loss of faculty and the minimum loss is considered as 10 percent. (Byssinosis cases are handled in a very special manner.) In cases of hearing loss there is no compensation unless the disablement is found to be 20 percent or more.

Since the schedule creates very strong presumptions for listed diseases and occupations, it is hardly surprising that the British schedule contains gaps in coverage. The primary responsibility for adding to or modifying the schedule lies with a subcommittee of the Industrial Injuries Advisory Council. The council consists of a chairperson and sixteen other appointees, four of whom are drawn from the labor community and four who represent management's views. The balance are drawn from other areas and most of them are physicians. Their recommendations for changes must be consistent with the directions of the Social Security Act of 1975 (Section 76(2)):

A disease or injury may be prescribed in relation to any employed earners if the Secretary of State is satisfied that — (a) it ought to be treated, having regard to its causes and incidence and any other relevant considerations, as a risk of their occupations and not as a risk common to all persons; and (b) it is such that, in the absence of special circumstances, the attribution of particular cases to the nature of the employment can be established or presumed with reasonable certainty.

Although the TUC continues to work to widen the schedule, recently pushing to include bronchitis, it appreciates that a virtually complete listing of all possible diseases and employments would undermine the current practice of the very strong presumption involving diseases and employments on the schedule. The TUC finds this aspect of the system satisfactory.

Other Programs

Aside from the available remedies already described, the majority of British workers are covered by provisions for sick pay, most of which are the results of collective bargaining. There are no hard data on the extent of coverage, however, the TUC reports on a 1964 study that estimated that 55 percent of the work force was covered, as well as a 1970 survey that indicated about 70 percent coverage.[1] Such schemes all provide for some offsets, partial or full, for benefits received under the National Insurance scheme. Sick pay benefits are also offset in the calculation of any awards for tort damages.

British workers may also attempt to supplement National Insurance benefits through civil remedies. Such actions are not related to the National Insurance scheme except that damage awards will be reduced by one-half of the benefits paid under the program for up to five years.

When the exclusive remedy was dropped in 1948, the traditional law was modified to enhance the possibility of a claimant's winning such a suit. The fellow-servant defense, that is, that injury was due to the negligence of another worker, was no longer permitted to be used by employers and the assumption of risk defense was sharply curtailed. The only traditional defense remaining of the "unholy trinity" was contributory negligence, which still is used and can serve to either defeat claims or, more commonly, reduce the size of damages awarded. To win such an action the employee, or a survivor, must prove that the employer was negligent and consequently caused the injury in question. A 1973 decision in the courts allowed damages to a worker who had contracted the unscheduled diseases bronchitis and emphysema, which were held to be the result of a workplace exposure caused by employer negligence.[2] Tort damages may be awarded for loss of earnings, loss of amenities including disability, pain and suffering, loss of life expectancy, and special expenses incurred.

There are no hard data available on the number of persons receiving damages. In a

Table 6.1
Distribution of settlements and court award

Amount of Damages (£)	Total Cases (%)
00– 99	20
100–249	25
250–499	18
500–749	10.5
750–999	6.5
1000 and over	19

Source: Trades Union Congress, for the Royal Commission on Civil Liability and Compensation for Personal Injury: Injuries in the Course of Employment, unpublished report, undated, p. 18.

survey in 1971 to 1972 of TUC members, it was estimated that 16 percent of the persons receiving industrial injury benefits also received damages, but some analysts have placed the appropriate proportion at under 10 percent and others have estimated it at above 16 percent.[3] Whatever the correct proportion is, the TUC further estimates that 95 percent of the recipients of such damage awards receive them through settlements with employers-insurers rather than through the courts.[4] The TUC survey for 1970 to 1971 found that there was a tendency for damage cases to involve the more serious injuries and illnesses. The distribution of awards reported is shown in table 6.1.

The average award was approximately £540.[5] British employers are required by the Employers Liability Act of 1969 to insure against tort liabilities. The TUC report cites a 1973 study (from the London School of Economics) that estimates the total costs of the tort system for industrial injuries and diseases at £60 million per year.[6] The costs of administering the system may be as high as 50 percent of the total insurance paid by employers.[7] The presence of such an adversary procedure makes the British experience in this sector comparable to all of workers' compensation in the American states.

Workers' compensation in Great Britain is not very closely tied to matters of occupational health. The primary responsibility for assuring that workers are employed in safe and healthful establishments falls upon the HM Factory Inspectorate and Health and Safety Commission. Workers are neither strongly urged nor effectively forced out of employment when continued exposures will exacerbate existing health problems. The Coal Board requires miners to regularly submit to X-rays and in several industries, nuclear power, lead, and ionizing radiation, workers must be periodically examined.

In broad terms the pattern of occupational disease cases in England is comparable to that of the United States and several other nations (table 6.2). New cases in 1974–1975 were approximately 2.3 percent of injuries due to accidents. The largest number of cases of diseases involve dermatitis. About one-third of the cases involve problems of the joints or inflammations of the hand and forearm. There are only a trivial number of cases involving infectious disease or cancer.

The data in table 6.2 do not indicate the number of claims brought that were denied nor any cases involving medical or other treatment but no time lost from work. The British data indicate that occupational diseases are more serious than injury-by-accident cases. The estimated median duration of incapacity for new cases of accidents and diseases in 1974–1975 was fifteen and eighteen days respectively for males, and sixteen and twenty-six days respectively for female workers.[8]

Table 6.2 does not include cases involving pneumoconioses. Unpublished data are available and demonstrate that such diseases represent a significant proportion of the

Table 6.2
Spells of certified incapacity commencing in 1974 to 1975, provisional data

Work-related accidents	577,000	
Prescribed diseases	13,585	(2.3% of accidents)
poisoning by lead	36	(0.3% of diseases)
squamous cell skin cancer	9	(0.1% of diseases)
bursitis or subcutaneous cellulitis, hand, knee, or elbow	1,126	(8.3% of diseases)
traumatic inflammation, tendons of hand or forearm	3,264	(24.0% of diseases)
tuberculosis	51	(0.4% of diseases)
inflammation or ulceration, mucous membrane of the mouth or upper respiratory passages due to dust, liquid, or vapor	35	(0.3% of diseases)
Noninfective dermatitis of external origin (excluding that due to ionizing particles or electromagnetic radiations)	8,929	(65.7% of diseases)
Other diseases	136	(1.0% of diseases)

Source: *Social Security Statistics 1975,* Department of Health and Social Security, U.K., 1977, tables 20.50, 20.59.

work load for program administrators. In 1974 there were 10,340 new claims and 18,244 examinations by the pneumoconiosis medical boards (this includes new cases and reevaluating older cases).[9] There were 914 new cases diagnosed by the medical boards as involving pneumoconioses. If such cases were added to the total 13,585, shown in table 6.2, they would account for over 6 percent of the number of new disease cases that year.

Summary

There is a workers' compensation system in England, however, it is significantly different than the one that set the pattern for many of the states in the United States. The availability of comparable benefits for workers that do not meet one of the tests of compensability provides a meaningful alternative to many workers. This system is entirely free of an adversary procedure, but the right of workers to sue employers means that many issues of safety and health are highly controversial.

The British do not compensate a large number of occupational disease cases even in the absence of an adversary process. In large part, the doors have been kept from opening widely by a schedule that is relatively restrictive and by special provisions, as in the cases of hearing loss (the twenty-year to one-year rules), byssinosis, etc. What distinguishes the British and American systems, however, is the very high degree of certainty that characterizes claims in the former. The use of strong, though rebuttable presumptions means that controversion need not occur commonly. Because of this and due to active union involvement and assistance to workers in need, there are very few cases involving attorneys outside the tort damages area.

France

The Workers' Compensation System

In 1898 the country's first workers' compensation law was put into effect. It replaced a fault system that had provided few injured workers or their survivors with compensation. From 1898 on occupational diseases posed a problem since the early law required that an "accident" must have occurred, yet there was no definition of the term in the legislation. In 1919 the law was explicitly expanded to cover occupational diseases.

The present French statute, along with virtually all of France's social insurance programs, was restructured after World War II so that the current workers' compensation law is essentially the one that was passed in 1946. Separate programs to deal with work injury provide coverage to workers in agriculture, mining, railroads, public utilities, the public sector, seamen, and self-employed persons. Few persons who work are not covered by one workers' compensation program or another. No distinction exists either in coverage or the handling of a claim between native and foreign persons working in France.

Benefits and Financing
Benefits are paid to workers with industrial injuries or occupational diseases. Workers unable to work for either reason collect compensation of 50 percent of lost wages subject to a maximum from the first day for up to twenty-eight days and from then, 66.66 percent of lost wages subject to a maximum from the twenty-ninth day on. (These benefits closely parallel those provided to workers under the national sickness insurance program, though the maximum potential benefits are lower under the more inclusive program.)

When a condition stabilizes, a permanently disabled worker begins to draw disability benefits that are the product of the previous wage and the degree of disability. Compensation in France is provided for disability (the socioeconomic loss), not for impairment (the physiological loss only). For disabilities ranging from 10 percent to 50 percent, the benefit is set at one-half the level of disability times the previous average annual wage (subject to a maximum). For disabilities in excess of 50 percent, the formula for benefits is set at 25 percent, plus 1.5 times the increment over 50 percent, times the worker's previous annual wage level (subject to a maximum). All medical expenses are covered under workers' compensation in France, which makes the program more generous than the national health insurance for non-occupational illnesses or injuries.

By American standards social insurance payroll taxes on employers in France are very high. Although subject to a maximum wage level for purposes of calculating such taxes, the total tax rates on employers, exclusive of workers' compensation, is approximately 30 percent of payroll. The workers' compensation premium varies by the firm's risk category (in some instances based on the firm's own experience) and the size of the establishment and is paid solely by the employer. Small establishments pay premiums based on industry experience, medium size establishments pay rates based both on industry and their own experience, and large establishments pay on the basis of their own previous record over the past three years. On the average, a French employer pays a tax of about 3.5 percent of payroll for workers' compensation.

Occupational Diseases
Diseases in France are covered by workers' compensation with few exceptions, if and only if they conform to a highly detailed schedule. The schedule is complex and, at

times, quite comprehensive. Sixty-four "diseases" are enumerated. Not each of these is a disease, since many of the listings are actually hazardous substances; item number 4 is simply "illnesses caused by benzene and its homologues (toluene, xylenes, and so forth)." It is more appropriate to say that the French schedule contains sixty-four tables, each covering a different class of substances or diseases. For each set of diseases or hazards the table presents at least three things in matrix form: specific illnesses (a list of nine is in the benzene table), the time period from last exposure for which the workers' compensation system is liable (a separate listing for each sickness associated with benzene is in the table, ranging from three days to ten years), and a list of tasks which would be presumed to be linked to the disease. Because the list is so detailed and the system is not "mixed" (a disease must be listed in order for workers' compensation to be applicable), changes in the list occur relatively frequently. These changes, however, may take the form of minor modifications, such as the rule on time limits since last exposure or in the work tasks (occupations) shown.

The French schedule has several significant omissions. Heart disease is not shown, though it may be compensated occasionally as an injury due to accident. Coal workers' pneumoconiosis does not appear, but some cases are being compensated as pulmonary fibrosis (since some free silica is present in the coal mines). To clear up potential problems caused by this indirect means, the disease will probably be added to the schedule shortly. Byssinosis does not appear and is likely not to be compensated in France. Arsenic is found in the table (number 20) but there is no indication that it is recognized as carcinogenic. Urinary cancers are associated with contact with aromatic amines, however, the last exposure must have occurred within the previous fifteen years in order to be compensable. This may be adequate for the coverage of some workers; it is not long enough to provide protection to all persons previously exposed to such workplace hazards.

Other shortcomings exist with the French schedule. Minimum exposure rules exist for a few listed diseases, including a five-year rule for pneumoconioses, though there is a provision that this can be waived by a panel of three doctors in cases of silicosis and asbestosis. There is also a five-year last (or most recent) exposure rule for the pneumoconioses, which is adequate for most workers but serves as an absolute bar to compensation for some others. Where a worker is disabled by a disease not on the schedule, he is not barred from civil action against his employer, though such cases are very rare.

When several factors, including preexisting conditions, contribute to causing a disease as long as one of the factors is drawn from the schedule, the worker will be compensated. The presence of the other contributing factors, however, can reduce the extent of the disability award. Cigarette smoking would not be considered a contributing factor so it has no direct impact on the disability rating.

There is flexibility in the French schedule in the description of occupations or work tasks. Aside from being very open-ended, in some claims they are construed to be indicative rather than definitive. When a worker claims to suffer from an occupational disease that arose while he was employed in a task not shown in the table, the person need only receive certification from his employer or a labor inspector that he had exposure to a (listed) hazard on the job. (Obviously the exposure and a specifically listed illness must match up in a table.) In cases involving hearing loss or infectious diseases, however, the list of occupations is definitive and must be adhered to rigorously. Since the French use a two-stage hearing-loss test for compensability, and the second test comes only after the employee has been removed from the hazard for six months, it is not surprising that few claims for hearing loss materialize.

The schedule is flexible when a claim would be covered by a planned revision that has not been officially put into effect. In such transitionary periods the claim may be allowed but it is rare.

Claims for workers' compensation in France go through the regional or national Social Security Administration. The law requires that doctors report all cases of illness that are occupational (even if not on the schedule) to a labor inspector or other government agent for reporting to the ministers of labor and social affairs. In many instances compliance with the law triggers the filing of a claim by a sick worker. Cases that are appealed from the social security office can go to the courts, though the procedure depends on the issue involved. There is a separate, technical Social Security Court to hear appeals on certain issues, such as the extent of disability, regardless of whether the cause is injury or illness. It is not unusual to have disparate testimony from doctors representing either the claimant or the government fund. Issues of causality, however, are not heard in this court and are generally resolved by the court's appointment of a medical expert whose decision is binding and cannot be appealed further. Decisions of this court may be reversed by a general appellate court but only on matters of law.

Revisions in the schedule occur frequently because of its significance in handling occupational diseases. An Industrial Hygiene Commission made up of civil servants, technical specialists, and representatives of labor and management has a subcommittee on industrial diseases. The subcommittee has working groups composed of physicians and health personnel. Recommendations for changing the schedule come from the commission and are made to the minister of labor, who seeks the advice of the National Social Security Fund whose directors come from management and the unions. Advice is sought also from the Conseil d'Etat on the legal implications of modifications in the schedule. The process of change involves the key interest groups at one stage or another. It takes from two to four years to make an addition to or change in the schedule. Even in the case of vinyl chloride and angiosarcoma, when the matter developed quite quickly in the scientific community, it took more than a year of activity to have it added to the schedule.

Other Programs
There are a variety of social insurance and other transfer payment programs available to injured or sick workers whose disability does not arise from the workplace. Totally disabled workers may receive 50 percent of their average annual earnings for the previous ten years with minimum and maximum salary levels set at the same levels that exist for workers' compensation. Partial disability benefits and cash benefits are also available during periods of illness. Unlike workers' compensation these other social insurance programs require that the person work for some time period before coverage begins. Although coverage is not as wide nor benefits as large, a disabled worker who does not collect workers' compensation usually has a slightly less attractive alternative in terms of medical-health costs and income maintenance.

Programs to hire the handicapped are specified by law. Any firm employing ten or more workers must reserve 3 percent of its positions for the handicapped. This has led some employers to interpret the term handicapped very broadly. All firms employing 5,000 or more employees are required to create and maintain sheltered workshops. Firms have been made to comply with the letter of the law, but a number of them do little more than maintain such facilities. Workers who are sixty or older and disabled are rarely rehabilitated and are encouraged to seek retirement and a public pension.

Occupational safety and health in France are maintained in several ways. The Labor Inspectorate has a relatively small staff charged with enforcing a variety of labor codes in areas including wages, strikes, and industrial relations, as well as safety and health conditions. They are empowered to raise payroll tax rates on employers operating dangerous enterprises or shut down particularly dangerous establishments. In recent years employers operating very hazardous plants where accidents occurred have been jailed, with substantial notoriety given to these cases.

Aside from the Labor Inspectorate there are regional and local representatives of the social insurance fund who provide technical assistance and consultation to firms in matters of safety and health. These funds employ approximately 400 engineers, hygienists, and other technicians, some of whom are specialists in certain types of industry.

Plant safety and health are also the responsibility of the occupational physician. Whenever a firm hires a new employee, a preemployment (sometimes during the employment probationary period) physical examination must be provided. A plant doctor usually determines what the examination should entail, but for certain occupations the law requires that the examination include X-rays or other specific tests. Quarry workers and sand blasters must receive chest X-rays at least every six months, workers exposed to iron oxide and asbestos and rubber and chemical workers must be examined at least once each year. Approximately 5,000 occupational physicians exist in France, about one-half of whom devote a majority of their work time to this practice. Occupational medicine is a required course of study in French medical schools and every French firm has its own physician either employed by or under retainer to it.

It is difficult to force an employer or employee to stop exposing that worker to a hazard that has already shown signs of undermining his health. The employer is encouraged where possible to transfer such a worker. At one time such a worker received a bonus from the Social Security Fund to change jobs if there was no transfer available to him within the firm, but the program no longer exists. If the employer releases the worker, rather than transferring him, the employee may become eligible for disability benefits under workers' compensation.

Another factor that some believe may contribute to reducing industrial illnesses in France is the physician-reporting requirement. Medium-sized and large establishments are partially or fully experience rated, which may lead to fewer injuries and diseases due to work.

Experience
Data in table 6.3, drawn from a limited portion of the French labor force and only from cases involving the payment of some indemnity, reveal that occupational diseases were only a tiny part of the compensation picture in 1973. Illnesses accounted for less than one-half of 1 percent of all cases and fewer than 1 percent of work-caused fatalities (excluding traffic accidents). The exclusion of data on the mining sector is significant since over 3,500 cases of silicosis began to receive compensation in 1973. Of the 4,580 compensable cases of disease in 1973, 2,640 came from only two industrial sectors, construction and metals. The sources of many of these are shown in table 6.4, which also indicates, broadly, the causes of the eighteen recorded fatality claims in 1973.

Table 6.3
Workers' compensation in France, 1973

Covered wage earners[a]	13.5 million
Accidents[b]	
Accidents with lost work time	1.1 million
Fatalities	2,246
Days lost due to temporary incapacity	29.0 million
Occupational diseases	
Illnesses recorded	4,580
Permanent disabilities	1,681
Fatalities	18
Days lost due to temporary incapacity	330,500

Source: Ministry of Labor, unpublished memorandum, undated.
a. Excludes separately funded and administered programs such as mining, railroads, government, and agriculture.
b. Excludes traffic accidents.

Table 6.4
Sources of compensable disease claims and fatalities, 1973

Claims compensated (n = 4,580)[a]	
Silicosis (exclusive of mining)	607
Viral hepatitis	533
Dermatoses (due to lubricants)	230
Ethylene chlorides	210
Lead	199
Bursitis (knees)	174
Noise	147
Brucellosis	121
Aromatic amines	103
Epoxy resins	100
Fatalities by source (n = 18)	
Benzene	8
X-rays	5
Lead	2
Viral hepatitis	2
Asbestosis	1

Source: Ministry of Labor, unpublished memorandum, undated.
a. Shown only when 100 or more cases involved.

Summary
A prevailing view in Europe is that occupational safety and health as well as workers' compensation in France are far more advanced in statutory form than in practice. It was not possible to assess the extent to which French law is actually enforced. The system is not as free of dispute and contention as others in Europe but is more so than in the United States. The French schedule is applied rigorously so that employer-union disputes focus on the development of the schedule and not on its application. Aside from silicosis, there are few claims for occupational disease in France. Although many of the diseases on the French schedule have only recently become recognized in the United States, they involve few claims, particularly ones involving fatalities. The differential between survivors' benefits under workers' compensation and that available in other situations is sufficiently large to make it worthwhile to seek such claims. Nevertheless, there are far more public alternatives available to support injured or sick workers in France than in the United States. The French schedule misses a number of diseases that could be compensated in other western European nations.

Belgium

The Workers' Compensation System
Belgium is the only country studied in this book that totally bifurcates the compensation of occupational diseases from injuries due to accidents at the workplace. For purposes of financing and administration the approaches taken for the compensation of either are totally separated. Belgium could serve as a model for those who advocate that occupational diseases in the United States should be dealt with by a system not tied to a larger workers' compensation system.

The first workers' compensation law in Belgium was passed in 1903 without provision for occupational diseases. In 1927 a new law was passed that set up an institution, the Fund for Occupational Diseases (FMP), to compensate workers with such illnesses. Coverage of workers in Belgium is very broad, and employers are required to secure insurance, either through private carriers or in some instances through public associations, for injuries due to workplace accidents. Protection for occupational diseases is compulsory and only available through the FMP. With this bifurcated compensation system, together with approximately twenty-five different public or semipublic insurance schemes covering various related programs such as sickness, disability, veterans' pensions, and family allowances, there is a potential problem of overlapping jurisdictions. The issue is exacerbated by the presence of both private and public insurers in programs that inevitably cover neighboring territories. Claims rejected under one system are frequently filed subsequently with other systems. There is a tendency, however, for the public sector's FMP to accept jurisdiction readily in cases that might be covered by other insurance programs, including injuries that might be covered under workers' compensation. When a dispute arises over which system of insurance has responsibility, it is resolved in the courts. An effort is made, however, not to delay compensating a claimant where the only matter at issue is that of determining the responsible carrier. When this is only one of several issues in dispute, there may be delays for the worker in receiving payments.

Benefits and Financing

Benefits for occupational diseases are funded by a uniform rate payroll tax of 0.75 percent, assessed on all payrolls (subject to a wage maximum), excluding civil servants, the self-employed, and railway workers, and paid by employers. The Belgian government also has provided special subsidies for the program, for example, 60 percent of the costs of miners' pneumoconiosis is paid from a federal fund. Otherwise the fund is self-supporting and tax rates have not been raised for some time.

Benefits for injuries or diseases arising from work are essentially the same. There is no incentive for the worker to prefer having a disability labeled an occupational disease or an injury. Benefits can be collected from the first day of incapacity. The wage replacement rate for temporary total disability is full pay for the first week of disability and thereafter 90 percent of the worker's average daily wage. When the condition stabilizes or the individual returns to work, he may be eligible for a permanent disability award. The cash benefit is set as a proportion of the worker's previous annual wage subject to a maximum equal to the extent of disability; a 75 percent award for a 75 percent disability.

In the case of occupational diseases the worker's wage is considered from the time the disease was thought to have begun to be manifested. Supplementary benefits are available to workers with a very low income to assure minimum benefit levels. Disability ratings are set on the basis of medical and in some instances economic criteria. Unlike some other systems, permanent disability benefits can be paid for disability ratings as low as 1 percent. Benefits can be supplemented with an allowance for persons who attend a disabled worker, but the total benefit may not exceed 150 percent of the worker's average previous wage. When the disability rating is below 10 percent, lump-sum payments are compulsory at the end of periodic review periods.

Surviving spouses receive pensions that are set at 30 percent of the deceased worker's base wage. Orphans receive 15 percent each of the base wage with a maximum set at 45 percent (three children) and an overall maximum in the case of death of 75 percent where there is a spouse and at least three children. Pensions can also be paid to other surviving family members.

Occupational Diseases

There is a special need for a careful delineation between injuries and diseases since occupational diseases are compensated from a different source than are injuries due to workplace accidents. The Belgians attempt to accomplish this by using an exclusive schedule of diseases instead of through rigorous definitions. Diseases that are unscheduled are either not compensated or in some instances are compensated as accidents. Heart disease, for example, except where it is associated with a listed disease such as coal workers' pneumoconiosis, can only be compensated as an accidental injury.

The Belgian schedule is very similar to that of Switzerland. Its first portion lists approximately fifty substances or classes of substances and for most identifies industries (in a few cases occupations) in which disease would be covered. For these substances specific diseases are not listed. The second part of the list covers skin illnesses caused by substances not listed elsewhere on the schedule. No specific diseases are identified (though skin cancer is specifically mentioned), but instead a variety of substances, industries, and occupations are identified, and some are listed as subsets of each other. The third part of the schedule covers occupational illnesses caused by the inhalation of substances and agents not listed elsewhere. The list includes silicosis, asbestosis, and other specific diseases and for each identifies industries and/or occupations covered. Curiously, it specifically lists lung cancer associated with asbestosis, though some medical evidence has shown that the former can occur in the absence of the latter. In the third section the schedule also covers "pulmonary disorders caused by the inhalation of dusts of cotton, lint, hemp, jute, sisal, and bagasse" and although the substances are rather specific, a variety of diseases could be covered. The next section of the schedule covers infectious and parasitic diseases. Specific diseases are listed and for each, specific industries and occupations are identified. Tetanus is specifically listed but coverage is available only to sewage workers. The list does have substantial gaps. The final section of the schedule covers illnesses caused by physical agents. Only four sets of such agents are covered: ionizing radiation, noise, compression, and vibration. Agents such as sunlight, heat, and cold are excluded.

The list is exclusive, however, the FMP has used some flexibility in interpreting and using the list subject to explicit government direction. Suicide has been compensated when committed by a person with disabling silicosis. Mental disorders are compensated when they occurred in workers previously exposed to carbon disulfide, trichloroethylene, and so forth. Emphysema is compensable for workers in occupations that exposed them to cadmium, manganese, or vanadium. Welders will not be compensated for emphysema unless they have been exposed to nitrous oxide. Asthma is treated as an occupational disease when it occurs in workers having exposures to certain hazards appearing on the schedule. A few of these practices are tied to minimum exposure rules. Bronchitis and asthma are compensable for persons working with flax for ten years or more. It is presumed not to be an occupational disease when the exposure was for less than ten years. Workers exposed to asbestos are compensated for lung cancer only in the presence of asbestosis, according to the law. The Belgians will compensate mesothelioma of the pleura but not of the peritoneal cavity in workers exposed to asbestos. Flexibility of the schedule allowed Belgium to compensate vinyl chloride workers with angiosarcoma when the problem became known without changing the schedule itself.

Decisions of the sort described above are made by the FMP. These emerge from a Technical Council of the FMP named by the Crown in the following way: Four physicians are selected from lists submitted by each of the country's major universities. Two physicians are selected from a list prepared by the FMP's administrative council. Two other physicians, whose fields are hygiene and occupational medicine, are appointed from names provided by the Ministry of Labor. An engineer and a chemist are selected on the basis of their skills in the area of disease prevention, two civil servants with skills in social insurance, and the head of medical services of the FMP are also named. This council not only has the basic responsibility for interpreting the list, it also is charged with recommending changes in the schedule to the minister of Social Affairs. The minister can modify the schedule at his discretion and without receiving support from the Parliament. Acceptance by the minister of the Technical Council's recommendations are not pro forma and some have not been accepted.

Once a disease is on the schedule or accepted through interpretation of the schedule by the FMP, the worker has no responsibility for proving etiology. The worker must simply demonstrate that he has been exposed to the hazard in question. Belgian law assumes that the worker was fit at the time of hire, so that given the evidence that an exposure has occurred and a sickness is diagnosed, the worker can expect to be compensated. For compensation to be denied the FMP would have the burden of proof that the disease was not work related and the FMP rarely, if ever, pursues such a course.

The FMP is a largely autonomous institution, directed by a fifteen member board selected by the Crown. A president is appointed (presumably a neutral) as are fourteen other members, seven each drawn from a list submitted by employers and workers' organizations. This group has the responsibility for running the FMP, but the technical matters pertaining to occupational disease are in the hands of the Technical Council.

Decisions by the FMP may be appealed by claimants to a Labor Court. In such instances the court will call on its own medical expert and rarely find against the decision of its own appointed specialist. From there appeals may go to the Supreme Court but only on matters of law and not fact. Even when the claimant loses an appeal, court costs are borne by the FMP and not the worker.

Other Programs

The FMP administers a significant social insurance program, and it is not the center of controversy as such an institution would be in the United States. The reason for this is that sick and disabled workers in Belgium who are not compensated by FMP have significant alternative sources of income. Employees who are unable to work due to illness are entitled to 100 percent wage replacement from their employer for seven to thirty days (depending on their occupations) and 60 percent of their earnings (subject to a maximum lower than that under workers' compensation) for up to one year. If the individual is disabled beyond one year, he is entitled to an invalidity pension set at 43.5 percent of his wage (where there are no dependents) up to 65 percent of the wage (with dependents and subject to a maximum). Although coverage is not as broad—due to minimum working time requirements—nor benefits as large, the vast majority of workers have acceptable alternatives if they are denied compensation. Also the FMP is aware that if it makes an adverse decision the claimant has other sources of social insurance that are close to comparable to workers' compensation benefits. Moreover, the costs of medical and health care are provided for almost all Belgian workers, regardless of the source of the illness. These benefits, however, can expire before workers' compensation benefits would.

Belgium has active rehabilitation and reemployment programs. Firms with twenty or more employees are required to provide a certain fraction of their positions to the handicapped. The Belgians are especially active in moving persons away from hazards that cause workers to begin to manifest symptoms of occupational disease. Even when the employee has no "symptoms" but begins to show some predisposition to a disease or some radiological changes occur, the worker is "urged" to change jobs if he is unable to transfer to another site in the firm where he will not continue to be exposed. If the worker refuses to move, he may be told that he can count on workers' compensation only for the existing level of disability, if any, and none for any higher level that might result from continued exposure to the hazard. When a worker does change jobs, he receives 100 percent of his previous wage for three months even if he suffers no loss of earnings at all in making the job change. The Belgians believe that such a bonus for prevention may, in the long run, save the fund money, and it is consistent with the view that prevention is more desirable than compensation. After the three months pass, the worker is eligible for compensation based on earnings lost when changing to a more healthful but lower-paying job. Workers who have unhealthy (for them) employments receive counseling, job training, and encouragement to find other work. If no work is found, the person is eligible for unemployment insurance along with workers' compensation. Belgium also applies this program, the Écartement (separation), to pregnant women if they or their unborn babies are at risk due to an occupational hazard. In 1974 an écartement was proposed in 1,327 cases, and 1,084 of them were accepted. Such écartements were proposed in 498 cases involving skin problems, 387 cases involving lead, 140 cases of pneumoconioses, 124 cases involving hearing loss, and the balance in other areas.[10]

Occupational health is a responsibility given to the plant doctors. Every enterprise in the country must have a designated physician either in its employ or under contract. Small firms usually use doctors through intra or interindustry services. Belgium has approximately 1,000 occupational physicians (a labor force of about 2.5 million in 1975). The system, which only began to operate in 1968, involves the plant doctor providing preemployment and periodic examinations, as well as taking some responsibility for health and safety. Originally it was anticipated that the physician would pass on the safety of new products and processes in the plant and help oversee safety and health practices in the shop. That aspect of the program is less ambitious today in most enterprises, and physicians are largely involved in examining, diagnosing, and treating workers. The Ministry of Labor and not the FMP coordinates the plant doctor program. The FMP, therefore, is in a deferential position in dealing with the doctors and providing them with information and research findings.

Experience

Substantial data exist on occupational diseases in Belgium due to the bifurcated approach to workers' compensation. Since the FMP handles only occupational disease cases, its own annual report is filled with material pertaining exclusively to such illnesses. In 1974, 10,328 claims were filed, 94 percent from male workers and 36 percent from foreign nationals.[11] During 1974 the FMP made 15,167 decisions based on the initial

Table 6.5
Number of cases accepted for reparations by cause, 1974

Cause of Disease	Temporary Total	Permanent Incapacity	Fatalities
Chemical agents	166	6	12
Skin diseases caused by chemicals not otherwise shown	159	4	6
Inhalation of substances not otherwise shown	0	3,275	1,869
(Silicosis)	0	3,228	1,859
Infectious or parasitic	151	0	2
Physical agents	1	86	0
Total	477	3,371	1,889

Source: Rapport Annuel, Exercice 1974, (Brussels: Fonds des Maladies Professionnelles), pp. S-2–S-4.

filing of claims (as compared to reassessing the extent of disability, for example) and rejected 6,557 cases (43.2 percent). At least 70 percent of the rejections were based on a determination by the FMP that the worker was not suffering from an occupational disease. If one excludes silicosis in coal miners (which in Belgium includes coal workers' pneumoconiosis), there were 4,741 first decisions made by the FMP in 1974, of which 3,038 (64 percent) were rejected for compensation.[12] In 1974, 626 cases were brought to the labor courts and 949 appeals were decided by that court.[13] Of those, 528 (56 percent) involved the court's modifying or rejecting a decision of the FMP, but many of these did not involve the basic issue of compensability. More than 44 percent of the cases modifying or rejecting an FMP decision involved the question of the extent of disability.

A major source of occupational disease in Belgium is the mines. Mining has been a declining industry in Belgium for a number of years (150,000 miners out of a labor force of 2 million in 1958, and only 30,000 miners were employed out of 2.8 million in 1975), but claims continue to come in from exposures incurred in earlier years. In 1963 the FMP began to compensate miners for pneumoconioses, and from 1964 to 1972 there were 130,422 claims for such diseases.

The data in table 6.5 describe the incidence of occupational disease in Belgium based on claims accepted in 1974. It is evident that the occupational disease problem in Belgium is almost entirely one of silicosis (including coal workers' pneumoconiosis). Of the 1,889 new fatalities accepted by the FMP in 1974, all but 30 are due to silicosis. And of the 3,371 new cases involving a permanent incapacity, 3,228 (96 percent) were due to silicosis.

The relatively small number of claims for skin disorders is due to three factors. A number of cases are included with illnesses due to specific chemical agents and, hence, are included in row 1. A number of workers disabled by a skin condition due to an "accident," such as a splash burn due to a caustic agent, are compensated but not as occupational diseases. Many relatively minor skin cases never come before the FMP since the worker receives 100 percent of his wage from his employer during an initial period of disability. Thus many cases that would involve workers' compensation in other countries never enter the Belgian compensation program.

The relatively small number of deaths compensated, aside from silicosis, occurs in part because heart cases are only compensated as injuries due to accident. Belgian employers are not experience rated and so have little or no stake in fighting claims for occupational diseases. Despite some limitations of the schedule, the very small number of cases of permanent disability and death reflect either the absence of a problem or the inability of medical science to detect them. The absence of such cases in Belgium cannot be attributed to efforts by employers or insurers to deny compensation to worthy claimants nor the lack of an industrial base that would expose workers to a variety of occupational hazards. There is a striking parallel between the United States and Belgium in the enormous volume of claims that developed when the laws covering coal workers' pneumoconiosis were broadly extended. It is instructive that a relatively liberal system such as Belgium's has shown no other signs of substantial claims outside the limited area of mining.

Summary

Historically, occupational diseases have been relegated to a minor area of workers' compensation in most countries. With 98 percent or more of the claims involving injuries due to accidents, occupational diseases were a neglected area in the compensation programs of most countries. Belgium created entirely separate systems and so has assured that professional and institutional attention be given to the area of health and compensation.

The Belgians have removed the controversy between employers and workers over the troublesome and complex questions of etiology, diagnosis, preexisting conditions, and the like by totally separating the financing of compensation and payment of benefits. Critics of such a separation will focus on the removal of incentives for employers to maintain healthy working environments. Firms that create disease potential do not bear a proportionate share of the costs of maintaining the system, and some economists may argue that the system will produce excessive illnesses. Neither the Belgians nor other Europeans, however, believe there is a particularly high incidence of disease in that country. The system is far from harsh, and occupational diseases constitute a small problem for the country by absolute standards or relative to accidents and work injuries, as long as the historic problem of the mines is held aside.

There is a problem of workers selecting the appropriate compensation jurisdiction. The requirement that disease claims conform to the schedule prevents chaos. In this way the system has prevented the largest share of those workers who are denied compensation in one forum from automatically seeking benefits in another. Both systems can work in a less stressful environment aware that uncompensated claims do not mean that the worker has no reasonable alternatives.

Benefits in the Belgian law are clear and the proportion of lost earnings replaced is high. The system may be judged as a strict one on the basis of the restrictive schedule, but the program is fair to Belgian workers. The FMP and the system for dealing with occupational illnesses are sensitive to their responsibilities and the needs of disabled workers.

Denmark

The Workers' Compensation System
The forerunner of the present Danish workers' compensation system was a liability system that first gave way in 1898 with the passage of the Industrial Injuries Insurance Act. That law covered only certain trades and industries and was gradually supplemented by other statutes extending protection to other classes of workers. The Industrial Injuries Insurance Act of 1916 consolidated each of the statutes and required that every employer covered by the act purchase insurance from a state approved (private) carrier. The law was the basis for the contemporary Danish workers' compensation system. In a major revision in 1933 occupational diseases came under the system. The present law compensates workers, according to a no-fault principle, for illnesses and injuries arising out of and in the course of employment. The program is administered centrally but financed largely through the use of private carriers.

Coverage under the Danish law is very broad. It includes some self-employed individuals, working wives of employers, state and local government workers, and residents and inmates of workhouses, mental hospitals, preventive detention centers, and prisons. Private employers are required to have insurance, which must be purchased from the small number (perhaps three dozen) of mutual liability or stock companies that the government has approved. A second method of insurance, found in limited situations such as the fishing and shipping industries, is the use of insurance associations for all firms in the industry. A few employers are permitted by the Minister of Social Affairs to self-insure. When an employer is not insured, the firm is liable to a disabled worker for compensation costs, but if the firm is insolvent the Directorate of Industrial Injuries Insurance (within the Ministry of Social Affairs) compensates the worker out of a fund assessed against all insurers.

Workers' compensation insurance covers disabilities that reduce or limit one's working capacity due to injuries and illnesses arising out of and in the course of employment. Injuries incurred while going or coming to work or (despite the no-fault system) caused by the worker due to intoxication, gross negligence, or by failing to observe existing safety rules are not compensated. Not only does the latter undermine the customary no-fault approach to workers' compensation, where the employer has been grossly negligent, the employee has a right to sue for civil damages. Suits are not common.

Benefits and Financing
The Industrial Injuries Insurance provides five types of benefits: medical treatment and rehabilitation, daily cash benefits, an industrial injuries benefit, survivors' benefits, and funeral benefits. The directorate actively supervises medical care and rehabilitation, and a worker who refuses to submit to recommended treatment may lose some or all of his right to compensation. Daily benefits replace three-quarters of the worker's lost wages, subject to a maximum, payable after a three-day waiting period. When the employer provides sick pay equivalent to wages during time lost, the employer is entitled to the daily cash benefit. These benefits are paid until the worker returns to work at his predisability level or remuneration, death, or when the condition stabilizes and a disability determination is made.

If a worker suffers an injury that reduces his earnings capacity by 5 percent or more, he is entitled to an industrial injuries benefit. The decision regarding this is made within one year of the time of the injury but may be delayed as long as three years. When a worker has a 100 percent loss of earnings capacity, he receives an annual pension of two-thirds of his previous earnings. For partial disability, benefits are also determined as two-thirds of loss of earnings capacity. No such benefit is payable when the disability is determined as 0 to 5 percent. When it falls between 5 and 50 percent, the pension is paid as a lump sum, and above 50 percent it is paid as an annual pension.

Survivors' benefits are paid when the employee's injury is fatal. Surviving spouses, without dependent children, receive 50 percent of the worker's wage for the first two years after death, and this falls to 30 percent in subsequent years. The size of the award increases if there are additional dependents. In no case can benefits exceed 50 percent of the deceased worker's wage after the first two years have passed. A surviving widow is given a lump sum equivalent to three years of benefits on remarriage, and payments cease thereafter. Funeral benefits are also provided under the statute.

Benefits paid on a continuing basis to disabled workers or to survivors are indexed to the cost-of-living. The government provides funds to cover adjustments for injuries that occurred prior to April 1, 1947.

Costs of compensation are borne by employers only, except that the state provides a subsidy for the premiums paid by very small employers. The government regulates insurance rates and since 1927 has operated under a rule requiring that at least 75 percent of the premiums received be applied to benefit payments. When a carrier's premium income exceeds benefit payouts by more than one-third, the excess must be returned to policy holders. Individual firms are not experience rated in Denmark, but high risk industries can be subjected to higher premiums.

Occupational Diseases

On July 1, 1976, the Danish law was modified so that coverage is no longer being limited to those occupational diseases appearing on their schedule. The new law has moved the Danes into virtual conformity with the European Economic Community (EEC) recommendations. The list is almost the same and the system is now "mixed"; diseases not on the schedule may be compensated. A disease is considered occupational when, according to medical and technical opinion, a worker has a higher degree of risk of contracting it than an ordinary person. The schedule links certain diseases to specified occupations or industries. Occupations or industries are identified with specified diseases, and the former are cited as examples and are not exclusive. Until now only persons in those medical-technical occupations cited would be eligible for compensation for infectious diseases. Under the new "mixed" system, other employees may now find such diseases compensable.

There is very little or no chance that compensation will be denied when a scheduled disease is contracted. It is too early to determine what the impact will be of opening up the system in 1976 to unscheduled illnesses. When the disease is not scheduled, the burden of proof shifts to the claimant, whereas the presence of a scheduled disease created a very strong presumption — that has been rarely challenged — in the worker's favor.

When an individual believes that he has an occupationally caused illness, he notifies the National Social Security Office, an arm of the Ministry of Social Affairs. The ministry provides the claimant with the name of a physician who examines the worker and reports to the agency. Hospitalization is free in Denmark and most medical expenses are provided by one insurance arrangement or another, however, if a specialist's medical fee is not already covered, the insurance carrier will be responsible in cases where the illness is deemed occupational. If the physician and the social security office believe that an occupational disease exists, the ministry notifies the employer and the insurer, who may appeal, as may the worker if the judgment is that there is no compensable claim. Such appeals go to the directorate of Industrial Injuries Insurance, located within the Ministry of Social Affairs. From this level further appeals may be made to the twelve-member Industrial Injuries Insurance Council, whose chairperson is appointed by the Crown. Two council members must be physicians, one a surgeon and the other a neurologist or a psychiatrist, and the other members are drawn from management and labor. Decisions of the council are final. Certain questions of law but no issue of fact may be appealed from the directorate level directly to the minister of Social Affairs and then may be appealed in the courts. Matters of fact are initially and solely determined within the Ministry of Social Affairs.

Practically no cases, according to the ministry, are formally appealed by insurers or employers. Employees are more likely to appeal decisions, primarily on the issue of extent of disability. Hearings and appeals are not held in an adversary manner and attorneys rarely are involved in such cases. The directorate requests information needed to make a determination, and disputes are not common.

For several reasons the date of the injury may be significant to the claimant. The relevant date for purposes of disease cases involves either the date when symptoms were first manifested, or the date a physician informs a worker that a disablement is work connected, or the date when the disease results in repeated periods of lost time from work. The National Social Security Office is required by statute to select the date most beneficial to the claimant.

According to Danish practice, there is no apportionment among employers or carriers, and the last employer generally takes full responsibility for a claim. There is apportionment in cases where a work-related disability combines with a preexisting noncompensable condition to cause a loss of earnings capacity. In this situation only the loss due to the work-related disease is compensated.

The system operates on an earnings capacity loss principle, so there are no benefits provided for diseases involving reproduction, such as miscarriages, still births, and infant abnormalities. Diseases that cause less than a 5 percent loss in earnings capacity are not compensated (except during periods of temporary total disability).

Prior to July 1, 1976, the exclusive schedule of occupational disease could be modified only by statute. Under the new law, the schedule is no longer exclusive and can be altered administratively by the National Social Security Office. At least once every two years, the entire schedule must be reevaluated by this office. The minister of social affairs appoints an advisory committee of seven persons, each appointed for three years, to assist in the process. The committee's membership must be selected from persons recommended by the following groups: one member recommended by the National Social Security Office, one from the National Health Service, one from the Labor Inspectorate, two members recommended by the Danish Employers' Confederation, and two from the National Confederation of Danish Trade Unions. It is not evident why the

Table 6.6
Compensated occupational diseases

Silicosis	46
Lead poisoning	6
Skin disorders	229
Asthma	20
Other	46

Source: Unpublished materials, Ministry of Social Affairs.

statute requires that a full-scale evaluation of the schedule be considered at least every two years given the presence of the groups represented by the advisory committee.

Other Programs
Perhaps the reason that so little controversy exists in Denmark's program is that although there is an industrial injury insurance program, there are significant supplements to and substitutes for it. A variety of social security schemes operate in conjunction with privately purchased insurance (paid by employers, employees, and in some instances subsidized by government). These guarantee most workers that medical, hospital, and associated expenses are provided, as well as income maintenance programs covering periods of sickness, invalidity, unemployment, old age, and death. The programs are not duplicative, so the range of benefits available to workers is limited, but the availability of some form of benefit is not. Denmark also has an extensive system of vocational and other rehabilitation programs available to disabled persons.

Denmark has an occupational safety and health program that dates back to 1873 but operates today in conformity with legislation passed in 1954. Under it, an employer cannot hire a worker eighteen years or under without first providing a medical examination. The Labor Inspectorate that enforces the law may ask employers to transfer workers to other work environments if it appears that not to do so will further jeopardize a worker's health. In the case of silicosis, although the Social Security Office cannot force the employee to transfer to a less hazardous environment, he may be threatened with the loss of his invalidity pension — or future increases in it — if he does not leave such an environment. Safety committees in quarries and shops will also attempt to persuade the employer or employee of the desirability of eliminating continuing exposures to hazards that threaten to exacerbate an individual's existing health condition. The Social Security Office requires a medical examination at least biennially for persons with silicosis and other work caused impairments.

Experience
Relatively few cases of occupational disease are compensated in Denmark, even in the absence of an adversary procedure. From July 1, 1974 to June 30, 1975, 347 cases were "recognized" (table 6.6).

Occupational cancer is rarely, if ever, seen. The case load may begin to expand because the recent statutory change requires for the first time that physicians and dentists report occupationally caused diseases to the Social Security Office.

Summary

The deep divisions and hostile confrontations that characterize labor-management relations on occasions in most nations are largely absent in Denmark, and there is relatively little controversy over matters such as workers' compensation and occupational illnesses. Cases are dealt with in a nonadversary system with the bulk of the responsibility for administration and decision making in the Ministry of Social Affairs. Despite this there is still a role for private insurance carriers.

As in most other Western European countries there are ample alternatives for sick or injured workers whose claims are found to be noncompensable. There was little dissatisfaction with the system prior to 1976, but the Danes decided to open up the system by eliminating the exclusivity of the schedule. They do not anticipate a flood of new cases based on the change though it is too early to evaluate their forecasts.

The incidence of occupational illness in Denmark is very small based on the number of claims compensated. Some of this may be attributable to the comparatively safe and healthy work conditions that Danish civility may foster. Partly it must be traced to the industrial composition of the country, which has spared Denmark many of the traditionally high-risk sectors, coal mining, tunneling, and so forth. The cause is not the unwillingness of employers or the government to compensate sick workers.

Germany

The Workers' Compensation System

In November 1881, Bismarck read an imperial proclamation to the German Parliament that laid the groundwork for his country's social insurance programs, the first of their type in the world. The proclamation led to health insurance, unemployment compensation, retirement schemes, and workers' compensation, the latter becoming effective in 1884. Prior to this the Germans depended on a liability system that had been overhauled in 1871 but was deficient in several respects and inconsistent with Bismarck's broad goals for worker protection.

In most ways the 1884 innovation is still the basis of Germany's law. It closely parallels the laws developed later in other Western European countries and the United States. The German law provided for employer financed insurance to be paid to injured workers for injuries occurring on the job without regard to issues of fault. Even when an injury occurred due to a worker's negligence or his violation of an employer or government prescribed regulation, the worker was still entitled to compensation. Only in 1925 was the German law modified to explicitly cover occupational diseases.

In one respect at least the German approach is quite unlike that of the United States or several of the European nations discussed in this book, although it closely resembles the Swiss system of administration. Social insurance in Germany has been based on the principle of "collective self-provision." Primary responsibility for operating and administering workers' compensation rests with the various industrial injury insurance institutes *(Berufsgenossenschaften)* that operate quite autonomously with minimal government involvement. These nonprofit public corporations cover all branches of private industry and agriculture. There are thirty-six separate institutes organized on the basis of industry or industry by region and nineteen corporations in agriculture. For example, there is an institute for mining, two of them for iron and steel (delineated by north and south), and seven in the building industry (each for a different region). These institutes are self-governing with their rules emerging from formal representatives' assemblies *(Vertreterversammlung)* and carried out by their own managing boards *(Vorstand)*. In industry, membership in the industrial insurance institutes is equally divided between representatives of labor and employers. In agriculture these responsibilities are split three ways with the third group composed of self-employed individuals. This balancing of power has allowed the German government to play a minimal role in the activities of the institutes and workers' compensation.

Coverage of persons under workers' compensation in Germany is extremely broad. Workers not covered by the industrial or agricultural injury insurance institutes include public sector employees, railway, and postal employees, who are covered by special specific programs. Self-employed persons can be covered, as can employers and spouses of employers, in some of the industrial insurance institutes. Domestic workers are covered, as are persons in cottage industries, fishermen, and other groups frequently not covered in other countries. One of the few sets of groups still uncovered are self-employed physicians, dentists, and pharmacists.

Protection in Germany is extended to cover injuries sustained while the worker travels to or from work, or if the person is injured while storing, moving, or repairing his tools or equipment necessary for work. This approach, which has widened the scope of the law considerably, goes back to 1925 when occupational diseases also became covered.

Any new employer is required to affiliate with the appropriate insurance institute. It is the employer's responsibility to notify the institute of his existence and any changes in his operation that affect his status with that institute. Workers' compensation in Germany is the "exclusive remedy" although third party actions are allowed.

Benefits and Financing

If a worker in Germany is injured or ill there are a wide variety of programs that provide for health care or wage replacement. As in a number of other European countries the issue of work-relatedness is often only an academic matter to the specific worker. The problem of assessing whether an illness is an occupational disease is much less frequently raised in Germany than in the United States, for example, for purposes of determining compensability. Most German wage and salary workers are covered by compulsory sickness insurance. The major exceptions are those salaried and self-employed persons whose earnings exceed 25,000 DM per year (1975). The latter are eligible for voluntary coverage, however.

When a covered employee becomes ill — regardless of whether it is work-connected or not — he is entitled to his full earnings (100 percent wage replacement) for up to six weeks. If after this period the employee is still unable to work, he is entitled to 80 percent of his previous wage for up to seventy-eight weeks regardless of whether the workplace is the source of the disablement. There are, however, several ways in which work relatedness does become an issue after the initial six-week period. The source of the benefit will either be a sickness insurance fund or an industrial injury insurance institute, depending on the cause of the illness. The maximum benefit is higher under workers' compensation than under the sickness insurance, which will affect the higher wage worker at least. A small share of medical care costs are born by the individual covered by sickness insurance, but an occupationally caused illness involves no health care expenses for the worker. Under either system there are some limits imposed on the worker's choice of a physician, with greater restrictions in the work-connected case. Regardless of how the worker is injured or made sick, the sickness insurance fund pays the necessary medical care costs during the first eighteen days of lost time. Thereafter the costs are shifted to the relevant injury insurance institute if the cause is work related. If the worker is not covered by a sickness insurance fund, health care costs are immediately the responsibility of the institute.

If after the period of temporary total disability benefits, the worker is at least 20 percent disabled for thirteen weeks or more, he is eligible for a permanent disability award. For covered persons disabled through non–work-connected causes, disability must be at least 50 percent to be eligible to receive an invalidity pension. The 20 percent level is very restrictive by American state workers' compensation standards, although the 50 percent cutoff is liberal in contrast to social security standards. Disability, in theory at least, is based on the loss of earnings capacity rather than on physical impairment only. In permanent disability cases compensation is awarded as two-thirds of the evaluated level of disability, subject to a maximum predisability earnings level of 36,000 DM (1976). Thus a worker with a 75 percent disablement would receive 50 percent of his predisability earnings but no more than 18,000 DM per year. This represents the legislatively determined payment, however, the various injury insurance institutes are free to alter their charters to pay amounts that exceed the statutory maximum. In 1976 all of the thirty-six industrial injury insurance institutes had made such a modification to pay more than the legislated maximum. The majority of industrial injury insurance institutes voluntarily raised the maximum wage base to 60,000 DM.

In addition to the two-thirds wage replacement in permanent cases, allowances for dependent children are paid when disability is "severe" (in excess of 49 percent). The benefit is increased by 10 percent for each child rather than providing a sum of money not tied to the workers' previous wage.

A widow (or widower) is given a lump sum of one month's pay, a provision for funeral expenses, and 30 percent of the deceased worker's previous earnings, subject to the same maximum as in permanent disability cases. Only if the survivor is forty-five years or older, an invalid, or caring for a dependent child will the benefit be raised to 40 percent. Dependent children are each entitled to 20 percent of the worker's previous earnings, subject to a maximum for the family of 80 percent. The law also makes provision for benefits to dependent parents. Benefits in death cases look very small in comparison to the American states' compensation for younger widows particularly, and those who have no dependent children. German wage replacement rates for those with dependent children can reach 80 percent, a high figure by international norms. Temporary and permanent disability, as well as death benefits, are readjusted annually through statute to reflect increasing wage levels throughout the economy.

The injury insurance institutes are responsible by law for providing compensation, health care, and rehabilitation benefits and safety services. To carry out these functions each institute levies an assessment on member firms; there is no employee contribution. Each institute is self-sustaining and must maintain a sizable reserve fund to assure that future payments will not be jeopardized by economic or other exigencies. Despite these safeguards, individual institutes have occasionally encountered financial difficulties, the most serious and recent case involving mining. As in many countries (for example, Belgium and the United States) employment in the sector has contracted sharply — employment fell from approximately 650,000 in 1955 to about 250,000 in 1975 — while compensation expenses have not fallen correspondingly, due largely to older cases. When insurance assessments reached 14 percent of the wage bill, the federal government intervened and provided subsidies to the mining insurance institute, as it had previously done in some cases in agriculture. The industrial injuries insurance institutes regarded this involvement as unwelcome and inconsistent with the principles of the program. They jointly agreed on a procedure whereby mutual assistance is provided to any member who encounters certain defined financial difficulties. In this way the solvency of each institute is further protected and the potential for expanded governmental intervention is checked.

Insurance premiums are set by each institute, but they are not uniform across constituent employers. Rates are levied on the firm's wage bill (a product of total employment and average wage rates) and vary by degree of risk set on the basis of the enterprise's activities. Not only is an individual firm rated by its group's experience, the law requires that the institutes provide rebates or special assessments when a firm performs respectively at better or worse than the average of other firms within its own "hazard class." Assessments in Germany bear a close resemblance to financing practices found in the United States even to the extent that the average employer expense, approximately 1.5 percent of payroll, is in line with U.S. levels.

Occupational Diseases

At the present time, the question of occupational disease is resolved through the use of a schedule. Until January 1, 1977, the Germans used a schedule listing forty-seven items. This, their seventh such list, was modified by the order of December 8, 1976. The most recent version of the schedule has several new items on the list (byssinosis, farmer's lung, "white-finger" syndrome, and mesothelioma) and has changed its format. According to the new decimalized list there are fifty-five entries. Unlike some other European schedules, there is no mention of specific occupations or activities. In most instances only a causative agent is identified, for example, illness caused by lead or its compounds. Some specific diseases, such as silicosis or typhus, are indicated without reference to a causative agent. Only in a few instances is an illness linked to a specific hazard, for example, cataracts due to heat radiation. The entry for bursitis in miners specifies a minimum period of underground exposure for three years in order to be found compensable.

The Germans routinely follow their schedule, however, there is an open-ended provision (number 541.2) that allows the injury insurance institutes to compensate unlisted diseases. The provision is rarely used but is thought of as a mechanism allowing for the rather infrequent changes in or additions to the schedule. Between the time that it became widely accepted that mesotheliomas were linked to asbestos and it actually was placed on the schedule, claims were compensated under this provision. In 1974 there were only ten initially compensated claims paid under this provision. For all purposes the list is virtually an exclusive one.

The German list is seldom modified; they currently are operating with only their seventh list. The lists have always tended to become more liberal, but the current list is not as progressive as it could be. Heart cases are not considered diseases and only serious or chronic skin diseases are compensable. Yet many of these cases are covered by the very generous sick-pay provisions available for most workers. Claims involving difficult questions of etiology or diagnosis are resolved within the individual injury insurance institute. These are based on practices that emerge from the work of staff physicians and experts retained by the institute. The management of these institutes is in most cases (excluding agriculture) a reflection of both management and labor. Not only do practices vary among institutes because of different staffs, relative influence by labor and employer groups, and past records of performance, the types of diseases and workers involved, by industry and occupation, vary systematically. There is far less controversy regarding the handling of claims in Germany than in the United States, partly because the parties understand what will be compensable.

The criterion for adding a disease to the schedule — though this may mean identifying a hazard — is comparable to provisions found in numerous statutes in American states; an illness that, according to up-to-date medical knowledge, is more prevalent in or peculiar to certain types of occupations and arises out of and in the course of employment. The schedule is embodied in the workers' compensation statute. It can be modified, as was done in 1976 to 1977 on the recommendation of the minister of labor by the federal chancellor. Authority to do this comes from prior parliamentary consent. The source of changes in the schedule is a Labor Ministry's Medical Commission, an advisory subcommittee on occupational illnesses. The group consists of government physicians (both federal and provincial), academics, and others who have special expertise in this area. The desirability of changing the schedule is argued in this group, largely on scientific-medical grounds. Beyond the technical level, however, economic and other issues may influence the labor minister's decision on whether to modify the schedule.

If a worker develops a listed disease (or a disease due to a scheduled hazard), there is a strong presumption that it is occupational if the worker can show he has been exposed to the risk at the workplace. The law specifies that every case is unique and each claim must be evaluated on the basis of facts applicable to it. When a worker has a covered disease and demonstrates some exposure, there is rarely a challenge to the claim. In most cases payments begin as soon as disability manifests itself (or the sickness insurance ends), but in some instances the worker needs to file a claim with the relevant insurance institute. If the claim is ultimately rejected by, or a dispute cannot be resolved within, the institute, cases go to provincial courts that hear social security cases. There is less than an adversary process here to resolve disputes because the court plays a very active role in seeking facts to render a verdict. The court usually will seek out and direct that expert witnesses appear. Beyond this there is an appellate court, which is seldom called on, and beyond this is a federal court, which is called on to decide only questions of law and not of fact. Such instances are very rare.

Other Programs

One of the legal obligations of the institutes is to prevent accidents and illnesses at the workplace. The managing board of an institute is allowed to impose large fines on member firms that deliberately or negligently violate the safety codes. The thirty-six industrial injury insurance institutes alone employ over 1,000 engineers to assure that safe and healthy working conditions prevail. These individuals specialize in such matters, and government inspectors are responsible for similar matters, as well as observing that other labor laws (pollution control, employment standards, and so on) are followed. The institutes enforce not only the legal codes but those imposed by the institutes themselves.

The law of 1963 also calls for a system of safety officers appointed by the employer in consultation with the local works committee. This institutionalized a practice that the industrial injury insurance institutes had carried out for many years. The safety officers receive technical training by the institutes, and although they have no special authority, they are expected to work with both management and labor to improve health and safety at the workplace. By 1976 the industrial injury insurance institutes had trained over a quarter of a million safety officers.

As in several other European countries Germany has recently (1973) passed a law requiring widespread use of occupational physicians. Large scale establishments (3,000 employees or more) are expected to employ their own physicians, and smaller establishments are participating in medical centers. Very small firms need only assure that workers are subject to regular physical examinations. Since the law has created an unmet demand for occupational physicians, the institutes have given short training courses to those who participate but who have no medical specialty. These physicians are responsible for observing work practices, monitoring the environment, and working with the safety officers of the plant. They periodically administer physical examinations to workers in the establishment. Rules regarding the frequency and content of these

Table 6.7
Occupational injuries and diseases, preliminary data, 1975

	Cases Reported	First Time Compensated
Work injuries[a]	1,741,602	61,365
Occupational illnesses	35,374	5,974
Fatal work injuries		3,058
Fatal occupational diseases		184

Source: Bericht der Bundesregierung über den Stand der Unfallverhütung und das Unfallgeschehen in der Bundesrepublik Deutschland-Drucksache 7/4668, 1-29-76, pp. 211, 212, 213.
a. Excludes occupational illnesses

examinations are set by the government and the institutes. In cases where the physician believes that a worker's health will be (further) impaired by continued contact with a hazard at the workplace, he will urge the employer (and the worker) to relocate him (to relocate himself). When such a move is made and wage loss is suffered, the employee can be compensated for two-thirds of any lost wages.

The institutes have developed extensive research and data gathering programs as a part of their health and safety programs, as well as to assist in future workers' compensation decisions. In certain higher risk industries a worker who is periodically exposed to a hazard is issued a card that describes the type and extent of the exposure. The card is held in the files of the personnel officer but if the worker changes employment the card is transferred with the worker. In asbestos all workers' health files go to a central asbestos documentation center. When a worker leaves the industry, he is monitored medically on a regular basis. (This should eventually provide epidemiologists with a wealth of data.)

The insurance institutes also have responsibility for the care and rehabilitation of sick and injured workers. The institutes maintain hospitals, training and rehabilitation centers, and other facilities in order to carry out these activities. The impression given by the German insurance institutes is that rehabilitation is a very significant part of their activity and it pays, economically, to engage actively in such programs. Aside from this, German law requires that firms employ handicapped persons in proportion to their total employment. The source of the disablement need not be work related.

Experience

The data describing the German experience emerge from the various injury insurance institutes. In terms of detail and explicitness they compare very favorably with data available from other industrialized nations. In 1975 approximately 24.5 million workers were covered by workers' compensation (table 6.7).

The very large number of work injuries, relative to cases involving compensation, reflects the many injuries dealt with through sick-pay coverage. A work injury is reported if it involves at least three lost working days, although compensation is not paid until sickness insurance benefits cease after eighteen days. Not every reported case is ultimately found to be compensable. Only 3.5 percent of reported injuries ultimately result in compensation, and 16.8 percent of reported occupational diseases involve some indemnity payments. This suggests that the occupational diseases reported tend to involve relatively more serious cases than do work injuries. (Only serious and chronic dermatitis is considered an occupational disease in Germany.) Overall, 8.9 percent of initially compensated claims in 1975 were for occupational disease, a very high figure by international standards.

Tables 6.8 and 6.9 provide a breakdown of the types of claims for occupational diseases encountered by the Germans in 1974. In terms of new cases reported and claims initially filed, hearing loss is the largest single source of disease. There has been, however, a striking increase in this problem in recent years so that as recently as 1967 there were only 1,123 new reported cases and 173 initially compensated cases. Silicosis claims have dropped substantially; a post-World War II high for new cases compensated was 1953 when the figure reached 10,385. From 1950 to 1960 there were almost 60,000 new claims compensated for this disease. Much of the problem is associated with employment in Germany's coal mines, which has fallen off considerably in recent years. Many of the claims can be traced to exposures before and during World War II, when safety and health considerations were sacrificed to national needs for coal.

The relatively small number of skin diseases is well below comparable data for other nations, but this reflects the handling of such cases more than it does any health or safety features found in Germany. The number of infectious illnesses both reported and compensated is surprisingly large by comparative standards but indicates some looseness in the schedule. Infectious diseases are compensable in Germany when contracted by employees in health centers, laboratories, or where the person's duties particularly expose the worker to such illnesses. The latter is sufficiently open-ended to allow the numbers of reported and compensated cases.

Over the long run there has been a substantial decline in the rate (per thousand covered workers) of injuries and of diseases, either reported or compensated. Much of the decline in disease cases came from the declining influence of silicosis.

The rapid growth in hearing-loss cases, however, suggests that an increase in the rate of occupational disease may begin again. The Germans are giving considerable attention to this problem, but it will take several years before the influence of past hazardous exposures to noise cease to result in claims.

Summary

Germany has the oldest workers' compensation system in Europe, but it is one of the most energetic. The system combines the very small role of government with active and aggressive compensation administration. Either aspect is attractive to conservative and liberal groups respectively in other nations, and the approach has existed in Germany for generations. The equal roles of labor and management in directing the injury insurance institutes assure that consensus is needed in the formulation of their policies.

Table 6.8
Occupational diseases, 1974

	Cases Reported	First Time Compensated
Hearing loss	9,890	1,589
Skin diseases	7,756	501
Silicosis	5,726	1,208
Infectious disease	3,437	1,072
Miners' knee	1,712	746
Tendonitis, etc.	1,274	6
Other	6,329	950
Total	36,124	6,072

Source: Bericht der Bundesregierung über den Stand der Unfallverhütung und das Unfall-geschehen in der Bundesrepublik Deutschland-Drucksache 7/4668, 1-29-76, p. 169.

Table 6.9
Fatalities initially compensated, 1974

Silicosis, silicosis-tuberculosis	117
Asbestosis in connection with lung cancer	14
Infectious diseases	11
Carbon monoxide	10
Arsenic and related compounds	9
Haiogenated hydrocarbons	8
Bronchial asthma	7
Animal carried diseases	6
Other	19
Total	201

Source: Bericht der Bundesregierung über den Stand der Unfallverhütung und das Unfall-geschehen in der Bundesrepublik Deutschland-Drucksache 7/4668, 1-29-76, pp. 170–173.

There are relatively few occupational diseases in Germany, particularly when one neglects hearing-loss and silicosis claims. Undoubtedly, some illnesses are not noted because they have not been scheduled (for example, byssinosis until 1977). Given the widespread use of occupational physicians and physical examinations, the medical monitoring of high-risk occupations, and a law requiring that health practitioners report all occupational diseases to the provincial health authorities, it is difficult to understand why workers are not filing more claims. The nonserious cases of disease are simply being unrecorded in cases where sickness insurance is providing short-run compensation benefits and health care costs.

The German schedule is a strict one by European standards. It is changed infrequently and virtually no claims are paid for diseases that do not appear on the schedule. Some specific items on the schedule, such as infectious diseases, are relatively open to claimants.

Overall the system is free of litigation though attorneys may be found in the process. The vast majority of claims are disposed of either automatically or after a hearing within the insurance institutes rather than in the courts. It suggests that labor and management can cooperate effectively so as to jointly operate and administer an inherently complex program. Both parties will occasionally make uncomfortable compromises for the sake of some other issue, but the rights of the worker and the employer are protected by their own representatives serving as decision-makers within the institutes. These difficult claims are resolved through the use of "inside" professionals and technicians in a manner akin to the grievance procedure found in many American collective bargaining arrangements.

Switzerland

The Workers' Compensation System

Every country's workers' compensation program is unique, but Switzerland's bears less resemblance to that of any country covered here—aside from Holland, which has no such program. The Swiss system most closely parallels that of New Zealand because of its unusual coverage provision; although far older than New Zealand's, it has received much less attention in the United States. Administratively and legally the Swiss system closely parallels Germany's.

The Swiss Compulsory Accident Insurance Law was passed in 1911 and substantially modified in 1918. The same law, basically, exists today. Persons employed in covered establishments are protected from disability due to accidents, regardless of whether the injury was work-connected, and from occupational diseases. Insurance benefits for occupational or non-occupational injuries and occupational diseases do not vary regardless of the source of disability. The Swiss Compulsory Accident Insurance law provides covered disabled workers with insurance except in cases of illnesses that are not occupational. The determination of what is an occupational disease becomes an important matter, particularly since other supplementary social insurance programs for workers are very limited.

One of the unusual features of the Swiss law, compared to other countries, is the relatively narrow coverage. The act provides coverage for firms in specified industries and certain high-risk occupations. Only about two-thirds of Switzerland's employees are covered by the law . Many of those who are not covered by the act have some protection through privately purchased insurance. Separate compulsory accident insurance programs, some administered through the cantons and not at the federal level, exist for agricultural workers and crews of seagoing Swiss ships.

Because coverage under the law is mandated for certain establishments, their workers are protected even if the firm has not made premium payments. Employees begin to be covered from the beginning of the day when they first start, or should have started to work, in a covered establishment. For persons in long-term employment, the insurance lapses on the thirtieth day after entitlement to wages has ended. For persons employed twelve days or less, coverage ends on the last day of work. In either case the insurance may be temporarily extended beyond such time limits in specified situations, including when the individual has ceased work due to a disability.

The Swiss system is administered by SUVA (from the German acronym) or CNA (its initials in French). SUVA operates all aspects of the program including raising revenues and making expenditures. Although charged with administering a law, SUVA is an institute that is fully autonomous. It is run by directors drawn from labor, management, and the civil service, and the statute specifies clearly that SUVA is not an agency of government. Thus the approach closely parallels the one used by Germany.

Benefits and Financing

In the event that a worker is injured or becomes ill due to an occupational illness, he becomes eligible for benefits to replace 80 percent of his lost wages, subject to a maximum, after an initial two-day waiting period. Temporary total disability benefits are continued until the individual returns to work or when the condition stabilizes. If the individual retains a permanent disability that will affect his earning capacity, he is entitled to a pension that is scaled according to the extent of disability. If the employee is permanently and totally disabled, the benefit is set at 70 percent of his prior wage earnings, subject to a maximum, and a possible supplement of up to 30 percent of his wage when constant attendance is needed. Pensions are increased automatically as the cost of living increases. However, when a person is found to be one-third or less permanently disabled, benefits are not escalated with increases in costs of living. The compulsory accident insurance provides all needed health costs as long as health services can appreciably help to improve the individual's condition.

Funeral benefits are available in a lump sum. Survivors' benefits are 30 percent of the worker's wages paid to a widow and 15 percent to orphans below the age of eighteen. Other dependents may receive benefits also, but the maximum to be paid in survivors' benefits is 60 percent of the wage.

Switzerland, unlike many other Western European countries, does not treat disabled, covered foreign nationals in the same manner as its own citizens. When Switzerland has no agreement with foreign states and such countries provide fewer benefits to resident Swiss nationals than Switzerland does, permanent disability and survivors benefits are reduced by 25 percent.

Coverage and benefits for disabled workers do not vary if the cause is occupational, however, the costs of the system are carefully separated between occupational and non-occupational causes. Workers are assessed a payroll tax that fully covers the cost of non-work-related injuries. Rates do not vary by risk but a slight difference can be set by sex, depending on the fund's experience. From 1968 to 1972 the payroll cost per employee under this program was 0.97 percent.[14] Work-caused injuries and occupational diseases are funded entirely by employer contributions, and firms are experience rated. From 1968 to 1972 the average employer cost under this program was 1.13 percent of covered payroll.

Occupational Diseases
Occupational diseases in Switzerland are compensated by conforming to a short and simple schedule embodied in the law. The schedule consists of two parts, the first being a list of approximately 120 hazardous substances. The second part is divided into two sections; the first lists a dozen classes of illnesses, such as diseases of ionizing radiation and conditions related to compressed air, and applies to all exposed workers. The second section identifies seven other classes of illness, for example, pneumoconioses, infectious diseases, and tropical illnesses, and for each of these seven there is a list of types of work covered. In comparison to the highly detailed and explicit schedule of some other countries, such as France, the Swiss schedule is a model of simplicity.

According to the Swiss officials, the only exclusion from Swiss coverage that keeps it from conforming to the International Labor Organization's recommended schedule is silicosis-tuberculosis.

The Swiss schedule is set by statute and is rarely modified. Partly for this reason and to deal with illnesses not covered in the schedule but obviously a consequence of the workplace, compensation can be provided to sick workers voluntarily. The compensation agency, SUVA, is free to accept cases as occupational disease under the statute if it believes that the illness was caused exclusively and with certainty at work and could not be caused by other (nonwork) conditions. Thus the Swiss schedule is not exclusive and allows covered employees with uncovered illnesses to be compensated. From 1968 to 1972, 27.2 percent of all compensated occupational disease cases came from illnesses or hazards that were not on the schedule but were voluntarily accepted by SUVA.[15] These tended to be less expensive types of claims and accounted, disproportionately, for only 7.3 percent of the costs of all occupational disease cases.[16]

"Heart" cases are not covered as occupational diseases nor are they considered injuries due to accident. Mental illnesses are not covered as occupational illnesses either. Deafness can be compensated as an occupational disease and, as is common in the United States and elsewhere, is treated as an exception because benefits are paid even in the absence of wage loss. "Occupational" cancers are compensated but cases are rare, averaging approximately two cases per year over the past sixty years. The majority of these involved persons employed in the chemical industry.

Decisions regarding compensability, extent of disability, and so on are made by SUVA. Appeals can be made to a cantonal tribunal and these decisions, in turn, may be appealed to the Swiss Supreme Court. Approximately one case in a thousand is appealed to the tribunal level. A frequent cause of such appeals is when SUVA finds that a preexisting condition contributed to the extent of the disability. The Swiss law permits apportionment so that benefits are not provided for preexisting conditions, so the issue is largely one of the size of an award, not the basic matter of compensability. From 1968 to 1972 an average of 5,300 cases per year (work-related claims) were denied compensation, or about 2 percent of the cases that were accepted.[17] Because the vast majority of Swiss citizens, including workers, are protected by one of a number of voluntary illness insurance plans, some or most of their medical expenses are provided even if they are denied compensation by SUVA. The Swiss social insurance system provides invalidity benefits, so a worker denied benefits by SUVA may still receive some cash payments.

In the fall of 1973 a commission of experts made its report on the Swiss accident insurance system.[18] Although it gave its blessing to the manner in which occupational disease claims were handled—it supported continuation of the schedule and the voluntary acceptance of cases not covered by the schedule—it made a strong recommendation regarding future legislation. The experts urged that workers be able to legally challenge cases where SUVA chose not to voluntarily cover an unscheduled disease. Currently, because SUVA's acceptance of such claims is voluntary, workers are unable to seek legal remedies when their case is not accepted. The recommendation has not yet had an effect on the law.

Workers' compensation (the compulsory accident insurance) is the exclusive remedy but, as in the United States, an injured or sick worker may seek damages from third parties. In instances where damages are awarded, SUVA is reimbursed for expenses already incurred in the case.

The Swiss government has given SUVA the primary responsibility for promoting health and safety at the workplace. SUVA is empowered to issue rules regarding work practices and is able to raise insurance premiums for firms that do not comply with such standards. There is an active program to prevent occupational diseases, particularly silicosis. SUVA directs which firms and industries must administer preemployment physical examinations and periodic check-ups after employment. SUVA directs under what conditions a worker may not be employed. These decisions may be appealed by the worker to the Social Security Office. Standards are high.

SUVA will direct a firm to transfer an employee found to be developing a disease to a better environment or, if necessary, to let the worker go. In the latter case, the worker can be compensated for actual wage loss for up to a maximum of 300 times his daily wage. Much of this prevention effort is directed at reducing the incidence and severity of silicosis cases. Workers tend to resist such relocation efforts.

Findings
From 1968 to 1972 approximately 2.6 percent of all nonminor claims (and excluding those due to accidental injuries not due to one's work) were for occupational diseases (table 6.10). Silicosis (due to quartz) is specifically included in table 6.10 because of its severity in Switzerland (it accounted for 0.2 percent of all nonminor claims). Occupational diseases accounted for 3.1 percent of all new compensated cases for permanent disability over this period and 75 percent of these (2.4 percent of all such cases) were due to silicosis. During this period 554 out of 2,919 recorded fatalities (19.0 percent) were for occupational diseases, and of all fatalities silicosis accounted for about one death in every six attributable to the workplace. Because occupational diseases, and

Table 6.10
Occupational diseases and occupational injuries due to accidents, Switzerland, 1968–1972

	Minor Claims Accepted	All Other Claims Accepted	Total Claims
Occupational accidents only	657,340	689,234	1,346,574
Occupational diseases	5,214 (0.8)	18,642 (2.6)	23,856 (1.7)
Silicosis (quartz)	0	1,593 (0.2)	1,593 (0.1)

	Permanent Disabilities	Fatalities	Expenses for medical costs and earnings replaced[a]
Occupational accidents only	19,182	2,365	1,614.6
Occupational diseases	622 (3.1)	554 (19.0)	115.6 (6.7)
Silicosis (quartz)	471 (2.4)	485 (16.6)	71.3 (4.1)

Source: Résultats de la Statistique des Accidents, pp. 59, 59, 72, 83, 103, 104.
a. In millions of Swiss francs.
Note: Items in parentheses are the percent of occupational accidents plus occupational diseases.

Table 6.11
Compensated occupational diseases, Switzerland, 1968–1972

	Number of Cases	All Occupational Disease Cases (%)	Cost per Case (Swiss francs)
Poisoning (listed)	1,510	6.3	7,713
Poisoning (not listed)	390	1.6	5,072
Skin diseases (listed)	7,653	32.1	1,760
Skin diseases (not listed)	3,911	16.4	938
Sickness due to physical agents	5,776	24.2	1,033
Other sicknesses (listed)[a]	2,163	9.1	35,146
Other sicknesses (not listed)	2,453	10.3	1,150
Total	23,856	100.0	4,845

Source: Résultats de la Statistique des Accidents, pp. 102–103.
a. Category includes silicosis cases.

silicosis in particular, tend to involve a significant number of the serious claims (permanent disabilities and deaths) they account for a disproportionate share of system costs in Switzerland. If silicosis claims were excluded from the occupational disease category, disease claims would involve a lower share of permanent disabilities, deaths, and costs than the proportion of all compensated cases involving occupational disease. The reasons for this are evident in table 6.11. First, 48.5 percent of all claims were for skin diseases. These claims, particularly the ones not listed but that SUVA accepted voluntarily, are relatively inexpensive. Dermatological disorders are the preponderant occupational disease in Switzerland (as in most countries) and their cost is well below that of most other sources of disease. For each of the three categories where SUVA identifies the source of illness, where it accepts claims voluntarily and the schedule is not pertinent, less expensive claims are involved. This reflects a number of possibilities deserving some exploration by the Swiss authorities.

Summary
The Swiss system should not be considered a workers' compensation scheme except for occupational diseases. The coverage of accidental injuries, regardless of cause, makes the Swiss system far broader than that of the United States, however, its exclusion from coverage of approximately one-third of the workers in Switzerland is viewed as a serious shortcoming by conventional U.S. values. The system involves little disputation beyond the level of SUVA, relatively few claims are denied, apparently because most parties understand what will or will not be compensated. The system is generous by U.S. standards, except in the case of widows, but the premiums that are levied to finance the program are very low by European standards.

Ontario

The Workers' Compensation System
The Workmen's Compensation Act of Ontario was first enacted in 1914 and took effect on January 1, 1915. It is a product of the same era that witnessed the development of comparable laws in the majority of American states. The original act is thought to be the product of Sir William Meredith, appointed by the provincial government in 1912 to study ways to deal with industrially caused disabilities and deaths. The original law provided only for the replacement of lost earnings, and as in many of the states the law was soon amended to provide benefits for medical and health related costs (1917).

In many ways the present Ontario scheme is similar to those in most or all of the states. An employee who is disabled faces the arising-out-of-and-in-the-course-of test, benefits are financed by employers (who may be experience-rated), wages are fractionally replaced by tax-free benefits, private insurance carriers serve some employers, and the central government plays almost no role in the entire system. Despite these obvious similarities the differences between Ontario and the fifty states are fundamental. The scope and finality of decisions by the Ontario's Workmen's Compensation Board are unparalleled in the states' programs.

Virtually all workers in Ontario are covered by the Workmen's Compensation Law. A major exception is domestic workers. Employees are covered by dint of working in industries that are specifically enumerated in the statute. Should a person be injured in a nonlisted industry, he is allowed to seek tort damages under the statute's "Part II" provisions. Industries not listed in the statute may be added for coverage purposes by the board on the application of the employer.

Benefits and Financing

As of 1976 benefits in Ontario are generous relative to those in most of the states. In cases of temporary total disability an injured or sick worker receives 75 percent of his weekly wage (benefits are tax free) up to a weekly maximum payment of $216.35. However, when a worker's wage is below $90 per week there is 100 percent replacement and when weekly wages exceed $90, the benefit must be at least $90.

In cases of permanent disability, determinations of the extent of disability are made after maximum recovery has occurred. Benefits are paid as monthly pensions unless the disability is rated as no more than 10 percent; then a lump-sum payment is made. Benefits are based on a board-determined rating of disability (which takes into account the socioeconomic condition and the physician's evaluation) rather than simply impairment. The basis for the assessment is the worker's previous annual earnings and the extent of disability, up to a maximum of 75 percent of those earnings for total disability. In this case the maximum benefit allowed in 1976 was $937.50 and the minimum, $400 per month. In neither temporary nor permanent disability cases are there dependents' benefits.

There are a variety of benefits in death cases including a lump-sum payment of $600, burial expenses of up to $600, and a monthly pension of $286.00 per month paid to a widow or widower until remarriage. Each dependent child is entitled to a monthly pension of $77. As in most Western European countries, workers' compensation is far less generous to survivors than it is in cases involving disablement, reflecting a combination of factors including the availability of other benefit schemes and the attempt to preclude having survivors become totally dependent on these transfer payments.

The financing of benefits in Ontario operates in a bifurcated manner. Covered industries are specifically listed in the statute and these are split into schedule 1 and schedule 2. Most private industry and the large majority of employees are under schedule 1; schedule 2 includes employees of provincial and local government and some persons in communications and transportation. Employers covered by schedule 2 (or their insurers) pay injured workers or survivors directly, as is in the United States. Firms under schedule 1 are assessed periodically by the board and these funds support the accident fund out of which the board pays medical and indemnity benefits. The Workmen's Compensation Board administers the program for workers covered by either schedule, but under schedule 1 payments are made directly by the board. Schedule 1 firms are taxed on the basis of the experience of the industry in which they operate and in some cases on the firm's own experience also. Because firms have an obvious stake in keeping the costs of compensation for their employees low, the board has established a Second Injury and Enhancement Fund, so the compensation system does not create another barrier for the handicapped and disabled. In the case of occupational disease, this second injury fund is the source of some portion or all of the costs of compensating an employee whose disability resulted from the aggravation of a preexisting condition. The statute gives the board enormous latitude in setting rates and assessments, as it has in most other areas of administering this law.

Occupational Diseases

The Ontario statute defines an industrial disease as "any of the diseases mentioned in Schedule 3 and any other disease peculiar to or characteristic of a particular industrial process, trade or occupation." Schedule 3 lists fifteen diseases and for each disease there is an associated "process." The list is far broader than this number suggests; one disease is "poisoning and its sequelae," and seventeen items are specifically enumerated including the chlorinated hydrocarbons. Another listed disease(s) is "the pneumoconioses other than silicosis" (listed elsewhere) with no specific or relevant "process" listed.

Two points are the basis of understanding how the schedule is applied by the board. It is not an exclusive list, so persons with unlisted diseases can be compensated so long as the board can be shown that the disease is peculiar to or characteristic of a particular line of work. This does not mean that the burden of proof rests solely with the worker.

If a physician employed by the board reports that this is the case, there is no special burden placed on the employee. Second, even when a person has a listed disease, compensation is not necessarily granted by the board. If it can be shown that the disease was not due to the nature of the employment, compensation need not be given. The schedule does not create an irrefutable presumption, though it is very rare for a worker with a listed disease to be denied compensation.

Decisions regarding the compensability of a disease are made by the board in a non-adversary setting. Employers, private physicians, and others may submit information pertinent to the determination of etiology or on the matter of the extent of disability, but the board weighs the evidence, including input from its own medical staff, in a nonlitigious environment. Attorneys are rarely used, and a board official interviewed reported with pride that all of the legal fees paid during the course of a year due to workers' compensation matters would not be enough to support the needs of a single attorney in Toronto.

In cases of disease brought to the board that are not routine, much of the board's thinking is guided by the findings and research of its own staff and consultants. These experts recommend to the board what action to take on hearing various types of claims. The following is an excerpt of recommendations made in 1976 by some medical staff for an unscheduled illness:

(1) That lung cancer for coke oven workers in the steel industry be accepted as an industrial disease under Section 118 and Section 1 (1) (L) of the Act as peculiar to and characteristic of exposure to coke oven emissions in the steel industry.

(2) That based on medical studies lung cancer claims be favourably considered when the following circumstances apply:

2.1 Persons employed 5 or more years in full time top side jobs.

2.2 Persons employed as bench level workers in an oven of "old design" and who are in the 40–50 year age group and have 10 or more years of exposure.

2.3 Employees who have been non-smokers for a minimum of 10 years preceding the diagnosis of lung cancer and who were working partially on ground and partially at bench level, with 10 or more years exposure.

2.4 Employees who have been non-smokers for a minimum of 10 years duration preceding the diagnosis of lung cancer and who are retired coke oven workers and who have worked 20 or more years at ground and bench level.

2.5 Employees who are smokers or who have stopped smoking in less than 10 years prior to the diagnosis of lung cancer not included in 2.1 or 2.2 and who have worked partially at top side, bench level, and ground level for 20 years or more.

(3) Claims which do not meet the criteria in "2" be individually judged on their own merits in view of the variations in exposures which could cause lung cancer and where it seems reasonable that the lung cancer resulted from exposure to coke oven work in the steel industry, consideration be given to these cases. The benefit of reasonable doubt applies.

Because lung cancer is not on Ontario's schedule, the proposed presumptions would lead to compensation under the "peculiar to" provision of the law. The proposed rule would include a variety of specific quantitative restrictions, but the board is urged to judge cases falling outside these limits "on their own merits" and to apply the "benefit of reasonable doubt."

The extraordinary flexibility granted to the board is not even restricted by concerns regarding precedent. The law instructs the board to base decisions on the "real merits and justice of the case," and it "is not bound to follow strict legal precedent." The board will take evidence that may not be admissible in courts of law.

In cases involving dust diseases the board receives an evaluation from a special panel of physicians through the Provincial Department of Health. These persons—drawn from the universities, government agencies, and private practice—examine all such cases and provide the board with a consistent set of criteria to evaluate etiology and the extent of disability in these particularly problematic areas.

Heart cases are considered diseases in Ontario unlike most of the European countries. For the calendar year 1975 out of 395,000 claims brought to the board, approximately 120 were for heart cases; 36 were successful in being found compensable. There were almost twenty times that number of successful claims for hearing loss, a source of rapidly increasing claims as in Europe. Hearing loss due to traumatic events has always been compensable under the Ontario law, but only in 1947 did loss due to chronic exposure become compensable. The board has acquired data on the extent of noise in various establishments and sites throughout Ontario, and these are checked when a claim is filed and hearing loss is indicated. When no such data exists, the Environmental Health Branch of the Ministry of Health conducts a noise survey with the information going both to the board and the employer.

A worker's hearing is tested in a variety of ways, and Ontario tests for loss after the worker has been removed from his work environment for at least forty-eight hours. The board will pay a worker for any wages lost during this period, and for that reason the test is given after there is some initial evidence presented that the worker has a hearing-loss problem. Total deafness in one ear is judged to be a 5 percent disablement, and the condition for both ears warrants 30 percent. As of 1976 the average claim cost

$5,000 and some have cost up to $20,000. As is the case in many countries claims have grown sharply in recent years, probably due to the increasing awareness of the availability of compensation for such losses and a tendency over time for a larger share of claims to receive pensions. From 1950 to 1955 only 10 claims were received, in 1960 there were 28 claims, in 1966 100 claims, in 1970 there were 301 claims, and from January to August of 1976 1,632 claims were received. During the mid-1970s the number of new pensions awarded has been roughly 40 to 45 percent of the new claims in that year. Board staff expect claims will level off and even decline in the near future as the result of improved working environments. The level of consciousness in Ontario industry regarding hearing loss is high. All large employers in the province administer audiometric tests during preemployment screening. If the job applicant shows signs of having impaired hearing at that time, it will serve to undermine claims for workers' compensation in later years.

The only infectious diseases included in the schedule are anthrax and tuberculosis (and specific occupations are shown for the latter). Nevertheless, the board will compensate some claims where the worker shows that the illness was "peculiar to or characteristic of" a particular industry or occupation. The board has exercised its accustomed flexibility in this regard, but it has not pursued an open-door policy. In 1975 there were 187 successful new claims due to infectious diseases with hepatitis being the most common (41 cases) and including mumps (10), chicken pox (8), pertussis (8), measles (7), and infectious mononucleosis (6). The board has accepted even the most ordinary of the contagious sicknesses when it was convinced that the cause was work related.

The board has shown a progressive leaning in some matters relative to the United States, while trying to avoid opening up some potentially large and troublesome areas. Against the recommendation of its staff, the board gave workers' compensation for an abortion when a schoolteacher contracted German measles. The board approved a claim for skin cancer in a lighthouse keeper. Yet the staff believes that the chances for compensation due to depression or suicide in workers exposed to carbon disulfide, xylene, or toluene would be minimal. Compensation for "mental-mental" disabilities are also very low.

Decisions made by the Ontario Workmen's Compensation Board are virtually never appealed. On the average one or two decisions a year are challenged on the basis of law in the courts. If a party feels grieved by a decision made by an operating division, this can be challenged, thus bringing the Appeals Board process into effect. An appeals examiner first hears the matter and reports the findings to a commissioner for a decision.

That judgment may be appealed further to the Appeals Board, a body of three commissioners. An opportunity for a hearing is provided by the Appeals Board, whose decision is final. Members of the board (commissioners) are named by Ontario's lieutenant governor in council, who also designates who is to be chairman, vice-chairman, and commissioner of appeals. Commissioners are appointed for five-year terms and may be reappointed. The lieutenant governor in council sets the remuneration and benefits for the appointees.

Because of the board's ability to deal with each claim on the basis of its own merits, there is no compelling need to modify the schedule as medical science finds new evidence linking the workplace and specific illnesses. Consequently the schedule has been amended infrequently. The responsibility for modifying the schedule belongs to the board; the Ontario statute provides that the board, subject to the approval of the lieutenant governor in council, may amend the schedule as necessary.

Other Programs
Ontario's Workers' Compensation system differs from many others in that it has a very active role to play in issues of occupational safety and health. Although it shares these responsibilities with other government agencies, the board's role is an active and aggressive one. Several pieces of evidence demonstrate this; therefore a statute gives the board the authority to enter an employer's premises to determine the health and safety conditions therein (section 97). The board also seeks to facilitate the movement of workers from certain hazardous occupations when continuing exposure will (further) undermine their health. For a number of years the board tried to induce silicotics to leave mining and take rehabilitation that prepared them for other lines of work. If such workers suffered any wage loss due to a job change of this sort, some compensation benefits were available to replace a share of lost income. A major change and innovation occurred in 1975 when the program was extended to those workers who did not yet have silicosis but whose X-rays showed signs of subtle changes preceding the disease's development. Such persons (called code 4s) are encouraged to leave hazardous occupations through retraining programs and stipends for lost earnings. It is too early to judge the program's effectiveness, but the staff of the board feels that it is "moderately successful" and some persons are leaving hazardous work prior to the onset of disease. Funding for this program comes from an industry-wide assessment by the board and not by a tax levied specially on the worker's own employer.

The Ministry of Health has issued regulations requiring workers to be regularly

examined by a "qualified medical practitioner" if their work exposes them to a concentration of lead, mercury, beryllium, asbestos, isocyanates, silica, enzymes, fluorides,
benzol, "or other substances of similar toxicity that is likely to endanger his health."
As long as the worker who has been so exposed remains in the establishment, his health
is monitored and a record maintained. The examination is done by a physician retained
by the firm, but it must conform to guidelines set by the ministry. Plant conditions
are also periodically monitored by industrial physicians from the ministry. When the
physical examination reveals that a worker's health has been impaired, the Ministry
of Health can issue an order requiring that the worker not be further exposed to the
damaging substance for a specified period of time. The worker receives 75 percent of
any lost wages subject to the maximum prevailing at the time. In the case of lead,
movement out of the workplace or returning thereto is largely governed by the worker's
blood and urine lead levels. For miners, these regular screening examinations are the
basis for identifying potential code 4s.

Experience
The Ontario system covers over 2.5 million workers. In 1975 there were approximately
400,000 claims reported, not all of which were allowed. Of these, there were 4,990
industrial disease claims allowed (table 6.12). The data are comparable to those for
the United States. The bulk of the successful claims involve similar types of disease
categories and there are very few cases of the more serious disorders. This is also evident
when the number of successful cancer claims in Ontario is examined (table 6.13).

The number of compensated respiratory cancer claims probably exceeds the experience of every state in the United States, but taking into account population, the
overall number of 239 cases during the life of the Ontario statute is an average of only
about four cases per year. Many of these cases resulted from exposures in mining, an
industry that has employed a more significant share of Ontario's work force than in
many other jurisdictions. However, compensation for exposure to either nickel or
arsenic has been relatively rare in the past in the United States, unlike the experience
in Ontario. The data in table 6.13, although limited to respiratory diseases only, corro-
borate an observation made by a staff person. He commented that he was confident that
workers presently or formerly exposed to hazardous substances in the primary sectors
are aware of their rights to compensation when certain types of diseases strike them.
Workers not so directly exposed to hazards in some manufacturing and services sectors,
however, are unaware of the links that may tie their conditions to the workplace.

Table 6.12
Allowed claims for industrial diseases, Ontario, 1975

	Claims Allowed	Percent
Occupational dermatitis	1242	24.9
Fume toxicity	1062	21.3
Welding flashes, conjunctivitis, and keratitis	958	19.2
Occupational noise deafness	639	12.8
Tendonitis, tenosynovitis, bursitis, etc.	566	11.3
Infectious diseases	187	3.7
Silicosis	73	1.5
Asbestosis	41	0.8
Heart cases	36	0.7
Lead	30	0.6
Ionizing radiation—Radium	22	0 4
Malignancies	16	0.3
Other	118	2.4
		100.0

Source: Ontario Workmen's Compensation Board, 1976, unpublished report.

Table 6.13
Allowed claims for respiratory cancers in all years until June 30, 1976

	Lung	Sinus	Mesothelioma
Uranium	21		
Nickel	100	39	
Asbestos	26		15
Arsenic	23		
Coke oven	3		
Gas	12		
Total	185	39	15

Source: Ontario Workmen's Compensation Board, internal reports.

Summary
The Ontario system has certain characteristics that superficially look like those found in the United States. There are such common features as private insurance carriers, experience rating, a system not closely tied to social security, provincial rather than federal preeminence, and certain common language such as the "arising out of" or "peculiar to or characteristic of" provisions. The commonalities were emphasized further when in 1972 the chairman of the Ontario board became president of the IAIABC, the organization of state workers' compensation administrators. Yet Ontario's approach has much less in common with that of the states than the foregoing suggests. The central difference is the nonadversary approach to resolving issues used by the Canadians under the direction of a strong and very active board. This role is particularly significant in the administration of claims for occupational diseases where the technical issues of etiology and diagnosis are dealt with primarily by professionals representing neither a plaintiff nor defendant. With the board as the final arbiter in virtually every compensation issue that arises, the agency can act with authority and confidence that decisions should be sought in each case solely on the merits of that situation.

Ontario's commitment to its workers' compensation program is well illustrated by the size of the program. The board has over 1,900 employees and of these at least 45 are physicians. Most state agencies in the United States employ fewer than 100 persons, many have staffs below 50, and even certain large states such as Pennsylvania have under 100 employees. It is true that this neglects the activities of persons employed in state rehabilitation agencies, insurance commissions and the courts, but there is still no comparison with the scope of the program in a province with about eight million persons.

There is an obvious pride in Ontario in its system of workers' compensation. There is the view, however, that although the system works well, it would be difficult to replicate in the United States. The absence of the adversary process is now a familiar scheme to industry, labor, and the health communities in Ontario, just as is the litigation and contention that characterizes the state systems in the United States. The absence of a meaningful role for the trial lawyer in Ontario poses obvious obstacles to any state attempting to replace its current approach with one patterned on that of Ontario.

The Netherlands

The System
There is no workers' compensation program in the Netherlands. In 1967 the Dutch government abolished the system and replaced it with one that provides workers with

Table 6.14
Relationship of benefits to incapacity

Incapacity for Work (%)	Benefits (as percent of 100/107 daily wage)
Under 15	No benefits
15–25	10
25–35	20
35–45	30
45–55	40
55–65	50
65–80	65
80 or more	80

Source: Social Security in the Netherlands, Ministry of Social Affairs, 1976.

disability protection that does not differ regardless of whether the injury was job-connected. A Dutch worker (the programs available for nonworkers will not be described) receives coverage for disability without regard to the issue of "arising out of and in the course of employment." Such an approach greatly simplifies the administration of a compensation program, particularly in occupational disease cases where the etiology may be unknown. The Dutch system, however, is a very complex one with a variety of interrelated programs, each filled with highly detailed provisions.

Beginning in 1903 the Netherlands enacted its first social insurance law, providing workers' compensation for persons employed in high-risk establishments. By 1921 the law was modified to cover all occupational risks and occupational diseases. A Sickness Benefit Insurance Act in 1930 provided income maintenance to persons unable to work due to illness or injury. Unlike the workers' compensation program, which could provide benefits to a disabled worker for his lifetime, the Sickness Benefits Insurance Act provided support for no more than one year. On July 1, 1967, the Dutch ended this bifurcated approach so benefits no longer vary because of the source of the disability.

Benefits and Financing
There are four major programs providing protection from the effects of injury or disease: the Sickness Benefits Insurance Act (ZW), Disablement Insurance Act (WAO), General Widows and Orphans Act (AWW), and the Health Insurance Act (ZFW). If a worker is injured or ill, beginning with the third day he is eligible to receive 80 percent of his daily wage, subject to a maximum wage (since January 1, 1976) of 185.19 Fl per day (approximately $75 a day). Benefits terminate when the individual returns to his employment or after 52 weeks.

If the worker is unable to return to work within one year or his disability sufficiently limits his ability to earn income (table 6.14), he is entitled to disablement insurance that continues until he is close to fully restored occupationally, dies, or reaches the age of sixty-five, when the General Old Age Pensions Act begins to provide benefits. (The latter benefits are uniform, that is, not tied to previous wage levels, nor is coverage limited by previous employment status.) Under the pre-1967 scheme of workers' compensation, benefits could be paid to employees who suffered a permanent partial disability without any wage loss. Under the current disability insurance scheme, benefits are paid only if there is actual wage loss and then only if the loss is 15 percent or more. Disability benefits, as of January 1, 1976, were based on actual wages or a minimum of (approximately) $32 per day and a maximum of (approximately) $75 per day.

Table 6.15
Financing of Dutch social insurance, January 1, 1976

Scheme	Employer Tax Rate (%)	Employee Tax Rate (%)	Maximum Income[a]
Sickness Benefits Act	7.45	1.25	$74/day
Disablement Insurance Act	6.65	3.55	$74/day
General Widows' and Orphans' Act		1.5	$14,240/yr
Compulsory Health Insurance Act	4.8	4.8	$40/day

Source: Social Security in the Netherlands, Ministry of Social Affairs, 1976.
a. Approximation based on 1 Fl = $0.40.

A worker's survivor is eligible for continuation of sickness or disability insurance for the remainder of the month and for two more months if either benefit was being paid. Thereafter benefits are paid to eligible survivors of any socially insured person, regardless of current employment status. These benefits are not tied to any previous wage or earnings levels but depend solely on the number and ages of dependent survivors. Even in the event of the death of an employed spouse, a widow who is under the age of forty and has no dependent children is not eligible for benefits other than a temporary widows' benefit, paid for from six to nineteen months only.

The Health Insurance Act provides medical and health insurance to all workers whose income on January 1, 1976, was below 30,900 Fl per year (approximately $12,400). Many workers with earnings above this level participate in voluntary health insurance schemes, some of which provide narrower coverage (no dental insurance) than does the compulsory plan for lower wage workers. Thus unlike workers' compensation in most countries, health benefits are not automatically provided to injured or sick workers in Holland. Prior to 1967 an injured worker coming under the workers' compensation system was provided with full medical and health insurance. The benefits under the Dutch scheme are largely, though not fully, provided by financing that is partially shared by employers and employees (table 6.15).

Several other forms of social insurance are provided in the Netherlands. When all these were taken into account, the average employer in 1976 had social insurance taxes of approximately 26 percent of his payroll (up to some maximum wage in every case), and an employee had payroll taxes on his wages of approximately 22 percent. This does not include a new General Incapacity Allowance Insurance that went into effect on October 1, 1976, and set a payroll tax on employers of 1.6 percent. The costs of such taxes can be gauged by noting that there are few low-wage workers in Holland; the broadly applicable statutory minimum wage for workers between ages twenty-three and sixty-five years of age was approximately $130 per week and $575 per month in 1976.

Administration

The determination of whether an illness is "occupational" is no longer necessary. Only in rare cases, for example, when a person becomes ill after retiring from work but before age sixty-five, might such a question arise. When the individual becomes sixty-five, his eligibility for the old-age pension means that he is no longer entitled to a disability or sickness insurance benefit.

The Dutch system is one of social insurance, however, much of it is not directly administered by the Social Security Fund but is managed by twenty-six separate occupational associations (fifteen of which operate under a single joint administration). The Ministry of Social Affairs classifies every Dutch industry and trade into one such association. Labor and management are represented in these associations and their decisions may be appealed to "Boards of Appeal" created by the ministry and ultimately to the courts that handle social insurance matters.

Aside from social insurance remedies, injured workers or survivors have rights to sue employers although such suits are not common. First, the injured worker must show that the employer has been grossly negligent. In death cases, damages in successful suits involve only lost earnings, less social insurance benefits being provided, and there is no award for nonmaterial losses (pain, loss of a loved one, and so on). In cases of illness or injury not resulting in death, a grossly negligent employer may be assessed for such nonmaterial losses. Awards are not frequently sought and tend to be small when they are won. Court costs may have to be borne by an unsuccessful claimant, although legal aid is customarily made available through a union or from the state.

Summary
Staunch supporters of workers' compensation schemes can point to a number of areas where Dutch workers are worse off today than in the presence of such a program. Medical benefits may not be available or only provide limited benefits under voluntary insurance programs for higher income workers. Prior to 1967 benefits for disability could be continued for a lifetime whereas, currently, they are supplanted at age sixty-five by an old-age pension that is generally substantially lower. Other injured workers are worse off in the new Dutch scheme because they suffer less than a 15 percent disability or no wage loss and so receive no benefits beyond sickness insurance. Prior to 1967 and in many other workers' compensation systems, they would have been eligible to receive some benefit.

As the Dutch system further develops and experience accumulates, it seems certain that a significant focus of concern will be on the costs of the various programs and on work incentives. Recent descriptions of the social insurance programs in *The Economist* and *Washington Post* describe skepticism in Holland and abroad about the country's ability to sustain them.[19] "One of the statistics that tends to unmask the problem is that roughly 18 percent of the Dutch work force—some 740,000 persons—on any one day are either out sick or on a disability—a figure almost double what it was five years ago. When the country's record 240,000 jobless are added to this, an amazing 22 percent of the work force is not working. They are, however, getting paid."[20]

Conclusions

Judging by the size of some of the efforts to describe American workers' compensation programs, the very short sketches of eight differing approaches to work injuries and illnesses must be viewed as introductory. There are serious limits to generalizing about all or even most of them because the eight systems are so heterogeneous. Considerable caution is needed before one argues that because a system, or subsystem, works well in one country that it should be adopted by another. The success of a system elsewhere does not assure that it can be replicated in an entirely foreign and unfamiliar environment. The customs and institutions that allow a program to function satisfactorily, as well as the complementary programs that have operated jointly with it in the past, may be essential to assure that a transplanted approach will survive. Nevertheless, in several respects the Europeans and Ontarians operate occupational disease systems containing fewer problems than exist in the American states, and there are some valuable lessons from them.

The most common and significant thread running through each of these workers' compensation systems (this excludes Holland) is that administrators depend heavily on a schedule or list of covered diseases. Even when the list is not an exclusive one, it defines the range of compensable illnesses. The administrators who were interviewed depend on the guidance of the schedule and acknowledge that it would create serious difficulties for them if no such list were available. The direction such a list provides for the administrators of compensation programs also gives much more certainty to workers, their representatives, and employers about the advisability of filing a claim. Although the presumptions (of varying degrees of strength) that the schedule gives to a claim assures compensability in many cases, the presumption against a worker with an un-listed illness allows him to immediately seek other sources of assistance. Even when there is an exclusive schedule, the system must evaluate claims, some of which will not be compensable. Nevertheless, the list allows a large range of (potential) claims to be quickly removed from the area of uncertainty and controversion. Some of these would be difficult claims by current American practices.

It may surprise some in the United States that the Europeans (and Ontarians) depend heavily on their lists, since the use of such schedules has been the target of attack by American reformers, many of whom know that social insurance programs in the United States generally are less progressive than in Europe. There is no anomaly here. The basic criticism of the use of exclusive schedules by American states relates to the narrowness of the schedule (excluding significant occupational diseases or categories of coverage) and to the infrequency with which such schedules are changed, despite the findings of the medical health community. The Europeans (and Ontarians) have shown that such schedules need not systematically deprive deserving workers of compensation. One can opt for either an exclusive schedule that is appropriately modified in the light of new scientific evidence or one can slowly alter the schedule when there is a provision in the law that eliminates the exclusivity of the list.

The schedule plays a crucial role in the determination of what is regarded as an occupational disease, and it is edifying that most of the countries depend heavily and formally on the medical-scientific community. Recommendations for changes usually are evaluated first within a professional panel—frequently consisting of specialists who may represent the interest groups—rather than being initially evaluated in legislative hearings. Scientists are forced to provide evidence to persuade other scientists, rather than attempting to convince legislators directly. The result overall has been that most occupationally caused illnesses, aside from the infectious diseases, are listed and routinely compensated where a claim is made. Every system also has some blind spots; other nations may currently "accept" the disease but that country's system is still debating the legitimacy of adding it to the schedule. No country has thrown open its doors so widely that a mass of illness claims with dubious links to the workplace will financially or otherwise undermine the compensation system, yet most legitimate diseases are covered by the various systems.

Benefits under the eight systems do not vary between workplace injuries and occupational illnesses, and are roughly comparable to those in the United States. Aside from the matter of the maximum level of compensation, wage replacement approaches are similar to those in the American states. The Europeans are harsher in some of their limits on compensating minor permanent partial disabilities and compensation of survivors, particularly those without dependent children.

The most striking difference in benefits between the eight programs and the United States is the availability abroad of significant and relatively generous alternatives to and supplements of workers' compensation benefits. These programs are particularly significant to persons whose disabilities are not work connected, and so are especially important in cases of disease. Benefits are always more generous when the disablement is due to an occupational disease (except Holland), however, the next best alternative is often only slightly less substantial when the illness is not occupational in origin. The availability of alternatives must make it less difficult for a compensation administrator to rule against a claimant and a worker or a survivor to accept such a decision. Many decisions need never be made because some of these alternatives to workers' compensation provide the initial temporary support to workers without regard to the arising-out-of-and-in-the-course-of test. In many instances before benefits expire the person has been fully restored to his previous position and the issue of the source of the condition is never raised.

There is a clear distinction between the United States and the eight jurisdictions involving the process or method by which decisions regarding compensability are made. Only in the American states does one find the adversary procedure used as a way to resolve disputes, including such issues as diagnosis, etiology, and the extent of impairment. The common practice in Europe and Ontario is to hold hearings and find fact without using attorneys and, commonly, without a private insurer or employer challenging a claimant's position. Claims are subject to challenge in some form everywhere, but it is usually the social insurance agency that does this rather than a private party. The appellate process is typically restricted beyond the first or second hearing level, to matters only of law and not of fact, and to an agency or a court specializing in social insurance issues. At the other extreme are the states where the highest appellate court in the state will evaluate issues of fact as well as law (approximately twenty-three), where the states may permit trial de novo in the appellate process (approximately seven). In Ontario and Europe there is a commonly shared sense of disbelief that complex medical-scientific issues in workers' compensation cases are regularly contested in such settings. Although the British do not tolerate this any more than others do outside the United States, when an employee sues his employer for negligence some of that process resembles a workers' compensation claim in the United States.

Unlike in the United States, the key determinant of compensability in technically difficult claims is the position taken by professionals (such as physicians and epidemiologists) who are not witnesses for the plaintiff or for the defense but are employees or regular consultants to the compensation agency. There is a tendency for these professionals to specialize in certain areas where problems frequently occur, for example, respiratory diseases, and for them to know precisely what it is that the compensation administrator needs to know. The agency's quest for truth need not involve efforts to reconcile vastly different technical perspectives that partially or fully reflect the interests of one of two contending parties. Nor must an enormous amount of resources be diverted to support a process of controversion and litigation.

The Europeans and Ontarians all recognize the significant links between occupational safety and health programs and workers' compensation. One of the new practices that has developed in several of the European countries, the required use of occupational physicians, deserves close scrutiny and evaluation by governments responsible for assuring healthful and safe workplaces. The proponents of this approach believe that the new system will lead to reduced numbers of occupational illnesses and earlier diagnoses and treatment when such sicknesses do occur. It is too early to judge how effective these programs will be. Beyond this, Ontario and several of the European countries have been vigorous in attempting to remove workers from exposures that will exacerbate existing health conditions. The compensation system is used to induce employees not to further jeopardize their health or lives by continuing contact with the substances that have already been harmful to them. Several American states have related types of legislation, but the workers' compensation agencies have not been aggressive about using them. The Federal Occupational Safety and Health Administration in the United States is finally attempting some preliminary steps along these lines in lead exposures.

The varieties and magnitudes of occupational disease have differed considerably in the eight jurisdictions outside the United States. Some of these differences reflect disparate industrial-occupational mixes, some are a function of the alternative systems of compensation, and some reflect different reporting procedures and requirements. There are two strong similarities extending across all jurisdictions, however, and both may hold significant import for U.S. policy. At the present time there is not a serious problem of occupational disease in any country, reflected in the workers' compensation data. Some speculation has been offered to explain this phenomenon in the United States and many of the same reasons must apply in these other jurisdictions. What differs is that workers do not face potentially hostile and contentious employers (or private insurers) in most of the eight settings. There is no adversary process in any of these seven countries and Ontario nor are employers even involved through experience rating in several instances. It might be expected that many more employees are filing or winning compensation claims than is actually taking place. For whatever reasons this is true, it is incorrect to place the responsibility for these missing or nonexistent claims on the shoulders of specific employers seeking to undermine them.

The second observation regarding the magnitude of the disease problem relates to the relatively large, residual incidence of silicosis and other diseases associated with mining, particularly in coal, that exists in a number of the jurisdictions. In the light of the post-1969 U.S. experience the existence of this problem is not surprising. The huge outpouring of workers' compensation claims with the passage of the federal Black Lung Law causes one to wonder how many other such occupations or industries exist. As a policy issue it raises the question, Would a new solicitous federal law in other occupational disease areas bring forth similar masses of successful claims as in the Black Lung Program? The prospects of the potential numbers must cause some apprehension for legislators who are concerned about the financial ability of taxpayers or employers to sustain programs comparable in scope to black lung. The European and Ontarian experience is instructive here. Bearing in mind all of the usual qualifications about international comparisons, the problems of mining, especially coal, seem to be unique, and the black lung experience will almost certainly not be replicated simply by extending coverage to other diseases and industries. Even when countries (or Ontario) have demonstrated a considerable liberality in the acceptance of claims for occupational disease, only mining stands out as a major source of serious claims. (The only exception has been the rapid growth of hearing-loss claims in several situations; however, in a number of respects these are systematically unlike other occupational disease claims.) It would be folly to argue that no other large reservoir of potential claims exists that would become evident if and when a black lung-like statute were to be passed, but it is inappropriate to shun such a program solely on an extrapolation from the experience in coal mining.

Summary

A brief restatement of some of the significant findings thus far provides the background for an assessment of the system and the policy recommendations that follow.

There are various estimates of the dimensions of occupational disease in the United States but all of these are seriously limited. Much of the problem derives from inadequate data and medical-scientific uncertainties regarding etiological, diagnostic, and other matters. These often make estimates of the incidence of even single diseases problematic. A more fundamental difficulty is the lack of a common definition of occupational disease. The absence of a shared starting point makes meaningful comparisons of estimates more challenging.

Recognition of these issues may allow one to avoid joining the ranks of those who have made quantitative estimates of the dimensions of occupational disease. It does not, however, excuse one from arguing that there are large and significant disease problems at the workplace. By example even if the proportions of cases of cancer and cardiovascular diseases attributable to exposures on the job were small, such as a few percentage points (and this is not liberal), these two categories of diseases alone would account for thousands of deaths annually. Estimates of 100,000 deaths or more per year may be too high (or in retrospect may prove to be too low), however, in absolute terms the occupational disease problem is a large one.

The evidence suggests that the workers' compensation system in the United States is dealing with very few cases of occupational disease. In most states such cases are perhaps 1 or 2 percent of all claims encountered. Much rarer, even in absolute terms, are disease claims involving very serious disablements or death. Statistics on these cases are fragmentary and not readily comparable on an interstate basis. Yet as the scientific-medical community identifies increasing morbidity and mortality occurring due to workplace exposures, the compensation system specialist still sees little of this reflected in workers' claims. A similar situation prevails in Western Europe and Ontario despite vast differences in their approaches to compensation.

When claims for occupational disease are made, there is a bifurcated response in the system. Those cases that have characteristics similar to common injuries due to accidents — and are relatively inexpensive — are handled like most other claims. Other types of disease claims, usually involving more serious disabilities, frequently involve extended controversy (and primarily these disputes are over the basic issue of compensability), very long periods between filing and first payment, and represent disproportionate costs of administration to the system as a whole. For such claims the system retains many of the undesirable features of the tort system that workers' compensation was supposed to supplant.

The contentiousness, delays, and uncertainty that exist in dealing with occupational disease claims are rooted in the nature of the illnesses. Although claimants must show that disability occurred due to a disease arising out of and in the course of employment, the causes of many serious illnesses are not known. Even when certain health hazards are known, the extent of the exposure and the amount needed to account for the disability are frequently not understood. Persons are exposed to the hazards away from the workplace. Thus noise, stress, and radiation can each contribute to disability, but even in those rare instances where records exist indicating past exposure levels, scientific uncertainties exist that force each party to disagree and litigate.

A variety of technical and scientific problems exist in administering occupational disease claims, but a number of difficulties particularly for workers derive from the statutes and their judicial interpretations. A partial list includes such barriers as unrealistic time and exposure limitation rules, exclusive and narrow schedules of covered diseases, arbitrary and special limits on benefits for certain types of diseases, eliminating certain illnesses due to their "ordinariness," and evaluating some claims for the presence of some accidental occurrence. The bases for some of these rules may have been to satisfy some problems encountered in a state's early compensation experience or perhaps were developed as part of some quid pro quo established between the interest groups, but their presence undermines or prevents claims by persons whose disability arose out of and in the course of employment.

The various states are not alone in wrestling with the issue of how to fairly compensate persons with occupational illnesses. The European and Ontarian systems have technical problems that are similar to ones found in the United States, however, there are also profound differences. At least one country (Holland) has simply scrapped the workers' compensation system and avoids many of the special problems of occupational illness. None of the other countries depend on an adversary process to determine the compensability of and extent of a disability as does the United States. In most cases employers have little or no direct stake in the outcome of a case nor are they (or a private insurer) involved in the claims process. Outside the United States, sick and disabled workers have readily available alternative benefits to workers' compensation that may be equal to or only slightly less than the latter. The question of compensability presents administrators and courts with a less dramatic and compelling alternative in this situation. The data suggest that even when there is no private economic stake in contesting a worker's claim the incidence of occupational diseases abroad is not very great, particularly when considering serious claims. This generalization has even more validity if one excludes claims that arise out of the mining industry.

Assessment and Recommendations

The broad goals of workers' compensation initially set forth in *The Report of the National Commission on State Workers' Compensation Laws* provide some framework for evaluating the operation of the system and suggesting needed changes. The degree to which the states' laws conform to these goals serves as a benchmark and identification of needed reforms.

Income Maintenance Goals
The National Commission argued that workers disabled by circumstances arising out of and in the course of employment should be adequately and equitably compensated. The extent to which states are meeting this goal can be debated though the commission found considerable room for improvement. The preponderance of criticism in recent years of workers' compensation laws has focused on the inadequate levels of compensation benefits.[1] There are at least four areas requiring remediation in order to bring equity to workers with occupational diseases.

Differentiated Benefits There is no valid reason to provide a different type of benefit to a worker with an occupational disease than with injury caused by accident. These disparities may have been necessary at one time to gain legislative approval for extended disease coverage, but such expedients are unwarranted today. The principle to apply is to link compensation with the extent of the disability and not with its source. It makes no sense, nor is it fair, to provide a different level of compensation to two workers with the same degree of hearing loss when one of them suffers the loss due to a long-term exposure and the other's occurred because of a single, traumatic event. It is anachronistic for special limits to be placed on benefits paid to workers with specific diseases, such as silicosis or asbestosis, when those limits are set below levels available to persons with equal levels of disability caused by accidental injuries or other diseases.

The primary argument for supporting such changes involves the matter of horizontal equity, that is, the equal treatment of equals. The only argument that could be made against the elimination of such differentiated benefits is that some employers will necessarily have to pay higher compensation costs. An effort to eliminate such disparities could be phased in over a period of several years. Because the primary area of such discrimination involves dust diseases and the number of such cases is not large, such a change would be relatively inexpensive.

Permanent Partial Disability   Some states do not compensate workers for occupational disease where the worker is only partially disabled. As with differentiated benefits, there is no compelling argument for the discriminatory treatment of disease claims for permanent partial disability. Many problems exist in most states regarding permanent partial disability claims in general, and these issues will not be raised here. But however a state resolves its permanent partial system, it ought not to distinguish between claims for injuries and those for diseases, much less for some arbitrarily selected group of diseases. Workers with occupational diseases should be eligible for benefits, the level of these should not differ systematically from those for accidental injuries, and the length of time that a worker could receive such benefits should not differ simply because a specific disease caused the disability. The arguments for and against moving toward more horizontal equity in the system are the same as in the case of differentiated benefits.

Impairment with No Disability   With some exceptions, occupational diseases are not being compensated in the absence of wage loss. The absence of compensation when impairment occurs without disability is a pragmatic device to limit benefits and simplify administration by setting benefits in terms of some standard wage loss. This has been not only a basic principle of compensation from its origin in the United States, it is also a characteristic of many programs in other industrialized countries. We quarrel here not with the principle but only with its inconsistent application. In some instances benefits are paid for occupational disease even in the absence of actual or hypothetical wage loss. By permitting retirees to receive benefits for hearing loss or giving benefits to survivors of persons who are stricken and die from an occupational disease after retirement, the principle is being violated. Even if we quarreled with such exceptions, and we do not, it would be unrealistic to suppose that such provisions could be eliminated where they already exist. In the case of very serious diseases that may remain latent for a number of years, compensation benefits to retirees or their survivors may have a beneficial (though very likely slight) impact on the safety and health practices of employers. Nevertheless, how can such practices be consistent with existing practices that deny compensation to workers with impaired health and no wage loss? For example, consider impairments to the reproductive system resulting in sterility, miscarriages, and deformed or otherwise damaged children.

There are two possible solutions. Existing liability laws could be modified to increase the likelihood that a worker (or spouse) can successfully gain common-law relief in such cases. The second alternative would be to provide workers' compensation benefits to families whose health problems occurred due to a hazard encountered at the workplace. Should the latter approach be used, benefits could be paid according to a schedule. When a worker suffers an impairment without a wage loss, such as damage to the person's reproductive system, there is no justification for tying the cash benefit to an existing wage level. A child who is poisoned by lead due to the hazard brought home from work by a parent should be compensated at a level independent of the parent's earnings. However, when one worker becomes disabled due to a hazard encountered at the workplace by another family member, benefit levels could appropriately be linked to lost earnings.

This proposal will be viewed as radical by traditional compensation specialists. In the event workers' compensation does not extend its coverage to provide such benefits, it is reasonable to anticipate that costly, time-consuming liability actions will be more commonplace. Moving such cases under the umbrella of workers' compensation undoubtedly will raise system costs, but the alternative is even higher future costs through a liability approach. Workers' compensation already provides benefits to some persons in the absence of wage loss. This proposal does not violate some current, absolute principle on which the whole system rests but poses a challenge and provides an opportunity for the compensation system.

The Wage Replacement Formula The basis for setting benefits is not uniform when a disease of long latency is identified as occupational. Some states have used a worker's wage level of the period two or three decades earlier as the basis for current wage replacement. The case of a totally disabled former beryllium worker who received only $13.33 per week in the 1960s, based on her earnings in 1941 to 1942, is hardly an example of the compensation system at its finest.[2] The problem is not very widespread because many states use a less severe method for determining wage loss and so few diseases of very long latency are being compensated.

Benefits in long latent disease cases could be based on several factors. One possible formula could use the worker's most recent full-time wage. Another could be to estimate the ratio of the worker's earlier wage to the maximum prevailing then and apply that proportion to the current maximum. A third approach would tie the earlier wage to a cost-of-living index and adjust it accordingly. To base compensation benefits on earnings levels that reflect no change for inflation is tantamount to admitting that a state's compensation program is totally inflexible. For those relatively few workers affected by such a change, the system would be providing much fairer treatment.

Health and Safety

The National Commission identified the achievement of a healthful and safe workplace as a second goal of a workers' compensation system. Supporters of workers' compensation have often pointed to the incentives the system provides for improving health and safety on the job. The evidence does not clearly indicate that this has been effective. There is some evidence that for a variety of reasons certain health hazards are not as widely prevalent as they were, but many others have not vanished at all from the workplace. New agents and processes are emerging in the industrial environment constantly. Information in this area is scarce, but a particular problem undoubtedly exists with long latent diseases such as cancer. Even if a hazard is suspected of jeopardizing the workers' health, the stockholders, managers, firm, or insurers may no longer exist when claims are made eventually.

Even when claims are anticipated and the management does not take a short-sighted approach, the mathematics of the discounting process implies that the present value of a claim to be made twenty or thirty years hence is very small. Thus a profit-maximizing firm must evaluate the costs incurred in the present period of providing a healthier environment or alternative production techniques against the marginal benefits to it of lower workers' compensation costs twenty years from now. For these and other reasons, society cannot depend on this very delayed process to provide healthier working conditions.[3] It is not surprising that Smith, who strongly rejects OSHA's role as a safety policeman, argues that the agency must continue to function as it does when health hazards involve long latent diseases.[4] *Workers' compensation creates no adequate incentive for improving health at the workplace to prevent long latent diseases.* The primary responsibility for healthy working conditions must remain with agencies like NIOSH and OSHA and not the compensation system. Nevertheless, there are at least five ways in which the compensation system can contribute to reducing the disease problem.

Waivers A number of states still allow workers to waive their rights to compensation, presumably so employers will not be discouraged from hiring workers with preexisting conditions. In the absence of waivers, the fear of potential workers' compensation claims may make such workers unemployable. The issue of waivers is a sensitive one since workers and employers both support their use or at least endorse the right of either party to enter into contracts freely. When the labor movement is ambivalent or silent about such waivers, however, it is not being consistent with its strong opposition to "yellow-dog contracts" which were declared unenforceable in federal courts by the Norris-LaGuardia Act (1932). This issue is particularly difficult for workers and their organizations because the inability to find or retain work seems more serious than the alternative, the agreement by the impaired worker to continue in some hazardous occupation and/or forego his rights to compensation.

There are no simple solutions, but waivers involving the worker's yielding all rights to compensation should be eliminated. This could be done directly or indirectly, that is, making such contracts unenforceable in the courts. When the waiver shifts responsibility for possible eventual damages to a second injury fund and away from the employer, at least the worker has the prospect of some financial protection against disablement. The latter is clearly preferable to the former, but if either situation encourages the return to a hazardous situation by a disabled worker who then risks much graver consequences to his health, the system is violating a basic goal.

Instead of condoning waivers the state must assure its citizens that they will not be forced, through lack of alternatives, to continue in a workplace setting that will exacerbate an existing health problem. Libertarians would argue that this is an infringement on individual freedoms. This view can be rejected for three reasons. If a person with a disease seeks to reexpose himself to the hazard, it suggests that the individual's options are so limited that they do not constitute a genuine choice. If the individual eventually becomes more seriously ill or dies, it will create an economic burden for society since compensation costs rarely cover the full costs of the disease. The worker should not be forbidden to reenter the hazardous occupation, but the compensation system should do nothing to contribute in a positive manner to such a decision.

Removal from Hazardous Occupations A few states allow the compensation agency to deny payment of benefits if a worker returns to a hazardous occupation. The agency is able to cut off assistance to partially disabled employees unless they cease exposing themselves to the hazard that has already disabled them. This approach should be adopted by all states in the presence of other conditions cited below, and it ought to be used much more widely than it has been in those states already permitting it. To sanction compensation payments to a sick worker who continues to threaten his health undermines a basic goal of the system.

This is not a significant problem at present because the number of workers collecting permanent partial benefits for such occupational illnesses is small. Employers and insurers are in an ambivalent position on this issue. If a worker collects benefits for a partially disabling dust disease and returns to a hazardous working environment, there is the potential that a far costlier claim — for permanent total disability or death — may result. Yet so long as the employee is unable to find a suitable job, his claim may be for total disability and at least temporarily involve higher compensation costs than for permanent partial disability. The core of the problem is that by providing only very limited benefits to partially impaired workers, a worker may feel that no alternative exists but to become employed again in the occupation in which he was exposed.

The purpose of this recommendation is not to raise new barriers to sick workers receiving compensation nor help to limit the long-run costs of compensation to employers; it is to prevent further undermining of an individual's health from the workplace. The recommendation may appear harsh and will often be so unless it is adopted in conjunction with other measures. If a worker is removed from his employment for a partially disabling illness — or because medical evidence suggests that a disease condition is likely to develop — he should be eligible to receive temporary total disability benefits until a new, safe, regular position can be secured for the employee. In that way the worker is provided with an alternative to staying in an especially hazardous occupation.

The key to using this approach successfully is an aggressive, involved state compensation administration. Only a few states actively encourage workers under their workers' compensation law with early and nondisabling diseases to seek healthier employment elsewhere by providing benefits to do so. All states should take such aggressive action to reduce the risks of serious health problems to workers.

Programs of this type are much more extensively used in Western Europe and Ontario. The key to their success is to encourage employers to find other work within their establishments that does not force the employees to continue to expose themselves to risk. When this cannot readily be done, a problem particularly in smaller establishments or mines, a retraining program is usually needed and is often provided abroad. Stipends for retraining could come from workers' compensation insurance (as a form of rehabilitation) or from manpower programs designed to assist the hard-to-employ. In the absence of adequate financial support it is likely that many workers will be unable to participate in such efforts.

Information to Workers on Hazards Not all workers feel compelled to work under hazardous circumstances, and if they were aware of the risks they encountered, they might change their employment accordingly. If the only result of this greater awareness would be to raise employee turnover, it would not be desirable per se. It is likely that a better awareness of hazards would force an improvement in conditions at the workplace. There are several reasons why such information might lead to a healthier work environment. Labor turnover is a costly matter for employers and the prospects of increased levels due to worker dissatisfaction can be expected to have some salutary effects on working conditions. When workers are informed of the hazards, they may, through the collective bargaining process, force employers to provide heathier surroundings. If the employer finds that his firm's image in the community suffers because of the conditions under which his employees operate, he may have an additional incentive to clean up the workplace. This effect most likely will be felt in larger, publicly held corporations that have evidenced some concerns about their "images." NIOSH could develop a list of substances that, if used in the establishment, would be prominently posted for workers to see. Such information will shift the labor supply curve to the left. Not only will recruiting costs increase, but wages may have to rise to attract adequate numbers of workers. Such potential increases in costs provide an incentive to the employer to reduce the hazards to health in his establishment.

The primary agencies who disseminate information about hazards are NIOSH, OSHA, EPA, and some others, but it would be reasonable for the workers' compensation system to exchange information and data with these groups. Regardless of which agency provides the information, its increased dissemination will result in less occupational disease. With some cost constraints, there is no reason to deny to any worker information regarding the nature of the substances to which he is being exposed at the workplace. Taken by itself this recommendation will not be a panacea for the problem of unsafe or unhealthful work environments, but it can be an important supplement to more direct measures.

Smoking and Interaction Effects Multiple causes of disability are more prevalent in occupational diseases than elsewhere in workers' compensation. Some states partially deal with the issue by using apportionment schemes whereby the employee, or other employers aside from the primary one, bear some of the costs of disability; other states do not apportion costs at all. There are solid arguments for using either approach. When the disease is partially caused or exacerbated by the workers' cigarette smoking, the burden of compensation ought not to fall entirely on the employer because a disability that is intentionally or willfully inflicted is not customarily compensable. There is ample precedent for such special treatment as in cases where a worker was injured while under the influence of alcohol or drugs. An employer cannot force an employee to cease smoking even if that person works in an uranium mine, on a coke oven, as an asbestos installer, or at a copper smelter. The medical evidence is so overwhelming that cigarette smoking is a virulent hazard that allowing the employee to escape any share of the burden of compensation in these cases seems grossly uneven. The recommendation may seem radical because this concept may be more broadly applied to other risks intentionally incurred, but it is not troublesome as long as the legislature limits the application to the self-destructive aspects of certain non-work-related activities.

The aim is not to have this issue used to decide the matter of compensability. It would be used solely *to apportion* the responsibility for disability. This would further the goal of a workers' compensation system that helps produce a healthy and safe work environment. If the compensation system clearly states that it will apportion benefits on this basis, it should lend added weight to all other arguments against cigarette smoking.

Opponents of such a recommendation will point to the many problem areas in which the role of cigarette smoking as a primary causative factor or cofactor in disease is still subject to scientific debate. They will likely be concerned by the potential of such a rule to increase litigation and/or frustrate otherwise worthy claims. These concerns are warranted but can be overcome by statutorily identifying the specific types of claims where such apportionment would be applied. It would be limited to occupations or industries, which the health community has already identified, *where cigarette smoking is especially hazardous. The use of apportionment should only be applied where such issues have largely been resolved.*

Another criticism made by employers or insurers might be that the proposal is too modest because the financial responsibility would, largely, still rest with the employers. If the disease would not have developed (or been exacerbated) in the absence of cigarette smoking, why should the employer bear any of the costs. This contention would be reasonable, however, solely if the only source of the disease were cigarette smoking and the workplace was not involved at all.

A third criticism is that it would be unfair to workers to change rules in the middle of the game. Workers in hazardous occupations who already smoke could be denied some benefits without having been alerted either to the risks of smoking, hazards they encounter at work, or changing rules of responsibility. For this reason alone it seems fair to phase in the rules gradually, but for the sake of the workers' health this could begin to be implemented immediately.

A fourth criticism is that such an apportionment approach would create an undue hardship on the worker or his family. Several states already use apportionment formulas in cases where claimants had preexisting conditions. If such an apportionment approach is rejected, it does not deal with the costs that the employer must shoulder because of a worker's preference for the health risk. For states that recognize the legitimacy of such concerns but are unwilling to move toward an apportionment rule, an alternative is that a fund could be established, out of which some of these compensation costs could be paid. The resources for such a fund, logically should come from a tax levied on the sale of cigarettes.

Information on Hazards to Employers It is wrong to suppose that all employees are subjected to health hazards because of the indifference or callousness of their employers. In some instances employers know little more than their employees about the hazards to which they are exposed. Schoenberg and Mitchell found that many employers were unaware that asbestos was used in their shops.[5] Moreover, many employers are unaware of the toxicity of the substances used. Although a number of agencies have the task of providing information to the many employers who would voluntarily eliminate such hazards, the workers' compensation agency could obviously play a constructive role here. At a minimum it can provide those agencies charged with protecting workers' health with information regarding illnesses occurring on the job. The end result should be fewer claims.

Adequate Medical Care

Many individuals regard the primary goal of workers' compensation programs to be the rapid restoration of the worker, as fully as possible, to the condition of health enjoyed prior to disablement. The goal can be achieved by providing a full array of medical, hospital, and rehabilitative services to the damaged employee. Cases of occupational diseases and injuries resulting from accidents differ little in this respect. A limited number of recommendations are made because there is little to differentiate the handling of disease.

Medical Benefits A few states still place arbitrary limitations on either the length of time medical benefits must be provided or the dollar amount of such benefits in cases of specified occupational diseases. Such limits contradict the purposes of the compensation system and have no place in it. Medical care is not a free good to be squandered frivolously, but it makes little sense to say that after some time or dollar limit has passed, a silicotic worker must find other means to support medical treatment. There is no medical or other health literature to support the contention that a discrete and predictable level of health care expenditure will restore any worker suffering from occupational disease.

Educating Physicians on Workers' Compensation When a worker is injured by accident at the workplace, his friends, the local union representative, the employer, plant physician, or others may formally or informally advise the person of his rights to compensation. In many instances the worker is aware of this right even in the absence of such assistance. The situation with diseases is significantly different. No one else at the workplace may know that the worker is ill or the type of illness he has. The only person outside his immediate family who may know that he is disabled is the worker's physician. The physician's problems in evaluating etiology or in some instances correctly diagnosing the illness have been stressed. Yet if the physician knew that the worker might be entitled to certain benefits because of his disability, many doctors would so advise their patients. This matter is more complicated when the treatment is provided by a company physician. This role of alerting a worker to his rights is inescapably the physician's for there is no other source that can readily link the illness to the workplace. Unfortunately most physicians do not understand how the systems work and could not be expected to satisfactorily fulfill this role at present.

In some instances workers will seek out the services of a plant physician. Without judging the diagnostic and restorative skills of such professionals, there is an obvious problem for them in suggesting that the worker may have a compensable claim in cases that are not clear-cut. This problem may not affect the patient's likelihood of receiving medical treatment, even at no charge to himself, but it can lower the probability that a claim for compensation will follow.

It is the responsibility of the compensation agency to seek out and inform health professionals about the rights of workers, so that in turn a disabled worker can be alerted to them. Oregon has such a program where the compensation agency provides informative literature on compensation to doctors.[6] Outreach programs by the state agency could begin with efforts directed to medical and nursing students, local medical societies, and hospital groups. A mechanism should be developed so that the doctor will recognize that he may be the only one who can alert a worker to his rights. Once the worker recognizes that he may have a compensable claim, the physician's role will have largely ended except in terms of rehabilitating his patient.

The Delivery System

A workers' compensation system is expected to deliver decisions — and where applicable, benefits — with speed, consistency and equity, justice and the protection of basic rights of all involved parties, and without a large expense for administration. To accomplish all this is no simple matter, yet to aspire to provide less violates the principles on which the system rests. Were a system to deal with occupational disease designed anew and independent of injuries caused by accidents, it could be totally reshaped. So long as the basic framework for dealing with injuries is not altered, or until it is redesigned, recommendations for handling occupational diseases are made within the current context. With the goal of achieving an adequate delivery system in mind, the following steps are recommended.

Time Limitation Rules There are few aspects of workers' compensation law that so overtly discriminate against persons disabled by occupational disease as the various time limitation rules in bringing claims. Medical science is gradually learning about the almost incredible delays that occur between the time a worker is exposed to a hazard and the time when the disease is manifested. Few hard rules regarding latency periods have emerged other than they vary widely even for the same substance and the same disease. In the light of such findings, it might be supposed that the states would have loosened their rules on time limitations but many have not. These still require that one or more unreasonable time rules be met in order for the claim to be compensable. Whether the rule is that the claim must be filed within some time of the last exposure to the hazard, or it requires that some arbitrary time must have been spent exposed to the hazard at work, the limits are not in accord with the medical knowledge about etiology or the latency period of disease. A triple-barreled rule for certain diseases, found in a number of states, requires that the worker has been exposed for a minimum of five years, this cumulative exposure occurred within the previous ten years, and at least two of the five years have been spent exposed in the particular state. Other rules are more unidimensional but may be even more restrictive.

A number of years ago the Atomic Energy Commission launched an effort to eliminate such restrictive rules because a number of health disorders caused by radiation exposure involved latency periods that assured that affected workers could not be compensated. That effort was relatively successful if the criterion used to evaluate it is the number of states with special time provisions for the filing of radiation claims. However, even when states have provided more liberal limits for radiation cases, the period granted may still be inadequate. Every state should adopt some type of "discovery rule" so that the time limit for filing a claim does not begin until the claimant learns or should have learned of the potentially compensable nature of his disease. Legislated limits on periods of exposure should be dropped entirely or written for specific diseases on the basis of modern medical knowledge. The former is strongly recommended on the grounds of simplicity and clarity and because in the latter it would be necessary to rewrite the law periodically. Laws such as the one stating that any disease contracted in less than one year on the job is presumed not to be occupational should be dropped. These limits are comparable to coverage requirements in unemployment insurance, Social Security, and welfare rules, and they are antithetical to the principle that protective coverage for the employee begins the instant he begins employment.

Opponents of such changes may argue that they will increase the number of claims (and thus the costs) of workers' compensation. This cannot be disputed, however, it is not the goal of the system to limit or minimize claims, but to provide compensation for illnesses and injuries that arise out of and in the course of employment. Probably relatively few persons would be affected by this type of liberalization in state laws, but regardless of the number justice demands that these arbitrary limits be removed. This recommendation does not suggest that no time limit be set for the filing of claims but that such restrictions be attached to "discovery rules," and they be applied liberally.

Resolution of Medical Questions The no-fault concept that characterizes workers' compensation was supposed to remove substantial areas of contention from the process of assisting injured workers. Anyone familiar with the current system understands that there is still substantial litigation, particularly in cases of serious and expensive disability. The primary issue for litigation in accidental injuries is largely a question of the extent of the disability. Regardless of the suitability of the technique developed by each state to resolve this matter, the medical issue of etiology (and to some extent diagnosis) is frequently far more complex than that of the extent of disability.

Etiological problems in occupational diseases are so technical and challenging that the compensation adjudicator is unequipped to resolve many of them. Indeed it would not be surprising if most nonmedical persons currently charged with deciding such matters would prefer not to have to do so. As an alternative a panel of health specialists in each system could be formed, whose function would be to receive evidence on the questions of etiology and the extent of disability in all occupational disease claims and report on these two matters to the compensation adjudicator. Although responsibility for decisions regarding compensability would still rest with the boards and the courts, questions of medical fact should be resolved by the panel of health specialists. It is not uncommon now for the courts to review only matters of law and, thus, not hear appeals from decisions of fact made by the compensation board. On medical questions of fact the decisions should be made by such a panel, then provided to the board for its use in resolving claims, and the parties could not challenge the panel on such questions. Aside from the several obvious benefits from such an approach, it could result in a greater willingness by health specialists to come forward and involve themselves in such matters. These persons might still find themselves subjected to an adversary proceeding, however, it would be carried out under the aegis of other health professionals.

There are various arguments that challenge this recommendation. It may be said that questions of etiology are not so complex that they cannot be resolved before compensation boards or in the courts. This line might point out that judges and juries are required already to decide difficult scientific questions in areas such as patents, medical malpractice, and products liability. A second objection might be that medical panels are not without biases (of a professional sort) and that, as such, their decisions should not be inviolate. Also, skilled medical-scientific personnel are so highly compensated that it would be too costly to recruit and use such panels.

Each of these arguments has some merit. Yet the evidence points to the extraordinarily difficult etiological questions inherent in compensating occupational illnesses, and these matters mostly involve scientific and not legal questions. There is no evaluation of how well the medical malpractice or other comparable areas are functioning, but the compensation system is not well equipped to resolve these controversies. It is frequently capricious with the rewards allocated to those with the more sympathetic, experienced, or articulate health experts available to testify for an appropriate retainer. These panels would not make law; they would provide the expertise to better carry out the directions provided by the legislature.

Professional biases may present problems when using the panel approach, but this argues more for evaluation and peer review of panels than it does against their use. Ontario's experience is encouraging. Since 1929, a medical panel there has evaluated all dust disease claims. Were there to be an underlying bias in their assessments, it would be apparent to medical practitioners in the province, who in turn might be expected to raise some form of protest. Instead it is believed that this scrutiny minimizes such biases from being manifested, while at the same time providing continuity and consistency in decision making. The same results could be expected here. A balanced, even-handed panel should reflect not simply the views of physicians with labor and management backgrounds, but it should also contain other types of health specialists including hygienists and rehabilitation specialists. Obviously, panelists need not be involved in matters ranging beyond their areas of professional expertise.

Medical panels may be expensive to maintain, but they might not be costlier than the current method of resolving medical issues. Moreover scientific consistency in decision making might lead to a reduction in the future litigation over questions of etiology and diagnosis, and so reduce other administrative costs. The extraordinary degree of controversion on the basic issue of compensability in occupational disease claims attests to the substantial costs already imposed in attempting to resolve some of these questions. These costs already are being borne by the system, and it is difficult to conceive that a panel approach would substantially raise them.

Aggressive Administration The workers' compensation agency should implement the law that protects disabled workers by seeking them out and advising them of their rights. The agency's role would expand well beyond the one it currently takes in some jurisdictions of simply hearing cases and occasionally having notices posted on factory walls. There can be no rational objection to the agency providing information to covered employees about their rights and the qualifications for benefits so long as a reasonable cost constraint is observed.

The explicit agency goal should be to provide more and better information to workers and employers and not simply to raise its case load. The information could be disseminated through the media, with instructional programs for workers and their representatives, possibly under the auspices of state labor education programs, at schools, and so on. The agency could meet with employers or their trade organizations to inform them of their rights, as well as of recent developments in compensating occupational health claims. The short-run effects of such a program would be to increase the volume of compensated claims for occupational disease by picking up cases that are currently being missed. In the longer run the program could lead to a reduced number of cases as greater emphasis is placed on safety and health programs.

An objection to this recommendation could be that workers' compensation agencies do not have the resources to undertake such programs. Other agencies such as state departments of labor might be better equipped, or are already operating these kinds of programs. Such programs must entail added costs for the agency through the need for more staff; yet to oppose this recommendation on these grounds would not be economically sound if the benefits from such aggressive administration would exceed these costs. There is no strong evidence to support either side but the benefits of having safer and healthier workplaces, better informed employers and workers, and so on is potentially impressive. Society places a significant value on raising the probability that existing individual rights and entitlements be received by making their availability known to the parties concerned. The issue of other agencies within the state being better equipped to provide such services needs to be resolved ad hoc on a state by state basis.

Proof   Aside from the matter of presumptions, the burden of proof in workers' compensation cases rests with the claimant. The burden can be an extremely difficult one in the case of occupational disease, and it results in claims being denied and a reduced volume of claims being filed. The issue does not lend itself to simple remedies, but O'Toole is correct in his analysis:

... more nearly consonant with traditional notions of justice and with the special purposes of workmen's compensation laws would be a more wide and generous application of the principle that the compensation claims are to be disposed of by interpreting the law liberally in favor of the employee whenever the facts permit. While such liberal interpretation appears not to go so far as a presumption in favor of the employee, it serves to benefit the employee not simply on the issue of causation but on all issues, including the issue of exposure.[7]

Many states have not acted in accordance with the view expressed in an Indiana case over three decades ago: "Occupational disease acts, being humane in purpose, are to be liberally construed and applied to extend protection to the ultimate good of the greatest number of workers."[8] Laws in the future should be construed in a manner consistent with this Indiana decision.

Autopsy Use   A number of commentators, who have examined the problems of occupational disease, have concluded that wider use of autopsies would improve the decision-making process. A number of states require that an autopsy be conducted on the request of the workers' compensation agency, but the use of the procedure is still relatively rare. Because better etiological and diagnostic decisions will follow, the wider use of such practices is recommended, except when to do so violates a religious or ethical precept.

Data Needs   A recurring theme has been the deplorable lack of data in the areas of occupational health and workers' compensation. The primary problems in the former area involve the recent development of major federal programs and the inability of medical science to provide a sufficient framework for developing such data. Important progress in recent years on both fronts promises that substantial improvement will occur. In the area of workers' compensation, however, there has been very little progress. The development of an adequate data system, particularly one that is uniform on an interstate basis, is not a simple or inexpensive task, however, this shortcoming has been painfully evident to interested observers for sixty years. Usable data are the sine qua non of any management information system and for legislatures and others who wish to evaluate the program. Moreover, if the federal government undertakes some role in the field, a uniform data system must be developed to assure that states are monitored on the basis of comparable criteria.

As data sources are improved, attention should be given to the problems of occupational diseases and hazards. Although the number of cases is still relatively small in each state, they are almost certain to grow in scope and in interest and need to be monitored separately from injuries caused by accident.

Exposure Records   As medical science continues to learn more about occupational health, it will become increasingly important for purposes of workers' compensation to know the extent to which an employee has been exposed to various workplace hazards. There are many reasons for establishing a national registry of individuals who have been exposed to various toxins (or suspected toxins), and a significant one would be to improve the functioning of the compensation system. Developing such a registry would discourage the use of many of the substances included. It would also alert workers to the risks that they were running in the course of work. It would be a potential source of evidence in future compensation claims, providing the panel of specialists with some parameters regarding past levels of exposure. A registry of exposures would create new record-keeping burdens for both the private and public sectors. It would have to be limited to something less than the full list of toxic substances that NIOSH has published. These factors imply added costs and difficult decisions in rating hazards. Yet such a system has been developed for many workers exposed to radiation, and though still imperfect it provides data that have been used in numerous compensation proceedings.[9] Cole has recently proposed such a registry for all laboratory workers who are exposed to carcinogens and mutagenic agents.[10] Germany currently monitors, longitudinally, all workers there who have had exposure to asbestos.

Such data would enter a national pool and would be shared by state health and compensation agencies. It could well be integrated into an ongoing program of transmitting information on hazards and disease characteristics between the federal government and all the states. For a number of reasons the registry and the dissemination of information could be undertaken by NIOSH most reasonably, although that agency's contacts with state workers' compensation agencies is currently minimal.

Broad Coverage

The compensation system should provide broad coverage of workers and the diseases that disable them. Many states give lip service to the notion of broad coverage of occupational diseases, but there is little evidence that this exists. The problem is definitional to some extent. Although most states no longer use restrictive schedules and thus appear to cover all occupational diseases, coverage is still effectively limited by one device or another. An obvious example is when states evaluate the compensability of a disability, caused by what any rational person would consider a disease, in terms of the injury-by-accident criterion. No matter where the line is drawn between an occupational disease and an ordinary disease of life, litigation and contention will develop. The lines need to be redrawn, not in the interests of preserving the system but to permit the essential goals of the system to be met. Perhaps the handling of occupational diseases has always been more imperfect than that of injuries caused by accident. Changing scientific knowledge has outpaced changes in the practices by various jurisdictions, and the situation has been made even more unsatisfactory, particularly in terms of coverage.

No issue is more disturbing than the realization that many workers who are disabled and killed because of their work receive no medical or indemnity benefits. Although at present no one can correctly estimate the number of workers so disabled or the proportion of these who receive compensation, it is clear that the system is not adequately covering all workers. If many of these workers never even file a claim, a host of secondary issues, such as the size of benefits paid, arbitrary limits on medical benefits and so on, are moot. To deal with this significant problem of occupational disease, it must be understood why cases are being missed so mechanisms for wider, more appropriate coverage can be developed. There are perhaps eight separate reasons why so many cases of occupational disease do not enter the workers' compensation systems. The first four reasons are more significant than the last four.

Ignorance   The difficulties of establishing the medical cause of many diseases has been stressed. A correct diagnosis may be hard to reach, making it even more unlikely that an occupational cause will be suspected. When a disease has a long latency period, the employee may not recall or be able to learn what hazards he encountered at work. The employee is not aware that the source of his disability is the workplace because of the lack of information and the inadequacies in medical science. Even if the physician suspects the workplace, and if he so advises the patient, a worker or a retiree may not be aware of his legal entitlement to compensation. The relative rarity of occupational disease claims may cause as well as reflect a widespread belief that workers' compensation is designed exclusively for injuries.

Statutory Limits   The entire history of occupational disease and workers' compensation indicates a prevailing fear that relatively broad coverage would swamp the system and thereby jeopardize the existing coverage. Legislatures and the courts have gone to great lengths to prevent "unworthy" diseases from being compensated. By drafting and interpreting codes excluding coverage for so-called ordinary diseases, the system has leaned away from covering such cases. There is no such sickness as an "ordinary disease of life," but there are probabilities ranging from 0 to 1.0 that a given sickness for a specific worker was caused by a hazard encountered at the workplace. Medical science is gradually replacing the one cause–one disease approach. This suggests that when several hazards may contribute to disability, such probabilities become particularly difficult to estimate. Yet some states still cling to the position that certain diseases ought not to be compensated on the grounds that they are per se ordinary. Others have discarded such antiquated views, but it is still difficult to secure compensation for certain types of diseases. Obvious examples are infectious diseases, certain pulmonary ailments, and cancer.

Time Limitations on Claims Potentially worthy claims are blocked from entering the system due to various time limitation rules. In view of the knowledge about the latency period of diseases, such limitations are inequitable. When states set arbitrary limits that can easily be exceeded before many diseases and/or ensuing disabilities are manifested, it only supports the contention that the injured worker is not the primary beneficiary of the compensation system. Limitations on the time to file claims that are peculiar to specified diseases and unrealistic in terms of their applicability attest more to the power of certain interests than to the realities of modern medical science.

Problems of Proof If a worker (or his physician) believes that a disability is due to a disease contracted at the workplace, he must then prove it to the satisfaction of the system. The burden of proof is not particularly cumbersome for most injuries caused by accident, but it can be an enormous barrier to a successful claim for occupational disease. Claims are not being filed if workers, perhaps on the advice of an attorney, believe that they do not have adequate proof to support a claim. Not every person who files a claim is certain of winning benefits, but as the problems of providing sufficient proof are more burdensome, a larger proportion of potential claimants will not file.

Disability Provisions In most cases where compensation benefits are paid, workers must demonstrate not only that they have been medically impaired but also that they have suffered a disability. Occupational disease is somewhat different in this regard, but this provision of compensation generally applies. Discher, Kleinman, and Foster report finding occupational disease cases that are not being compensated.[11] Yet who would not find it anomalous that compensation is given to a worker with impaired hearing but no earnings loss, while a person who has been sterilized, has been subject to a miscarriage, or has borne a deformed infant cannot be compensated because no "disability" has occurred? The worker may seek redress in a liability action, but why force this alternative on one worker but not on the other? In any case, with many diseases, particularly those involving some chronic but not disabling condition, no claim enters the system.

Delays One of the aims of workers' compensation is to provide a speedy and certain remedy for the employer (or insurer) and the employee whose disability arises out of and in the course of employment. Both parties yielded certain rights when this type of system first was established. Despite this, the process does not always operate as planned, and protracted disputes are not unusual in potentially costly occupational disease claims. Such delays may not intimidate all claimants, but it will cause some to not file at all or to drop the matter before it is resolved. More important, attorneys may not take such cases thus discouraging potential claims. If the attorney's income depends primarily on a rapid turnover of clients, a prolonged and difficult claim may not merit his time, and the volume of potential claims is further reduced.

Economic Fears of Workers A worker may be aware that a work-related health condition is partially and/or gradually disabling him but still be reluctant to file a workers' compensation claim because of economic insecurity. The employee may fear retaliation by a vindictive employer or may be threatened with loss of work if he admits to a physiological disorder. Simply revealing the presence of some illnesses may force the employer to transfer him to an occupation that is less hazardous but lower paying, and perhaps reducing his seniority.

Even if the worker is confident that a claim will be successful, he may not select this remedy if prolonged delays in getting benefits pose an economic threat to him, the maximum will replace only a small portion of lost wages, or the loss of work jeopardizes important fringe benefits, including health and life insurance. Much of this also applies to disabilities due to injurious accidents, but the problem is worse in the occupational disease area because the manifestation of illness is very gradual and health treatment delayed or postponed by the worker. Unlike most injuries, diseases may not even appear until after the worker has retired. If the employee receives a pension and is uncertain how secure it is, he may be reluctant to press a claim even after retirement.

The Physician's Apprehension Although a number of physicians specialize in occupational medicine or compensation medicine, many others seem to want as little contact as possible with the workers' compensation system. Some physicians find such processes unacceptably time consuming. No doubt a number of doctors have little taste for the adversary process wherein their professional views are challenged openly by attorneys and other physicians. His own uncertainty regarding the possible source of a patient's illness may cause a physician with little or no experience in workers' compensation matters to believe that the worker could not get any benefits. For any of these reasons a physician may not advise a worker that the source of his illness is work connected and potentially compensable. Without this counsel the worker is unlikely to file a claim.

Many workers with occupational disease do not seek or receive workers' compensation benefits, so the system must be faulted on the grounds that it is not performing the vital function assigned to it by the stated principles of workers' compensation. The system is under little pressure to change only as long as the public believes that workers are being protected satisfactorily. There is a growing awareness of the myriad health hazards at the workplace and, consequently, more attention will be directed to the system that is supposed to compensate workers for their resulting disabilities.[12] In order to survive the scrutiny that must eventually come, the system will have to demonstrate that most of the persons covered by it can count on protection if they are disabled by disease. Not every worker with a sickness should file a claim nor should he be guaranteed some compensation for the system to satisfy some criterion of broad coverage. Nevertheless the system must be rationalized so that its services are rendered in a rapid, consistent, equitable, and inexpensively administered manner.

The following recommendations would further improve the coverage of workers and diseases.

Schedules   Medical science has recorded hundreds of diseases that it regards as occupational and many thousands of substances that it recognizes as toxic, but a handful of states still limit compensable occupational diseases to a tiny list. Such laws make a mockery of the past 100 years of research in medical science. Several of these states use some limited flexibility in interpreting their statutes; however, these restrictive schedules are testimonials to apathy, indifference, or greed. As they are currently constructed, the schedules in states where they still exist undermine any pride attached to the workers' compensation system. They should be replaced immediately.

There are three possible alternatives to these types of schedules. One option would be to eliminate them entirely and not stipulate by statute which diseases are compensable. The advantage of this approach is that it provides full flexibility to the compensation authorities and the courts. A very serious disadvantage is that it creates considerable uncertainty as to what will be found compensable.

A second option is to use schedules but to make them comprehensive and, equally important, responsive to changing medical-scientific knowledge. Virtually all of the western European nations use such comprehensive lists and extend them relatively quickly on the heels of new scientific findings. These schedules usually prescribe diseases and a pertinent cross listing of occupations and/or hazards with such illnesses. The disease is frequently indicated in the broadest possible way, for example, "illness caused by arsenic or its compound." When a disease occurs from such a hazard or in a specified occupation, and these are being broadly construed, a presumption is made that the disability is compensable. This approach has considerable merit but its relevance for the state systems is questionable. The countries in Europe using this approach believe that the schedules can be both comprehensive and rapidly updated when necessary, involving a minimum of contention among the economic interests. It may be impossible to achieve such a climate here in the near future.

A third possibility is to use both a schedule and a catchall provision allowing compensation for unscheduled occupational diseases. New York uses such an approach, as do a number of European countries. The New York schedule, however, carries at best a weak presumption (unlike the European schedules), and the catchall provision creates room for considerable uncertainty. This approach has the virtue of being most responsive to new developments; in Germany vinyl chloride workers were able to be compensated for angiosarcomas even before the government modified the schedule of diseases.

Each of the options is preferable to a situation where a state depends on restrictive schedules, however, the last option is the best. Broad coverage and a good delivery system imply that workers, employers, and insurers are given substantial certainty about the range of compensable diseases. Ideally the schedule should identify specified hazards (by class or singly), occupations and industries (where such limits are realistic), and specific diseases alongside occupations and industries. The schedule should be based on scientific evidence, including epidemiological studies, and should create very strong presumptions in favor of the claimant. The pertinent statute would indicate that a heavy burden of proof falls on the insurer when a worker has a scheduled disease in order for the claim to be denied. The defense would be able legally to contest the claim, but the presumption in favor of the employee would be very difficult to challenge.

Alternatively when a claim is made by a worker for an unscheduled disease or when the employee is in the "wrong" occupation or industry, there would be a presumption that the illness was not occupational. Some European countries reject such cases or attempt to cover them as an injury by accident. It would be better to handle these claims as the Germans or Swiss do and compensate them under a catchall category. The burden of proof would be entirely on the employee as it is now, and unlisted illnesses would be presumed to be non-occupational. Unlike the restrictive practices existing currently in many states, however, such presumptions would not bar a person from bringing a claim and having a hearing. Some of these might be difficult to win, but they would at least have a chance of success. Scheduled cases should be handled routinely and the issue of compensability rarely raised, but insurers would not be barred from raising this challenge. Ideally such challenges would be made only in exceptional circumstances.

Several elements are essential to meet the necessary criterion of acceptability by the various interests. The schedule must be sound and kept current as health science uncovers new candidates for inclusion. Although the development of such a schedule initially may appear to be an enormous challenge, several good models exist abroad. The schedule must be supplemented by a variety of operational rules (diagnostic tests, the types of illnesses resulting from arsenic exposure, and so on) that would be developed by the health panels. The catchall category should be limited to the very special cases not included on the schedule because of their rarity and the "new" diseases that have only been uncovered recently and will be added to the schedule.

The approach just sketched out would reduce litigation, speed up the claims process, remove the need for expensive attorney services, and allow the system to operate as it was originally conceived to do. The savings effected by eliminating much of the contentiousness and haphazardness of the current system could allow more resources to flow directly to compensate victims of injuries or illness. Much of the difficult burden of resolving unanswerable medical and health matters would be removed from the shoulders of the compensation adjudicators.

The By-Accident Provision   Many states have sought to keep coverage from expanding until it protected all workers, past and present, from all sicknesses by precluding compensation for ordinary diseases of life. Although the fear of mushrooming may have been justified, it forced many jurisdictions to evaluate diseases in terms of a criterion of accidental injury. This procedure should be dropped, at least as it is currently used. By seeking the accident in the event that triggers a disability, the basic concept behind the provision is destroyed and violates any rational person's sense of the meaning of occupational disease. The arising-out-of-and-in-the-course-of test should be applied and the accident provision either dropped or used to preclude benefits only when the worker intentionally contracted the disease. Infectious diseases should be evaluated on the basis of these criteria just as cases of lead poisoning or dermatitis should be.

Diseases with Unknown Etiology   The problems raised by the ways the various state systems have grappled with the tough issues of etiology are so great that a policy of status quo cannot be defended. Basic changes should be made that explicitly confront the issues of unknown etiology. Those diseases whose etiology is unknown should not be covered in the manner that currently prevails in most states. For courts or juries to decide etiological matters when science does not have any answers creates an unacceptable burden for them and necessarily results in capricious decisons. The vast majority of heart and cancer cases cannot yet be linked scientifically to the workplace. In each case states have responded in an indirect way by arbitrarily limiting coverage. In heart cases they have limited compensability to those rare instances where the attack has occurred by chance during or very shortly after working hours. For cancer, time limitation rules or its consideration as an ordinary disease of life has served the same end.

Until health science develops more and better information, the system ought not to be maintained in its current form. Consistent with the American Heart Association's recommendation, all heart cases should be dropped from coverage until medical science can provide better answers that link work and cardiovascular disease. (Obviously there must be exceptions, as in situations involving cor pulmonale or heart stoppage due to electrical shocks.)

Most cancer cases should be excluded from coverage by workers' compensation systems. Unlike most cardiovascular diseases, a great deal is known about the links between certain hazards and/or occupations or industries and specific cancers by site. In light of this, states should include these hazards, occupations or industries, and specific forms of cancer in their schedule. Thus if such cancer develops subsequent to a proven workplace exposure, there would be a very strong presumption in the claimant's favor. Urinary system cancers would always be compensable in cases where past exposures to beta-naphthylamine can be shown to have occurred. All forms of cancer known to be associated with exposure to asbestos would be compensable in cases where a worker has had contact with the substance.

Claims involving heart disease or cancers where there is no "known" occupational cause would not ordinarily come into the system and when they did would usually be denied. As better information is found that links a form of disease to the workplace it should be added to the schedule. The catchall category would be available for those claims until the schedule was modified.

Implementing Recommendations

The limitations of the current workers' compensation systems are significant, and some elements have been identified that should be added or removed to allow workers' compensation to meet five basic goals. For those familiar with workers' compensation and the various efforts to improve it in the past, there is a recognition that the toughest nut to crack may well be to find a technique to implement and enforce proposed reforms. It is particularly difficult to address that issue in relation to occupational diseases because they involve such a small share of all compensation claims. Whatever form an improved system will take, it is likely to be shaped largely in terms of the shortcomings for 98 percent of the cases rather than for the 2 percent or so involving illnesses.

There are four possible routes that could lead to the improved handling of cases involving occupational disease. They can be classified as voluntary reform, imposed reform, a separated system, and an integrated approach.

Voluntary Reform

This approach would entail all of the individual states moving on their own toward improving their own system. All of the previous recommendations could be fitted into the current state systems, but it is extremely remote to expect that states will do so. This view is based on the inadequate response by the states to meet the nineteen essential recommendations enumerated in the Report of the National Commission. The commission recommended in 1972 that unless the states met these criteria by July 1, 1975, the federal government should impose the criteria on them as standards. As late as 1979 the average state had not met even two-thirds of the recommendations. Although voluntary reform by the states could be the least complicated path to reform, it is unlikely that the states will adopt all or most of the recommendations suggested here.

Imposed Reform

A state-administered law, changing none of the basic features of the compensation system but meeting minimum, federally-set standards is the imposed reform solution. Several unsuccessful attempts have been made to legislate such standards, all foundering under pressure from the interest groups and primarily vulnerable on the political and constitutional issues of how to enforce state compliance. For those who have attempted to develop such legislation, it is clear that the enforcement techniques that are most likely to emerge will force Congress to focus on simple, quantitative standards, such as benefit maxima and waiting periods, and eschew possible administrative and qualitative standards. Most of the problems involving occupational diseases involve nonquantitative issues so it will not be a simple matter to reform this area through federal minimum standards. For example, the creation of health boards and panels could be made mandatory in the law, but it would be very difficult for the federal government to determine if such a measure were being implemented according to criteria that would have to be developed administratively and legislatively.

A federal standards bill could most directly deal with a number of obvious legislative problems, such as inadequate statutes of limitation, restrictive schedules, and benefit limitations for certain specified diseases, but the knottiest problem would be to assure broad coverage of legitimate occupational diseases. The statute would need to either specify or allow an administrator such as the secretary of labor to identify which workers and/or diseases would have to be covered. In the absence of such a provision there could be little assurance that workers with diseases involving difficult etiological or diagnostic problems would receive appropriate compensation.

A minimum standards law allowing an administrator to set occupational disease rules raises a number of difficult questions. Politically, the uncertain but potentially very high costs would draw very serious fire from industry. The standard-setting process would be a focal point of criticism for many if not all of the interest groups. Would such disease standards emerge mostly from health professionals or would socioeconomic considerations be built into the process at the formulative stage? Who would initiate the inquiry that might ultimately yield a standard? How would other interested parties and agencies within a political administration affect the standard-setting process? Would standards be limited to etiological and diagnostic matters or would they also be applied to evaluating the extent of disability (not simply impairment)?

From a political perspective it seems likely that a federal standards-setting procedure will preclude most states from taking actions that move them very far in front of the minimum set by Washington. When a state is debating whether to modify its practices with respect to compensating a certain disease or type of worker based on recently established scientific evidence, opponents of change would probably point to any federal inaction as proof that the matter is still unresolved. If the standard setter would operate in an excessively cautious manner, the outcome might mean that the procedure actually inhibits reform that might have occurred in its absence in some states.

The preferable reform is a federal minimum standards bill allowing for the development of occupational disease standards that must be met by all states through the use of whatever enforcement device applies for other standards contained in such a law. There is much to be said for having the standards emerge from a body that is independent of the old-line federal agencies, particularly when the latter are closely identified as primarily serving the interests of certain limited segments of society. Such a body should contain, explicitly, persons with backgrounds in labor, commerce, insurance, and public administration and be broader than simply drawing on members of the medical profession. Professionals from other health and non-health disciplines should be represented, and their appointment would be made by the president. The standards that the group would ultimately issue could be made subject to the approval or rejection in toto by either the president or a cabinet-level person based on the record used to establish the recommendation.

The bulk of the standards issued by such a body would result in changes and additions to the states' schedules and would go beyond the strong presumptions mentioned earlier. The way that specific standards would emerge cannot be easily forecast without first observing how states would respond to the initial elements of workers' compensation reform. If a series of standards imposing the use of strong presumptions on the states are evaded by compensation agencies and/or the courts, more definitive rules would certainly follow. In that case presumptions could become irrebuttable.

Separated System

A separated system would involve either creating many black-lung type programs that would effectively remove certain problem diseases from state workers' compensation systems or, following the Belgian model, create a wholly separate (and presumably federal) system of compensation for diseases. In either case some very difficult choices would have to be made. By selectively covering diseases — as was the case in black lung — one has to choose which disease cases are not worthy of inclusion. The political realities are such that Congress would likely be asked by employee and employer interests to move to cover the broadest range of illnesses conceivable. By selecting one illness, a single industry, and only miners, Congress has been able thus far to limit its extension into the occupational disease area. However, if the doors are opened for persons with brown or red lung, with cancer, with radiological illnesses and so on, it is difficult to imagine that any significant illnesses will be excluded. If such federal legislation promises to move the immediate burden for compensation from the private sector to the United States Treasury, many employers could be expected to support such a move.

A separated system, whether it involves a handful of diseases (if that limit could be achieved) or all diseases, creates the following concerns:

What is the basis for having the federal government shoulder what has been the financial responsibility of employers till now?

How does one distinguish the areas of coverage? If the federal government would supplant the states in the occupational disease area, how would one resolve the myriad claims that would involve some elements both of disease and accidental injury? Would "cumulative trauma" back cases go to one jurisdiction, and sudden, accidental back strains go to another? One could imagine some hearing loss or eye damage or heart cases going to either or both jurisdictions, depending on the assessed probability of winning a claim and the size of the indemnity payments awarded by either jurisdiction. Could claims lost in one jurisdiction be later, or even concurrently, brought in the other?

What is the need for the federal government to replace existing systems for the most commonly seen claims that are currently being processed in a fashion similar to the typical injury-by-accident case? Since these dermatitis, retinitis, and comparable cases pose no special problems for the states now, would those be excluded from federal coverage?

If the federal government were to administer its own occupational disease program, what assurances are there that it would deal with the tough, technical questions of etiology, diagnosis, and so on in some exemplary way? It would probably not approach such questions through an adversary type process, and it would likely depend far more than the states currently do on authoritative medical opinion. Yet there are few if any federal compensation programs that could be used as models for an extension of this sort by the central government. This issue hinges not on a comparison of the various strengths of different levels of government but on their comparative inadequacies.

Integrated Approach
A variety of programmatic changes all of which would break some of the existing boundaries across programs would be an integrated approach. One version would replace workers' compensation as we know it with medical and income maintenance programs for all workers — essentially twenty-four-hour protection — by eliminating the arising-out-of-and-in-the-course-of provisions as a test of eligibility. This is the way that Holland and New Zealand have gone and that some other countries are close to providing.

Another version would integrate the myriad transfer-payment and insurance-based programs into some type of rational and equitable scheme. Workers' compensation might be coordinated with temporary disability insurance, unemployment compensation, survivor, disability, medicare, and retirement benefits under Social Security, veterans' benefits, welfare programs, and so on. Such a rationalization would have to give attention to the tax-free income associated with most of these programs.

It is difficult to quarrel with this approach except that the political obstacles to fulfillment that would emerge (and have emerged) seem insurmountable at present. All groups that currently benefit from one or more of these programs will examine recommendations jeopardizing their continuance with suspicion or open hostility. An integrated approach may also be threatened by a society that is unwilling to fund it appropriately once the full costs of supporting such a unified or integrated system are known. It may be easier to maintain public acceptance of scattered, overlapping programs even if overall costs are actually higher using this approach, and fragmentation means that some needy individuals fall "in between the cracks" and are missed and others are eligible for benefits from multiple sources.

A discussion of a basic overhaul of the public health and income maintenance programs should be reserved for a fuller treatment of prevailing conditions. If twenty-four-hour protection were provided, however, there would still be problems of occupational disease coverage. No doubt, avoiding having to demonstrate arising-out-of-and-in-the-course-of would eliminate many of the system's present difficulties. Instances where illness develops after the person has left work would still need to be evaluated when previous occupational exposure or incidents were potentially a contributing factor. This issue disappears only when benefits are provided regardless of work attachment. In that case, however, where injured or sick workers are compensated no differently than nonworkers, system costs can be expected to explode, and employees may insist that the elimination of workers' compensation should imply that their common-law rights to actions against their employers be restored. The Europeans have avoided this by allowing higher benefits for injured or sick persons who are workers when the source of the disability is the workplace, but then they are forced to identify diseases as occupational.

To summarize, four classes of change that would alter the handling of occupational diseases in the United States are conceivable. Two of these, which curiously range from the least to the most extreme in terms of their impact on the current system, are least likely to occur. That is, states are not moving towards voluntary reform, nor will the next few years bring an integrated, rationalized system. While Black Lung has put us on the path towards a separated system, problems with that program will likely impede further extensions of this approach. What is left then is either the status quo or imposed reform.

Costs

Cost estimates have not been made due to the absence of precise information on occupational diseases and compensation systems. The implications of the recommendations would probably, in the short run, lead to relatively large increases in the costs of compensation of occupational diseases in certain states. When these costs are evaluated against current expenditures for all of workers' compensation (injuries by accident and diseases) the increase is much less dramatic.

In the longer run occupational diseases will become increasingly important in workers' compensation. Because these cases are more expensive than injuries due to accident, system costs will rise even more quickly than the proportion of disease claims compensated. A number of the recommendations are aimed at using the compensation system to improve health conditions at work or reduce the degree of disability when disease occurs. These can hold down the anticipated growth in costs of compensating diseases.

The costs to society, and to employers, of occupational diseases are already being borne even if they are not being compensated.[13] Suffice it to note here that private insurance schemes and public programs help provide health and income benefits where illness or death are not considered compensable. Morbidity and premature mortality reduce total output through foregone product, a major cost of disability. When diseases occur, costs must be incurred, regardless of how workers' compensation chooses to treat them. Thus many of the arguments asserting that society cannot afford certain reforms neglect that society already bears such losses, and the real issue is only who will shoulder the direct and immediate burden for them.

APPENDIX A
CLAIM SURVEY

INTERDEPARTMENTAL WORKERS' COMPENSATION TASK FORCE - CLAIM SURVEY

OMB NO. 44-S75026
Approval Expires 11/31/75

General Instructions

1. **Multiple Choice Questions** - In all such questions, select the one (1) most correct answer and enter that number in the box provided to right. In questions 19.d, 21, 41 and 43, you may select more than one (1) answer, entering the number or numbers in the boxes to the right.

2. **Dates** - when a date is required, enter the month, day and two digits of the year. If the month or day requires less than two (2) characters, insert a zero in the first column. EXAMPLE: March 7, 1975 M D Y $\boxed{0}\boxed{3}$ $\boxed{0}\boxed{7}$ $\boxed{7}\boxed{5}$

3. **Dollar Amounts** - Should be rounded up or down and entered in whole dollars only: Insert zeros in any unused boxes to the left of the proper entry. EXAMPLE: \$683.72 would be: $\boxed{0}\boxed{0}\boxed{0}\boxed{6}\boxed{8}\boxed{4}$

4. **Don't Guess** - Unless you are reasonably certain of the answer, do not enter a dollar amount, date, yes, no, etc.; enter the number choice for "unknown" or leave the answer box blank. If a question does not apply, enter the number choice for "NA" (not applicable) or leave the answer box blank. If you have to correct an answer make sure your correction is legible.

5. **Occupational Disease** - for O.D. claims you do not have to answer questions 5 and 15.b denoted by an asterisk*, but you should complete questions 40 to 43.

6. **In Question 2**: use the following two digit standard insurance industry numerical code corresponding to the Post Office two letter code listed in alphabetical order: AL-01, AK-54, AZ-02, AR-03, CA-04, CO-05, CT-06, DE-07, DC-08, FL-09, GA-10, HI-52, ID-11, IL-12, IN-13, IA-14, KS-15, KY-16, LA-17, ME-18, MD-19, MA-20, MI-21, MN-22, MS-23, MO-24, MT-25, NE-26, NV-27, NH-28, NJ-29, NM-30, NY-31, NC-32, ND-33, OH-34, OK-35, OR-36, PA-37, RT-38, SC-39, SD-40, TN-41, TX-12, UT-43, VT-44, VA-45, WA-46, WV-47, WI-48, WY-49, Federal Acts other than DC-53. EXAMPLE: Wisconsin would be $\boxed{4}\boxed{8}$

7. **Physical Rehabilitation** in question 16 means treatment beyond the necessary medical and surgical treatment ordinarily provided for the healing of wounds; for example, the purchase of and the fitting and training for use of prosthetic devices, or whirlpool therapy to promote muscle use.

8. **Psychological Counselling** in question 17 means therapy or treatment by a Psychiatrist, Psychologist, or other professionally accredited Psychiatric Therapist.

9. **Vocational Rehabilitation** in question 18 involves vocational counselling and placement as well as vocational training for new employment.

10. **Contested or Controverted** in question 20 means a claim for which a formal or informal hearing was held to resolve any issues in question.

11. **Settled by Agreement** in question 24 includes compromise and release, "C & R", redemptions, stipulations, etc.

12. **The Carrier or Self Insured I.D. #** is one that has been assigned to your company and you should obtain it from whoever forwarded the questionnaire to you. The Claim # is your own company Claim File #. If it is more than 10 digits, use the 10 that will enable you to best identify the claim.

Carrier or Self-Insured ID #   1 ☐☐☐☐☐

Claim # 7 ☐☐☐☐☐

1. Type of Insurer:
(1) Stock (2) Non-Stock
(3) State Fund (4) Self-Insurer   17 ☐

2. State or jurisdiction under which benefits paid. (See Instruction 6 above.)   18 ☐

3. Age at time of injury.   20 ☐☐

4. Sex: (1)Male(2)Female(3)Unknown   22 ☐

5. *Date of injury: 23 (*Means question does not need to be answered in OD case. See Instruction 5.)   M D Y ☐☐ ☐☐ ☐☐

6. a. Date lost time began.   29 M D Y ☐☐ ☐☐ ☐☐
   b. Temporary lost time was: (1) Continuous(2)Intermittent(3)None   35 ☐

7. If injury or disease resulted in death, date of death.   36 M D Y ☐☐ ☐☐ ☐☐

8. Date notice of injury or disease received by insurer (or employer if self-insured.)   42 M D Y ☐☐ ☐☐ ☐☐

9. How was notice or knowledge first received by insurer (or employer, if self-insured)?(1) Report by employer to insurer (2) Report by employee to self-insurer (3) Notification by attorney or fee paid specialist (4) Notification by state industrial accident or W.C. organization (5) Filing of a petition for benefits (5) Medical Report (7) Other   48 ☐

10. Date on first indemnity check sent to injured employee or beneficiary.   49 M D Y ☐☐ ☐☐ ☐☐

11. a. Average weekly wage prior to injury or disability from which weekly indemnity rate was determined. (If wage not known, but was above maximum, give maximum.)   55 ☐☐☐
    b. Weekly wage: (1) Below maximum (2) Above or equal to maximum (3) Unknown (4) N.A.   58 ☐

12. Did employee return to work for same employer? (1) Yes (2) No (3) Unknown   59 ☐

13. Date of return to work, if permanent, and known.   60 M D Y ☐☐ ☐☐ ☐☐

14. Weekly wage upon return to work, if known.   66 ☐☐☐

15. Injury: a. Part of body: 69 ☐
(01) Head (02) Back (03) Chest (04) Abdomen (05) Side (06) Hip (07) Groin (08) Leg, Knee (09) Ankle (10) Foot, Toe (11) Arm, Elbow, Wrist (12)Hand,Thumb,Finger, (13) Face (14) Eye (15) Heart (16) Multiple (17) Other (18) NA
b. *Nature of Injury: 71 ☐☐
(01) Fracture (02) Sprain/Strain (03) Laceration/Abrasion(04)Puncture Wound (05)Contusion or Swelling (06)Foreign Body In (07) Hernia or herniated (08) Heart Attack (09) Paralysis (10) Burn (11) Amputation (12) Multiple (13) Other (14) NA

16. Was physical rehabilitation other than normal medical and surgical procedures provided? (1) Yes (2) No (See Instruction 7.)   73 ☐

17. Was psychological counselling provided by a professionally recognized therapist? (See Instruction 8.)(1)Yes (2)No   74 ☐

18. Was Vocational Rehabilitation provided by: (1) Carrier (2) State V.R. Organization (3) Other (4) No V.R. provided. If none, skip to 20. (See Instruction 9.)   75 ☐

Continued on reverse side.

19. Did V.R. include:
    a. Vocational Counseling:
    (1) Yes (2) No   76
    b. Vocational Training:
    (1) Yes (2) No   77
    c. Vocational Placement:
    (1) Yes (2) No   78
    d. Was V.R. paid for, in whole   79
    or in part by:
    (1) Carrier (2) State V.R. Org.
    (3) State Emp. Service (4) Em-   5
    ployer (5) Other (Use 2nd box
    if necessary.)

20. Was case ever contested or con-   6
    troverted? (1)Y (2)N (See In-
    struction 10) If No skip to 24.

21. If claim was contested or
    controverted, or hearing   11
    held, what was the most impor-
    tant reason(s)? (1) Hearing re-   12
    quired by law, no dispute (If 1
    skip to 24.)(2) Compensability
    (3) Jurisdiction (4) Degree of
    impairment (5) Medical diagno-
    sis in doubt (6) Length of dis-
    ability (7) Multiple liability
    (8) Coverage (9) Other (If
    more than one use second box.)

22. If the claim was contested
    or controverted was   13
    employee's position:
    (1) Sustained (2) Denied (3) Modi-
    fied by decision (4) Settled by
    agreement (5) Dismissed (6) Other

23. If claim was contested
    or controverted, at what level   14
    was the issue resolved? (1) In-
    formal procedure (2) Formal hear-
    ing, 1st level (3) 2nd level (4)
    Civil Court, 1st level (5) 2nd
    level (6) Final level (7) Not con-
    tested

24 Was case settled by a formal   15
    compromise agreement, e.g.,
    "compromise and release", "re-
    demption", "stipulation", etc.?
    (1) Yes (2) No

25 a. Was request for informal or form-
    al hearing filed? (Include hearings
    required by statute even though no
    dispute was involved.)(1)Y(2)N   16
    If No skip to 27
    b. Was hearing held? (1)Y (2)N   17

26. If hearing held:
    a. Date first   M D Y
    requested (if not   18
    required by law):
    b. Date of first   M   D   Y
    hearing: 24
    c. Date issue fi-   M   D   Y
    nally resolved: 30

27. Was claimant represented by:
    (1) Atty. (2) Fee paid special-   36
    ist (3) Union official (4)
    Other (5) None (If none skip to 32.)

28. Was there a dispute before
    an attorney, specialist,   37
    etc., represented claimant?
    (1) Yes (2) No (3) Don't know

29. Were there legal and other liti-
    gation expenses to claimant?   38
    (1) Yes (2) No (If No skip to
    31.) (3) Unknown

30. If "Yes" to 29, were any claimant
    litigation expenses deducted from
    W.C. benefits payable to clai-
    mant? a. (1) Yes (2) No   39
    b. If yes, what was
    dollar amount?
                                   40

31. Were any claimant litigation expenses
    paid by employer or insurer in addi-
    tion to W.C. benefits paid?
    a. (1) Yes (2) No   45
    b. If Yes, what was
    dollar amount?   46

32. Have all expected benefit pay-
    ments in this case been made?   51
    (1) Yes (2) No

33. What has actually
    been paid?
    a. Medical :   52
    b. Indemnity to
    claimant: 57
    (Aggregate payments to claimant, clai-
    mant's attorneys, and dependents
    including penalties and interest,
    but not payments to second injury
    or other special funds, or other
    case expenses which are not benefits.)

34. Indicate under which of the follow-
    ing categories indemnity payments
    were made, and (if applicable) what
    the weekly payments and number of
    whole weeks paid were (round off).
                  Category
    (1) Temporary partial (2) Temporary
    total (3) Permanent partial (4) Per-
    manent total (5) Death benefit to
    survivors.
    (If payments were made under more
    than one category, use 2nd, 3rd or
    4th line. Do not use more than a
    single line for a category, e.g. if
    there were two levels of permanent
    partial payment take the average
    over the total number of weeks.)
    Category   Weekly rate   Weeks
    63   64   67
    70   71   74
    77   11   14
    17   18   21

35. Lump Sum Payment:
    a. Amount of   24
    directed or com-
    promise settlement:(Not commutation,
    advance or specific, or scheduled
    award, or death benefits. Do not in-
    clude payments to claimant's attor-
    neys or any temporary benefits paid
    previous to lump sum.)   30
    b. Was there a release?(1)Y(2)N
    c. Amount of other   31
    lump sum payment:
    (Advance, commutation, catch-up or
    scheduled award, etc.)

36. If this is a claim on which a direct-
    ed or agreed-upon decision on the
    amount of future payments has been
    made, but payments are not yet com-
    plete, provide the following infor-
    mation on payments not yet made:

    (Question 36 continued in next col.)

    a. Lump sum pay-
    ment of any kind 37
    b. Weekly payments: 43
    c. Fixed period of weekly   46
    payments remaining
    (if specified):
    d. Life time payments (1)Y(2)N   49
    e. Are payments to?(1) Injured
    (2) Beneficiary   50
    f. If to beneficiary:
    Present age of principal
    beneficiary: 51
    Sex of beneficiary:
    (1)Male (2)Female (3)Unknown   53

37. Was there a third party subro-
    gation action? (1) Yes (2) No   54

38. Percentage impairment paid:
    (Scheduled injuries only)   55
    a. (1) Whole body (2) Injured
    member(s)
    b. Percent: 56
    (If more than one give largest %.)

SELF-INSURERS ONLY:

39. Supplemental Weekly-Indemnity:
    Was supplemental weekly indemnity
    paid to employee in addition
    to W.C. benefit?
    a. (1) Yes (2) No   59
    b. Date of first   M   D
    payment: 60
    c. Total weekly
    payment as a percent   66
    of salary:
    d. Total number of weeks   69

QUESTIONS 40 TO 43 TO BE COMPLETED
FOR OCCUPATIONAL DISEASE CASES ONLY

40. Was acceptance of the occupa-   72
    tional disease claim deferred?
    (1) Yes (2) No (if No skip to 42)

41. If "Yes", why? (Select up to 3   73
    choices.) (1) Reported late to
    insurer or self-insured employer
    (2) Time required for medical   74
    and lay investigations
    (3) Possible liability of more   75
    than 1 carrier or self-insurer

42. Following investigation, was the
    O.D. claim: (1) Accepted volun-   76
    tarily (2) Disputed

43. Disease involved (select up to 2):
    (1) Occupational skin diseases and
    disorders,e.g., dermatitis, eczema.
    (2) Dust diseases of the lungs (pneu-
    moconioses)e.g.silicosis, asbestosis
    (3) Respiratory conditions due to
    toxic agents, e.g.pneumonitis, phar-
    yngitis, rhinitis. (4) Poisoning,
    systematic effects of toxic agents,
    e.g.,metals, gases, organic solvents
    (5) Disorders due to physical agents
    (other than toxic materials), e.g.,
    heat stroke, frost bite, effects   77
    of radiation (6) Disorders due
    to repeated trauma,e.g., noise-
    induced hearing loss, synovitis,   78
    bursitis,(7) occupational can-
    cers and tumors, e.g., lung,
    liver (8) Other

Occupational Diseases

This section provides information on the kinds of occupational hazards that exist, the illnesses they cause, and the occupations most likely to be involved. Because this closely parallels textbooks dealing with occupational health or industrial medicine, a reference to helpful sources is provided. Additionally, a gap that appears in the literature is dealt with here.

There are no diseases that are purely occupational, and there are no diseases that are purely non-occupational except most of those that can only be transmitted genetically. A number of states have held cases involving venereal disease, and varicose veins as compensable, and in 1972 the State of Michigan allowed compensation for "tennis elbow."[1] (The disease arose out of and in the course of employment for a brick mason.) Itemizing occupational diseases involves some arbitrary judgments about the inclusiveness of the field. In theory, since virtually all diseases can arise out of and in the course of employment, any list that does not include every known (non-hereditary) illness may be considered incomplete. Inevitably, then, a corresponding list of health hazards or of occupations involved must also be arbitrary.

Aside from the problem of scope, any listing of hazards, occupations, or diseases runs the risk of being outdated rapidly. Research in areas such as occupational medicine, carcinogenesis, and environmental health is burgeoning and the exploding literature causes the lists to become obsolete quickly. It is also becoming apparent that many health problems at the workplace are due to the interaction of multiple hazards, not exposures to single substances.

Descriptive material has linked either hazards and illnesses or hazards and workers by occupation or industry. Rarely have illnesses and specific occupations been linked. When such associations have been reported, the disease has often been some form of cancer. A number of excellent sources of information, some of which may already have been used in workers' compensation proceedings, deal with workplace hazards.

NIOSH Criteria Documents The first of these, on asbestos, appeared in January 1972. NIOSH is publishing about ten to fifteen of these each year. Each document deals with a specific hazard and reviews the acute and chronic disorders resulting from exposures to the substance. The reviews are scrupulously thorough in reporting the evidence from animal experiments, epidemiological research, and published medical findings. Many *Criteria Documents* provide lists of occupations exposed to such hazards, but most of them are drawn from the badly dated work by Gafefer, and occasionally from even older sources.[2]

Other NIOSH Information In December 1973, the *President's Report on Occupational Safety and Health* listed fifty-seven specific hazards and indicated briefly the sorts of medical disorders related to each substance.[3] A short sketch was provided of how the substance was primarily used in industry. Though the hazard was not linked to specific occupations, some industries could be easily identified as major users of the substance. An estimate of the quantity of the substance produced and/or used in industry and the number of workers exposed to it was also provided.

Mancuso's Appendix As an appendix to his 1958 paper on the medical aspects of occupational diseases, Mancuso prepared a list of fourteen specific chemicals and their compounds, relating them to the occupations involved and the symptoms of industrial poisoning.[4] Although the list of chemicals is limited, his paper provides elaborate occupational detail. Almost 100 occupations are shown as exposed to chlorine and hydrochloric acid.

"Modes of entrance" are also indicated. The data are based partly on exposures expected in Ohio and so there may be a few occupations that are excluded because they are absent from the economy of Ohio. The paper, along with its appendixes, is an important contribution, and it is particularly significant that it was published in a law journal. An express purpose of the piece was to ". . . broaden the knowledge of attorneys concerning the scope of occupational illnesses and provide them with some understanding of the chemicals and occupations involved in the industries of Ohio."[5]

Guide for Decision Making A recent paper developed under contract for NIOSH is explicitly designed to assist workers' compensation administrators in the area of occupational disease.[6] It includes a list of fifteen specific agents (three are the same as in Mancuso's appendix), describes illnesses, symptoms, laboratory evaluations, and gives a detailed list of occupations in which the hazard may be found. The manual is a convenient reference source for persons who are not health professionals. It is as thorough as Mancuso's appendix in identifying exposed occupations, but only fifteen hazards are indicated.

Stellman's and Daum's Book The emphasis in all of the sources previously cited is on one or more specified hazards, however, Stellman and Daum use occupation as the point of departure.[7] They list almost 400 occupations ranging in specificity from "agricultural workers" or "rubber makers and workers" to "phthalic anhydride makers" and "plasma torch operators," and they indicate the hazardous substances encountered by each. This impressive list extends over fifty pages. It focuses primarily on chemical substances and, although it includes heat and cold as explicit hazards, it excludes noise. Seventy-two substances are indicated as hazards for rubber makers and rubber workers, although only sixteen hazards are shown for the

category "miners," including one identified only as "dusts: rock, metal."[8] Such unevenness detracts only slightly from the substantial contributions made by the authors. Stellman and Daum do not list either symptoms or specific diseases, but this is still an extremely useful reference for persons concerned with workers' compensation administration.

Gafefer's Book The Gafefer volume is one of the few sources that attempts to relate occupations to specific hazards and link these to diseases.[9] Because the book has a number of different authors for the separate chapters, there is some variation in the presentation. Some chapters focus on specific categories of disorders, and others approach the issue from the hazard. A chapter on occupational dermatoses lists approximately 150 occupations (some very broadly and some very narrowly defined) and identifies hazards in each that may cause skin disorders. Another chapter identifies ten poorly understood sources of pneumoconioses and describes ten others that are better known to the health community, but no occupations are identified with either of the sources. A chapter on chemical hazards itemizes 191 separate chemicals and lists some effects of various toxic agents. Additional chapters discuss five categories of pesticides; fourteen plastics and synthetic resins; physical hazards including radiation, abnormal air pressure, defective illumination, abnormal temperatures, and noise and vibration; biologic hazards including a list of specified diseases and occupations at risk; and one dealing with plant and wood hazards, which also lists occupation and specified diseases. The Gafefer volume is more encyclopedic than any other listed, but it is also more uneven in its format and is no longer timely.

Others There are a large number of other sources that list, categorize, or inventory hazards, illnesses, and/or workers at risk. None combine breadth of coverage and specific detail as do those already mentioned. Because of the special kinds of problems associated with cancer, however, some of the most recent sources have identified industrial carcinogens: Pochin,[10] Cole and Goldman,[11] the National Cancer Institute,[12] and Dinman[13] have identified industrial carcinogens. Except for Dinman, they identify a body site and group of occupations involved for each agent. Some disagreement exists about which are proven sources of cancer so it is not surprising that differences appear among these lists, although overlap is the usual circumstance. Yet the differences are noteworthy because each of these sources was published in 1974 or later. Discrepancies among them are due to different standards of proof among scientists that a substance is carcinogenic. Thus iron oxide appears on three of the lists but not on that of Pochin. Pochin lists cadmium though it appears on none of the other lists. (In the case of these two substances, the questions are significant because hundreds of thousands of workers are known to be exposed to both in the United States.) Cole and Goldman is the only source to indicate that hypoxia (a condition of inadequate oxygen in the blood) is a source of bone cancer in caisson workers. Dinman is the only one of the four sources to indicate that beryllium is carcinogenic. The beryllium case is a most interesting one because the substance has been known to be harmful due to its acute and chronic effects since 1933. It has been widely studied and is one of the better known occupational hazards. In 1970 Mancuso reported that, in addition to the problem of berylliosis in cases of chronic exposure, there was evidence of significantly elevated incidence of lung cancer among those who had worked with beryllium for very short periods of time years earlier.[14] Although these workers apparently left their employment as a result of developing acute respiratory

reactions to beryllium, it is unlikely that this link would ever be discovered except through a followup of all workers known to have ever been exposed to beryllium. But beryllium is generally excluded from recent lists of carcinogens. In a pamphlet published in 1976 for distribution to workers and their employers, OSHA reports: "There is also some indication that beryllium exposure may increase the risk of developing certain types of cancer. For instance, some recent research has revealed higher death rates from lung cancer among workers who had beryllium disease. There is also evidence that workers previously exposed to beryllium have unusually high proportions of cancer of the liver, gall bladder and bile ducts — other organs where beryllium is deposited."[15]

The only apparent reason for beryllium's characterization as carcinogenic by some writers and not by others is the tentative nature of the findings thus far, despite the close scrutiny given to it for several decades. It is uncertain if beryllium will some day routinely appear on such lists or if new evidence will develop that eliminates it as a cause of cancer, but it is certain that the number of recognized occupational carcinogens will grow rapidly. A major impetus for such findings is the effort by NIOSH. The National Cancer Institute's bioassay program also seeks to identify and evaluate chemical carcinogens, particularly those deemed to be of environmental and occupational significance. Because each bioassay requires at least three years to complete and a minimum of $100,000, there are limits to the speed with which new agents will be identified. But during 1975, 540 chemicals were in some stage of testing. Eighty-two of these are industrial chemicals, 94 are pesticides and agricultural chemicals, and 36 are metallic compounds.[16] Based on past findings, about 10 to 15 percent, conservatively, will be found to be carcinogenic.[17] Thus of the 212 industrial chemicals, pesticides and agricultural chemicals and metallic compounds now under analysis, rough 20 to 30 may be expected to be found carcinogenic.

Cancer is not the only danger being created by new substances and processes or being uncovered by new research findings. Background Information Letters from NIOSH warn of the (noncancerous) toxicity of polychlorinated byphenyls,[18] and the toxic hepatitis found to be associated with exposure to 4, 4' diaminodiphenylmethane.[19] The increasingly evident link between many chemicals found in the workplace and coronary heart disease and other cardiovascular disorders has a far wider implication. Plunkett mentions only as examples, anilines, nitrobenzenes, ethylene, chloroform, trichloroethylene, azides, carbon disulfide, nitroglycerine, ethylene glycol dinitrate, carbon monoxide, cyanide, butyraldoxmine, ammonia, chlorine, phosgene, the chloroformates, and heat and cold.[20] Should cardiovascular disease, the nation's leading source of mortality, be found to be substantially tied to substances encountered at the workplace, the recently prevailing emphasis on the search for occupational carcinogenics will surely be shared or supplanted.

To fill a gap that exists for most occupational diseases other than cancer, a listing of occupational diseases has been prepared, cross-classified by those occupations most likely to be involved (Appendixes C and D). Mindful of the difficulties noted earlier about the inseparability of occupational and non-occupational diseases, it seemed appropriate to leave the decision as to what to include to medical experts in the field. The list was prepared by itemizing every disease and occupation mentioned in the voluminous classic by Donald Hunter, *The Diseases of Occupation,*[21] supplemented by two other widely used texts in the field.[22] Although there are shortcomings to any such attempt at classification, and workers'

compensation systems may deal more often with some "non-occupational diseases" than with others appearing on the list, these are the diseases that the medical community links to workplace exposure. The enormous breadth of the problem is one more indication of the incredibly diffuse and complex burden that the workers' compensation system has been asked to shoulder.

APPENDIX C
DISEASES OF OCCUPATIONS

Disease	Key
Abattoir workers	
sulfureted hydrogen	
poisoning	H4:661
undulant fever (brucellosis)	H4:711
Q fever	H4:712
louping ill	H4:713
orf	H4:714
Weil's disease	H4:738
erysipeloid of Rosenbach	H5:710
Accountants	
writers' cramps	H4:879
Acetaldeyhde makers	
mercury poisoning	TM:654
Acetic-acid makers	
mercury poisoning	TM:654
Acetone (synthetic) makers	
mercury poisoning	TM:654
Acetylene workers	
carbon disulfide poisoning	TM:642
Acid chlorides and	
anhydrides manufacturers	
phosgene poisoning	H4:680
Acid polishers and treaters	
(glass factories)	
chlorine and hydrochloric	
acid poisoning	TM:644
Acrobats	
callosities	H5:752
Acrylamide workers	
acrylamide poisoning	H4:637
Acrylonitrile workers	
acrylonitrile poisoning	H4:633

Disease	Key
dermatitis	H4:636
Aerosal bombs workers	
fluorine and hydrofluoric	
acid poisoning	H4:683
fluorocarbon poisoning	H4:703
Agricultural implements	
industry workers	
lead poisoning	TM:649
zinc poisoning	TM:659
Agricultural laborers	
arsenic poisoning	H4:336
brucellosis	H4:711
farmers' lung	H5:1036
hookworm	H5:713
lime burns, dermatitis, lime	
hole, cornea, and conjunc-	
tiva injury, symblerpharom	H4:367
traumatic tenosynovitis	H4:809
Weil's disease	H4:738
Agricultural silo workers	
carbon dioxide poisoning	H4:654
silo fillers' disease	H4:675
silo disease	MM:126
farmers' lung	H5:1036
Air bag builders (rubber tires)	
benzol poisoning	TM:638
Air conditioning workers	
fluorine and hydrofluoric	
acid poisoning	H4:683
fluorocarbon poisoning	H4:703
Aircraft covering men	
benzol poisoning	TM:638

Sources: H4 and H5: Donald Hunter, *The Diseases of Occupations,* 4th and 5th editions (London: The English Universities Press, Ltd., 1969 and 1975).

MM: May R. Mayers, *Occupational Health: Hazards of the Work Environment* (Baltimore: The Williams and Wilkins Co., 1969).

TM: Thomas F. Mancuso, "Medical Aspects of Occupational Disease," *Ohio State Law Journal,* 19, no. 4 (1958): 612–667.

Numbers after source are page references.

Disease	Key
Aircraft industry workers	
lead poisoning	TM:649
zinc poisoning	TM:659
Aircraft mechanics	
burns	H4:601
cyanosis	H4:602
methyl bromide poisoning	H4:599
Aircraft spray operators	
benzene poisoning	H4:512
Aircraft upholstering men	
benzol poisoning	TM:638
Air hammer operators	
decalcification of carpus bones	H4:887–888
injury to soft tissues of hands	H4:887–888
osteoarthritis	H4:887–888
Raynaud's phenomenon	H4:887–888
Airline pilots	
air contamination	MM:173
frostbite	MM:171
heat stress	MM:173
hypoxia or aeroembolism	MM:165–166
labyrinth dysfunction with vertigo	MM:162
"microsleep"	MM:159
motion sickness	MM:165
personality changes	MM:166
snow blindness	MM:171
thermal stress	MM:169
Airmen	
aviation deafness, aviation pressure deafness	H4:873
ear block, rupture of the tympanic membrane, aero-otitis media, sinus block, aerodontalgia	H4:847
Airplane dope workers	
carbon tetrachloride poisoning	TM:644

Disease	Key
Airplane engine manufacturers	
mica pneumoconiosis	H5:991
Alabaster miners	
scoliosis	H4:373
Alcohol (synthetic) makers	
mercury poisoning	TM:654
Aldehyde pump men	
methyl alcohol poisoning	TM:656
Alkali power manufacturers	
chlorine poisoning	H4:678
Alkali-salt makers	
hydrogen sulfide poisoning	TM:648
Alkaline accumulator manufacturers	
cadmium poisoning	H4:447
Aluminum fluoride manufacturers	
fluorine and hydrofluoric acid poisoning	H4:685
fluorosis of the skeleton	H4:687
Aluminum workers	
chlorine and hydrochloric acid poisoning	TM:645
fluorosis of the ligaments and skeleton, anemia, dental fluorosis, fluorine, and hydrofluoric acid poisoning	H4:689–690
staining of the fingernails	H5:758
Amalgum workers	
mercury poisoning	H4:290
Ammonia workers	
ammonia burns and poisoning, eye injury	H4:672–673
Ammonium chloroplatinate workers	
platinosis	H4:483
Ammonium-salts makers	
carbon disulfide poisoning	TM:642

Disease	Key
Ammunition mixers	
chlorine and hydrochloric	
acid poisoning	TM:645
Ammunition workers	
lead poisoning	TM:650
zinc poisoning	TM:659
Analysts (lime, cement, and	
artificial stone)	
chlorine and hydrochloric	
acid poisoning	TM:645
Anesthetists	
gamma ray exposure	MM:181
radio dermatitis, leukemia	
and other cancers, radia-	
tion cataracts, reduced	
lifespan, and genetic	
mutations	MM:183
Aniline dyes and explosives	
workers	
anemia with punctate	
basophilia	H4:541
aniline poisoning	H4:567
bladder cancer	MM:237
cyanosis	MM:64
dermatitis	H5:735
methemoglobinemia	MM:64
methyl alcohol poisoning	TM:539
nitro benzene poisoning	H4:539
papilloma of the bladder	H4:834
Aniline workers	
aniline poisoning	H4:567
dermatitis	H5:735
methyl alcohol poisoning	TM:656
papilloma and cancer of	
the bladder	H4:834
Animal charcoal makers	
anthrax	H4:721
Annealers (foundries)	
chlorine and hydrochloric	
acid poisoning	TM:644
manganese poisoning	TM:652

Disease	Key
Anthracene workers	
skin cancer	H4:818
tar melanosis, tar mollusca	H4:819
Anthroquinone manu-	
facturers	
skin cancer	H4:822
Antifreeze makers	
methyl alcohol poisoning	TM:656
Apple pickers	
inhaling dust	MM:36
apple sorters' disease	H5:731
Apprentice boys in jewelry	
industry	
cyanide poisoning	TM:646
Aromatic arsines workers	
skin lesions and vesication	H4:350
Aromatic nitro and amino	
derivatives workers	
anilism and anilinism	
methaemoglobinaemia	H4:534
Arsenic packers	
arsenic poisoning	H4:335
skin cancer	H4:339
Arsenic sifters	
arsenic poisoning	H4:335
skin cancer	H4:339
Arsenic workers	
arsenic dermatitis, arsenic	
ulcers, arsenic hyperkera-	
tosis	H5:350
organic arsenic compounds:	
methyl dichlorasine, ethyl	
dichlorarsine, diphenyl	
chlorarsine, chlorovinyl	
dichlorasine, phenyl	
chlorasine, diphenyl	
cyanoarsine, phenarsazine	
chloride	H5:729
skin cancer	H4:339
Art glass workers	
methyl alcohol poisoning	TM:656

Disease	Key
Artificial cryolite manufacturers	
fluorine and hydrofluoric acid poisoning	H4:685
Artificial flower makers	
cramps	H4:878
mercury poisoning	TM:654
Artificial silk makers	
carbon disulfide poisoning	TM:642
hydrogen sulfide poisoning	TM:648
methyl alcohol poisoning	TM:656
sulfureted hydrogen poisoning	H4:661
Artificial stone slabs and blocks makers	
mica pneumoconiosis	H5:991
zinc poisoning	TM:659
Asbestos, cement workers	
mesothelioma	H5:986
Asbestos, textile workers	
lung cancer	H4:818
asbestosis	H5:972
Asbestos workers	
asbestosis	MM:48
asbestos warts	H5:978
Boeck's sarcoid	MM:46
lung cancer	MM:50
mesotheliomata of the peritoneum	H5:972
mesotheliomata of the pleura	MM:295
pulmonary asbestosis	H4:818
Asphalt and roofing materials industry workers	
lead poisoning	TM:649
Asphalt testers	
carbon disulfide poisoning	TM:642
Asphalt workers	
cancer of the skin	H4:819
color changes of the skin	H5:760

Disease	Key
tar melanosis	H4:819
tar mollusca	H4:819
Asphyxiants (workers dealing with)	
tissue hypoxia	MM:57
Assemblers	
chlorine and hydrochloric acid poisoning	TM:645
Assemblers (instruments)	
mercury poisoning	TM:654
Assemblers (suit, coat and overalls industry)	
cyanide poisoning	TM:646
Assembly line girls (electrical machinery)	
mercury poisoning	TM:654
Assistant supervisors (chemicals)	
methyl alcohol poisoning	TM:656
Assistant technicians (dairy products)	
mercury poisoning	TM:654
Auramine workers	
cancer of the bladder	H4:827
Auto accessories industry occupations: cementer patchers	
benzol poisoning	TM:638
Automatic lathe operators	
skin cancer	H4:819
Automobile factory workers	
chlorine and hydrochloric acid poisoning	TM:645
lead poisoning	TM:649
manganese poisoning, bluers	TM:652
methyl alcohol poisoning, painters	TM:656
zinc poisoning	TM:659

Disease	Key
Automobile painters	
methyl alcohol poisoning	TM:656
Aviation ground crews	
aviation deafness and avia-	
tion pressure deafness	H4:873
hearing loss	MM:175
Aviation petrol and	
methanol manufacturers	
chromium poisoning	H4:454
Aviators	
aviation deafness and	
aviation pressure deafness	H4:873
bends	H4:842
hypoxia and aeroembolism	MM:165,166
motion sickness	MM:165
thermal stress	MM:169
Babbitting machine	
operators (brass factories)	
antimony poisoning	TM:636
Babbitt pourers (foundries)	
antimony poisoning	TM:636
Bacteriologists	
infections	
pulmonary tuberculosis	MM:181
typhoid, diptheria,	
gonorrheal opthalmia, strept	
throat, bacteriaemia,	
primary chancre of the	
finger, poliomyelitis,	
anthrax, typhus, cholera,	
plague	H4:709
Bagasse workers	
bagossis	H5:1040
lobar pneumonia and	
chemical pneumonitis	H4:707
Bakelite makers	
phenol poisoning	TM:657
Bakers	
asthma	MM:285
callosities	H5:752

Disease	Key
dermatitis	H5:730
posterior polar cataracts	H4:865
Bakers (electrical machinery)	
mercury poisoning	TM:654
Ballet dancers	
pes cavus	H5:753
shortening and thickening	
of the tendo Achillis and	
callosities	H5:753
Banana planters	
hookworm	H5:713
Banbury operators	
antimony poisoning	TM:636
Band saw operators (brass	
factories)	
antimony poisoning	TM:636
Bar automatic shop workers	
multiple-pigmented	
hyperkeratosis, scrotal	
cancer	H4:825
Barbed wire manufacturers	
cuts, abrasions, infections	H4:707
Barge men	
Weil's disease	H4:738
Barium carbonate workers	
hydrogen sulfide poisoning	TM:648
Barley workers	
barley itch	H5:745
dermatitis	H5:733
Barmen	
pulmonary tuberculosis	H4:706
Barometer makers	
mercury poisoning	TM:654
Barometer manufacturers	
mercury poisoning	H4:290
Barrel burnishers	
cyanide poisoning	TM:646
Baryta grinders and packers	
baritosis	H5:1015
Baryta miners	
baritosis	H5:1015

Disease	Key	Disease	Key
Battery makers		furnaces)	
manganese poisoning	TM:652	phenol poisoning	TM:657
Battery men (garages)		Beryllium workers (mining,	
chlorine and hydrochloric		extraction, metallurgy)	
acid poisoning	TM:645	pneumonitis	H5:403
Bauxite smeltors		beryllium disease	MM:45
aluminosis	H5:1016	Boeck's sarcoid	MM:46
shaver's disease and pneu-		pneumonitis	H5:403
mothorax	H5:1017	pseudotuberculoma sili-	
Beaders (tin and enameled		coticum	H5:1020
ware)		pulmonary granulomatosis	MM:237
antimony poisoning	TM:636	Beta-naphthylamine	
manganese poisoning	TM:652	workers	
Bead makers (rubber tires)		bladder cancer	MM:278
chlorine and hydrochloric		Bichromates workers	
acid poisoning	TM:645	stained hands and finger-	
Bean sorters		nails	H5:756
allergic rhinitis, asthma	H5:1046	Bin room attendants	
Beef workers in abattoirs		(storage batteries)	
undulant fever (brucellosis)	H4:711	manganese poisoning	TM:652
Beer vat varnishers		Biscuit makers	
blindness	H4:583	dermatitis	H5:730
methyl alcohol poisoning	H4:580	Blacksmiths	
Beet sugar factory workers		acoustic trauma	MM:95
sulfureted hydrogen		blacksmiths' deafness	H4:872
poisoning	H4:661	callosities	H5:752
Bench workers (brass		cyanide poisoning	TM:646
factories, dental supplies,		posterior polar cataracts	H4:864
and foundries)		Blank books and paper	
chlorine and hydrochloric		products industry workers	
acid poisoning	TM:645	lead poisoning	TM:649
mercury poisoning, dental		zinc poisoning	TM:649
supplies	TM:654	Blast furnaces (benzol	
phenol poisoning, dental		house operators, chemists,	
supplies	TM:657	and laborers)	
Benzene workers		benzol poisoning, chemists,	
benzene poisoning	H4:508	tinners and wire drawers	TM:638
Benzidene workers		carbon dioxide poisoning	H4:654
cancer of the bladder	H4:827	carbon monoxide poisoning	H4:646
Benzol house operators		chlorine and hydrochloric	
(charcoal and coke, blast		acid poisoning	TM:644

Disease	Key	Disease	Key
Blast furnaces (continued)		Body men (automobile	
phenol poisoning, benzol		factories)	
house operators	TM:657	chlorine and hydrochloric	
Blast furnace bottom makers		acid poisoning	TM:645
manganese poisoning	TM:652	Boiler cleaners	
Blast furnace machine		vanadium poisoning	H4:497
operators and machinists,		carbon dioxide	H4:654
oilers		Boilermakers	
antimony poisoning	TM:637	acoustic trauma	MM:95
carbon dioxide poisoning	H4:654	boilermaker's deafness	MM:96
carbon monoxide poisoning	H4:656	Boiler scaler	
Blast furnace workers		rheumatoid pneumo-	
hydrogen sulfide poisoning	TM:648	coniosis	H5:1007
lead poisoning	TM:649	Bone-button workers	
zinc poisoning	TM:659	erysipeloid of Rosenbach	H5:110
Bleachers (cotton cloth)		Bone charcoal manu-	
chlorine and hydrochloric		facturers	
acid poisoning	TM:645	anthrax	H4:721
Bleachers (rayon and		Bone meal manufacturers	
artificial silk)		anthrax	H4:721
cyanide poisoning	TM:646	nitrogen dioxide poisoning,	
Bleach powder manu-		edema of the lungs	H4:675,676
facturers		Bone workers	
chlorine poisoning	H4:678	anthrax	H4:721
manganese poisoning	TM:652	lobar pneumonia and	
Blenders (paint and		chemical pneumonitis	H4:707
varnish factories)		Book binders	
manganese poisoning	TM:652	methyl alcohol poisoning	TM:656
Blockers (hats)		Bookkeepers	
carbon tetrachloride		writers' cramp	H4:879
poisoning	TM:643	Boot industry workers	
mercury poisoning	TM:654	pulmonary tuberculosis	H4:706
Blowers (felt hats)		Boot welders	
mercury poisoning	TM:654	scoliosis of the thoracic	
Bluers (automobile		spine	H5:803
factories)		Bottle finishers	
manganese poisoning	TM:652	glassworkers cataract	H4:863
Boat building industry		Bottle kilns firers	
workers		firemen's eye	H4:863
zinc poisoning	TM:659		

Disease	Key	Disease	Key
Bottle makers (blast furnaces)		Brazers	
manganese poisoning	TM:652	chlorine and hydrochloric acid poisoning	TM:645
Bottle sorters (soft beverages)		Braziers	
chlorine and hydrochloric acid poisoning	TM:645	boilermakers' deafness	H4:872
Bottlers (mineral water)		Breeders of dogs and cats	
hydrogen sulfide poisoning	TM:648	ringworms, ectothrix trichophyta	H4:710
Bowlers		Brewers	
cramps	H4:878	phenol poisoning	TM:657
Boxers		Brewers' draymen	
cauliflower ears (also nose may be flattened, scarred	H5:760	pulmonary tuberculosis	H4:706
eyebrows, opaque corneas,		Brewery workers	
dislocated thumbs)	H5:761	ammonia burns and poisoning, eye injury	H4:672–673
Brake linings manufacturers		carbon dioxide poisoning	H4:654
mesothelioma	H5:986	onychomycosis	H5:736
Braiders		sulfureted hydrogen poisoning	H4:661
traumatic tenosynovitis	H4:809	Brick, tile and terra cotta industry workers	
Brass dippers		lead poisoning	TM:649
nitrogen dioxide poisoning, edema of the lungs	H4:675–676	manganese poisoning	TM:652
Brass factories (babbitting		Brick workers	
machine operators, band saw		bricklayers' callosities	H5:753
operators, die cast operators,		hookworm	H5:713
hand tool operators, meltors,		olecranon bursa	H5:803
moulders, multicut saw		subacromial bursa (hodmen's shoulder)	H5:803
operators, receiving clerks,		Brine workers	
shakeout men, cleaners)		leuconychia	H5:756
antimony poisoning	TM:637	Britannia metal workers	
chlorine and hydrochloric acid poisoning	TM:645	antimony poisoning	HEW:35
lead poisoning	TM:649	Briquette makers	
zinc poisoning, workers in general	TM:659	skin cancer	H4:818
Brass founders		Bronzers	
metal fume fever	H4:422	hydrogen sulfide poisoning	TM:648
rheumatoid pneumoconiosis	H5:1007	mercury poisoning	TM:654
		metal fume fever	MM:38
		methyl alcohol poisoning	TM:656
		zinc shakes	MM:38

Disease	Key
Broom manufacturers (and strawboard)	
grain itch	MM:124
Browners (gun barrels)	
mercury poisoning	TM:654
Brush makers	
anthrax	H4:721
methyl alcohol poisoning	TM:656
Brushers (felt hats)	
mercury poisoning	TM:654
Budgerigar breeders	
bird-breeders' lung or bird-fanciers' lung	H5:1047
Buffers (electroplating)	
cadmium poisoning	TM:641
Buffers (metal furniture and optical goods)	
cyanide poisoning	TM:646
Buffers (other metals)	
antimony poisoning	TM:636
Builders (who use lime)	
dermatitis, lime hole, conjunctiva and cornea injury, symblepharon	H4:367
lime burns	H4:367
perforated nasel septums	H4:371
Bullion refiners	
lead colic and lead anemia	H4:286
Burnt sugar workers	
stained hands and fingernails	H5:756
Butchers	
anthrax	H4:721
erysipeloid of Rosenbach	H5:710
glanders	H4:733
orf	H4:714
verucca or lupus necrogenia, butchers' tubercle	H4:707
Weil's disease	H4:738

Disease	Key
Cabinet makers	
callosities	H5:752
cramps	H4:878
Cable manufacturing workers	
cancer of the bladder	H4:828
Cable splicers	
hydrogen sulfide poisoning	TM:648
Cadmium alloys welding	
cadmium poisoning	H4:447
Cadmium and cadmium compound makers	
cadmium poisoning	TM:641
Cadmium handlers	
yellow ring on teeth	H5:801
Cadmium platers	
cadmium poisoning	TM:641
Cadmium salts workers	
color changes of the skin	H5:760
Cadmium sulphoselenide pigments manufacturers	
cadmium poisoning	H4:447
Cadmium-vapor-amp makers	
cadmium poisoning	TM:641
Caisson workers	
aseptic necrosis of bone	H4:844
bends, erythema of the skin with pruritis, the itch or prickles, vertigo, "the staggers," nausea, vomiting, tinnitus, and nystagmus	H4:843
caisson disease	MM:152
carbon dioxide poisoning	H4:654
ear block, aero-otitis media, sinus block, aerodontalgia	H4:847
fatal distension of the heart with gas, subcutaneous emphysema	H4:846
nitrogen embolism	H4:846
osteoarthritis	H4:845
rupture of the tympanic membrane (rare)	H4:847

Disease	Key
Calcium carbide workers	
mucous membrane and	
conjunctiva injury	
necrotic skin ulcers	H4:367
Calcium cyanamide workers	
papular dermatitis, vesicles	
weeping excoriations,	
ulcers on the mucous	
membranes of the mouth,	
rhinitis, gingivitis, con-	
junctivitis	H4:368
Calico printers	
antimony poisoning	TM:636
aniline poisoning	H4:567
cadmium poisoning	TM:641
dermatitis	H5:730
manganese poisoning	TM:652
mercury poisoning	TM:654
methyl alcohol poisoning	TM:656
phenol poisoning	TM:657
Canal workers	
Weil's disease	H4:738
Cane cutters	
traumatic tenosynovitis	H4:809
Canners of citrus fruits,	
vegetables, meat, fish	
dermatitis	MM:24
Cap loaders	
mercury poisoning	TM:654
Car and railroad shop	
workers	
lead poisoning	TM:649
zinc poisoning	TM:659
Carbanilide makers	
carbon disulfide poisoning	TM:642
Carbon disulfide makers	
(disculphide)	
carbon disulfide poisoning	TM:642
headaches, somnolence,	
acute mania, symmetrical	

Disease	Key
polyneuritis	H4:629
hydrogen sulfide poisoning	TM:648
Carbon tetrachloride	
workers	
centrolobular necrosis of	
the liver	MM:272
chemical pneumonitis	MM:250
edema of the lungs, carbon	
tetrachloride poisoning,	
retrobulbar neuritis, toxic	
amblyopia, necrosis of the	
liver	H4:607–610
pulmonary edema	MM:272
Carbonizers (woolens and	
worsteds)	
chlorine and hydrochloric	
acid poisoning	TM:645
Carborundum wheel	
operators	
vascular disorders (Ray-	
naud's phenomenon)	H4:891
Carcass handlers	
anthrax	H4:710
Card room workers	
byssinosis, "weaver's	
cough"	MM:39
strippers' and grinders'	
asthma	H5:1024,1031
Cardiologists	
radiodermatitis, leukemia	
and other cancers, radiation	
cataracts, possible reduced	
lifespan, genetic mutations	MM:183
Carpenter	
blisters, abrasions,	
callosities	MM:115
dermatitis	H5:730
lung cancer	H4:816
traumatic tenosynovitis	H4:808
Carpet workers	
anthrax	MM:117

Disease	Key
Carroters (felt hats)	
mercury poisoning	TM:654
Carters	
glanders	H4:733
Cartridge makers	
mercury poisoning	TM:654
Case hardeners (electrical	
machinery)	
cyanide poisoning	TM:646
Case hardeners of metal	
hydrocyanic acid poisoning	H4:663
cyanide poisoning	TM:646
Cattle workers	
undulant fever (brucellosis)	H4:711
Q fever	H4:712
Caulkers	
Raynaud phenomenon	H4:895
Ceiling plasterers	
miners' nystagmus (not	
in U.S.)	H4:856
Cellarmen	
pulmonary tuberculosis	H4:706
Cellar, vault, wells, tanks,	
cistern, ship's hold workers	
carbon dioxide poisoning	H4:654
Celluloid solvent workers	
diethylene dioxide	
poisoning, anorexia,	
albuminuria, acute	
hemorrhagic nephritis,	
uremia	H4:623–624
Cellulose acetate workers	
diethylene dioxide	
poisoning, anorexia,	
albuminuria	H4:623
tetracholorethane poisoning,	
toxic jaundice, toxic poly-	
neuritis	H4:615–616
Cellulose extractors	
hydrogen sulfide poisoning	TM:648

Disease	Key
Cellulose sprayers	
aplastic anemia	H4:517
Cellulose workers	
carbon disulfide poisoning	TM:642
hydrogen sulfide poisoning	TM:648
Cement industry workers	
dermatitis, conjunctivitis,	
cornea injury	H4:371
manufacturers' diethylene	
dioxide poisoning, ano-	
rexia, albuminuria, acute	
hemorrhagic nephritis	H4:623–624
manufacturers' lead	
poisoning	H4:239
nodular silicosis	H4:371
perforation of the nasal	
septum	H4:371
uremia	H4:623–624
zinc poisoning	TM:659
Cementers (rubber shoes)	
carbon disulfide poisoning	TM:642
carbon tetrachloride	
poisoning	TM:644
methyl alcohol poisoning	TM:656
Cementers (suit, coat, and	
overalls industry)	
benzol poisoning	TM:638
methyl alcohol poisoning,	
shoe industry	TM:656
Cement mixers (rubber	
industry)	
carbon disulfide poisoning	TM:642
Centrifugal machine	
operators (cube sugar)	
callosities	H5:752
Centrifugal operators	
(paint and varnish factories)	
manganese poisoning	TM:652
Ceramics workers	
chromium poisoning	H4:454

Disease	Key	Disease	Key
Ceramics workers (continued)		Chemical operators, plater	
fluorosis of the skeleton	H4:687	pressmen, pressmen, and	
pneumoconiosis (from talc)	H5:987	wrappers	
Cereal crop sprayers		benzol poisoning	TM:638
DNOC poisoning	H4:561	chlorine and hydrochloric	
Chain makers		acid poisoning	TM:645
heat: rash, cramps, syncope,		Chemical plumbers	
stroke, neurosis	MM:93–94	lead poisoning	H4:238
dehydration	MM:93	Chemical industry press	
posterior polar cataracts	H4:864	operators	
respiratory infections	MM:95	phenol poisoning	TM:658
Charcoal and coke industry		Chemical process men	
(benzol house operators,		cadmium poisoning	TM:641
and chemists)		chlorine poisoning	H4:680
benzol poisoning	TM:638	phosgene poisoning	H4:680
zinc poisoning, workers		Chemical storage men,	
in general	TM:659	packers	
Checkers (fertilizer factories)		antimony poisoning	TM:637
cyanide poisoning	TM:646	Chemical warfare manu-	
Chemic users (cleansing		facturers	
agent used at the end of		chlorine poisoning	H4:679
the day)		phosgene poisoning	H4:680
alkali dermatitis	H5:734	Chemical workers and	
Chemical assemblers		foremen, mixers	
antimony poisoning	TM:636	ammonia burns and	
Chemical engineers		poisoning, eye injury	H4:672–673
aplastic anemia and myeloid		antimony poisoning	TM:637
leukemia	H4:911	burns	H5:755
manganese poisoning	TM:652	carbon disulfide poisoning	H4:629
Chemical factory repairman		chlorine poisoning	H4:680
phosgene poisoning	H4:681	cyanide poisoning	TM:646
Chemical foundrymen,		dermatitis	H5:730
assemblers, foremen,		ethylene chlorhydrin	
foundrymen, fuse assem-		poisoning	H4:620
blers, packers, storage men		lead poisoning	TM:649
antimony poisoning	TM:637	methyl alcohol poisoning	TM:656
Chemical machinery		phenol poisoning	TM:657
cleaners		platinum dermatitis for	
sulfureted hydrogen		chemical technicians	H5:450
poisoning	H4:661	severe strain on normal	
		homeostatis mechanisms	MM:225

Disease	Key
Chemical workers (continued)	
trichlorethylene toxemia	MM:56
zinc poisoning, workers in	
general	TM:659
Chemical-works' laborers	
burns	H5:659
Chemists	
acute chemical poisoning	MM:178
air contamination	MM:178
carbon monoxide poisoning	MM:178
carbon tetrachloride	
poisoning	TM:643
dermatitis	H5:730
lung cancer	H4:817
mercury poisoning	MM:179
methyl alcohol poisoning	TM:656
phenol poisoning	TM:657
platinum dermatitis	H5:450
platinum poisoning	H4:482
radiation fibrosis, fibrosis	
of lungs	H4:921
selenium poisoning	H4:488
Chemists (blank books and	
paper industry, blast	
furnaces, dental supplies,	
electrical machinery, lime,	
cement and artificial stone)	
chlorine and hydrochloric	
acid poisoning	TM:645
cyanide poisoning (electrical	
machinists)	TM:646
Chemists (brick, tile, and	
terra cotta; paint and	
varnish factories)	
manganese poisoning	TM:652
Chemists (chemicals, dye-	
stuffs, ink)	
chlorine and hydrochloric	
acid poisoning	TM:645
methyl alcohol poisoning	TM:656
phenol poisoning	TM:657

Disease	Key
Chemists (metal furniture, pat-	
ent medicine, and drug industries)	
phenol poisoning	TM:657
Cherry processors	
chlorine and hydrochloric	
poisoning	TM:645
Chief technicians (dairy	
products)	
mercury poisoning	TM:654
Chimney sweeps	
chimney sweeps' cancer	H5:780
pigmented scars	H5:760
scrotal cancer	MM:294
skin cancer	H4:818
Chiselers of hard steel	
rollers (flour mills)	
color changes of the skin	
(dark blue spots)	H5:760
Chloride of lime users	
(cleansing agent used at the	
end of the day)	
dermatitis	H5:734
Chlorine workers	
bleaching of hair and beard	H5:760
chlorine poisoning	H4:678
manganese poisoning	TM:652
mercury poisoning	TM:654
Chlorinated naphthalene	
workers	
chloronaphthalene acne,	
jaundice, hepatitis	H4:617–619
Chlorinated naphthalenes	
and diphenyls workers	
acute yellow atrophy of	
the liver	MM:273
Chloroform manufacturers	
methyl chloride poisoning	H4:596
Chloronapthalene workers	
chloronapthalene acne,	
chloracne, halowax, cable	
rash, blackhead itch	H5:580

Disease	Key
Christmas-cracker makers	
conjunctivitis	H4:411
generalized argyria	H4:411
Chromates workers	
chrome dermatitis, chrome	
holes, chrome ulcers	H5:422
lung cancer	H4:818
stained hands and finger-	
nails	H5:756
Chrome pigment workers	
chrome dermatitis, ulcers,	
and holes	H5:422
chromium poisoning	H4:454
lung cancer	H4:818
Chrome platers	
chrome dermatitis, ulcers,	
and holes	H5:422
Cigarette rollers	
asthma	H5:1033
callosities	H5:752
cramps	H4:878
Cigar makers	
asthma	H5:1033
cramps	H4:878
Clay shovelers	
spinal fractures	MM:115
Clay workers	
zinc poisoning	TM:659
Cleaners (brass factories,	
foundries, tin, and enameled	
wares)	
chlorine and hydrochloric	
acid poisoning	TM:645
cyanide poisoning, in brass	
factories	TM:646
dermatitis, cleaners in	
general	H5:730
Cleaners (copper factories,	
electrical machinery)	
cyanide poisoning	TM:646

Disease	Key
Cleansing preparations	
manufacturers	
fine punctate mottling and	
coalescence of the lungs,	
pulmonary changes	H5:992
Clergymen	
pre-patellar bursa	H4:803
Clock and watch factories	
repairmen	
benzol poisoning	TM:638
Clock and watch makers	
mutilation of the fingernails	
by trauma	H5:758
zinc poisoning	TM:659
Closers (paint and varnish	
factories)	
manganese poisoning	TM:652
Clutch-facings manu-	
facturers	
mesothelioma	H5:986
Coachmen	
animal sarcoptes infestation	H5:744
glanders	H4:733
ischial bursa	H4:803
Coach painting	
lead poisoning	H4:239
Coal-getters (bottom-holers)	
beat disorders	H4:806
zinc poisoning	TM:659
Coal miners	
albuminuria	H4:854
bursitis or beat disorders	H4:806
coal workers' pneumo-	
coniosis, pinhead mottling,	
complicated pneumoconiosis,	
focal emphysema, tubercu-	
losis, melanoptysis, massive	
fibrosis	H5:999–1005
dermatitis	H5:735
heat	H4:853

Disease	Key
Coal miners (continued)	
hookworm	H5:712
miners' cramp	H4:853
miners' nystagmus	H4:857
oscillation of lights, psycho-	
neurosis, tachycardia, ble-	
pharospasm, and head	
tremor	H4:858
right heart hypertrophy,	
death from congestive heart	
failure, bronchopneumonia,	
pulmonary arterial throm-	
bosis, rheumatoid pneumo-	
coniosis (Caplan's syndrome),	
rheumatoid granulomata	H5:1006–1007
vertigo	H4:858
Weil's disease	H4:738
zinc poisoning	TM:659
Coal trimmers (working in	
ships)	
pneumoconiosis and focal	
emphysema	H5:1004
Coal workers (in general)	
phenol poisoning	TM:657
zinc poisoning (charcoal)	TM:659
Cobalt workers	
hard metal disease	H4:478
Cobblers	
callosities	H5:752
modifications of the teeth	
due to abrasions	H5:802
Cocoa planters	
hookworm	H5:713
Coffee planters	
hookworm	H5:713
Coffee roasters	
stained hands and fingernails	H5:756
Coil solderers (electrical	
machinery)	
chlorine and hydrochloric	
acid poisoning	TM:645

Disease	Key
Coke furnace workers	
carbon monoxide poisoning	H4:656
Coke industry workers	
zinc poisoning	TM:659
Coke oven workers	
carbon dioxide poisoning	H4:654
hydrogen sulfide poisoning	TM:648
Collieries workers	
hookworm	H5:713
Colliers	
color changes of the skin	H5:760
Collodion cloth manu-	
facturers	
dental erosion	H4:591
Color grinders	
phenol poisoning	TM:657
stained hands and finger-	
nails	H5:756
Color makers	
antimony poisoning	TM:637
cadmium poisoning	TM:641
mercury poisoning	TM:654
Color mixers	
phenol poisoning	TM:657
Color developers	
eczematous eruptions	H4:572
lichenoid eruptions	H4:572
Compo conveyors (shoes)	
benzol poisoning	TM:638
methyl alcohol poisoning	TM:656
Compositors	
cramps	H4:878
Compounders (patent	
medicine and drugs industry)	
phenol poisoning	TM:657
Comptometer workers	
cramps	H4:878
traumatic tenosynovitis	H4:809
Condenser manufacturers	
chloronapthalene acne,	
jaundice, hepatitis	H4:617–619

Disease	Key	Disease	Key
Condenser manufacturers (continued)		Copper smeltors	
mica pneumoconiosis	H5:991	hair and beard dyed dark	
Coners (felt hats)		green	H5:760
mercury poisoning	TM:654	Copper stayers	
Confectionary workers		Raynaud phenomenon	H4:895
dermatitis	H5:730	Coppersmiths	
limonene dermatitis	H5:736	acoustic trauma	MM:95
sugar dust	MM:36	phenol poisoning	TM:657
Control men (foundries)		Copper workers	
chlorine and hydrochloric		selenium poisoning	H4:488
acid poisoning	TM:645	teeth stained green	H5:801
Convey turners		tellurium poisoning	H4:490
beat knee	H4:806	Copra (dust) workers	
Cooks (who cook fish)		copra itch	H5:745
erysipeloid of Rosenbach	H4:745	dermatitis	H5:733
fish handlers' disease	H4:745	Corundum producers (from	
Cooks (who skin rabbits)		bauxite)	
tularemia	H4:711	pneumothorax	H5:1017
Copper burnishers		shaver's disease	MM:44
hair and beard dyed dark		Cosmetic manufacturers	
green	H5:760	diethylene dioxide	
Copper dippers		poisoning, anorexia, albumin-	
nitrogen dioxide poisoning,		uria, acute hemorrhagic neph-	
edema of the lungs	H4:675–676	ritis, uremia	H4:623–624
Copper factories workers		mercury poisoning	TM:654
lead poisoning	TM:649	Cotton cloth spreaders	
zinc poisoning	TM:659	(and other textiles)	
Copper filers		benzol poisoning	TM:638
hair and beard dyed dark		Cotton cloth workers	
green	H5:760	lead poisoning	TM:649
Copper planishers		Cotton defoliant workers	
phenol poisoning	TM:658	pentachlorphenol	
Copper refiners		poisoning	H4:532
selenium poisoning	H4:488	Cottonfield laborers	
tellurium poisoning	H4:490	hookworm	H5:713
Copper retiners		Cotton-mule spinners	
antimony poisoning	TM:637	scrotal cancer	H4:822
Copper rollers		skin cancer	H4:819
metal fume fever	MM:38	Cotton strippers and grinders	
zinc shakes	MM:38	strippers' and grinders'	
		asthma	H5:1024

Disease	Key	Disease	Key
Cotton twisters		Crystal violet workers	
cramps (cotton twisters'		dermatitis	H5:735
cramps)	H4:885	Cupola tenders (foundries)	
Cotton weavers		cadmium poisoning	TM:641
cotton weavers' deafness	H4:872	manganese poisoning	TM:652
weavers' cough, asthma	H5:1027	Curriers	
Cotton workers (also		laborers' spine/Osteo-	
hemp and flax)		arthritic spondylitis	H5:755
benzol poisoning	TM:638	Cuttermen	
byssinosis	MM:38	beat knee	H4:806
chlorine and hydrochloric		Cyanogen makers	
acid poisoning	TM:645	hydrogen sulfide	
hookworm	H5:713	poisoning	TM:648
lobar pneumonia and		mercury poisoning, gas	
chemical pneumonitis	H4:707	makers	TM:654
mill fever, weavers'		Cyclotron workers	
cough	H5:1021,1031	radiation cataracts	H4:868
Cowmen			
dairymen's itch	H5:744	Dairy attendants	
dermatitis (sensitization		anthrax	H4:721
and aureomycin	H5:736	dairymen's itch	H5:744
ectothrix trichophyta,		farmers' lung	H5:1038
ringworms	H4:710	Dairymen	
undulant fever (brucellosis)	H4:711	anthrax	H4:721
Crane men (blast furnaces)		dairymen's itch	H5:744
chlorine and hydrochloric		farmers' lung	H5:1037
acid poisoning	TM:645	Q fever	MM:136
Crane men (fertilizer		Dairy-products, pasteurizers	
factories)		and technicians	
cyanide poisoning	TM:646	chlorine and hydrochloric	
Creosote workers		acid poisoning	TM:645,646
skin cancer	H4:818	mercury poisoning,	
tar melanosis, tar mollusca	H4:819	technicians	TM:654
Crucibles manufacturers		Dairy-products, workers	
beryllium poisoning	H4:430	lead poisoning	TM:649
Cryolite workers		Dancers	
fluorosis of the ligaments		cramps	H4:878
and skeleton, anemia, den-		shortening and thick-	
tal fluorosis, fluorine and		ening of the tendo	
hydrofluoric acid		achillis and callosi-	
poisoning	H4:689–690	ties	H5:753

Disease	Key
Decorators	
callosities	H5:753
manganese poisoning (in	
potteries)	TM:652
Degreasers (textiles)	
carbon tetrachloride	
poisoning	TM:644
diethylene dioxide	
poisoning, anorexia,	
albuminuria, acute	
hemorrhagic neptritis,	
uremia	H4:623–624
Dental supplies (bench	
workers, laboratory	
workers, and laborers)	
benzol poisoning	TM:638
carbon tetrachloride	
poisoning	TM:643
chlorine and hydrochloric	
acid poisoning	TM:645
zinc poisoning, workers	
in general	TM:659
Dental surgeons	
dermatitis	H5:730
mercury poisoning	H4:290
Dental technicians	
carbon tetrachloride	
poisoning	TM:643
chlorine and hydrochloric	
acid poisoning	TM:645
dermatitis	H5:730
mercury poisoning	TM:654
phenol poisoning	TM:657
Dentists	
radiodermatitis, leukemia	
and other cancers,	
radiation, cataracts,	
possible reduced lifespan,	
genetic mutations	MM:183
mercury poisoning	H4:290
dermatitis	H5:730

Disease	Key
Derris workers	
lobar pneumonia and	
chemical pneumonitis	H4:707
Detonator cleaners	
mercury poisoning	TM:654
Devil operators (felt hats)	
mercury poisoning	TM:654
Di-isocyanates workers	
rhinitis, pharyngitis,	
bronchitis, bronchiolitis	
obliterans, breathlessness	
and cough, fatigue, night	
sweats, rhonchi, râles,	
cyanosis	H4:526
Diamond cutters	
cramps	H4:878
lead poisoning	MM:66
Diamond and metal	
polishers	
rheumatoid pneumo-	
coniosis	H5:1007
Die makers (foundries)	
cyanide poisoning	TM:646
Die and tool makers (foundries)	
manganese poisoning	TM:652
Diethylene dioxide workers	
diethylene dioxide	
poisoning, anorexia,	
albuminuria, acute	
haemorrhagic nephritis,	
uraemia	H4:623–624
Digestion-house workers	
(pulp and paper)	
hydrogen sulfide poisoning	TM:648
Diluents in conjunction with	
epoxy resins workers	
dermatitis	H5:735
Dimethylnitrosamine (DMN)	
workers	
centrilobular necrosis of	
the liver	H4:593

Disease	Key
Dinitrobenzene (DNB) workers	
anemia	H4:544
bronze tinting of the hair	H5:760
color changes of the skin (yellowing)	H5:760
DNB poisoning	H4:542
headache, cyanosis, vertigo	H4:544
jaundice and necrosis of the liver	H4:545
Dinitro-orth-cresol (DNOC) workers	
cataracts	H4:871
DNOC poisoning	H4:559
Dinitrophenol (DNP) workers	
DNP cataracts	H4:871
DNP poisoning	H4:555
Dinner-fork filers	
color changes of the skin	H5:760
Dioctylphthalate workers	
dermatitis	H5:735
Dippers (aluminum products, brass factories, other manufacturing plants)	
chlorine and hydrochloric acid poisoning	TM:645
Dippers (potteries, tin and enameled ware)	
manganese poisoning	TM:652
Dippers (rubber tires)	
cyanide poisoning	TM:646
Direct-current electric meters manufacturers	
mercury poisoning	H4:290
Disinfectant makers	
mercury poisoning	TM:654
phenol poisoning	TM:657
Distemper manufacturers	
pneumoconiosis (from talc)	H5:987

Disease	Key
Distilling apparatus workers	
benzene poisoning	H4:508
Divers	
bends, decompression sickness (if fatal, called taravana), bleeding (from the nose, ears, and mouth)	H4:840
divers' palsy (paraplegia)	H4:844
ear block, rupture of the tympanic membrane (rare), aero-otitis media, sinus block, aerodontalgia	H4:847
nitrogen narcosis	H4:849
oxygen poisoning	H4:850
Dock laborers	
anthrax	H4:721
copra itch, general dock laborers handling copra	H5:745
fig-mite dermatitis	H5:746
grocers' itch	H5:745
swelling and deformity of the upper part of the pinna on both ears	H5:801
Dope shop workers	
benzene poisoning	H4:512
Dough mixers	
dermatitis	H5:733
Drapers	
cramps	H4:878
Dress designers	
modifications of the teeth by abrasion	H5:802
Dressers	
anthrax	H4:721
Dressmakers	
modifications of the teeth due to abrasions	H5:801
Driers (electrical machinery)	
cyanide poisoning	TM:647
Driers (in general)	
methyl alcohol poisoning	TM:656

Disease	Key	Disease	Key
Driers (rubber industry)		polyneuritis	H4:615–616
carbon disulfide poisoning	TM:642	trichlorethylene toxemia	MM:56
Drivers of horse-buses and		Dryers (brass factories)	
trams		chlorine and hydrochloric	
glanders	H4:733	acid poisoning	TM:645
Drug manufacturers		Dry-pan feeders (potteries)	
ammonia burns and		manganese poisoning	TM:652
poisoning, eye injury	H4:672–673	Dry-smokers (butchers)	
Drummers		callosities	H5:752
cramps	H4:878	Dustmen	
Dry battery makers		bursitis (dustmen's	
mercury poisoning	TM:654	shoulder)	H4:803
Dry cell paste mixers		callosities	H5:753
(storage batteries)		dermatitis	H5:730
manganese poisoning	TM:652	Dye makers	
Dry cleaning and dyeing		antimony poisoning	TM:637
industry finishers, furniture		hydrogen sulfide poisoning	TM:648
cleaners, rug cleaners, and		methyl chloride poisoning	H4:596
spotters		Dye works employees	
benzol poisoning	TM:638	chlorine poisoning	H4:678
carbon tetrachloride		manganese poisoning	TM:652
poisoning (finishers,		mercury poisoning	TM:654
spotters)	TM:643	methyl alcohol poisoning	TM:656
dry cleaning carbon disul-		papilloma of the bladder	
fide poisoning	TM:642	and renal pelvis, cancer	
Dry cleaning workers		of the bladder	H4:829
benzol poisoning	TM:638	Dyers (cotton cloth, dry	
carbon disulfide poisoning	TM:642	cleaning and dyeing, textile	
carbon tetrachloride		dyeing and finishing,	
poisoning	MM:70	woolens and worsteds)	
dermatitis, polyneuritis,		chlorine and hydrochloric	
corneal anesthesia and		acid poisoning	TM:645
ulceration, cranial nerve		color changes of the skin	H5:760
palsies, narcosis	H4:603–606	dermatitis	H5:730
edema of the lungs,		ethylene chlorhydrin	
retrobulbar neuritis, toxic		poisoning	H4:620
amblyopia, necrosis of the		manganese poisoning, in	
liver	H4:607–610	general	TM:652
lead poisoning	H4:284	phenol poisoning, in	
tetrachlorethane poisoning,		general	TM:657
toxic jaundice, toxic			

Disease	Key	Disease	Key
Dyestuffs (chemists and laborers)		galvanizers, hot tin coaters, insulators, maintenance	
benzol poisoning	TM:638	tinners, metal cutters,	
Dyestuffs (ink, etc.) workers		picklers, platers, repairmen,	
lead poisoning	TM:649	service men, sheet metal	
zinc poisoning	TM:659	workers, solders, switch	
		assemblers, testers)	TM:645
Electric accumulators manu-		Electrical machinery meter	
facturers		assemblers and moulders	
lead poisoning	H4:239	antimony poisoning	TM:637
Electric arc welders		Electrical machinery	
nitrogen dioxide poisoning		workers	
and edema of the lungs	H4:675–676	lead poisoning	TM:649
Electric lamps manufacturers		mercury poisoning	TM:654
mercury poisoning	H4:290	zinc poisoning	TM:659
Electric light bulb clouders		Electrical porcelain	
fluorine poisoning	H4:683	manufacturers	
Electric wire insulators		beryllium poisoning	H4:430
chloronapthalene acne,		pneumoconiosis (from	
jaundice, hepatitis	H4:617–619	talc)	H5:987
Electrical fitter		Electrical shock victims	
electrical cataracts	H4:869	electrical cataracts	H4:868
Electrical fixtures picklers,		Electricians (auto factories	
platers and solderers		and blast furnaces)	
chlorine and hydrochloric		callosities, in general	H5:753
acid poisoning	TM:645	chlorine and hydrochloric	
Electrical fixtures workers		acid poisoning	TM:645
lead poisoning	TM:649	Electrolytic metal refiners	
zinc poisoning	TM:659	fluorine and hydrofluoric	
Electrical machinery		acid poisoning	H4:685
(assembly line girls, bakers,		Electrolytic metal stripping	
foremen, letter foremen,		process men	
letter-out men, oven tenders,		nitrogen dioxide poisoning,	
packers, pump boys, pumpers		edema of the lungs	H4:678
and testers)		Electroplaters	
mercury poisoning	TM:654–655	acute ungual eczema	H5:736
Electrical machinery (coil		antimony poisoning	TM:637
solderers and etchers,		carbon disulfide poisoning	TM:642
finishers fabricators)		carbon tetrachloride	
chlorine and hydrochloric		poisoning	TM:644
acid poisoning (hot			

Disease	Key
Electroplaters (continued)	
chlorine and hydrochloric	
acid poisoning	TM:646
chromium poisoning, chrome	
ulcers	H4:454
cyanide poisoning (metal,	
automobile factories,	
storage batteries, electrical	
machinery, electrical	
fixtures, foundries, potteries,	
brass factories, clock and	
watch factories, glass	
factories, jewelry, metal	
furniture, suits, coats, and	
overalls, printing, explo-	
sives, ammunitions and	
fireworks)	TM:647
fluorine and hydrofluoric	
acid poisoning	H4:685
hydrocyanic acid poisoning	H4:663
lead poisoning	TM:650
phenol poisoning (electri-	
cal machinery industry)	TM:657
platinum dermatitis, asthma	H5:450
zinc poisoning	TM:659
Embalmers	
mercury poisoning	TM:654
Embossers	
mercury poisoning	TM:654
Embroiderers	
callosities	H5:752
Embroidery and laces	
workers	
lead poisoning	TM:650
Embroidery stenciller	
anemia or lead poisoning	H4:288
Enamelers	
cramps	H4:878
cyanide poisoning	TM:647
manganese poisoning	TM:652

Disease	Key
Enamel workers (bakers	
and makers)	
antimony poisoning	TM:637
carbon disulfide poisoning	TM:642
fluorosis of the skeleton	H4:687
manganese poisoning,	
makers	TM:652
silicosis	MM:41
Engineers	
dermatitis	H5:730
oil folliculitis	H5:733
phenol poisoning, in	
chemicals industry	TM:657
Engravers (in general)	
callosities	H5:752
cramps	H4:878
lead poisoning	TM:650
zinc poisoning	TM:659
Engravers (jewelry)	
chlorine and hydrochloric	
acid poisoning	TM:645
Entomologists (in anti-	
locust research)	
urticaria, allergic rhinitis,	
asthma	H5:1046
Enzyme-containing deter-	
gents manufacturers	
allergic alveolitis	H5:1047
Epoxide workers	
dermatitis	H5:735
Etchers (blast furnaces,	
electrical machinery, and	
glass factories)	
chlorine and hydrochloric	
acid poisoning	TM:645
Etchers (foundries)	
methyl alcohol poisoning	TM:656
Etchers (in general)	
phenol poisoning	TM:657
Ethoxyline resins workers	
dermatitis	H5:735

Disease	Key
Ethylene chlorhydrin workers	
ethylene chlorhydrin poisoning, edema of the lungs, bronchopneumonia	H4:621–622
Ethylene dichloride workers	
ethylene dichloride poisoning	H4:612
leukocytosis, dermatitis	H4:613
Excavators (for foundations of pipes, river bridges, sky scrapers and tunnels)	
caisson disease	H4:839
Explosives workers	
carbon disulfide poisoning	TM:642
chlorine and hydrochloric acid poisoning, mixers	TM:645
dynamite encephalosis	H4:590
lead poisoning	TM:650
mercury poisoning	TM:654
methyl alcohol poisoning	TM:656
nitrogen dioxide poisoning, edema of the lungs	H4:675–676
nitroglycerine/dynamite headache	H4:587–588
phenol poisoning	TM:657
TNT dermatitis	H5:510
TNT poisoning and illness	H4:456
zinc poisoning	TM:659
Exterminators	
hydrocyanic acid poisoning	H4:664
Fabric stampers using Prussian blue	
hydrocyanic acid poisoning	H4:664
Fabricators (electrical machinery)	
chlorine and hydrochloric acid poisoning	TM:645

Disease	Key
Factory maintenance men	
callosities	H5:753
Farmers	
anthrax	MM:134
asthma	MM:124
bagassosis	MM:124
beef and pork tapeworms, roundworm, hookworm, ectoparasitic infestations, dermatoses	MM:134,137
bone fractures	MM:124
brucellosis, tetanus, encephalitis, Weil's disease	MM:155
byssinosis	MM:124
carbon monoxide poisoning	MM:123
convulsions	MM:127
cornpicker's hand	MM:124
dairymen's itch	H5:744
farmer's lung	MM:124
glanders	H4:733
grain itch	MM:124
hyperkeratoses	MM:122
leptosperosis, Q fever, rabies, salmonellosis, trichinosis, bovine tuberculosis, tularemia	MM:134
louping ill	H4:713
milkers' nodes	MM:122
orf	MM:133
parathion poisoning	MM:129
poison oak or ivy	MM:121
prickly heat, sunburn, keratoses, skin cancer	MM:121
ringworm	MM:133
rodent, snake and insect bites	MM:121
silo disease	MM:126
skin contamination	MM:128
swineherd's disease	H4:712

Disease	Key
Farmers (continued)	
telangiectases of the	
exposed skin	H5:754
thresher's lung	MM:125
typhoid, malaria, protozoan	
infections like amebic	
dysentary	MM:272
Fat renderers	
hydrogen sulfide poisoning	TM:648
Feather workers	
lobar pneumonia and	
chemical pneumonitis	H4:707
feather-pickers' disease or	
duck fever	H5:1046
methyl alcohol poisoning	TM:656
Fellmongers	
anthrax	H4:721
Felt-hat makers	
methyl alcohol poisoning	TM:656
Felt-hat manufacturers	
(blowers, brushers,	
carroters, coners, devil	
operators, hardiners,	
mixers)	
mercury poisoning	TM:654
Felt-hat sizers	
callosities	H5:752
Felt makers	
stained fingernails	H5:756
Fencers	
cramps	H4:878
Fermenting vats workers	
carbon dioxide poisoning	H4:654
Ferro-silicon transport	
workers	
arseniureted hydrogen	
poisoning or phosphoreted	
hydrogen poisoning	H4:385
Fertilizer industry workers	
ammonia burns and	
poisoning, eye injury	H4:672–673

Disease	Key
cyanide poisoning (bag	
hangers and printers,	
checkers, crane men,	
laborers, mixer-weighers,	
superintendents and	
weighers)	TM:646
fluorosis of the skeleton,	
hydrofluoric acid poisoning	H4:687
hydrogen sulfide poisoning	TM:648
lead poisoning	TM:650
manganese poisoning,	
manufacturers	TM:652
Fettlers (potteries)	
manganese poisoning	TM:652
Fiberglass workers	
irritations of the skin,	
conjunctiva and upper	
respiratory tract; parony-	
chia, secondary malforma-	
tion of the fingernails;	
and warts	H5:989
Field glasses bronzers	
mercury poisoning	H4:290
Field laborers	
dermatitis	H5:737
File cutters	
blisters, abrasions, callo-	
sities	MM:115
Filers	
antimony poisoning	TM:637
File makers	
mutilations of the finger-	
nails by trauma	H5:758
Fillers (paint and varnish	
factories, glass factories,	
patent medicine and drugs	
workers)	
manganese poisoning	TM:652
phenol poisoning (patent	
medicine and drug workers)	TM:657

Disease	Key
Filleters	
Weil's disease	H4:738
Filling machine operators	
benzol poisoning	TM:638
Filter pressmen (paint and varnish factories)	
manganese poisoning	TM:652
Fingerprint identifers	
mercury poisoning	H4:290
Finishers (electrical machinery)	
chlorine and hydrochloric acid poisoning	TM:645
Finishers (wood and wicker)	
benzol poisoning	TM:638
Fire extinguisher makers	
carbon tetrachloride poisoning	TM:644
methyl bromide poisoning	HA:598
Fire gilding (by gold-mercury amalgam)	
mercury poisoning	H4:290
Firemen	
carbon monoxide poisoning	H4:658
carbon tetrachloride poisoning	TM:643
dehydration	MM:93
heat cramps	MM:94
heat neurosis	MM:94
heat rash	MM:93
heat stroke	MM:94
heat syncope	MM:94
methyl alcohol poisoning	TM:656
respiratory infections	MM:95
Firemen (brick, tile, and terra cotta)	
manganese poisoning	TM:652
Firemen (chemicals industry)	
phenol poisoning	TM:657

Disease	Key
Firemen (stoking boilers, especially in ships)	
beat hand (subcutaneous cellulitis)	H4:807
Fireworks makers	
manganese poisoning	TM:652
mercury poisoning	TM:654
zinc poisoning	TM:659
Fireworks mixers	
chlorine and hydrochloric acid poisoning	TM:645
Fireworks workers	
lead poisoning	TM:650
zinc poisoning	TM:659
Fishbox repairers	
erysipeloid of Rosenbach	H4:745
Fish cleaners	
erysipeloid of Rosenbach	H4:744
salt hole	H5:733
Weil's disease	H4:738,740
Fishermen	
erysipeloid of Rosenbach	H4:744
telangiectases of exposed skin	H5:754
Fishermen (in waters polluted with organic mercury compound)	
Minamata disease	H4:325
Fish-lorry drivers	
erysipeloid of Rosenbach	H4:745
Fish-meal workers	
erysipeloid of Rosenbach	H4:745
Fishmongers	
erysipeloid of Rosenbach	H4:744
Weil's disease	H4:738
Fish porters	
bursitis (Billingsgate hump)	H4:803
erysipeloid of Rosenbach	H4:744
Weil's disease	H4:738
Fish processers	
erysipeloid of Rosenbach	H4:745

Disease	Key	Disease	Key
Fish workers		tulip fingers, lily rash,	
fish handlers' disease	H5:709	primrose family dermatitis	H5:738
Fitters		Flour bleachers	
oil folliculitis	H5:733	chlorine poisoning	H4:678
Fitters (shoes)		dermatitis	H5:730
methyl alcohol poisoning	TM:656	Flour packers	
Flap stickers (shoes)		dermatitis	H5:733
methyl alcohol poisoning	TM:656	Flour workers	
Flautists		dermatitis	H4:730
cramps	H4:878	lobar pneumonia and	
Flax mills workers		chemical pneumonitis	H4:707
byssinosis (pounce or		Fluoracetic acid workers	
pouncy chest)	H5:1025	fluoracetic acid poisoning	H4:703
hackling fever, flax		Fluoralcohols workers	
fever	H5:1024	fluoralcohols poisoning	H4:703
Flax-rettery workers		Fluorine workers	
hydrogen sulfide poisoning	TM:648	fluorine and hydrofluoric	
Flocculator manufacturers		acid poisoning	H4:684
acrylamide poisoning	H4:637	Fluoroscope operators	
Floor oil mixers (petroleum		x-ray burns	MM:102
refineries)		Fluorspar miners	
phenol poisoning	TM:657	lung cancer	H4:817
Floor polish manufacturers		Fluorspar workers	
anemia with punctate		fluorosis of the skeleton	H4:687
basophilia	H4:541	lung cancer	H4:817
methaemoglobinemia	H4:541	Flux men (blast furnaces)	
nitrobenzene poisoning	H4:539	chlorine and hydrochloric	
Floor sweepers		acid poisoning	TM:645
callosities	H5:752	Food industry workers	
Floor wax manufacturers		lead poisoning	TM:650
tetrachlorethane poi-		Food packers	
soning, toxic jaundice		traumatic tenosynovitis	H4:808
and toxic polyneuritis	H4:615–616	Food preparers	
Floormen (rayon and		salmonellosis	MM:135
artificial silk)		sulphur dioxide poisoning	H4:668
hydrogen sulfide poisoning	TM:648	Foremen (chemicals)	
Florists		methyl alcohol poisoning	TM:656
cramps	H4:878	Foremen (electrical ma-	
dermatitis	H5:730	chinery)	
hothouse primula obconica	H5:738	mercury poisoning	TM:654

Disease	Key
Foremen (metal furniture; suit, coat, and overalls industries)	
cyanide poisoning	TM:647
Foremen (paint and varnish factories)	
manganese poisoning	TM:652
Foremen (printing)	
methyl alcohol poisoning	TM:656
phenol poisoning, publishing	TM:657
Foremen (textile industries other than cotton)	
benzol poisoning	TM:638
cyanide poisoning (rayon and artificial silk)	TM:647
hydrogen sulfide poisoning (rayon and artificial silk)	TM:648
Forest workers	
caterpillar dermatitis or rash	H5:744
Forge-hammer workers	
dehydration	MM:93
heat (rash, cramps, syncope, stroke, neurosis)	MM:93–94
respiratory infections	MM:95
Formaldehyde manufacturers	
acute ungual eczema, dermatitis	H5:735–736
blindness	H4:583
methyl alcohol poisoning	H4:579
Forming room workers (electric accumulator factories)	
dental erosion	H5:802
Foundry cleaners	
carbon tetrachloride poisoning	TM:643
washers, chlorine and hydrochloric acid poisoning	TM:645

Disease	Key
Foundry etchers	
methyl alcohol poisoning	TM:656
Foundry workers	
antimony poisoning	TM:637
benzol poisoning (foundry painters)	TM:638
cadmium poisoning (cupola tenders)	TM:641
carbon tetrachloride poisoning (assemblers)	TM:643
casting burns	H5:755
chlorine and hydrochloric acid poisoning (acid treaters, annealers, cleaners, testers, tinners)	TM:644, 646
cyanide poisoning (blacksmiths, case hardeners, dye makers, electroplaters, foremen, machine operators, maintenance men, managers, metallurgists, picklers, punch press operators, spray painters, superintendents, and welders)	TM:646
heat cramps, heat syncope, heat stroke, heat neurosis	MM:94
heat rash, dehydration	MM:93
lead poisoning	TM:650
manganese poisoning	TM:652
methyl alcohol poisoning, etchers	TM:656
respiratory infections	MM:95
silicosis	MM:41
vascular disorders (Raynaud's phenomenon)	H4:889
zinc poisoning, in general	TM:659
French polishers	
dermatitis	H5:730
soda holes	H5:735

Disease	Key
Freshers and curers	
Weil's disease	H4:738
Fresh fish handlers	
Weil's disease, a lepto-	
spirosis	MM:155
Frit-kiln firers	
firemen's eye	H4:863
Fruit pickers	
dermatitis	H5:737
Fruit preservers	
sulphur dioxide poisoning	H4:668
Fuchsine preparers	
cancer of the bladder	H4:828
Fulminate of mercury	
manufacturers	
hydrocyanic acid poisoning	H4:664
mercury poisoning (ful-	
minate mixers)	TM:654
Fumigators	
hydrocyanic acid poisoning	H4:664
sulphur dioxide poisoning	H4:669
Fungicide workers	
sulphur dioxide poisoning	H4:669
Fur–felt hat manufacturers	
mercury poisoning	MM:83
methyl alcohol poisoning	
(felt hats)	TM:656
sulphureted hydrogen	
poisoning	H4:660
Fur felting	
mercury poisoning	H4:290
sulphureted hydrogen	
poisoning	H4:660
Fur fleshers	
onycholysis	MM:26
Fur workers	
asthma	MM:29
callosities	H5:752
lobar pneumonia and	
chemical pneumonitis	H4:707

Disease	Key
mercury poisoning (pre-	
parers and handlers	TM:654
pneumoconiosis (from	
talc)	H5:987
sulphureted hydrogen	
poisoning	H4:660
tetrachlorethane poisoning,	
toxic jaundice, toxic	
polyneuritis	H4:615–616
weeping eczema	MM:29
Furnace men	
chlorine and hydrochloric	
acid poisoning	TM:645
dehydration	MM:93
heat (rash, cramps, syncope,	
stroke, neurosis)	MM:93–94
posterior polar cataracts	
(iron furnacemen)	H4:864
respiratory infections	MM:95
Furnace room laborers	
(glass factories)	
manganese poisoning	TM:652
Furnace tenders (brass	
factories and foundries)	
manganese poisoning	TM:652
Furniture metal workers	
chlorine and hydrochloric	
acid poisoning	TM:645
Furniture polishers	
methyl alcohol poisoning	TM:656
staining of the fingernails	H5:758
Furniture industry workers,	
showcases, cabinets, etc.	
lead poisoning	TM:650
Furriers	
Callosities	H5:752
Garages (battery men, pump	
men, repairmen)	
benzol poisoning	TM:638

Disease	Key
Garages (continued)	
dermatitis	H5:730
methyl alcohol poisoning	
(pump men)	TM:656
Garage workers	
carbon monoxide poisoning	MM:63
carbon tetrachloride	
poisoning	TM:643
chlorine and hydrochloric	
acid poisoning	TM:645
dermatitis	H5:730
lead poisoning	TM:650
methyl alcohol poisoning	
(attendants)	TM:656
temporal or occipital	
headaches	MM:63
zinc poisoning, in general	TM:659
Galvanizers	
chlorine and hydrochloric	
acid poisoning	TM:645
metal fume fever	MM:38
staining (also thickening,	
fissuring, and ulceration)	
of the skin and fingernails	H5:758
zinc shakes	MM:38
Gardeners	
anthrax	H4:721
arsenic poisoning	H4:336
caterpillar dermatitis or	
rash	H5:744
dermatitis	H5:730
pinhead vesicles	H5:732
psittacosis	H4:715
tulip fingers; lily rash;	
primrose dermatitis; poison	
ivy, oak, sumac, elder, or	
ash; celery itch; pyrethrum	
dermatitis	H5:738-740
traumatic tenosynovitis	H4:809
Gas fitters	
lead poisoning	H4:239

Disease	Key
Gas illuminating workers	
hydrogen sulfide poisoning	TM:648
phenol poisoning	TM:657
Gas mask manufacturers	
tetrachlorethane poisoning,	
toxic jaundice, and toxic	
polyneuritis	H4:615-616
Gas purification workers	
sulphureted hydrogen	
poisoning	H4:660
Gaskets manufacturers	
(using asbestos)	
asbestosis, mesothelioma,	
lung cancer	H5:972-974
Gasworks workers (tar	
departments)	
carcinoma of the skin	H4:820
Generating plants workers	
carbon monoxide poisoning	H4:656
Glass blowers	
cadmium poisoning	TM:641
callosities	H5:753
cataracts	MM:99
dehydration	MM:93
glassblowers' cataracts	H4:862
heat (rash, cramps, syncope,	
stroke, neurosis)	MM:93-94
mercury poisoning (instru-	
ments)	TM:654
modifications of the teeth	
due to abrasion	H5:802
overexposure to infrared rays	MM:99
respiratory infection	MM:95
Glass colorers	
cadmium poisoning	TM:641
selenium poisoning	H4:486
Glass factory etchers	
chlorine and hydrochloric	
acid poisoning	TM:645
fluorine poisoning and	
hydrofluoric acid	H4:683

Disease	Key
Glass industry workers	
lobar pneumonia and	
chemical pneumonitis	H4:707
heat cramps	H4:852
lead poisoning	TM:650
zinc poisoning	TM:659
Glass mixers	
antimony poisoning	TM:637
manganese poisoning	TM:652
Glass wool handlers	
paronychia	H5:736
skin irritation, conjunctival	
irritation, upper respiratory	
tract irritation, secondary	
malformation of the finger-	
nails, warts	H5:989
Glaze makers for pottery	
and tile	
manganese poisoning	TM:652
Glazers (potteries)	
manganese poisoning	TM:652
Gliders	
mercury poisoning	TM:654
Glove manufacturing workers	
anthrax	MM:117
callosities	H5:752
Glue workers	
carbon disulfide poisoning	TM:642
diethylene dioxide poi-	
soning, anorexia, al-	
buminuria, acute	
hemorrhagic nephritis,	
uremia	H4:623-624
hydrogen sulfide poisoning	TM:648
sulphureted hydrogen	
poisoning	H4:660
Gold beaters	
cramps	H4:878
Gold extracters (from	
mineral ores)	
hydrocyanic acid poisoning	H4:663

Disease	Key
Gold miners	
pigmented scars	H5:760
Gold smelters	
posterior polar cataracts	H4:864
Gold telluride processors	
hydrocyanic acid poisoning	H4:663
Gold workers	
staining of the fingernails	H5:758
Grain porters	
grain fever	H5:1024
Grain workers	
grain itch and barley itch	H5:745
lobar pneumonia and	
chemical pneumonitis	H4:707
Grinders (chemical, paint	
and varnish, electrical fix-	
tures, and storage battery)	
manganese poisoning	TM:652
Grinders (electroplating)	
cadmium poisoning	TM:641
mutilation of the finger-	
nails by trauma, in general	H5:758
vascular disorders (Ray-	
naud's phenomenon)	H4:891
Grocers	
grocers' itch	H5:745
Fig-mite dermatitis	H5:746
Grooms	
animal sarcoptes infesta-	
tion	H5:744
glanders	H4:733
ringworms, ectothrix tri-	
chophyta, brucellosis	
(undulant fever)	H4:710-711
Gum arabic workers	
lobar pneumonia and	
chemical pneumonitis	H4:707
Guncotton manufacturers	
dental erosion	H4:592
Gunsmiths	
skin cancer	H4:819

Disease	Key
Gutters and picklers	
erysipeloid of Rosenbach	H4:745
Gymnasts	
callosities	H5:752
Gypsum workers	
hydrogen sulfide poisoning	TM:648
Hair curlers and sorters	
anthrax	H4:721
Hairdressers	
cramps	H4:878
Hair-dye workers	
dermatitis, asthma	H4:571
necrosis of the liver, toxic	
jaundice, refractory anemia	H4:572
paraphenylenediamine	
poisoning	H4:572
Hair workers	
anthrax	H4:710
lobar pneumonia and	
chemical pneumonitis	H4:707
Hammerers (hammer nails	
all day)	
traumatic tenosyno-	
vitis	H4:808
Hammermen	
cramps	H4:878
Handymen (paint and	
varnish factories)	
manganese poisoning	TM:652
Hardeners (felt hats)	
mercury poisoning	TM:654
Hardeners (foundries)	
chlorine and hydrochloric	
acid poisoning	TM:645
Harpists	
cramps	H4:878
Hatters	
callosities	H5:752
carbon tetrachloride	
poisoning	TM:643

Disease	Key
Hatters' furriers	
blackening of tooth enamel	H5:802
erosion of cutting edges of	
lower incisors and canines	H5:802
Hay workers	
lobar pneumonia and	
chemical pneumonitis	H4:707
Head blockers (blast	
furnaces)	
chlorine and hydrochloric	
acid poisoning	TM:645
Heat treaters (electrical	
machinery; car and rail-	
road shops, automobile	
factories, electrical fixtures,	
brass foundries, metal,	
printing)	
cyanide poisoning	TM:647
Heat treaters (foundries)	
manganese poisoning	TM:652
Heliogravure workers	
benzene poisoning	H4:512
Hemp, jute, and linen	
industry workers	
lead poisoning	TM:650
Hemp mill workers	
byssinosis (pounce or	
pouncey chest)	H5:1025
combers' fever	H5:1024
Herbicide workers	
pentachlorphenol	
poisoning	H4:532
Herders of sheep and goats	
(also see shepherds)	
hydatid cysts (sheep	
herders)	MM:142
Q fever	MM:136
Herdsmen (cows)	
dermatitis (sensitiza-	
tion and aureomy-	
cin)	H5:736

Disease	Key	Disease	Key
Hexamethylenetetramine workers		Household ammonia bottlers	
dermatitis	H5:735	ammonia burns and	
Hides disinfectors		poisoning, eye injury	H4:672–673
fluorine and hydrofluoric		Housemaids	
acid poisoning	H4:683	pre-patellar bursa (house-	
Hides handlers		maids' knee)	H4:803
anthrax	H4:710	Housewives	
Hoppers		psittacosis, orf	H4:714–715
traumatic tenosynovitis	H4:809	Hunters	
Hop pickers		tularemia	H4:711
dermatitis	H5:727	Hydrochloric acid makers	
lachrymation, conjunctivitis,		hydrogen sulfide poisoning	TM:648
edema of the eyelids (hop		Hydrocyanic acid manufacturers	
eye or hoppers' eye)	H5:734	hydrocyanic acid poisoning	H4:664
traumatic tenosynovitis	H4:809	Hydrofluoric acid workers	
Horn workers		fluorine and hydrofluoric	
anthrax	H4:721	acid poisoning	H4:684
lobar pneumonia and		fluorosis of the skeleton	H4:687
chemical pneumonitis	H4:707	Hydroquinone manu-	
Horse bean workers		facturing workers	
haemoglobinuria	H5:734	corneal and conjunctival	
Horsehair sorters		injury	H4:532
anthrax	H4:724	dermatitis	H5:735
Horse trainers			
glanders	H4:733	Ice manufacturers	
Horse workers		ammonia burns and	
glanders	H4:710	poisoning, eye injury	H4:672–673
Horticulturists		Ichthyol workers	
dermatitis	H5:737	color changes of the skin	H5:760
Hot galvanizers (electrical machinery)		Ink chemists and laborers	
		benzol poisoning	TM:638
chlorine and hydrochloric		Ink makers	
acid poisoning	TM:645	methyl alcohol poisoning	TM:656
Hot tin coaters (electrical machinery)		Insecticides makers	
		carbon disulfide poisoning	TM:642
chlorine and hydrochloric		dermatitis	H5:735
acid poisoning	TM:645	fluorine and hydrofluoric	
House painters		acid poisoning	H4:683
callosities	H5:753	OMPA, parathion, TEPP,	
lead poisoning	H4:239	and HETP poisoning (all	
		phosphate poisonings)	H4:396

Disease	Key
Insecticides makers (continued)	
pentachlorphenol	
poisoning	H4:532
thallium poisoning	H4:492
Instruments manufacturers	
(bench workers, press	
feeders and type setters)	
benzol poisoning	TM:638
lead poisoning	TM:650
Instrument repairmen	
(rubber tires)	
mercury poisoning	TM:654
Insulators (electrical	
machinery)	
chlorine and hydrochloric	
acid poisoning	TM:645
Iroks workers	
allergic dermatitis	H5:743,1032
Iron foundries workers	
rheumatoid pneumoconiosis	H5:1007
Iron and sheet iron casters	
heat cramps	H4:852
Iron smelters	
dehydration	MM:93
heat (rash, cramps, syncope,	
stroke, neurosis)	MM:93–94
respiratory infections	MM:95
Ironstone miners	
pigmented scars	H5:760
Ironers	
callosities	H5:752
cramps	H4:878
Ivory workers	
lobar pneumonia and	
chemical pneumonitis	H4:707
Janitors (printing)	
antimony poisoning	TM:637
Japanners	
methyl alcohol poisoning	TM:656

Disease	Key
Jet mechanics	
acoustic trauma	MM:96
Jet pilots	
metabolic rhythms dis-	
turbances	MM:224
Jewelers	
asthma	H5:450
chlorine and hydrochloric	
acid poisoning	TM:645
mercury poisoning	TM:654
platinum poisoning	H4:483
Jewelry apprentices	
cyanide poisoning	TM:646
Jewelry engravers	
chlorine and hydrochloric	
acid poisoning	TM:645
Jewelry workers, in general	
lead poisoning	TM:650
zinc poisoning	TM:659
Jute workers	
lobar pneumonia and	
chemical pneumonitis	H4:707
tetanus	H4:710
Kettlemen (textile dyeing	
and finishing)	
chlorine and hydrochloric	
acid poisoning	TM:645
Kitchen gardeners	
hookworm	H5:713
Knackers	
glanders (during early 20th	
century)	H4:733
Knife grinders	
siderosilicosis	H5:1012
Knife sharpeners	
cramps	H4:878
Knit goods industry workers	
zinc poisoning	TM:659
Knitters	
cramps	H4:878

Disease	Key
Labelers (patent medicine and drugs)	
manganese poisoning	TM:652
Laboratory assistants	
aplastic anemia	H4:911
manganese poisoning	TM:652
phenol poisoning, (patent medicine and drugs industry)	TM:657
x-ray cancer	H4:897
Laboratory "dieners"	
acute chemical poisoning	MM:178
Laboratory workers	
glanders	H4:733
lung cancer	H4:817
radiation fibrosis	H4:921
Rift Valley Fever, louping-ill	H4:712–713
x-ray cancer	H4:897
Laboratory workers (anti-locust research)	
urticaria, allergic rhinitis, asthma	H5:1046
Laboratory workers (dental supplies and electrical machinery)	
mercury poisoning	TM:654
phenol poisoning (dental supplies)	TM:647
Laborers	
cyanide poisoning (fertilizer factories)	TM:647
dermatitis, conjunctivitis, cornea injury, perforation of nasal septum	H4:371
Laborers (chemical, glass factories, electroplating, toys and unclassified novelties)	
cadmium poisoning	TM:641

Disease	Key
Laborers (dyestuffs, ink, patent medicines and drugs)	
phenol poisoning	TM:657
Lace work gilders and silverers	
hydrocyanic acid poisoning	H4:664
Lacquer manufacturers	
dermatitis	H5:737
ethylene chlorhydrin poisoning	H4:620
Lacquer solvent workers	
dermatitis	H5:737
diethylene dioxide poisoning, anorexia, albuminuria, acute hemorrhagic nephritis, uremia	H4:623–624
methyl alcohol poisoning	TM:656
Ladlers (blast furnaces, potteries, glass factories, tin and enameled ware, patent medicine and drugs)	
manganese poisoning	TM:652
Lamp black makers	
phenol poisoning	TM:657
Lamplighters	
callosities	H5:752
Lasters (shoes)	
methyl alcohol poisoning	TM:656
Lathe operators	
callosities	H5:752
oil folliculitis	H5:748
Laundresses	
posterior polar cataracts (rare)	H4:865
Laundries' spotters	
benzol poisoning	TM:638
carbon tetrachloride poisoning	TM:643
chlorine and hydrochloric acid poisoning	TM:646

Disease	Key
Laundry workers	
verruca or lupus necro-	
genia	H4:707
Layout men (foundries)	
chlorine and hydro-	
chloric acid poison-	
ing	TM:645
Lead burners	
lead poisoning	H4:238
Lead ferrocyanide workers	
color changes of hair	H5:760
Lead miners (in Spain)	
hookworm	H5:713
Lead smeltors	
antimony poisoning	TM:637
Lead workers	
antimony poisoning	TM:637
lead sulphide in gums pro-	
ducing a "lead line"	MM:277
wrist drop	MM:485
zinc poisoning	TM:659
Leather belts and goods	
manufacturers (case-makers,	
creasers, and sewers)	
benzol poisoning	TM:638
dermatitis	H5:730
Leather doper	
acute hyeloid lewpemia	H4:517
dermatitis	H5:730
Leather goods workers	
anthrax	MM:117
benzol poisoning	TM:638
corneal and conjunctiva	
injury and ocular staining,	
tanners	H4:532
dermatitis	H5:730
lobar pneumonia and	
chemical pneumonitis	H4:707
zinc poisoning	TM:659
Lemon squeezers	
limonene dermatitis	H5:736

Disease	Key
Letter foremen (electrical	
machinery)	
mercury poisoning	TM:654
Letter out men (electrical	
machinery)	
mercury poisoning	TM:654
Letter sorters	
cramps	H4:878
Lightermen	
ischial bursa	H4:803
Lime burners	
acute ungual eczema	H5:736
lime burns, dermatitis, lime	
hole, conjunctiva, and	
cornea injury, symblepharon	H4:367
Lime, cement and artificial	
stone industry workers	
zinc poisoning	TM:659
Lime kiln workers	
acute ungual eczema	H5:736
carbon dioxide poisoning	H4:654
carbon monoxide poisoning	H4:366
caustic burns	H4:366
dermatitis and lime hole;	
conjunctiva and cornea	
injury, symblepharon,	
lime burns	H4:367
Lime slakers	
acute ungual eczema	H5:736
lime burns, dermatitis,	
lime hole, conjunctiva, and	
cornea injury, symblepharon	H4:367
Linoleum fitters	
traumatic tenosynovitis	H4:808
Linoleum manufacturers	
chromium poisoning	H4:454
ethylene chlorhydrin poi-	
soning	H4:620
lead poisoning	H4:239
manganese poisoning	TM:652
methyl alcohol poisoning	TM:656

Disease	Key	Disease	Key
Linotype operators		Machine operators (exposed to cutting oils)	
antimony poisoning	TM:637		
burns	H5:755	multiple-pigmented hyper-	
lead poisoning	MM:66	keratosis, scrotal cancer	H4:825
Linseed workers		Machinists	
lobar pneumonia and		acoustic trauma	MM:96
chemical pneumonitis	H4:707	chloracne	MM:27
Lithographers		chlorine and hydrochloric	
chrome ulcers	MM:27	acid poisoning	TM:645
mercury poisoning	TM:654	cyanide poisoning	TM:647
Lithopone makers		dermatitis	H5:730
cadmium poisoning	TM:641	lesions (precancerous and	
Loaders (brick, tile and terra cotta)		cancerous)	MM:27
		phenol poisoning (petroleum	
manganese poisoning	TM:652	refineries)	TM:657
Locksmiths		Magenta workers	
callosities	H5:752	cancer of the bladder	H4:827
cramps	H4:878	color changes of the skin	H5:760
Loggers		Magnesium foundry workers	
cedar poisoning	H5:1032	fluorosis of the skeleton and	
Lorry drivers		ligaments	H4:697
callosities	H5:753	Maintenance men (foundries and electrical machinery)	
Lubricant manufacturers (using mica)		cyanide poisoning	TM:647
		Maintenance men (rayon and artificial silk)	
mica pneumoconiosis	H5:991		
Lumbermen		hydrogen sulfide poisoning	TM:648
scabies	H5:744	Maintenance tinners (electrical machinery)	
		chlorine and hydrochloric	
Machine hands		acid poisoning	TM:645
dermatitis	H5:730	Maize silo workers	
Machine operators (electrical fixtures)		silo-fillers' disease, nitrogen dioxide poisoning, edema of	
manganese poisoning	TM:652	the lungs	H4:675–676
Machine operators (foundries)		Malt workers	
cyanide poisoning	TM:647	lobar pneumonia and	
manganese poisoning	TM:652	chemical pneumonitis	H4:707
Machine operators (paper and pulp mills)		malt fever	H5:1024
		Managers (chemical)	
chlorine and hydrochloric acid poisoning	TM:645	methyl alcohol poisoning	TM:656
dermatitis	H5:730		

Disease	Key
Managers (foundries, electro-plating)	
cyanide poisoning	TM:647
Manganese bronze welders	
metal fume fever	H4:421
Manganese dioxide workers	
manganese poisoning	TM:653
Manganese steel manufac-turers	
manganese poisoning	H4:461
Manganese workers (mining, grinding, sorting, sieving, packing, and loading)	
manganese poisoning	H4:461
Mannequins	
pes cavus	H5:753
Manufacturing plants workers	
lead poisoning	TM:650
zinc poisoning	TM:659
Maple log peelers	
maple-bark disease	H5:1044
Market gardeners	
bursitis	H4:803
dermatitis	H5:737
Market men	
tularemia	H4:711
Masonia wood workers	
masonia wood bronchial spasms	H5:1032
Masons	
cramps	H4:878
Match dippers	
phossy jaw, abcesses, and sequestra	H4:378
Match factory mixers	
antimony poisoning	TM:637
carbon disulfide poisoning	TM:642
chlorine and hydrochloric acid poisoning (match factory tinners)	TM:646

Disease	Key
Match factory workers	
hydrogen sulfide poisoning	TM:648
manganese poisoning	TM:653
zinc poisoning	TM:659
Meat packers	
brucellosis	MM:137
Meat porters	
erysipeloid of Rosenbach	H5:710
swelling and deformity of the upper part of the pinna on both ears	H5:801
Mechanics (garages)	
carbon monoxide poisoning	MM:63
carbon tetrachloride poisoning	TM:643
chlorine and hydrochloric acid poisoning	TM:645
temporal or occipital headaches	MM:63
Mechanics (ice)	
chlorine and hydrochloric acid poisoning	TM:645
Mechanics (printing)	
cyanide poisoning	TM:647
Mechanics (rayon and artificial silk)	
hydrogen sulfide poisoning	TM:648
Medical men and technicians	
injuries from x-rays (ery-thema, swelling and necrosis of the skin, alopecia, chronic radio-dermatitis, x-ray burns, x-ray cancer, ulcera-tion of the skin, x-irradia-tion-caused cancer, cataracts, conjunctivitis)	H4:896
Melters (brass factories, found-ries, glass factories)	
manganese poisoning	TM:653
Mercury-alloy makers	
mercury poisoning	TM:654

Disease	Key
Meter repairmen (storage batteries)	
cyanide poisoning	TM:647
Methyl alcohol workers	
blindness	H4:583
methyl alcohol poisoning	H4:578
Methyl bromide workers	
burns	H4:601
cyanosis	H4:602
methyl bromide poisoning	H4:598
Methyl chloride workers	
methyl chloride poisoning	H4:596
Methylated spirit users (workers' cleansing agent at the end of the work day)	
dermatitis	H5:734
Mica (Muscovite) workers	
mica pneumoconiosis	H5:991
Microsurgeons	
skin burns from laser beams with possible carcinogenic effects, coagulation burns of the retina (chorioretinal burn)	MM:185
Mildewcide workers	
pentachlorphenol poisoning	H4:532
Milkers of cows	
cramps	H4:878
Mill hands (dyestuffs, ink, etc.)	
manganese poisoning	TM:652
Mill spinners	
byssinosis, "weaver's cough"	MM:39
Millers	
asthma	H5:1036
Millinery workers	
methyl alcohol poisoning	TM:656
Millmen (rubber)	
hydrogen sulfide poisoning	TM:648
Millstone dressers	
pigmented scars	H5:760
staining of the hands	H5:759

Disease	Key
Millwrights (textile industries other than cotton)	
benzol poisoning	TM:638
Mine roadways sprayers using calcium chloride solutions (dust suppression)	
indolent ulceration of the skin	H4:373
Mineral oil filterers	
fine punctate mottling and coalescence of the lungs; pulmonary changes	H5:992
Mineral water factories	
carbon dioxide poisoning	H4:654
hydrogen sulfide poisoning (bottlers)	TM:648
Miners	
albuminuria	H4:854
ankylostomiasis (hookworm)	H4:706
aseptic necrosis, "chokes," "staggers," bone necrosis	MM:153
asphyxia from fire damp inhalation	H4:652
athletes' foot	MM:142
beat elbow	H4:807
beat hand, beat knee, bursitis (miners' elbow), white fingers, dead fingers, Raynaud's phenomenon	MM:144
bends	MM:152
brucellosis, tularemia, malaria, protozoan infections	MM:272
black lung, silico tuberculosis, asthma, anthracosilicosis, and other pneumoconiosis	MM:150
caisson disease	MM:152
carbon dioxide poisoning	H4:655
carbon monoxide poisoning	MM:59
dermatitis	H5:730
falling and head injuries, burns	MM:142

Disease	Key	Disease	Key
Miners (continued)	mmm	and varnish factories' rubber	
hearing loss	MM:142	tires)	
heat cramps	H4:852	chlorine and hydrochloric	
hydrogen sulfide poisoning	TM:648	acid poisoning	TM:645
jaundice	MM:156	manganese poisoning	TM:653
lung cancer	MM:151	phenol poisoning	TM:658
massive fibrosis and emphy-		Mixers (felt hats)	
sema, exertional dyspnea	MM:151	mercury poisoning	TM:654
methane explosions	H4:651	Mixers (foundries, chemicals,	
miners' bunches and coolie		storage batteries, tin and	
itch	H5:715	enameled ware)	
miners' cramp	H4:853	manganese poisoning	TM:652
miners' elbow	H4:803	Mixers (petroleum re-	
miners' nystagmus (not in		fineries)	
U.S.)	H4:856	phenol poisoning	TM:658
prusitis, paralysis, abdominal		Mixers (rubber)	
cramps	MM:153	hydrogen sulfide poisoning	TM:648
psychoneurosis, tachycardia,		Molders (brass factories)	
blepharospasm and head		manganese poisoning	TM:653
tremor, oscillation of lights	H4:858–859	Money counters	
pulmonary tuberculosis, ty-		cramps	H4:878
phoid, dysentery	MM:141	Monochromates workers	
scabies	H5:744	lung cancer	H4:818
silicosis, acute silicosis	MM:149	Morbid anatomists	
subcutaneous cellulitis and		ankylosis and dissection	
acute bursitis	H4:807	wounds	H4:707
suffocation from black damp		pulmonary tuberculosis,	
or choke damp	H4:649	typhoid, dipheria,	
vertigo	H4:858	gonorrheal ophthalmia,	
Weil's disease	MM:155	strept throat, bacteriamia,	
zinc poisoning	TM:659	primary chancre of the	
Mirbane workers		finger, poliomyelitis, anthrax,	
nitrobenzene poisoning	H4:539	typhus, cholera, plague	H4:709
Mirror silverers		Mordanters	
mercury poisoning	TM:654	antimony poisoning	TM:637
Mixer-weighers (fertilizer		Motor-car body building	
factories)		lead poisoning	H4:239
cyanide poisoning	TM:647	Motor-car door flangers	
Mixers (explosives, ammu-		and clinchers	
nition and fire works; paint		Raynaud's phenomenon	H4:894

Disease	Key
Motor-car engine manu-facturers	
mica pneumoconiosis	H5:991
Motor-car industry workers (filers, assemblers, esp. where a wrench is used)	
traumatic tenosynovitis	H4:809
Mountain climbers	
pulmonary edema	MM:234
Mounters (rubber tires)	
chlorine and hydrochloric acid poisoning	TM:645
Mucilage makers	
phenol poisoning	TM:658
Munitions-works workers	
bronze-tinting of the hair	H5:760
mutilation of the finger-nails by trauma	H5:758
Muscovite (mica) workers	
mica pneumoconiosis	H5:991
Museum curators	
rhinorrhea and bronchial asthma (due to hyper-sensitivity to beetles)	H5:1046
Musicians	
callosities	H5:753
Naked divers (no diving apparatus)	
bends, decompression sickness (if fatal, called taravana), bleeding from the nose, ears, and mouth	H4:840
Nail makers	
cramps	H4:878
Naptha users (workers' cleansing agent used at the end of the day)	
dermatitis	H5:734
Needle finishers	
siderosilicosis	H5:1012

Disease	Key
Nevada desert workers	
heat cramps	H4:852
Newspaper folders	
cramps	H4:878
Nickel platers	
nickel itch (eczema)	H4:468
(see also Nickel workers)	
Nickel processors	
nickel-carbonyl poisoning	H4:473
(see also Nickel workers)	
Nickel refiners	
cancer of the ethmoid	H4:817
cancer of the lung and nasal sinuses	H4:476
(see also Nickel workers)	
Nickel workers	
cancer of the ethmoid	H4:817
cancer of the nose	H4:817
lung cancer	H4:814
nickel itch, nickel eczema, spectacle and suspender dermatitis	H5:435
teeth stained greenish-black	H5:801
Nicotine workers	
dermatitis	H5:735
Nitrate films and lacquers workers	
tetrachlorethane poisoning, toxic jaundice, toxic polyneuritis	H4:615–617
Nitrates manufacturers	
nitrogen dioxide poisoning, edema of the lungs	H4:678–679
Nitric acid manufacturers	
ammonia burns and poisoning, eye injury	H4:672–673
nitrogen dioxide poisoning, edema of the lungs	H4:675–676
Nitrobenzene workers	
anemia with punctate baso-philia	H4:541

Disease	Key
Nitrobenzene workers (con- tinued)	
cyanosis	H4:542
methaemoglobinaemia	H4:541
nitrobenzene poisoning	H4:539
Nitro-cellulose workers	
dental erosion	H4:592
Nitro-compounds manu- facturers	
nitrogen dioxide poisoning, edema of the lungs	H4:675–676
Nitro explosives workers	
nitrogen dioxide poisoning, edema of the lungs	H4:675–676
Nitroglycerine workers	
dynamite encephalosis	H4:590
nitroglycerine or dynamite headache	H4:587–588
Nitrolime workers	
papular dermatitis, vesicles, weeping excoriations, mucous membrane of the mouth ulcers, rhinitis, gingivitis, and conjunctivitis	H4:368
Nuclear researchers	
acute radiation syndrome	H5:886
criticality accidents (re- leasing penetrating ionizing radiation)	H5:924
neutron cataracts	MM:186
Nuns	
pre-patellar bursa (nuns' bursitis)	H4:803
Nurses	
aplastic anemia	H4:911
dermatitis	H5:730
dissection wounds and ankylosis	H4:707
flat feet	H5:753
gonads irradiation	MM:182

Disease	Key
herpetic whitlow	H5:758
phenol poisoning	H4:530
pulmonary tuberculosis, typhoid, diptheria, gonorrhaeal ophthalmia, strept throat, bacteremia, primary chancre of the finger, poliomylitis, anthrax, typhus, cholera, plague	H4:709
radio dermatitis, leukemia, other cancers, radiation cataracts, genetic mutation, reduced life span	MM:183
smallpox-handlers' lung	H5:1048
viral and serum hepatitis	MM:272
x-ray cancer	H4:897
Nurserymen	
arsenic poisoning	H4:336
dermatitis	H5:737
Nuts workers	
lobar pneumonia and chemical pneumonitis	H4:707
Oarsmen	
Dupuytren's contracture	H5:756
Oil extractors	
carbon disulfide poisoning	TM:642
Oil-flotation-plant workers	
hydrogen sulfide poisoning	TM:648
Oiling coolies	
scrotal cancer	H4:824
skin cancer	H4:819
Oil refiners	
dermatitis	H5:730
Oils workers	
dermatitis	H5:735
Oil-well workers	
hydrogen sulfide poisoning	TM:648

Disease	Key
Open-hearth men (blast furnaces)	
manganese poisoning	TM:653
Operators (blast furnaces; cotton cloth; dyestuffs, ink, etc.)	
chlorine and hydrochloric acid poisoning	TM:645
methyl alcohol poisoning (dyestuff, ink)	TM:656
phenol poisoning (dye-stuffs, ink)	TM:658
Operators (nemp, jute, and linen)	
methyl alcohol poisoning	TM:656
Operators (rubber tires)	
phenol poisoning	TM:658
Operators (welding, forging, heat treating)	
cadmium poisoning	TM:641
Ophthamologists	
skin burns from laser beams with possible carcinogenic effects, coagulation burn of the retina (chorio-retinal burn)	MM:185
Optical glass workers	
mutilation of the finger-nails by trauma	H5:758
Optical glass moulders	
burns	H5:755
Orange squeezers	
limonene dermatitis	H5:736
Orchestra conductors	
cramps	H4:878
Organists	
cramps	H4:878
Orthopedists	
radiodermatitis, leukemia, and other cancers, radiation	

Disease	Key
cataracts, possible reduced lifespan, genetic mutations	MM:183
Osmic acid workers	
vision impairment, headache, osmic acid poisoning	H4:479
Osmiridium refiners	
vision impairment, headache, osmic acid poisoning	H4:480
Osmium workers	
conjunctivitis, broncho-pneumonia, affects mucosa of nose, pharynx, and bronchi	H4:479
Ostlers	
glanders (early 20th century)	H4:733
ringworms, ectothrix tri-chophyta	H4:710
Oven tenders (electrical machinery)	
mercury poisoning	TM:654
Oxalic acid preparers	
hydrocyanic acid poisoning	H4:664
Packers (electrical machinery)	
mercury poisoning	TM:654
Packers (glass factories)	
manganese poisoning	TM:653
Packers (patent medicine and drugs)	
phenol poisoning	TM:658
Packers (printing industry)	
callosities (packers in general)	H5:753
carbon tetrachloride poisoning	TM:643
Paint and varnish factories (centrifugal operators, chemical engineers, closers, enamel and paint makers, fillers, filter pressmen, fore-men, grinders, handy men,	

Disease	Key
Paint and varnish factories (continued) laboratory assistants, mixers, paint mixers, testers, thinners, tinters, varnish makers, weighers)	
manganese poisoning	TM:652
Paint and varnish factories (laborers, printers' helpers, tank cleaners, testers and thinners)	
benzol poisoning	TM:638
chlorine and hydrochloric acid poisoning (mixers)	TM:645
chromium poisoning	H4:454
Paint color manufacturers	
lead poisoning (in general)	TM:650
manganese poisoning (blenders)	TM:652
Painters and paint makers	
aniline poisoning	H4:567
callosities	H5:752
carbon disulfide poisoning	TM:642
chromium poisoning	H4:454
cramps	H4:878
dermatitis	H5:730
manganese poisoning	TM:653
mercury poisoning	TM:654
methyl alcohol poisoning	TM:656
mica pneumoconiosis	H5:991
phenol poisoning	TM:658
pneumoconiosis (from talc)	H5:987
zinc poisoning	TM:659
Painters (foundries)	
benzol poisoning	TM:638
cadmium poisoning	TM:641
callosities	H5:752
cramps	H4:878
dermatitis	H5:730
manganese poisoning	TM:653

Disease	Key
Painters (glass factories, brick, tile and terra cotta)	
manganese poisoning	TM:653
Paint mixers	
manganese poisoning	TM:653
phenol poisoning	TM:658
Paint removers	
phenol poisoning	TM:658
Paper and pulp mills printers	
benzol poisoning	TM:638
Paper and pulp mill workers	
lead poisoning, workers in general	TM:650
Paper box factories workers	
lead poisoning	TM:650
Paperhangers	
callosities	H5:753
dermatitis, lime hole, conjunctiva and cornea injury, symblepharon	H4:367
lime burns	H4:367
Paper industry workers	
chlorine poisoning	H4:678
ethylene chlorhydrin poisoning	H4:620
pneumoconiosis (from talc)	H5:987
Paprika workers	
fibrosis of the lungs with bronchiectosis and right heart failure	H5:1043
lobar pneumonia and chemical pneumonitis	H4:707
paprika-splitters' lung	H5:1042
Parachute packers	
pneumoconiosis	H5:987
Paraffin users (workers' cleansing agent at the end of the day)	
dermatitis	H5:734
Paraffin workers	
carbon disulfide poisoning	TM:642

Disease	Key	Disease	Key
Parrafin workers (continued)		serum preparers)	
carbon tetrachloride		phenol poisoning	TM:657–658
poisoning	TM:644	Patent medicine and drug	
skin cancer	H4:819	fillers	
Paraphenylenedismine		carbon tetrachloride	
workers		poisoning	TM:643
necrosis of the liver	H4:572	phenol poisoning	TM:657
paraphenylenedismine		Patent medicine and drugs	
dermatitis	H5:533	labelers	
paraphylenedismine		carbon tetrachloride	
poisoning	H4:571	poisoning	TM:643
refractory anemia	H4:572	Patent medicine and drugs	
toxic jaundice	H4:572	printers	
Parasiticide manufacturers		benzol poisoning	TM:638
tetrachlorethane poisoning,		Patent medicine and drugs	
toxic jaundice, toxic		workers	
polyneuritis	H4:615–616	lead poisoning	TM:650
Parathion workers		phenol poisoning	TM:657
parathion poisoning	H4:397	zinc poisoning	TM:659
Paste makers		Pathologists	
carbon tetrachloride		glanders	H4:733
poisoning	TM:643	verruca or lupus necrogenica	
diethylene dioxide poisoning,		(prospectors' wart)	H4:707
anorexia, albuminuria, acute		Pattern makers (foundries,	
hemorrhagic nephritis,		pianos and organs)	
uremia	H4:623–624	chlorine and hydrochloric	
methyl alcohol poisoning	TM:656	acid poisoning	TM:645
phenol poisoning	TM:658	Pea shellers	
Pasteurizers (dairy products)		stained fingernails	H5:756
chlorine and hydrochloric		Pearl divers	
acid poisoning	TM:645	bends, decompression sick-	
Patent-fuel workers		ness (if fatal, called tara-	
pitch dust warts, scrotal		vana), bleeding from nose,	
cancer	H4:820	ears, and mouth	H4:840
Patent leather makers		Penicillin workers	
methyl alcohol poisoning	TM:656	dermatitis	H5:735
Patent medicine and drugs		Pentachlorphenol workers	
(chemists, compounders,		pentachlorphenol poisoning	H4:532
fillers, laboratory assistants,		Perambulator painters	
laborers, packers, pharmacists,		lead colic and anemia	H4:287

Disease	Key
Perfume makers	
aniline poisoning	H4:567
carbon tetrachloride	
poisoning	H4:644
dermatitis	H5:737
methyl alcohol poisoning	TM:656
phenol poisoning	TM:658
Pet shop salesmen	
psittacosis	H4:715
ringworm, ectothrix	
trichophyta	H4:710
Petrol users (workers'	
cleansing agent at the end of	
the day)	
dermatitis	H5:734
Petroleum ash (containing	
vanadium pentoxide) handlers	
vanadium poisoning	H4:997
Petroleum industry workers	
fluorine and hydrofluoric	
acid poisoning	H4:685
phenol poisoning	TM:657–658
Petroleum refineries (floor	
oil mixers, machinists, and	
mixers)	
phenol poisoning	TM:657–658
Petroleum refineries	
(operators and soapmixers)	
ammonia burns and	
poisoning, eye injury	H4:672–673
benzol poisoning	TM:638
hydrogen sulfide poisoning	TM:648
lead poisoning	TM:650
sulphur dioxide poisoning,	
refiners	H4:668
zinc poisoning	TM:659
Petroleum refineries water	
treaters	
chlorine and hydrochloric	
acid poisoning	TM:646

Disease	Key
Pharmaceutical compound	
manufacturers	
ammonia burns and	
poisoning, eye injury	H4:672–673
aniline poisoning	H4:567
ethylene chlorhydrin	
poisoning	H4:620
mercury poisoning	H4:290
Pharmaceutical workers	
ammonia burns and	
poisoning, eye injury	H4:672–673
carbon tetrachloride	
poisoning	TM:643
ethylene chlorhydrin	
poisoning	H4:620
overexposure to certain	
chemicals	MM:180
Pharmacists	
dermatitis	H5:737
phenol poisoning	TM:658
Phenol workers	
carbolmarasmus	H4:530
carboluria	H4:530
dermatitis	H5:735
phenic marasmus	H4:530
phenol poisoning	H4:530
Phenylenediamine workers	
dermatitis, asthma	H4:571
Phosphoric acid extractors	
hydrocyanic acid poisoning	H4:664
Phosphorus compound makers	
hydrogen sulfide poisoning	TM:648
Photoengravers	
lead poisoning	H4:188
methyl alcohol poisoning	TM:656
Photographers and photo-	
graphic workers	
callosities	H5:752
chrome ulcers	MM:27
chromium poisoning	H4:454
dermatitis	H5:730

Disease	Key
Photographers and photographic workers (continued)	
hydrocyanic acid poisoning	H4:663
lead poisoning	TM:650
mercury poisoning	TM:654
methyl alcohol poisoning	TM:656
platinum poisoning	H4:480
stained fingers and fingernails	H5:756
zinc poisoning	TM:659
Photographic chemicals manufacturers	
aniline poisoning	H4:567
Photogravure printers	
benzene poisoning	H4:511
Physicians	
ankylosis	H4:707
dermatitis	H5:730
dissection wounds	H4:707
phenol poisoning	H4:530
pulmonary tuberculosis, typhoid, diphtheria, gonorrheal opthalmia, streptococcal throat, bacteremia, primary chancre of the finger, poliomyelitis, anthrax, typhus, cholera, plague	H4:709
radiation leukemogenesis, radiodermatitis, other cancers, radiation cataracts, genetic mutation due to gonads irradiation, possible shortened life span	MM:183
smallpox-handlers' lung	H5:1048
viral and serum hepatitis	MM:272
Physicists	
skin burns from laser beams with possible carcinogenic effects, coagulation burns of the retina (chorioretinal burn)	MM:185

Disease	Key
Pianists	
cramps	H4:878
Piano and organ pattern makers	
chlorine and hydrochloric acid poisoning	TM:645
Pianos and organs industry (foremen, oiling off men, painters, rubbing men, and sprayers)	
benzol poisoning	TM:638
zinc poisoning, workers in general	TM:659
Piano keys makers	
anthrax (very rare)	H4:722
Picklers (blast furnaces, brass factories, electrical machinery, electrical fixtures, foundries, tin and enameled ware)	
chlorine and hydrochloric acid poisoning	TM:645
cyanide poisoning (foundries and tin and enameled ware)	TM:647
hydrogen sulfide poisoning	TM:648
Picric acid workers	
color changes of the skin	H5:760
dermatitis	H5:735
olive green tinting of the hair	H5:760
phenol poisoning	TM:658
Pig workers	
callosities	H5:752
Q fever	H4:712
undulant fever (brucellosis)	H4:711
Pigeon raisers or breeders	
bird breeders' lung or bird-fanciers' lung	H5:1047
Piggery workers	
Weil's disease	H4:738

Disease	Key	Disease	Key
Pigments manufacturers		Plate molders (printing and	
lead poisoning	H4:239	publishing industries)	
Pine resin workers		phenol poisoning	TM:658
dermatitis	H5:735	Plate trimmers (printing and	
Pipe laggers		publishing industry)	
mesothelioma	H5:986	phenol poisoning	TM:658
Pitch workers		Platers (auto factories,	
lachrymation, conjuncitivitis,		blast furnaces, brass factories,	
corneal ulceration, multiple		electrical machinery and fix-	
pitch warts	H4:820	tures, foundries, metal furni-	
pitch dust warts, scrotal		ture, other manufacturing	
cancer	H4:820	plants, pianos and organs,	
skin cancer	H4:818	printing, and storage battery)	
tar melanosis, tar mollusca	H4:819	chlorine and hydrochloric	
Planishers (copper factories)		acid poisoning	TM:645
phenol poisoning	TM:658	dermatitis	H5:730
Planning and milling tinners		Platers (foundries, welding,	
chlorine and hydrochloric		forging and heat	
acid poisoning	TM:646	treating, machine	
zinc poisoning, workers in		shops, brass factories,	
general	TM:659	electroplating, metal	
Planters (coffee, sugar,		furniture, printing	
bananas, cocoa, tobacco, tea)		and publishing, electrical	
hookworm	H5:713	machinery)	
Plant patrol men (electrical		cadmium poisoning	TM:641
machinery)		dermatitis	H5:730
carbon tetrachloride		Platers (signs)	
poisoning	TM:643	mercury poisoning	TM:654
Plasterers		Platinum electroplating	
callosities	H5:753	platinum poisoning	H4:482
dermatitis, lime hole, con-		Platinum miners and other	
junctiva and cornea injury,		workers	
symbupharon	H4:367	platinum poisoning	H4:482
lime burns	H4:367	Platinum salts workers	
Plasticizers workers		platinosis (platinum	
dermatitis	H5:735	poisoning)	H4:482
Plastics manufacturers		Polishers manufacturers	
fluorine and hydrofluoric		diethylene dioxide poisoning,	
acid poisoning	H4:683	anorexia, albuminuria, acute	
methyl alcohol poisoning	TM:656	hemorrhagic nephritis,	
		uremia	H4:623-624

Disease	Key
Pneumatic tool operators	
bursitis, tenosynovitis	MM:145
small areas of decalcification	
seen in x-rays of the bones	
of the carpus	H4:887
white fingers, dead fingers,	
Raynaud's phenomenon	MM:144
(pneumatic tools include	
air hammer, compressed-air	
chisel, compressed-air drill,	
jack hammer, pneumatic	
chisel, pneumatic drill,	
pneumatic hammer,	
pneumatic tool, pounding-	
up machine, riveting gun	
and tool, stone-cutters'	
hammer)	
Policemen	
flat feet	H5:753
Polishers (welding, forging,	
heat treating, brass factories,	
electroplating, metal furniture,	
printing and publishing, elec-	
trical machinery)	
cadmium poisoning	TM:641
Polishers (wood)	
methyl alcohol poisoning	TM:656
Polyurethane foam workers	
corneal lesions	MM:37
Porcelain mixers and sprayers	
(tin and enameled ware)	
manganese poisoning	TM:653
Porcelain or glass workers	
manganese poisoning	TM:653
mercury poisoning	TM:654
silicosis	MM:41
Pork workers in abattoirs	
undulant fever (brucellosis)	H4:711
Post-mortem attendants	
ankylosis and dissection	
wounds	H4:707

Disease	Key
verruca or lupus necrogenica	
(prosectors' wart)	H4:707
Potassium bichromate	
manufacturers	
perforation of the nasal	
septum and chrome ulcers	H4:457
Potmen	
prepatellar bursa	H4:803
Potters (before fritted lead	
glaze was used)	
callosities (potters in general)	H5:752
dermatitis	H5:730
Pottery dippers	
antimony poisoning	TM:637
Pottery manufacturers	
antimony poisoning	TM:637
dermatitis	H5:730
silicosis	MM:41
Pottery workers	
dermatitis	H5:730
hookworm	H5:713
lead poisoning	TM:650
rheumatoid pneumo-	
coniosis	H5:1007
zinc poisoning	TM:659
Poulterers	
erysipeloid of Rosenbach	H5:710
Poultry pluckers	
callosity	H5:751
Power makers	
phenol poisoning	TM:658
Precious metal refiners	
platinum poisoning, plati-	
num rhinorrhea, platinum	
asthma, and platinum	
urticaria, platinosis	H4:483
Pressers (dry cleaning	
and suits, coats and	
overalls industries)	
carbon tetrachloride	
poisoning	TM:643

Disease	Key
Press operators (chemicals industry)	
phenol poisoning	TM:658
Printers	
acoustic trauma	MM:96
benzol poisoning	TM:638
dermatitis	H5:730
lead poisoning	MM:66
methyl alcohol poisoning	TM:656
printers' asthma	H5:1033
zinc poisoning	TM:659
Printing and publishing industry (foremen, plate molders, and plate trimmers)	
phenol poisoning	TM:658
Printing industry (book bindery workers, compositors, delivery boys, hand make-up men, lock-up men, press feeders, press room devils, and printer's helper)	
benzol poisoning	TM:638
chlorine and hydrochloric acid poisoning (platers)	TM:645
dermatitis	H5:730
lead poisoning, in general	TM:650
zinc poisoning	TM:659
Printing melters	
antimony poisoning	TM:637
Propdrawers	
beat knee	H4:806
Prosectors	
verruca or lupus necro- genica (prosectors' wart)	H4:707
Publicans	
pulmonary tuberculosis	H4:706
Puddlers (iron)	
dehydration	MM:93
heat (rash, cramps, stroke, syncope, neurosis)	MM:93–94

Disease	Key
posterior polar cataracts	H4:863
respiratory infections	MM:95
Pulp-mill workers	
hydrogen sulfide poisoning	TM:648
Pump boys (electrical machinery and other manufacturing plants)	
mercury poisoning	TM:654
Pumpers (electrical machinery)	
mercury poisoning	TM:654
Punch press operators	
acoustic trauma	MM:96
cyanide poisoning (in foundries)	TM:647
Putty makers	
carbon disulfide poisoning	TM:642
Pyrites burners	
hydrogen sulfide poisoning	TM:648
Pyroxylin-plastics workers	
hydrogen sulfide poisoning	TM:648
Quinine manufacturing workers	
corneal and conjunctival injury, ocular staining	H4:532
Radioactive substances purifiers and producers	
lung cancer	H4:817
radiation fibrosis	H4:921
Radiographer	
basal-celled carcinoma of the skin	H4:900
(see also x-ray equipment operators)	
Radiologists	
fibrous atrophy of the testes	H4:901
profound refractory anemia	H4:901
reduced life span	H5:894

Disease	Key	Disease	Key
Radiologists (continued)		Radium workers	
squamous-celled carcinoma		aplastic anemia	H4:911
of the skin, basal-celled		myeloid leukemia	H4:911
carcinoma of the skin	H4:899	radium dermatitis	H4:910
x-ray cancer	H4:897	radium poisoning	MM:109
x-ray dermatitis (including		severe anemia, spontaneous	
acute erythema; striation,		fracture (radiation osteitis)	
fissuring, and brittling of		necrosis of the jaw, intrac-	
fingernails; warts; post-		table anemia, carcinoma of	
irradiation telangiectases;		the mastoid, facial neuralgia	
alopecia; paronychia; and		with anesthesia dolorosa,	
skin ulcers)	H4:898	ptosis of eyelid, total oph-	
(see also x-ray equipment		thalmoplegia, carcinoma of	
operators)		the paranasal sinuses	H4:914–916
Radio valves manufacturers		Railway loaders	
mercury poisoning	H4:290	grocers' itch	H5:745
Radium dial painters		Railway sleepers impregnators	
carcinoma of the mastoid,		(with creosote)	
facial neuralgia with		color changes of the skin	H5:760
anesthesia dolorosa,		Railway workers	
ptosis of the eyelid, total		deafness	H4:872
ophthalmoplegia	H4:916	Rangoon oil workers	
carcinoma of the paranasal		skin cancer	H4:823
sinuses	H4:913	Rat catchers	
radium poisoning	MM:109	Weil's disease	H4:738
severe anemia, aplastic		Raw stock preparation men	
anemia, necrosis of the		(textile industries other	
jaw, spontaneous fracture,		than cotton)	
sarcoma of bone, and		benzol poisoning	TM:638
intractable anemia		Raw vanilla workers	
(radiation osteitis)	H4:914	vanillism	H5:745
striation, fissuring and		Rayon-machinery cleaners	
brittling of the fingernails	H5:736	sulfureted hydrogen	
Radium preparations workers		poisoning	H4:661
aplastic anemia	H4:911	Reclaimers (rubber industry)	
radium dermatitis	H4:910	phenol poisoning	TM:658
Radium refiners		Red rubber workers	
radium poisoning	MM:103	antimony poisoning	TM:637
striation, fissuring, and		Reelers (blast furnace)	
brittling of the fingernails	H5:736	chlorine and hydrochloric	
		acid poisoning	TM:645

Disease	Key	Disease	Key
Refiners (metals)		Ricefield workers	
mercury poisoning	TM:654	hookworm	H5:713
Refinishers (wood, wicker,		Weil's disease	H4:738
etc.)		Rifle barrels burnishers	
methyl alcohol poisoning	TM:656	antimony poisoning	TM:636
Refractories manufacturing		Rinsers (brass factories)	
(using talc)		chlorine and hydrochloric	
pneumoconiosis	H4:987	acid poisoning	TM:645
Refrigerator reconditioners		Riveters	
carbon tetrachloride		acoustic trauma	MM:96
poisoning	MM:75	Road sweeper	
Refrigerator workers		callosity	H5:751
ammonia burns and		Rodenticide workers	
poisoning, eye injury	H4:672–673	cancer of the bladder	H4:828
fluorine and hydrofluoric		fluoracetic acid poisoning,	
acid poisoning	H4:683	fluoralcohol poisoning	H4:703
fluorocarbon poisoning	H4:703	fluorine and hydrofluoric	
methyl chloride poisoning	H4:597	acid poisoning	H4:683
sulfur dioxide poisoning	H4:670	thallium poisoning	H4:492
Repairmen (electrical		Root vegetable peelers	
machinery and foundries)		erysipeloid of Rosenbach	H5:710
chlorine and hydrochloric		Rotogravure workers	
acid poisoning	TM:645	benzene poisoning	H4:512
Research workers		Roughers (iron)	
acute radiation syndrome	H5:886	posterior polar cataracts	H4:864
aplastic anemia (due to		Rowers	
radium exposure)	H4:915	traumatic tenosynovitis	H4:809
x-ray cancer	H4:897	Rubber-coating workers	
Research workers (involving		benzol poisoning	MM:75
antilocust research)		carbon tetrachloride	
urticaria, allergic rhinitis,		poisoning	TM:644
asthma	H5:1046	dermatitis	H5:730
Research workers (involving		Rubber cold-curers	
parrots, parakeets, lovebirds,		carbon disulphide poisoning	H4:629
and budgerigars, or		dermatitis	H5:730
bacteriology)		Rubber compounders	
psittacosis	H4:715	dermatitis	H5:730
Resins (synthetic) makers		tellurium poisoning	H4:490
phenol poisoning	TM:658	Rubber factories (other than	
Resins workers		tires)	
dermatitis	H5:735	assemblers, bay makers,	

Disease	Key	Disease	Key
Rubber factories (continued)		bookers, buffers, builders,	
pressmen		cementers, checking machine	
benzol poisoning	TM:638	operators, cutters, dippers,	
carbon tetrachloride		dusters, experimental men,	
poisoning	TM:644	fillers, finishers, flag	
dermatitis	H5:730	sprayers, foremen, laborers,	
Rubber gloves dusters (with		millmen, mixers, painters,	
talc)		ply benders, printers,	
pneumoconiosis	H5:987	production men, repairmen,	
Rubber industry (cementer		resizers, shell coverers,	
patchers, commercial artists,		splicers, sprayers, stampers,	
dippers, and electrobrass		stock boys, stock preparers,	
platers)		supervisors, tapers, tire	
benzol poisoning	TM:638	study men and tread washers,	
carbon tetrachloride		truckers, tube curing men,	
poisoning	TM:644	type setters and valve stem	
dermatitis	H5:730	treaters)	TM:638
Rubber processors		carbon disulfide poisoning,	
aniline poisoning	H4:567	mixers	TM:642
dermatitis	H5:730	carbon tetrachloride	
leucodermia	H5:748	poisoning, builders	TM:643
Rubber reclaimers		chlorine and hydrochloric	
carbon disulfide poisoning	TM:642	acid poisoning, bead-makers,	
carbon tetrachloride		solderers, mounters, mixers,	
poisoning	TM:644	and machinists	TM:645
dermatitis	H5:730	cyanide poisoning, dippers	TM:647
phenol poisoning	TM:658	dermatitis	H5:730
Rubber tires compounders and		Rubber tires industry, workers	
mill men		in general	
antimony poisoning	TM:637	lead poisoning	TM:650
carbon tetrachloride		zinc poisoning	TM:659
poisoning	TM:643	Rubber tires and rubber goods	
dermatitis	H5:730	molders	
Rubber tires dusters (using		mica pneumoconiosis	H5:991
talc)		Rubber tires template makers	
pneumoconiosis	H5:987	and tinners	
Rubber tires industry		chlorine and hydrochloric	
benzol poisoning (airbag		acid poisoning	TM:646
builders, air bagmen,		Rubber workers	
assemblers, bias cutters,		antimony poisoning	TM:636
		cancer of the bladder	H4:828

Disease	Key
Rubber workers (continued)	xxx
carbon tetrachloride	
poisoning	TM:644
chlorine and hydrochloric	
acid poisoning	TM:645
chromium poisoning,	
coloring	H4:454
dermatitis	H5:730
lead poisoning	TM:650
leukoderma	MM:31
mica pneumoconiosis	H5:991
tetrachlorethane poisoning,	
toxic jaundice, toxic	
polyneuritis	H4:615–616
zinc poisoning	TM:659
Rugby players	
cauliflower ears	H5:760
Saddlers	
callosities	H5:752
cramps	H4:878
Safety equipment men	
(storage battery manufac-	
turers)	
carbon tetrachloride	
poisoning	TM:643
chlorine and hydrochloric	
acid poisoning	TM:645
Safety matches manufacturers	
chromium poisoning	H4:454
Sail makers	
cramps	H4:878
Sailors	
cramps	H4:878
deafness, in submarines	H4:873
telangiectases of exposed	
skin	H5:754
Sandblasters	
rheumatoid pneumoconiosis	H5:1007
silicosis	MM:41

Disease	Key
Sawyers	
cramps	H4:878
Scrap metal smelters	
selenium poisoning	H4:489
Scratchers (instruments)	
mercury poisoning	TM:654
Sculptors	
callosities	H5:752
Sealers (hunters of the sea	
mammals, seals)	
seal finger, erysipeloid of	
Rosenbach	H4:745
Sealers (instruments)	
mercury poisoning	TM:655
Sealers (storage batteries)	
manganese poisoning	TM:653
Seamstresses	
cramps	H4:878
modifications of the teeth	
due to abrasions	H5:802
Seamstresses (dry cleaning	
and dyeing industry)	
carbon tetrachloride	
poisoning	TM:643
laborers's spine or osteoar-	
thritic spondylitis, in	
general	H5:755
Secretaries (typists)	
cramps	H4:878
traumatic tenosynovitis	H4:809
Seeds workers	
lobar pneumonia and	
chemical pneumonitis	H4:707
Selenium workers	
selenium poisoning	H4:484
Serum preparers (patent	
medicine and drugs industry)	
phenol poisoning	TM:658
Service men (electrical	
machinery)	

Disease	Key
Service men (continued)	
chlorine and hydrochloric acid poisoning	TM:645
Sewage disinfectant workers	
chlorine poisoning	H4:678
Sewer workers	
chlorine poisoning	H4:679
hydrogen sulfide poisoning	TM:648
Weil's disease	MM:155
Sewing machine operators	
cramps	H4:878
traumatic tenosynovitis	H4:809
Shaders (paint and varnish factories)	
manganese poisoning	TM:653
Shake-out men (brass factories)	
manganese poisoning	TM:653
Shale oil workers	
skin cancer	H4:819
Sheep dip manufacturers	
carcinoma of the skin and bronchi	H4:818
louping ill	H4:713
lung cancer	H4:340
skin cancer	H4:339
Sheep handlers	
louping ill	H4:713
ringworm and suppurative mycoses (sheepskin handlers)	MM:133
orf, sheep shearers	H4:714
Sheet metal workers (blast furnaces, electrical machinery, foundries, furniture, showcases and cabinets, metal furniture, tin and enameled wares)	
chlorine and hydrochloric acid poisoning	TM:645

Disease	Key
Shepherds	
louping ill	H4:713
orf	H4:714
Q fever	H4:712
Rift Valley Fever	H4:712
Shinglers (iron)	
posterior polar cataracts	H4:864
Ship breakers	
lead poisoning	H4:238
mesothelioma	H5:986
metal fume fever	H4:421
Shipbuilders	
mesothelioma	H5:986
zinc poisoning	TM:659
Shipping clerks (chemical)	
carbon tetrachloride poisoning	TM:643
methyl alcohol poisoning	TM:656
phenol poisoning	TM:658
Shipping clerks (glass factories)	
manganese poisoning	TM:653
Ship, tunnel, tank, pits, or silo workers	
tissue hypoxia	MM:57
Shipyard workers	
acoustic after-images	H4:875
keratoconjunctivitis or shipyard conjunctivitis	H4:708
Shirts, collars, and cuffs general porters	
carbon tetrachloride poisoning	TM:643
Shirt, collar, and cuffs inspectors	
carbon tetrachloride poisoning	TM:643
Shoe cement manufacturers	
tetrachlorethane poisoning, toxic jaundice, toxic polyneuritis	H4:615–616

Disease	Key
Shoe industry (backers, cementers, compo conveyers, embossers, eyelet stayers, fillers, fitters, flap layers, insole men, laborers, leather skiving operators, leather workers, liners, operators, repairmen, sewers, sock liners, tapers and treers, and wood heel coverers)	
benzol poisoning	TM:638
lead poisoning and zinc poisoning, in general	TM:650
methyl alcohol poisoning (cementers, compo conveyors, fitters, flap layers, lasters, and tapers and treers)	TM:656
pulmonary tuberculosis (operatives)	H4:706
Shoemakers	
cramps	H4:878
modifications of the teeth by abrasion	H5:801
Shoemakers (shoe machinists)	
antimony poisoning	MM:75
benzol poisoning	MM:75
cramps	H4:898
shoemakers' stained fingernails	H5:756
vascular disorders (Raynaud's phenomenon)	H4:889
zinc poisoning	TM:659
Shoe polish manufacturers	
anemia with punctate basophilia	H4:541–542
cyanosis	H4:541–542
methaemoglobinaemia	H4:541–542
nitro benzene poisoning	H4:539
Shoe smiths	
glanders (during early 20th century)	H4:733

Disease	Key
Shot makers	
antimony poisoning	TM:637
Shredding machine operators	
bagossis	H5:1041
Shuttle-makers	
South African boxwood toxemia	H5:1032
Sign makers	
mercury poisoning	TM:655
Silage pits workers	
carbon dioxide poisoning	H4:654
Silica workers	
rheumatoid pneumoconiosis	H5:1006
shaver's disease	MM:44
silicosis	MM:41
silicotuberculosis	MM:43
Silk workers	
lobar pneumonia and chemical pneumonitis	H4:707
Sillimanite miners	
sillimanite pneumoconiosis	H5:989
Silver compound workers	
generalized argyria	H4:410
Silver dissolvers using nitric acid	
nitric acid burn and argyria	H5:747
Silver finishers	
welders' siderosis	H5:1012
Silver leaf workers	
localized argyria	H4:419
Silver nitrate manufacturers	
generalized argyria	H4:410
stained fingernails	H5:756
Silver refiners	
tellurium poisoning	H4:491
Silver workers	
argyria	H4:410
nitric-acid burn	H5:747
staining of the fingernails	H5:758
teeth stained greyish-brown	H4:801

Disease	Key
Silverers of glass beads	
generalized argyria	H4:410
Silvering men (glass	
factories)	
chlorine and hydrochloric	
acid poisoning	TM:645
Silversmiths	
localized argyria	H4:419
Sisal workers	
lobar pneumonia and chemi-	
cal pneumonitis	H4:707
Skins (animal) handlers	
anthrax	H4:710
Slaughter house workers	
anthrax	H4:721
orf	H4:715
Smiths	
blacksmiths' deafness	H4:872
boilermakers' deafness	H4:872
Smoke dryers	
erysipeloid of Rosenbach	H4:745
Smokeless powder makers	
carbon disulfide poisoning	TM:642
Soap factory printers	
benzol poisoning	TM:638
Soap manufacturers	
fine punctate mottling and	
coalescence of the lungs,	
pulmonary changes	H5:992
hydrogen sulfide poisoning	TM:648
lead poisoning	TM:650
manganese poisoning	TM:653
methyl alcohol poisoning	TM:656
zinc poisoning	TM:659
Soda ash users (workers'	
cleansing agent used at the end	
of the day)	
dermatitis	H5:734
Soda manufacturers using the	
Leblanc process	
hydrocyanic acid poisoning	H4:664

Disease	Key
hydrogen sulfide poisoning	TM:648
Sodium sulfide manufac-	
turers	
hydrogen sulfide poison-	
ing	TM:648
Soft beverage industry	
workers	
lead poisoning	TM:650
zinc poisoning	TM:659
Solderers	
cadmium poisoning	TM:641
chlorine and hydrochloric	
acid poisoning	TM:645
platinosis	H4:483
platinum dermatitis	H5:450
Solder makers	
cadmium poisoning	TM:641
Soldiers	
animal sarcoptes infestation	H5:744
cysticercus cellulose, cysti-	
cercosis of brain, subcu-	
taneous cysticerci	H4:756–760
phtheiriasis	H5:745
scabies, caterpillar rash	H5:744
Soldiers (who served in India)	
cysticercosis	H5:720
Sole stitchers	
mercury poisoning	TM:655
Solvent workers	
carbon disulphide poisoning	H4:629
dermatitis	H5:735
tetrachlorethane poisoning,	
toxic jaundice, toxic	
polyneuritis	H4:615–616
Sorters and spotters (dry	
cleaning)	
carbon tetrachloride	
poisoning	TM:643
chlorine and hydro-	
chloric acid poisoning	
(spotters)	TM:646

Disease	Key
South African boxwood workers	
South African boxwood toxemia	H5:741
Spark plug manufacturers (airplanes)	
mica pneumoconiosis	H5:991
Spinners (rayon and artificial silk)	
hydrogen sulfide poisoning	TM:648
Spotters (dry cleaning and dyeing)	
benzol poisoning	TM:639
carbon tetrachloride poisoning	TM:643
methyl alcohol poisoning	TM:656
phenol poisoning	TM:658
Spray operators	
damaged fingernails, loosening and separation of fingers	H5:758
Spray painters (foundries, tin, and enameled ware)	
antimony poisoning	TM:637
cyanide poisoning, foundries	TM:647
Sprayers (potteries, brick, tile, and terra cotta)	
manganese poisoning	TM:653
Stablemen	
glanders (during early 20th century)	H4:733
Weil's disease	H4:738
Starch makers	
hydrogen sulfide poisoning	TM:648
Station attendants (garages)	
methyl alcohol poisoning	TM:656
Steel engravers	
mercury poisoning	TM:655
Steel rollers	
infrared ray overexposure	MM:99

Disease	Key
Steel treatment workers	
ammonia burns and poisoning, eye injury	H4:672–673
Steel workers	
ammonia poisoning and burns, eye injury	H4:672–673
dehydration	MM:93
fluorosis of the skeleton	H4:687
heat (rash, cramps, syncope, stroke, neurosis)	MM:93–94
lobar pneumonia and chemical pneumonitis	H4:707
mercury poisoning (engravers)	TM:655
Stereotypers	
burns	H5:755
Stevedores	
callosities	H5:753
mesothelioma (if they handle asbestos)	H5:986
Stillmen	
phenol poisoning	TM:658
Stockmen	
ringworms, ectothrix trichophyta	H4:710
undulant fever (brucellosis)	H4:711
Stokehold workers	
heat cramps	H4:853
stokers' cramp	H4:853
Stokers	
color changes of the skin and callosities	H5:760
Stone breakers	
callosities	H5:752
Stone cutters, stone crushers	
blisters, abrasions, callosities	MM:115
silicosis	MM:41
vascular disorders (Raynaud's phenomenon)	H4:891
Stone masons	
callosities	H5:752

Disease	Key	Disease	Key
Stone setters (jewelry)		Submarine personnel	
chlorine and hydrochloric		deafness	H4:874
acid poisoning	TM:646	Sugarcane cutters	
Stone workers		heat cramps	H4:852
zinc poisoning	TM:659	traumatic tenosynovitis	H4:809
Storage battery (assemblers,		Weil's disease	H4:738
casters, checkers, element		Sugarcane workers in Uganda	
burners, foremen, foundry-		onchocerciasis	H4:706
men, general truckers, hand		Sugar confectioners	
moulders, inspectors, labora-		dermatitis	H5:730
tory assistants, loaders, ma-		limonene dermatitis	H5:736
chine builders and operators,		Sugar planters	
mechanics, mould cleaners,		hookworm	H5:713
oilers, packers, punch press		Sugar refiners	
operators, refiners, scalemen,		dermatitis	H5:730
stencilmen, strappers, strap		hydrogen sulfide poisoning	TM:649
supply men, sweepers, tool		sulphur dioxide poisoning	H4:668
makers, touch-up men,		Suits, coats, and overalls	
truckers, unloaders, and		industry workers	
wheelers)		lead poisoning	TM:650
antimony poisoning	TM:636–637	Sulfur extractors	
Storage battery manufacturers		carbon disulfide poisoning	TM:642
antimony poisoning	TM:636	Sulfide makers	
chlorine and hydrochloric		hydrogen sulfide poisoning	TM:649
acid poisoning, platers and		Sulfide ores smeltors	
tinners	TM:645	sulfide dioxide poisoning	H4:668
cyanide poisoning	TM:647	Sulfocyanide manufacturers	
lead poisoning	MM:66	hydrocyanic acid poisoning	H4:664
mercury poisoning	TM:655	Sulfur chloride makers	
zinc poisoning	TM:659	hydrogen sulfide poisoning	TM:649
Straw workers		Sulfur dioxide workers	
lobar pneumonia and chemi-		sulfur dioxide poisoning	H4:669
cal pneumonitis	H4:707	Sulfur dye manufacturers	
Streptomycin workers		sulfureted hydrogen	
dermatitis	H5:735	poisoning	H4:661
Stucco and concrete finishers		Sulfur miners (in Sicily, Rus-	
mica pneumoconiosis	H5:991	sia, and the Balkans)	
Students		hookworm	H5:713
bursitis	H5:803	hydrogen sulfide poisoning	
Subaquatic engineers		(anywhere)	TM:649
caisson disease	H4:839		

Disease	Key
Tar workers	
cancer of the skin	H4:818
color changes of the skin	H5:760
dermatitis	H5:730
phenol poisoning	TM:657
tar melanosis, tar mollusca	H4:819
tar warts, tar cancer, pitch	
cancer	H5:780
Taxidermists	
mercury poisoning	TM:655
Tea packers	
traumatic tenosynovitis	H4:808
Tea workers	
hookworm, planters	H5:713
lobar pneumonia and chemi-	
cal pneumonitis	H4:707
Technicians (in antilocust	
research)	
urticaria, allergic rhinitis,	
asthma	H5:1046
Teamsters	
glanders (during early 20th	
century)	H4:733
Technical men (chemicals,	
electrical machinery)	
cadmium poisoning	TM:641
Technicians (medical, x-ray)	
x-ray cancer	H4:897
x-ray dermatitis, carcinoma	
of the dorsum	H4:899
Teflon workers	
polymer fume fever	MM:38
polymeric fluorocarbon	
poisoning	H4:703
Telegraphists	
cramps (telegraphists' cramps)	H4:883
Telephone apparatus	
manufacturers	
mica pneumoconiosis	H5:991
selenium poisoning	H4:489

Disease	Key
Telephone linesmen	
lead poisoning	H4:239
Tellurium workers	
tellurium poisoning	H4:490
Testers (electrical machinery)	
mercury poisoning	TM:655
Testers (paint and varnish	
factories)	
manganese poisoning	TM:653
Tetrachlorethane workers	
tetrachlorethane poisoning,	
toxic jaundice, toxic	
polyneuritis	H4:615–616
Tetraethyl lead workers	
lead encephalophathy	MM:70
Tetryl workers	
color changes of the skin	H5:760
dermatitis	H5:532
tetryl poisoning (trinitro	
phenyl methyl nitramine)	H4:570
Textile degreasers	
carbon tetrachloride poisoning	TM:644
dermatitis	H5:730
diethylene dioxide poisoning,	
anorexia, albuminuria, acute	
hemorrhagic nephritis,	
uremia	H4:623–624
Textile dryers	
dermatitis	H5:730
Textile dyeing and finishing	
wash men	
carbon tetrachloride	
poisoning	TM:644
chlorine and hydrochloric	
acid poisoning (dyers)	TM:645
dermatitis	H5:730
lead poisoning, workers in	
general	TM:650
zinc poisoning	TM:659
Textile flameproofers	
dermatitis	H5:730

Disease	Key
Textile industries workers	
lead poisoning	TM:650
Textile printers	
dermatitis	H5:730
Textile solvent workers	
dermatitis	H5:730
diethylene dioxide poisoning,	
anorexia, albuminuria, acute	
hemorrhagic nephritis,	
uremia	H4:623–624
Thallium workers	
thallium poisoning	H4:494
Therapeutic radium	
laboratories' techni-	
cians	
lung cancer	H4:817
Thermometer fillers	
mercury poisoning	H4:655
Thermometer manufacturers	
mercury poisoning	H4:290
Thinners (paint and varnish	
factories)	
manganese poisoning	TM:653
Thorium workers (miners,	
metal fabricators, ore	
treaters)	
radiation	MM:104
Threshers	
aspergillosis	MM:136
threshers' lung	H5:1037
Tile makers	
hookworm	H5:713
pneumoconiosis (from talc)	H5:987
Timber creosoters	
cutaneous papilloma and	
carcinoma	H4:822
Timber porters	
bursitis (humpers' lump)	H4:753
callosities	H5:753
deal-runners' shoulder	H4:803

Disease	Key
Timber preservers	
cutaneous papilloma and	
carcinoma	H4:822
pentachlorphenol poisoning	H4:532
Tin and enameled ware	
(beaders, dippers, enamel	
makers, spray painters)	
antimony poisoning	TM:637
chlorine and hydro-	
chloric acid poisoning,	
cleaners, picklers,	
sheet metal workers	
and tinners	TM:645
lead poisoning, workers in	
general	TM:650
zinc poisoning, workers in	
general	TM:659
Tin miners	
hookworm (miners' bunches)	H5:715
pigmented scars	H5:760
Tinners (especially those	
who work with aluminum	
products, blast furnaces,	
electroplating, foundries,	
match factories, planing and	
milling, rubber tires, storage	
batteries, tin and enameled	
ware)	
chlorine and hydrochloric	
acid poisoning	TM:646
Tin oxide workers	
Stannosis	H5:1014
Tin-plate millmen	
posterior polar cataracts	H4:864
Tin refiners	
haemoglobinuria and haemo-	
lytic jaundice with anemia,	
arsenic poisoning	H4:346
Tinsmiths	
cramps	H4:878

Disease	Key	Disease	Key
Tinsmiths (glass factories; and suit, coat, and overalls industry)		Train despatchers miners' nystagmus (not in U.S.)	H4:856
chlorine and hydrochloric acid poisoning	TM:646	Transfer men (brick, tile, and terra cotta)	
Tinters (paint and varnish factories)		manganese poisoning	TM:653
manganese poisoning	TM:653	Transparent-wrapping-material workers	
Tinters (printing)		carbon disulfide poisoning	TM:642
methyl alcohol poisoning	TM:656	hydrogen sulfide poisoning	TM:649
Tobacco packers		Trawlermen	
traumatic tenosynovitis	H4:808	erysipeloid of Rosenbach	H4:745
Tobacco workers		Treers (shoes)	
dermatitis, tobacco poisoning, tobacco amblyopia, optic atrophy with partial blindness, tobaccosia	H5:1032–1033	methyl alcohol poisoning	TM:656
		Trichlorethylene users (workers' cleansing agent used at the end of the day)	
hookworm (planters)	H5:713	dermatitis	H5:734
lobar pneumonia and chemical pneumonitis	H4:707	Trichlorethylene workers	
		chemical pneumonitis	MM:250
Toilet powders manufacturers pneumoconiosis	H5:987	dermatitis, polyneuritis, corneal anaesthesia and ulceration, cranial nerve palsies, narcosis	H4:603–606
Toilet requisite manufacturers fine, punctate mottling and coalescence of the lungs, pulmonary changes	H5:992	pulmonary edema	MM:250
		Trimmers (wood, wicker, etc.) benzol poisoning	TM:638
Toolmakers (tools for cutting hard metals)		Trinitrotoluene (TNT) workers color changes of the skin (yellowing), bronze-tinting of the hair	H5:760
cyanide poisoning, brass factories	TM:647		
Toys and unclassified novelties (chemical mixers, stampers, pasters)		TNT poisoning, cyanoses, methaemoglobinaemia, sulfaemoglobinaemia, toxic gastritis, toxic jaundice, aplastic anemia, aplasia, hyperplasia of the marrow at necropsy, hemolysis of the red blood cells, necrosis of the liver, acute toxic purpura	H4:546–550
antimony poisoning	TM:637		
lead poisoning, workers in general	TM:650		
zinc poisoning, workers in general	TM:659		
Tradesmen's tricyclists cramps	H4:878		

Disease	Key
Tri-ortho-cresyl phosphate (TOCP) workers	
TOCP poisoning	H4:391
Tripe scrapers	
Weil's disease	H4:738
Truck drivers (chemicals)	
carbon tetrachloride poisoning	TM:644
methyl alcohol poisoning	TM:656
Truckers (dyestuffs, ink, etc.)	
manganese poisoning	TM:653
Trunks and suitcases (repairmen)	
benzol poisoning	TM:638
zinc poisoning, workers in general	TM:659
Tulip bulbs sorters and packers	
tulip fingers	H5:736
Tulip crop gatherers	
tulip fingers	H5:736
Tulip juice workers	
dermatitis	H5:733
Tung oil workers	
dermatitis	H5:735
Tungsten-molybdenum rod and wire manufacturers	
mercury poisoning	H4:290
Tunnel workers	
carbon dioxide poisoning	H4:654
hookworm	H5:713
hydrogen sulfide poisoning	TM:649
Tunnelers	
hookworm	H5:713
Turners	
cramps	H4:878

Disease	Key
Turpentine users (workers' cleansing agent used at the end of the day)	
dermatitis	H5:734
Type cleaners	
methyl alcohol poisoning	TM:656
Typists	
cramps	H4:878
traumatic tenosynovitis	H4:809
Underground workers	
chemical pneumonitis and lobar pneumonia	H4:707
Unloaders (car and radio shop)	
antimony poisoning	TM:637
Upholsterers	
Dupytren's contracture	H5:756
methyl alcohol poisoning	TM:656
modifications of the teeth due to abrasions	H5:801
traumatic tenosynovitis	H4:808
Uranium miners	
lung cancer	H4:814
Uranium workers	
lung cancer	H4:495
uranium nephritis	H4:495
Urea formaldehyde workers	
acute ungual eczema	H5:736
dermatitis	H5:735
Urologists	
radio dermatitis, leukemia and other cancers, radiation cataracts, possible reduced lifespan, genetic mutations	MM:183
Utility men (chemicals)	
benzol poisoning	TM:638
carbon tetrachloride poisoning	TM:644
methyl alcohol poisoning	TM:656

Disease	Key
Valve packings manu-facturers (using asbestos) asbestosis, mesothelioma, lung cancer	H5:972–974
Vanadium miners vanadium poisoning	H4:497
Vanadium ore grinders vanadium poisoning	H4:497
Vanadium pentoxide manu-facturers vanadium poisoning	H4:497
Varnish cookers (paint and varnish factories) phenol poisoning	TM:658
Varnishers aniline poisoning	H4:567
callosities	H5:752
manganese poisoning	TM:653
Varnish makers manganese poisoning	TM:653
zinc poisoning	TM:659
Vat cleaners benzene poisoning	H4:508
Veterinarians anthrax	MM:135
brucellosis	MM:138
Weil's disease	MM:155
Veterinary officers louping-ill	H4:713
Veterinary students animal sarcoptes infestation	H5:744
Veterinary surgeons dermatitis	H5:730
pulmonary tuberculosis, ectothrix, ringworms, erysipeloid of Rosenbach, glanders, psittacosis, swine erysipelas, tetanus, tuber-culosis, tularaemia, undulant fever, rabies, vaccinia	H4:709–710
Q fever	H4:712

Disease	Key
Vibrating tools workers small areas of decalci-fication seen in x-rays of the bones of the carpus, injury to the soft tissues of the hands, osteo-arthritis of the joints of the arms, vascular disturbance (Raynaud's phenomenon)	H4:888
Vicose-rayon manufacturers carbon disulfide poisoning	MM:84
Vine dressers arsenic poisoning	H4:336
Vineyard workers stained fingernails	H5:756
Violinists cramps	H4:878
Violincellists cramps	H4:878
Vulcanizers antimony poisoning	TM:637
benzol poisoning	TM:640
carbon disulfide poisoning	TM:642
carbon tetrachloride poisoning	TM:644
hydrogen sulfide poisoning	TM:649
methyl alcohol poisoning	TM:656
sulfureted hydrogen poisoning	H4:661
Waiters cramps	H4:878
flat feet	H5:753
Wallpaper manufacturers mica pneumoconiosis	H5:991
Wallpaper pigment manu-facturers fine punctate mottling and coalescence of the lungs, pulmonary changes	H5:992

Disease	Key	Disease	Key
Washers (automobile factories)		Welders	
manganese poisoning	TM:653	cadmium poisoning	TM:641
Washing-soda users (workers' cleansing agent used at the end of the day)		cyanide poisoning, in foundries	TM:647
		flash burns (ultraviolet rays exposure)	MM:100
dermatitis	H5:734	mercury poisoning	TM:655
soda holes	H5:735	welders' siderosis	H5:1012
Watchmakers		Welders of galvanized iron	
cramps	H4:878	metal fume fever	MM:38
Water disinfection workers		zinc shakes	MM:38
chlorine poisoning	H4:678	Western red cedar workers	
Water testers (electrical machinery)		asthma	H5:1032
methyl alcohol poisoning	TM:656	cedar poisoning	H5:1032
Water treatment workers (purification)		Whalers	
ammonia burns and poisoning, eye injury	H4:672–673	whale finger, erysipeloid of Rosenbach	H4:745
chlorine and hydrochloric acid poisoning, in petroleum refineries	TM:646	Wheat workers	
		farmers' lung, threshers' lung	H5:1037
Waxers (dental supplies industry)		White phosphorus manufacturing	
phenol poisoning	TM:658	phossy jaw (phosphorus caries and necrosis)	H4:383
Wax pressmen		White rubber gloves processors	
scrotal cancer	MM:294	leucodermia in blacks	H4:636
Weavers		Whitewashers	
callosities	H5:752	dermatitis, lime hole, conjunctiva and cornea injury, symblepharon	H4:367
cotton-weavers' deafness	H4:872		
deafness	H4:872		
ischial bursa or weavers' bottom	H4:803	lime burns	H4:367
Weighers (fertilizer factories)		Wicker workers	
		lead poisoning	TM:650
cyanide poisoning	TM:647	methyl alcohol poisoning, refinishers	TM:656
Weighers (foundries, paint and varnish factories, dyestuffs, ink, etc.)		Wild rabbit cleaners	
		tularemia, rabbit fever	MM:135
		Wine waiters	
manganese poisoning	TM:653	pulmonary tuberculosis	H4:706

Disease	Key
Wire drawers in blast furnaces	
chlorine and hydrochloric acid poisoning	TM:646
Wire picklers	
hydrofluoric acid and fluorine poisoning	H4:683
Wireless apparatus manufacturers	
mica pneumoconiosis	H5:991
Wood machinists	
callosities	H5:752
Wood polishers	
methyl alcohol poisoning	TM:656
Wood preservers	
mercury poisoning	TM:655
phenol poisoning	TM:658
Wood pulp bleachers	
sulfur dioxide poisoning	H4:668
Wood refinishers	
methyl alcohol poisoning	TM:656
Woodworkers	
allergic dermatitis	H5:743
asthma	H5:741
dermatitis	H5:733
lead poisoning	TM:650
lobar pneumonia and chemical pneumonitis	H4:707
mercury poisoning	TM:655
methyl alcohol poisoning	TM:656
South African boxwood toxemia	H5:741
wood toxemia	H5:741
Woodworking metal pattern makers	
chlorine and hydrochloric acid poisoning	TM:645
Wool, straw, and goat hair workers	
anthrax, wool sorters, combers and scourers	H4:721

Disease	Key
lobar pneumonia and chemical pneumonitis	H4:707
orf, louping-ill	H4:714–715
Q fever	MM:136
sulfur dioxide poisoning	H4:668
Woolens and worsteds, dyers	
chlorine and hydrochloric acid poisoning	TM:645
lead poisoning, workers in general	TM:650
Wrappers (storage batteries)	
manganese poisoning	TM:653
Wrestlers	
cauliflower ears	H5:760
Wrinkle pullers (textiles other than cotton)	
benzol poisoning	TM:640
Writers	
cramps (writers' cramp)	H4:879
X-ray apparatus manufacturing workers	
squamous-celled carcinoma of the skin, carcinoma of dorsum	H4:899–900
(see also x-ray equipment operators)	
X-ray equipment operators	
erythema, swelling and necrosis of the skin, alopecia, ulceration of the skin, conjunctivitis	H4:896
fibrous atrophy of the testes, profound refractory anemia	H4:901
gonads irradiation	MM:182
radiodermatitis, leukemia, other cancers, radiation cataract	MM:183

Disease	Key
X-ray equipment operators (continued)	
reduced life span and genetic mutations	MM:183
squamous-celled carcinoma of the skin, basal-celled carcinoma of the skin	H4:899
striation, fissuring and brittling of fingernails	H5:736
warts, post-irradiation telangiectases, paronychia, skin ulcers	H4:898
x-ray burns	MM:102
x-ray dermatitis, x-ray cancer	H5:858
X-ray technicians	
carcinoma of dorsum	H4:899
x-ray dermatitis	H4:899
(see also x-ray equipment operators)	
Xenylamine manufacturers	
cancer of the bladder	H4:827,829
carcinogenic effects	H4:636
Zinc chloride producers	
zinc chloride poisoning	H4:423
Zinc-electrode makers	
mercury poisoning	TM:655
Zinc galvanizers	
metal fume fever	H4:422
Zinc industry workers	
lead poisoning	TM:650
zinc poisoning	TM:659
Zinc miners	
manganese poisoning	TM:653
Zinc oxide manufacturers or zinc powder	
metal fume fever	MM;38
zinc shakes	MM:38
Zinc refiners	
antimony poisoning	TM:637

Disease	Key
cadmium poisoning	TM:641
Zinc smeltors	
antimony poisoning, chargers	TM:636
cadmium poisoning, chargers	TM:641
metal fume fever	MM:38
zinc shakes	MM:38
Zinc welders	
metal fume fever	H4:422
Zoo attendants	
anthrax	H4:721

APPENDIX D
OCCUPATIONAL DISEASES

Disease	Key
Abcesses	H4:378
Abdominal cramps	MM:153
Abrasions	H4:707
Acoustic afterimages	H4:875
Acoustic trauma	MM:95
Acrylonitrile poisoning	H4:633
Acute bursitis	H4:807
Acute chemical poisoning	MM:178
Acute conjunctivitus	MM:35
Acute erythema	H4:898
Acute hemorrhagic nephritis	H4:624
Acute hyeloid leukemia	H4:517
Acute radiation syndrone	H5:886
Acute toxic purpura	H4:550
Acute ungual eczema	H5:736
Acute yellow atrophy of the liver from carbon tetrachloride poisoning	MM:75
Aero-otitis media	H4:847
Aerodontalgia	H4:847
Aeroembolism	MM:166
Air contamination	MM:173
Albuminuria	H4:623
Alkali dermatitis	H5:734
Allergia alveolitis	H5:1036
Allergic dermatitis	H5:743
Allergic rhinitis	H5:1046
Alopecia	H4:896
Alveolitis	MM:35
Ammonia burns	H4:672

Disease	Key
Ammonia poisoning	H4:673
Anemia with punctate basophilia	H4:541
Aniline poisoning	H4:567
Anilinism	H4:534
Anilism	H4:534
Animal sarcoptes infestation	H5:744
Ankylosis	H4:707
Ankylostoma duodenale	H5:715
Ankylostomiasis	H4:706
Anthracine cancer	H5:783
Anthrax	MM:117
Anthrax meningitis	H4:731
Anthrosilicosis	MM:150
Antimony poisoning	TM:636
Antimony spots	HEW:33
Anuria	H4:347
Aplasia	H4:549
Aplastic anemia	MM:77
Apple-sorters' disease	H5:731
Argyria	H4:410
Arsenic dermatitis	H5:729
Arsenic hyperkeratosis	H5:729
Arsenic poisoning	H4:333
Arsenic ulcers	H5:729
Arseniuretted hydrogen poisoning	H4:385
Asbestosis	MM:48
Asbestos warts	H5:978
Aseptic necrosis	MM:153

Sources: H4 and H5: Donald Hunter, *The Diseases of Occupations,* 4th and 5th editions (London: The English Universities Press, Ltd., 1969 and 1975).

MM: May R. Mayers, *Occupational Health: Hazards of the Work Environment* (Baltimore: The Williams and Wilkins Co., 1969).

TM: Thomas F. Mancuso, "Medical Aspects of Occupational Disease," *Ohio State Law Journal,* 19, no. 4 (1958): 612–657.

Numbers after source are page references.

Disease	Key
Aseptic necrosis of bone	H4:844
Aspergillosis	MM:136
Asphyxia	H4:843
Asphyxia from firedamp inhalation	H4:652
Asthma	MM:29
Athlete's foot	MM:142
Aviation deafness	H4:873
Aviation pressure deafness	H4:873
Bacteremia	H4:709
Bagassosis	MM:124
Baritosis	H5:1015
Barley itch	H5:745
Basal-celled carcinoma of the skin	H4:899
Beat disorders	H4:806
Beat elbow	H4:807
Beat hand, beat knee	MM:144
Bends	MM:152
Benzene poisoning	H4:506
Benzol poisoning	TM:638
Beryllium dermatitis	H5:403
Beryllium disease	MM:45
Beryllium granuloma of the skin	H5:403
Blackening of tooth enamel	H5:802
Blackhead itch	H5:580
Black lung	MM:150
Blacksmiths' deafness	H4:872
Bladder cancer	MM:278
Blepharospasm	H4:859
Bleaching of hair and beard	H5:760
Blindness	H4:583
Blisters, abrasions, callosities	MM:115
Boilermakers' deafness	MM:95
Bovine tuberculosis	MM:134
Breathlessness and cough	H4:526
Bronchial asthma	H5:1046
Bronchiolitis oblitarans	H4:526
Bronchitis	H4:526

Disease	Key
Bronchopneumonia	H4:479
Bronze tinting of the hair	H5:760
Brucellosis	MM:134
Burns and explosions	MM:142
Bursitis	MM:113
Butchers' tubercle	H4:707
Byssinosis	MM:38
Cable rash	H5:580
Cadmium emphysema	H4:451
Caisson disease	MM:152
Callositis	H5:751
Cancer	MM:183
Cancer of the bladder	H4:827
Cancer of the ethmoid	H4:817
Canine leptospirosis	H4:742
Carbolmarasmus	H4:530
Carboluria	H4:530
Carbon dioxide poisoning	H4:655
Carbon disulfide arteriosclerosis	MM:84
Carbon disulfide poisoning	MM:83
Carcinogenic effects	H4:636
Carcinoma	H4:822
Carcinoma of the bronchi	H4:818
Carcinoma of the nose	H4:817
Carcinoma of the paranasal sinuses	H4:913
Carcinoma of the skin	H4:818
Carbon monoxide poisoning	MM:59
Carbon tetrachloride poisoning	MM:70
Casting burns	H5:755
Cataracts	H4:862
Caterpillar dermatitis or rash	H5:744
Cauliflower ears	H5:760
Caustic burns	H4:366
Cedar poisoning	H5:1032
Celery itch	H5:739
Centrolobular necrosis of the liver	MM:272
Chemical pneumonitis	MM:35

Disease	Key	Disease	Key
Chimney sweeps' cancer	H5:780	Cyanosis	MM:64
Choracne	MM:28	Cysticercosis	H5:718
Chlorine poisoning	TM:644		
Chloronapthalene acne	H4:617	DNOC poisoning	H4:559
Chlorovinyl dichlorasine	H5:729	Dairymen's itch	H5:744
Chokes	MM:153	Damaged fingernails	H5:758
Cholera	H4:709	Dead fingers, white fingers,	
Chrome dermatitis	Hg:422	Raynaud's phenomenon	MM:144
Chrome holes	H5:422	Deafness	H4:872
Chrome ulcers	MM:27	Deal-runners' shoulder	H4:803
Chronic nephritis	H4:259	Decompression sickness	H4:848
Coagulation burns of the		Dehydration	MM:93
retina	MM:185	Dental erosion	H4:592
Coal workers' pneumoconiosis	H5:1000	Dental fluorosis	H4:690
Color changes in the skin	H5:760	Dermatitis	H4:367
Combers' fever	H5:1024	Diethylene dioxide poisoning	H4:623
Complicated pneumoconiosis	H5:1001	Diethyl mercury poisoning	H5:319
Compressed air illness	H4:839	Dinitrobenzene poisoning	H4:542
Congestive heart failure	H5:1006	Dinitro-ortho-cresol	
Conjunctiva injury	H4:367	poisoning	H4:559
Conjunctiva irritation	H5:989	Dinitrophenol poisoning	H4:555
Convulsions due to exposure		Diphenyl chlorarsine	H5:729
to chlorinated hydrocarbon		Diphenyl cyanoarsine	H5:729
insecticide	MM:127	Diptheria	H4:709
Coolie itch	H5:715	Dislocated thumbs	H5:761
Copra itch	H5:745	Dissection wound	H4:707
Cornea injury	H4:367	Divers' paralysis	H4:839
Corneal anaesthesia	H4:604	Drowsiness	H5:741
Corneal lesions	MM:37	Duck fever	H5:1046
Corneal ulceration	H4:820	Dupuytren's contracture	H5:756
Cornpicker's hand	MM:124	Dustmen's shoulder	H4:803
Cotton-twisters' cramp	H4:885	Dynamite encephalosis	H4:590
Cotton-weavers' deafness	H4:872	Dynamite headache	H5:588
Cramps	H4:878	Dysentery	MM:141
Cranial nerve palsies	H4:604	Dyspnea	MM:151
Criticality accidents	H5:885		
Cutaneous anthrax	H4:723	Ear block	H4:847
Cutaneous papilloma	H4:822	Ectoparasitic infestations	MM:134
Cuts	H4:707	Ectothrix ringworms	H4:710
Cyanide poisoning	TM:646	Ectothrix trichophyta ring-	
		worms	H4:710

Disease	Key	Disease	Key
Eczematous eruptions	H4:572	Fluoracetic acid poisoning	H4:703
Edema of the eyelids	H5:734	Fluoralcohol poisoning	H4:703
Edema of the lungs	MM:35	Fluorine and hydrofluoric	
Electrical cataracts	H4:868	acid poisoning	H4:683
Emphysema	MM:151	Fluorocarbon poisoning	H4:703
Encephalitis	MM:134	Fluorosis of the ligaments	H4:689
Erysipeloid of Rosenbach	H4:710	Fluorosis of the skeleton	H4:687
Erosion of the cutting edges		Focal emphysema	H5:1003
of the lower incisors and		Frostbite	MM:171
canines	H5:802	Fulminate itch	H5:314
Erythema	MM:429	Fungus infections, skin	MM:124
Erythema of the skin with			
pruritis	H4:843	Gastrointestinal disturbances	
Erythema ab igne giving place		from carbon tetrachloride	
to livedo reticularis	H5:754	poisoning	MM:74
Erthropoiesis	HEW:39	Generalized argyria	H4:410
Ethyl dichlorarsine	H5:729	Genetic mutations	MM:183
Ethyl mercury chloride		Gingivitis	H4:368
poisoning	H5:319	Glanders	H4:710
Ethylene chlorhydrin		Glassblowers' cataract	H4:862
poisoning	H4:620	Glassworkers' cataract	H4:863
Ethylene dichloride		Gonorrheal optholmia	H4:709
poisoning	H4:612	Grain fever	H5:1024
Exertional dyspnea	MM:151	Grain itch	MM:124
Eye injuries	H4:672	Granulomatous fibrosis of	
Falls and head injuries	MM:144	the lungs	H4:440
Farmer's lung	MM:124	Grocers' itch	H5:745
Fatal distension of the heart			
with gas	H4:846	Hackling fever or flax fever	H5:1024
Fatigue	H4:526	Hair and beard dyed dark	
Feather-pickers' disease	H5:1046	green	H5:760
Fibrous atrophy of the testes	H4:901	Halowax acne	H5:580
Fig-mite dermatitis	H5:746	Hatlers' shakes	H4:297
Fine punctate mottling and		Headaches	H4:479
coalescence of the lungs	H5:992	Head tremor	H4:859
Firemen's eye	H4:863	Hearing loss	MM:142
Fish handlers' disease	H4:745	Heat cramps	MM:94
Flat feet	H5:754	Heat neurosis	MM:94
Flattened nose	H5:761	Heat rash	MM:93
Flax fever	H5:1024	Heat stress	MM:173

Disease	Key
Heat stroke	MM:94
Heat syncope	MM:94
Hemoglobinuria	H4:346
Hemolysis of the red blood cells	H4:550
Hemolytic jaundice with anemia	H4:346
Hepatitis	H4:619
Herpitic whitlow	H5:758
HETP poisoning	H4:396
Hodmen's shoulder	H4:803
Hookworm	MM:134
Humpers' lump	H4:803
Hydatid cysts	MM:142
Hydrochloric acid poisoning	TM:644
Hydrofluoric acid poisoning	H4:683
Hydrogen cyanide poisoning	H4:663
Hydrogen sulfide poisoning	TM:648
Hyperkeratoses	MM:122
Hyperplasia of the marrow at necropsy	H4:549
Hypoxia	MM:165
Indolent ulceration of the skin	H4:373
Infections	H4:707
Infrared ray cataracts	MM:186
Injury to the soft tissues of the hand	H4:888
Intractable anemia	H4:916
Ionizing radiation	MM:100
Ischial bursa	H4:803
"the itch"	H4:843
Jaundice	MM:156
Jaundice from carbon tetrachloride poisoning	MM:74
Kerato conjunctivitis	H4:708
Keratoses	MM:121

Disease	Key
Laborers' spine	H5:755
Labyrinth dysfunction with vertigo	MM:162
Lachrymation	H5:734
Lead anemia	MM:68
Lead colic	MM:66
Lead encephalopathies	MM:70
Lead line	MM:277
Lead poisoning	MM:65
Leptospiral jaundice	H4:742
Leptospiroses	MM:134
Leucodermia	H4:636
Leuconychia	H5:756
Leukemia resulting from benzol poisoning	MM:79
Leukemia from exposure to ionizing radiation	MM:183
Leukocytosis	H4:613
Leukoderma	MM:31
Lichenoid eruptions	H4:572
Lily rash	H5:738
Lime hole	H4:367
Limonine dermatitis	H5:736
Lobar pneumonia	H4:707
Localized argyria	H4:419
Loosening and separation of fingers	H5:758
Louping ill	H4:713
Lung cancer	MM:294
Lung disease	TM:629
Lupus necrogenica	H4:707
Malaria	MM:272
Malt fever	H5:1024
Manganese poisoning	TM:652
Maple bark disease	H5:1044
Masonia wood bronchial spasms	H5:1032
Massive fibrosis	MM:151
Melanoptysis	H5:1002

Disease	Key
Mercury dermatitis	H5:314
Mercury fulminate dermatitis	H5:314
Mercury poisoning	MM:79
Mesothelioma of the pleura and peritoneum	H5:982
Mesotheliomata	MM:295
Metal fume fever	MM:38
Metal platers' dermatitis	H5:435
Methane explosions	H4:651
Methemoblobinemia	MM:64
Methyl alcohol poisoning	TM:656
Methyl bromide poisoning	H4:598
Methyl bromide burns	H5:564
Methyl chloride poisoning	H4:596
Methyl dichlorarsine	H5:729
Methyl mercury hydroxide poisoning	H5:319
Methyl mercury iodide poisoning	H5:319
Mica pneumoconiosis	H5:991
Microsleep	MM:159
Milker's nodes	MM:122
Mill fever	MM:124
Minamata disease	H4:325
Miners' bunches	H5:715
Miners' cramp	H4:853
Miners' elbow (bursitis)	H5:803
Miners' nystagmus	H4:856
Modifications of the teeth by abrasion	H5:801
Motion sickness	MM:165
Mottled teeth (dental fluorosis)	H4:690
Mule-spinners' cancer	H5:783
Multiple neuritis	H4:387
Multiple-pigmented hyper-keratosis	H4:825
Multiple pitch warts	H4:820
Muscle cramps weakness	MM:113

Disease	Key
Mutilation of the finger-nails by trauma	H5:758
Myeloid leukemia	H4:911
Myelopoieses	HEW:39
Narcosis	MM:55
Nausea	H4:843
Necrosis of the jaw	H4:914
Necrosis of the liver	H4:545
Necrotic skin ulcers	H4:367
Neuritis	MM:113
Neutron cataracts	MM:186
Nickel carbonyl inhalation poisoning	H4:467
Nickel dermatitis	H4:468
Nickel dust inhalation leading to cancer of the lung and nasal sinuses	H4:467
Nickel salt solutions contact leading to dermatitis	H4:467
Night sweats	H4:526
Nitric acid burn	H5:747
Nitrobenzene poisoning	H4:539
Nitrogen dioxide poisoning	H4:674
Nitrogen embolism	H4:846
Nitrogen narcosis	H4:849
Nitroglycerine headache	H4:587
Nodular silicosis	H4:371
Non-ionizing radiation	TM:633
Nystagmus	H4:843
Ocular staining	H4:533
Oil folliculitis	H5:733
Olecranon bursa	H4:803
Olive-green tinting of the hair	H5:760
OMPA poisoning	H4:396
Onchocerciasis	H4:706
Onycholysis	MM:26
Onychomycosis of brewers	H5:736

Disease	Key	Disease	Key
Opaque corneas	H5:761	Phtheiriasis	H5:745
Optic atrophy with partial		Pigmented scars	H5:760
blindness	H5:1032	Pinhead mottling (in the lungs)	H5:1000
Orf	MM:133	Pinhead vesicles	H5:732
Oscillation of lights	H4:858	Pitch cancer	H5:780
Osmic acid poisoning	H4:480	Pitch dust warts	H4:820
Osteoarthritis of the joints		Plague	H4:709
of the arms	H4:888	Platinum dermatitis	H5:450
Osteoarthritis, osteoarthritic		Pneumoconiosis	MM:39
spondylitis	H5:755	Poison ivy and oak	MM:121
Other dusts	MM:36	Poison sumac, elder, or ash	H5:739
Oxygen poisoning	H4:850	Poliomyelitis	H4:709
Papilloma of the renal pelvis	H4:829	Polymer fume fever	MM:38
Papillomata of the bladder	H4:827	Polymeric fluorocarbon	
Paprika-splitters' lung	H4:1042	poisoning	H4:703
Papular dermatitis	H4:368	Polyneuritis	H4:391
Para-phenylenediamine		Portal cirrhosis of the liver	MM:70
poisoning	H4:571	Post-irradiation telangiectases	H4:898
Para-phenylenediamine		Posterior polar cataracts	H4:863
dermatitis	H5:533	Powder holes	H5:314
Paralysis	MM:153	Pre-patellar bursa	H4:803
Paraplegia	H4:849	The Prickles	H4:843
Parathion poisoning	MM:129	Prickly heat, sunburn	MM:121
Paronychia	H5:736	Primrose dermatitis	H5:738
Pentachlorphenol poi-		Printers' asthma	H5:1033
soning	H4:532	Profound refractory anemia	H4:901
Personality changes	MM:166	Prosectors' wart	H4:707
Pes cavus	H5:753	Protozoan infections	MM:272
Phenarsazine chloride	H5:729	Pruritis	MM:153
Phenic marasmus	H4:530	Pseudotuberculoma silicoticum	H5:1020
Phenol poisoning	TM:657	Psittacosis	H4:710
Phenol-related compounds		Psychoneurosis	H4:859
(cresol, tricresol, and creosote)		Pulmonary anthrax	H4:725
poisoning	TM:658–659	Pulmonary arterial thrombosis	H5:1006
Phenyl dichlorarsine	H5:729	Pulmonary changes	H5:992
Phenyl mercury acetate		Pulmonary edema	MM:234
poisoning	H5:318	Pulmonary emphysema	TM:631
Phosgene poisoning	H4:680	Pulmonary tuberculosis	MM:141
Phosphoreted hydrogen		Pyrethrum dermatitis	H5:740
poisoning	H4:383		
Phossy jaw	H4:377	Q fever	MM:136

Disease	Key
Rabbit fever, tularemia	MM:135
Rabies	MM:134
Radiation cateracts	MM:183
Radiation fibrosis	H4:921
Radiation osteitis	H4:916
Radiodermatitis	MM:183
Radium dermatitis	H4:910
Rales	H4:527
Raynaud's phenomenon, dead finger, white fingers	MM:144
Reduced lifespans due to exposure to ionizing radiation	MM:183
Refractory anemia	H4:572
Respiratory infections	MM:95
Retrobulbar neuritis	H4:610
Rheumatoid granulamata	H5:1007
Rheumatoid pneumoconiosis	H5:1006
Rhinitis	H4:368
Rhonchi	H4:527
Rhinorrhea	H5:1046
Rift Valley fever	H4:712
Right heart hypertrophy	H5:1006
Ringworm	MM:133
Rodent, snake, and insect bites	MM:121
Roundworm	MM:134
Rupture of the tympanic membrane	H4:847
Salmonellosis	MM:135
Salt hole	H5:733
Sarcoma of bone	H4:914
Scabies	H5:744
Scarred eyebrows	H5:761
Scoliosis	H4:373
Scoliosis of the thoracic spine	H5:803
Scrotal cancer	MM:294, H4:819
Secondary malformation of the fingernails	H5:989
Selenium poisoning	H4:484
Serum hepatitis	MM:272

Disease	Key
Severe strain on normal homeostatic mechanism	MM:225
Shale oil cancer	H5:780
Shaver's disease	MM:44
Shipyard conjunctivitis	H4:708
Shortening and thickening of the tendo achillis	H5:753
Siderosis	H5:1012
Silicosis	MM:41
Silicotuberculosis	MM:43
Sillimanite pneumoconiosis	H5:989
Silo disease	MM:126
Silo-fillers' disease	H4:675
Sinus block	H4:847
Skin abrasions	MM:284
Skin burns from laser beams with possible carcinogenic effects	MM:185
Skin cancer	MM:121
Skin contaminations	MM:128
Skin irritations	H5:989
Skin lesions	H4:350
Skin ulcers	H4:898
Small areas of decalcification seen in x-rays of bones of the carpus	H4:887
Smallpox-handlers' lung	H5:1048
Snow blindness	MM:171
Soda holes	H5:731
Soot wart	H4:819
South African boxwood toxemia	H5:741
Spectacle dermatitis	H5:435
Spinal fractures	MM:115
Spontaneous fracture	H4:914, H4:916
Squamous and horny carcinomas	H4:821
Squamous-celled carcinoma of the skin	H4:899
Staggers	MM:153

Disease	Key	Disease	Key
Stained fingernails and hands	H5:756	Tenosynovitis	MM:113
Stokers' cramp	H4:853	Tetanus	MM:134
Stannosis	H5:1014	Tetryl poisoning	H4:570
Streptococcal sore throat	H4:709	Thallium poisoning	H4:492
Striation, fissuring, and		Thermal stress	MM:169
brittling of the fingernails	H5:736	Threshers' lung	H5:1037
Strippers' and grinders' asthma	H5:1024	Tinnitus	H4:843
Subacromial bursa	H4:803	Tissue hypoxia	MM:57
Subcutaneous cellulitis	H4:807	TNT illness	H4:546
Subcutaneous cysticerci	H4:758	Tobacco amblyopia	H5:1032
Subcutaneous emphysema	H4:846	Tobacco poisoning	H5:1032
Suffocation from black damp or		Tobaccosis	H5:1033
choke damp	H4:649	Tolyl mercury acetate poisoning	H5:318
Sugar dust	MM:36	Tonsural bald areas	H5:760
Sulfaemoglobinaemia	H4:547	Toxic amblyopia	H4:610
Sulfur dioxide poisoning	H4:668	Toxic gastritis	H4:548
Sulfureted hydrogen poisoning	H4:660	Toxic jaundice	H4:548
Suspender dermatitis	H5:435	Toxic polyneuritis	H4:615
Swelling of the skin	H4:896	Traumatic tenosynovitis	H4:808
Swelling and deformity of the		Trichinosis	MM:137
upper part of the pinna on		Trichlorethylene toxemia	
both ears	H5:801	damage to the liver and kidneys	MM:56
Swine erysipelas	H4:710	Trinitrotoluene (TNT)	
Swineherd's disease	H4:712	poisoning	H4:546
Symblepharon	H4:367	Tuberculosis	H4:710
Tachycardia	H4:859	Tularemia (Rabbit fever)	MM:35
Tailors' ankle (bursitis)	H4:803	Tulip fingers	H5:736
Tapeworm	MM:134	Typhoid	MM:141
Tar cancer	H5:780	Typhus	H4:709
Tar helanosis	H4:819		
Tar mollusca	H4:819	Ulceration of the skin	H4:896
Tar warts	H5:780	Ulcers on the mucous mem-	
Taravana	H4:840	brane of the mouth	H4:368
TEPP poisoning	H4:396	Undulant fever	H4:710
Teeth stained green	H5:801	Upper respiratory tract	
Teeth stained greenish-black	H5:801	irritation	H5:989
Teeth stained greyish-brown	H5:801	Uranium nephritis	H4:495
Telangiectases of the exposed		Uremia	H4:624
skin	H5:754	Urticaria	H5:1046
Telegraphists' cramp	H4:883		
Tellurium poisoning	H4:490	Vaccinia	H4:710

Disease	Key
Vagabond's disease	H5:745
Vanadium poisoning	H4:496
Vanillism	H5:745
Vascular disturbance	H4:888
Verruca necrogenica	H4:707
Vertigo	H4:843
Vesication of the skin	H4:350
Viral hepatitis	MM:272
Vision impairment	H4:480
Vomiting	H4:843
Warts	H4:898
Weavers' bottom	H4:803
Weavers' cough	MM:124
Weeping eczema	MM:29
Weeping excoriations	H4:368
Weil's disease (leptospirosis)	MM:155
Welders' siderosis (iron-oxide lung)	H5:1012
Whale finger	H4:745
White fingers, dead fingers, Raynaud's phenomenon	MM:144
Woodcutters' disease	H5:1032
Wood toxemia	H5:741
Wrist drop	MM:485
Writers' cramp	MM:113
X-irradiation	H4:896
X-ray burns	MM:103
X-ray cancer	H5:860
X-ray dermatitis	H5:858
Yellow ring on teeth	H5:801
Zinc (and its compounds) poisoning	TM:659
Zinc shakes	MM:38

NOTES

Notes to Chapter 1

1. A fuller description of the history of New York's law is in Robert J. Chojnacki's "Occupational Disease Under the New York Workmen's Compensation Law," *St. John's Law Review* 42, no. 4 (April 1968): 473-507.

2. Patrick J. Kelley, "Statutes of Limitations in the Era of Compensation Systems: Workmen's Compensation Limitations Provisions for Accidental Injury Claims," *Washington University Law Quarterly* no. 4 (1974): 541-631.

3. Victoria M. Trasko, "Socioeconomic Aspects of the Pneumoconioses," *Archives of Environmental Health* 9 (October 1964): 521-528.

4. Ibid., p. 523.

5. This portion of New York's history is reported in *Report and Recommendations on Occupational Dust Diseases under Workmen's Compensation Laws* (1, 1966), Workmen's Compensation Board, New York.

6. Joseph C. Fagan, "The Incidence of Pulmonary Disease in Industry," *The Journal of Occupational Medicine* 10 (May 1968): 241-244.

7. J. Maynard Keech, *Workmen's Compensation in North Carolina,* 1929-1940 (Durham, N.C.: Duke University Press, 1942).

8. An excellent statement of the circumstances giving rise to the passage of OSHA can be found in Nicholas A. Ashford, *Crisis in the Workplace: Occupational Disease and Injury* (Cambridge, MA: The MIT Press, 1976).

9. Precise estimates of the toll at Gauley Bridge do not exist. The main contractor claimed that forty-eight men died from various diseases incurred through construction, while Representative Marcantonio of New York charged that 476 workers had died and 1,500 more were dying from silicosis alone. See *The New York Times,* January 23, 1936, p. 2.

10. *Criteria for a Recommended Standard: Occupational Exposure to Asbestos* (Rockville, MD: NIOSH, 1972).

11. *Criteria for a Recommended Standard: Occupational Exposure to Chloroform* (Rockville, MD: NIOSH, 1974).

12. Letter from John F. Finklea, director, NIOSH, "Current Intelligence Bulletin—Chloroform" (March 15, 1976).

13. *Criteria for a Recommended Standard: Occupational Exposure to Benzene* (Rockville, MD: NIOSH, 1974).

14. *Criteria for a Recommended Standard: Occupational Exposure to Cotton Dust* (Rockville, MD: NIOSH, 1974).

15. W. C. Hueper, *Recent Results in Cancer Research: Occupational and Environmental Cancers of the Respiratory System* (New York: Springer-Verlag, 1966), p. 8.

Notes to Chapter 2

1. Lloyd B. Tepper, "Commentary," *A Report on Federal-State Cooperation in Improvement of Workmen's Compensation Legislation and Proceedings of a Workshop,* vol. 1, Studies in Workmen's Compensation and Radiation Injury, Department of Labor, A.E.C. (1965), p. 27.

2. Ibid., p. 28.

3. Bertram D. Dinman, *The Nature of Occupational Cancer* (Springfield, IL: Charles C. Thomas, 1974), p. 7.

4. DHEW, "Limitation of Activity Due to Chronic Conditions, U.S. 1969 and 1970," *Vital and Health Statistics,* series 10, no 80 (April 1973): 34.

5. "Final Mortality Statistics, 1974," *Vital Statistics Report,* Supplement, 5. 24, no. 11 (February 3, 1976): 12.

6. DHEW, "Limitation of Activity," p. 34.

7. See, for example, Ronald E. Jones, "Alcoholism and the Workplace," *Manpower* (February 1975): 2–8.

8. Irving J. Selikoff, "Multiple Factor Interactions in Occupational Disease" (Paper presented at the Conference on Occupational Diseases and Workers' Compensation, Chicago, IL, February 10–12, 1976).

9. Ibid., p. 8.

10. *Criteria for a Recommended Standard: Occupational Exposure to Trichloroethylene* (Rockville, MD: NIOSH, 1973).

11. L. A. Sagan, "Radiobiological Problems Associated with Adjudication of Workmen's Compensation Claims," *Journal of Occupational Medicine* 11, no. 6 (June 1969): 338.

12. Selikoff, "Multiple Factor Interactions," p. 8.

13. *Riddle* v. *Broad Crane Engineering Co.,* 218 N.W. 2nd 845.

14. David P. Discher, Goldy Kleinman, and F. James Foster, *Pilot Study for Development of an Occupational Disease Surveillance Method,* HEW publication no. (NIOSH) 75–162 (Rockville, MD: NIOSH, May 1975).

15. This growing awareness is evidenced by a lengthy article by David Burnham, "Rise in Birth Defects Laid to Job Hazards," *The New York Times,* March 14, 1976, p. 1. Also see, Vilma R. Hunt, *Occupational Health Problems of Pregnant Women. A Report and Recommendations for Office of the Secretary,* DHEW, April 30, 1975.

16. The case described is *Hartford Accident & Indemnity Co.* v. *Industrial Commission,* 29 P 2d 142 (1934).

17. President, *The President's Report on Occupational Safety and Health* (Washington, D.C.: United States Government Printing Office, [GPO] , 1972), p. 111.

18. Information provided to the author by NIOSH personnel.

19. The material was provided to me in correspondence with Les Boden, Harvard University, August 1975. It was prepared by an unnamed panel for the National Institute of Health.

20. See, for example, "Man's Health and the Environment—Some Research Needs," *Report of the Task Force on Research Planning in Environmental Health Science,* National Institute of Environmental Health Sciences (March 1970), p. 147.

21. John M. Peters, "Occupational Health: Working Yourself Sick," in *The Challenges of Community Medicine,* ed. Robert L. Kane (New York: Springer Publishing Co., 1974), p. 262.

22. Letter from John M. Peters to Peter S. Barth, October 21, 1975.

23. Nicholas A. Ashford, "The Magnitude of the Occupational Health Problem" (Paper presented at the Conference on Occupational Diseases and Workers' Compensation, Chicago, Illinois, (February 10–12, 1976).

24. California Department of Industrial Relations, *California Work Injuries: 1974,* February 1976.

25. Ibid., table 21.

26. A number of shortcomings in the data have been eliminated, but the serious, largely inevitable ones described in a paper on this subject still exist. See Peter S. Barth, "OSHA and Workers' Compensation: Some Thoughts on Fatalities," *1975 Spring Meeting, IRRA Proceedings,* pp. 486–490.

27. Discher, Kleinman, and Foster, *Pilot Study.*

28. U.S. Department of Labor Press Release 75-647, November 19, 1975.

29. A helpful paper on this was delivered by Philip Enterline, "Methodological Problems in Measuring Dose in Studies of Asbestos and Cancer" (The American Public Health Association, 103rd Annual Meeting, Chicago, November 18, 1975).

30. For example see the first article using this approach, Thomas F. Mancuso and Elizabeth J. Coulter, "Methods of Studying the Relation of Employment and Long Term Illness, Cohort Analysis," *American Journal of Public Health* 49, no. 11 (November 1959): 1525-1536.

31. Carol K. Redmond, *Comparative Cause—Specific Mortality Patterns by Work Area Within the Steel Industry* (Rockville, MD.: NIOSH, 1975).

32. Thomas F. Mancuso and Elizabeth J. Coulter, "Methodology in Industrial Health Studies," *Archives of Environmental Health,* 6 (February 1963): 210-226.

33. Thomas F. Mancuso and A. A. El-Attar, "Cohort Study of Workers Exposed to Betanaphthylamine and Benzidine," *Journal of Occupational Medicine* 9, no. 6 (June 1967): 277-285.

34. Telephone interview with Harriet Hardy, January 1976.

35. Thomas F. Mancuso and A. A. El-Attar, "Epidemiological Study of the Beryllium Industry," *Journal of Occupational Medicine* 11, no. 8 (August 1969): 422-434.

36. See Enterline, "Methodological Problems."

37. Personal interview with Roy J. Steinfurth, administrator, Insulators Health Hazard Program (Asbestos Workers) November 4, 1975.

38. Philip Enterline and Vivian Henderson, "Type of Asbestos and Respiratory Cancer in the Asbestos Industry," *Archives of Environmental Health* 27 (November 1973): 314.

39. J. William Lloyd, "Long Term Mortality Study of Steelworkers," *Journal of Occupational Medicine* 13 (1971): 53-68.

40. Thomas F. Mancuso, "Medical Aspects" (Paper presented at the Conference on Occupational Diseases and Workers' Compensation, Chicago, Illinois, February 10-12, 1976).

41. Irving Selikoff and E. Cuyler Hammond, "Toxicity of Vinyl Chloride Polyvinyl Chloride," *Annals of the New York Academy of Sciences,* 246 (1975): especially p. 229.

42. Irving Tabershaw and William Gaffey, "Mortality Study of Workers in the Manufacture of Vinyl Chloride and its Polymers," *Journal of Occupational Medicine* 16, no. 8 (August 1974): especially p. 512.

43. S. Milham Jr., *Mortality Experience of the AFL-CIO United Brotherhood of Carpenters and Joiners of America 1969-70,* HEW publication (NIOSH) 74-129, (St. Lake City, July 1974).

44. A. J. McMichael, D. A. Andjelkovic, and H. A. Tyroler, "Cancer Mortality Among Rubber Workers," (Paper presented to the New York Academy of Sciences Conference on Occupational Carcinogenesis, March 24-28, 1975.

45. W. C. Hueper, *Occupational and Environmental Cancers of the Urinary System* (New Haven: Yale University Press, 1969).

46. Ibid., p. 129.

47. Alice Hamilton and Harriet L. Hardy, *Industrial Toxicology,* 3rd ed. (Acton, MA: Publishing Sciences Groups, 1974).

48. W. C. Hueper, *Recent Results in Cancer Research: Occupational and Environmental Cancers of the Respiratory System* (New York: Springer-Verlag, 1966).

49. E. E. Pochin, "Occupational and Other Fatality Rates," *Community Health* 6, no. 2 (1974): 2-13.

50. *Report and Recommendations on Occupational Dust Diseases Under Workmen's Compensation Laws,* Workmen's Compensation Board, New York (February 1, 1966).

51. Ibid., p. 37.

52. Ibid. p. 153.

53. Howard A. Buechner, "Hypersensitivity Pneumonitis," in *Occupational Medicine Symposia* GPO–NIOSH, Rockville, MD: 1975) pp. I-1–I-8.

54. Ibid. p. 1–5.

55. Ibid. p. 1–6.

56. Hamilton and Hardy, *Industrial Toxicology,* p. 472.

57. Discher, Kleinman, and Foster, *Pilot Study.*

58. See Suzan Q. Stranaham, "Why 115,000 Workers Will Die This Year," *Boston Globe,* March 21, 1976, p. 1.

59. Discher, Kleinman, and Foster, *Pilot Study,* p. 8.

60. Ibid., p. 9.

61. Ibid., p. 48.

62. Ibid.

63. Ibid.

64. A helpful summary of the details of this survey, as it pertains to workers' compensation, along with one of the Social Security Survey of the Disabled can be found in Monroe Berkowitz, "Sources of Information about Workmen's Compensation Recipients," in *Supplemental Studies for the National Commission on State Workmen's Compensation Laws,* vol. II (Washington, D.C.:GPO, 1973), pp. 109–162.

65. DHEW, National Center for Health Statistics, *Time Lost from Work Among the Currently Employed Population: U.S. 1968,* series 10, no. 71 (April 1962).

66. Ibid., tables 8 and 9.

67. *Health and Work in America: A Chart Book* (Washington, D.C.: American Public Health Association, 1975), p. 40.

68. DHEW, National Center for Health Statistics, *Prevalence of Chronic Circulatory Conditions: U.S. 1972,* series 10, no. 94 (September 1974).

69. *Chart Book,* p. 63.

70. The need for some qualification is regrettable but necessary. The APHA's *Chart Book* shows the incidence of hypertensive disease as 67.1 per 1,000 compared to 60.1 per 1,000 in the original source, and is depended on for the unpublished data on interoccupational differences.

71. Department of Labor, *Manpower Report of the President,* April 1974 (Washington, D.C.: GPO, 1974), p. 267.

72. Based on unpublished data of the Health Interview Survey in *Chart Book,* p. 63.

73. Hueper, *Occupational and Environmental Cancers of the Urinary System,* p. 15.

74. Thomas J. Mason, Frank W. McKay, Robert Hoover, William Blot, and Joseph J. Fraumeni, Jr., *Atlas of Cancer Mortality for U.S. Counties: 1950-1969,* DHEW Publication no. (NIH) 75-780 (Washington, D.C.: GPO, 1975).

75. Ibid., p. 3.

76. Ashford, "The Magnitude of the Occupational Health Problem."

77. Peters, *Challenges of Community Medicine,* pp. 267–270.

78. *The New York Times,* January 2, 1977, III.

79. President, *The President's Report on Occupational Safety and Health,* (Washington, D.C.: GPO, 1973), p. 119.

80. *Suspected Carcinogens: A Subfile of the Registry of Toxic Effects of Chemical Substances,* 2nd ed. (Cincinnati, Ohio: NIOSH, December 1976).

81. A. V. Roshchin, "Protection of the Working Environment," *International Labor Review,* 110, no. 3 (September 1974): 235–249.

82. "Working Women and Birth Defects," *The Washington Post,* April 17, 1976, p. B–2.

83. *The Report of the National Commission on State Workmen's Compensation Laws* (Washington, D.C.: GPO, 1972), p. 98.

84. Remarks by Andrew Kalmykow, (Conference on Occupational Disease and Workers' Compensation, Chicago, Illinois, February 10–12, 1976).

85. Hamilton and Hardy, *Industrial Toxicology,* section II.

86. *Criteria for a Recommended Standard: Occupational Exposure to Beryllium,* (Rockville, MD: NIOSH, 1972).

87. Woodward and Fondmiller Inc., "A Parallel Study on Workmen's Compensation Claims Arising from Exposure to Asbestos and Beryllium," *Studies in Workmen's Compensation and Radiation Injury,* vol. IV, DOL–AEC publication, undated.

88. Hamilton and Hardy, *Industrial Toxicology,* p. 461.

89. Ibid., p. 386.

90. Such sophistication and the remaining uncertainties are spelled out in Duncan A. Holaday, *NIOSH Technical Information: Evaluation and Control of Radon Daughter Hazards in Uranium Mines,* November 1974.

91. *Criteria for a Recommended Standard: Occupational Exposure to Benzene* (Rockville, MD: NIOSH, 1974).

92. Ibid., p. 23.

93. "Deaths are Blamed on Toxic Chemical," *The Hartford Times,* April 20, 1976; and Stuart Averbach, "6 Goodyear Workers' Deaths Probed," *The Washington Post,* April 21, 1976, p. A–3.

94. Ibid.

95. *Criteria for a Recommended Standard: Occupational Exposure to Inorganic Mercury* (Rockville, MD: NIOSH, 1973).

96. Ibid., p. 15.

97. Bill Richards, "Arsenic: A Dark Cloud Over 'Big Sky Country'," *The Washington Post,* February 3, 1976, p. 1.

98. Hueper, *Recent Results in Cancer Research,* p. 8.

99. Richards, *The Washington Post,* p. 1.

100. In a personal interview with Roy Steinfurth of the International Asbestos Workers, union members are aware of the extreme hazards posed by exposure to asbestos.

101. Hueper, *Occupational and Environmental Cancers of the Urinary System,* p. 85.

102. Ibid., p. 85.

103. Ibid., ch. 1.

104. H. J. Symanski, "Industrial Intoxication by Chlormethane Sulphonic Acid Trichloranilide in Europe," *Industrial Medicine and Surgery* (January 1967): 63.

105. Letter from John F. Finklea, *Current Intelligence Bulletin—Chloroform* (NIOSH, March 15, 1976).

106. "Priority List for Criteria Development for Toxic Substances and Physical Agents" (NIOSH, August 1974, unpublished.)

107. W. M. Gafefer, ed., *Occupational Diseases: A Guide to Their Recognition,* Public Health Service Publication, no. 1097 (Washington, D.C.: GPO, 1964).

108. U.S., Public Health Service, Environmental Control Administration, *Occupational Health Survey of the Chicago Metropolitan Area,* 1970.

109. For background on this study see *Survey Manual (1977), National Occupational Hazard Survey* (Rockville, MD: NIOSH, May 1974), and vols. II, III.

110. Letters by J. William Lloyd, NIOSH, July 7, 1975 and June 6, 1975 respectively.

111. *Criteria for a Recommended Standard: Occupational Exposure to Chrystalline Silica,* (Rockville, MD.: NIOSH, 1974), p. 17.

112. *Criteria for a Recommended Standard: Occupational Exposure to Asbestos* (Rockville, MD: NIOSH, 1972).

113. *The President's Report on Occupational Safety and Health* (December 1973); "Priority List for Critical Development for Toxic Substances and Physical Agents" (1974); and Letter from Finklea, "Current Intelligence Bulletin—Chloroform," March 15, 1976.

114. *Criteria for a Recommended Standard: Occupational Exposure to Inorganic Lead* (Rockville, MD:NIOSH, 1972), p. 111.

115. Ibid.

116. *Criteria for a Recommended Standard: Occupational Exposure to Cotton Dust* (Rockville, MD: NIOSH, 1974).

117; *Criteria for a Recommended Standard: Occupational Exposure to Coke Oven Emissions* (Rockville, MD: NIOSH, 1973).

118. *Survey Manual* (1974; 1977).

119. *Criteria for a Recommended Standard: Occupational Exposure to Cresol* (Rockville, MD: NIOSH, February 1978). pp. 22-23.

Notes to Chapter 3

1. The Report of the National Comission on State Workmen's Compensation Laws (Washington, D.C.: GPO, 1972).

2. In personal correspondence Henry Howe indicates that he believes this problem is less severe than in former years.

3. Seymour Jablon, "Radiation" in *Persons at High Risk of Cancer,* ed. Joseph F. Fraumeni, Jr. (New York: Academic Press, 1975), pp. 151-165.

4. *Criteria for a Recommended Standard: Occupational Exposure to Asbestos* (Rockville, MD: NIOSH, 1972).

5. L. A. Sagan, "Radiobiological Problems Associated with Adjudication of Workmen's Compensation Claims," *Journal of Occupational Medicine,* 11, no. 6 (June 1969): 335.

6. Ibid., p. 336.

7. Ibid., p. 338.

8. Michael J. McCormick, "Workers' Compensation—Quantum of Proof—A Recovery for Cancer, Allegedly Caused by Radiation Must be Based on a Reasonable Probability of Causal Connection," *St. Mary's Law Journal,* I (1969): 105-110.

9. *Criteria for Recommended Standard: Occupational Exposure to Benzene* (Rockville, MD: NIOSH, 1974).

10. *Legate* v. *Bituminous Fire & Marine Insurance Company,* 483 S.W. 2nd 488 (1972). A similar situation caused a Minnesota court to deny compensation in *Graver* v. *Peter Lametti Const. Co.,* 197 N.W. 2nd 443 (1972).

11. *Occupation and Disease—A Guide for Decision-Making,* Contract 210-75-0075 (NIOSH, February 1976), unpublished draft, p. 114.

12. *Carr* v. *Homestake Mining Co.,* 215 N.W. 2d 830.

13. See, for example, *Occupation and Disease—A Guide for Decision Making,* p. 114.

14. *Stevenson* v. *Castings, Inc.,* Colorado, District Court, City and County of Denver, No. C 39121, April 30, 1975.

15. *Report and Recommendations of Occupational Dust Diseases under Workmen's Compensation Laws,* Workmen's Compensation Board, New York (February, 1966).

16. Mobility data are from Herbert S. Parnes, *et al., The Pre-Retirement Years: A Longitudinal Study of the Labor Market Experience of Men,* vol. 1, Manpower Research Monograph No. 15 (Washington, D.C.: G.P.O., 1970), ch. 5.

17. W. C. Hueper, *Occupational and Environmental Cancers of the Urinary System,* (New Haven: Yale University Press, 1969), p. 169.

18. Philip Cole and Marlene Goldman, "Occupation," in *Persons at High Risk of Cancer,* ed. Joseph F. Fraumeni, Jr., (New York: Academic Press, 1975).

19. Liberty Mutual Loss Prevention Services, "Safety and the Younger Worker," *Supervisory Management,* 15, no. 6 (1970): 35-37.

20. Irving J. Selikoff, "Multiple Factor Interactions in Occupational Disease" (Paper presented at the Conference on Occupational Diseases and Workers' Compensation, Chicago, Illinois, February 10-12, 1976).

21. Ibid., pp. 2-3.

22. *Criteria for a Recommended Standard: Occupational Exposure to Zinc Oxide* (Rockville, MD: NIOSH, 1975), p. 33.

23. *Criteria for a Recommended Standard: Occupational Exposure to Sulphur Dioxide* (Rockville, MD: NIOSH, 1973), pp. 27-28.

24. See, for example, E. R. Plunkett, "Occupational Health Service," *Occupational Medicine Symposia* (Rockville, MD: GPO-NIOSH, 1975), pp. 11-12-11-16.

25. Thomas F. Mancuso, "Relation of D͏ ͏͏ion of Employment and Prior Respiratory Illness to Respiratory Cancer Among Beryllium Workers," *Environmental Research* 3, no. 3 (July 1970): 251-275.

26. Ibid., p. 270.

27. W. C. Hueper, *Recent Results in Cancer Research: Occupational and Environmental Cancers of the Respiratory System* (New York: Springer-Verlag, 1966), pp. 14-15.

28. Irving J. Selikoff, E. C. Hammond, and J. Churg, "Asbestos Exposure, Smoking and Neoplasia," *Journal of the American Medical Association* 204 (1968): 106-112.

29. Thomas F. Mancuso, Remarks at the Conference on Occupational Disease and Workers' Compensation, Chicago, Illinois, February 10-12, 1976.

30. Interview with Charles Stewart, Ontario Workmen's Compensation Board, September 30, 1976.

31. Alice Hamilton and Harriet Hardy, *Industrial Toxicology,* 3rd ed. (Acton, MA: Publishing Sciences Group, 1974), p. 465. This point, however, is subject to some debate. Mancuso, in personal correspondence has indicated his disagreement.

32. Jablon, "Radiation," p. 160.

33. Hueper, *Recent Results in Cancer Research* p. 14.

34. *Buchanan* v. *Allen-Hay Motor Co.,* 533 P. 2d 824.

35. *Fuentes* v. *Workers' Compensation Appeals Board,* 547 P. 2d 449 (1976).

36. D. J. Birmingham, Marcus M. Key, Duncan A. Holaday, and Vernon Perone, "An Outbreak of Arsenical Dermatoses in a Mining Community," *Archives of Dermatology* 91 (1964): 457-464.

37. Thomas J. Mason, Frank W. McKay, Robert Hoover, William Blot, and Joseph J. Fraumeni, Jr., *Atlas of Cancer Mortality for U.S. Counties: 1950-1969,* DHEW Publication no. (NIH) 75-780 (Washington, D.C.: GPO, 1975).

38. Hueper, *Recent Results in Cancer Research.*

39. Ibid, p. 13.

40. John W. Berg, "Diet," in *Persons at High Risk of Cancer,* ed. Joseph F. Fraumeni, Jr. (New York: Academic Press, 1975), p. 211.

41. Jablon, "Radiation."

42. Cited in Elmer H. Blair, "Occupational Disease," *Reference Guide to Workmen's Compensation* (St. Louis: Thomas Law Book Co., 1974), notes 18 and 19.

43. Duncan A. Holaday, *NIOSH Technical Information: Evaluation and Control of Radon Daughter Hazards in Uranium Mines,* November 1974.

44. John M. Peters, "Occupational Health: Working Yourself Sick" in *The Challenges of Community Medicine,* ed. Robert L. Kane (New York: Springer Publishing Co., 1974).

45. Ibid, p. 270.

46. Woodward and Fondmiller Inc., "A Parallel Study on Workmen's Compensation Claims Arising from Exposure to Asbestos and Beryllium," *Studies in Workmen's Compensation and Radiation Injury,* vol. iv, DOL-AEC publication, undated, pp. 14–15.

47. Janet B. Schoenberg and Charles A. Mitchell, "Implementation of the Federal Asbestos Standard in Connecticut," *The Journal of Occupational Medicine* 16, no. 11 (November 1974: 781-784.

48. *Marques* v. *Industrial Commission,* 517 P. 2d 1269 (1974).

49. *Studies in Workmen's Compensation and Radiation Injury,* vol. VI (Washington, D.C.: U.S. Atomic Energy Commission, 1972) p. 17.

50. John D. Repko, Ben B. Morgan, and John Nicholson, *Behavioral Effects of Occupational Exposure to Lead* (Cincinnati: NIOSH, May 1, 1975), p. 126.

51. See, S. V. Kasl and S. Cobb, "Blood Pressure Changes in Men Undergoing Job Loss: A Preliminary Report," *Psychosomatic Medicine* 32 (1970):19–38.

52. Robert B. Sleight and Kenneth Clark, *Problems in Occupational Safety and Health: A Critical Review of Select Worker Physical and Psychological Factors* (Cincinnati: NIOSH, November 1974), p. J-4.

53. Ibid., J-13.

54. Robert D. Caplan, *Job Demands and Worker Health* (Rockville, MD: NIOSH, April 1975).

55. "Report of the Committee on the Effect of Strain and Trauma on the Heart and Great Vessels," *Circulation* 26 (October 1962): 617.

56. *Carter* v. *General Motors Corp.,* 106 N.W. 2d 105 (1960).

57. *Baker* v. *Workmen's Compensation Appeals Board,* 96 Cal. Rptr. 279 (1971).

58. M. H. Brenner, "Patterns of Psychiatric Hospitalization Among Different Socioeconomic Groups in Response to Economic Stress," *Journal of Nervous Mental Disease* 184 (1969): 31–38.

59. Thomas F. Mancuso and Ben Z. Locke, "Carbon Disulphide as a Cause of Suicide," *Journal of Occupational Medicine* 14, no. 8 (August 1972): 595–606.

60. Nicholas Ashford, *Crisis in the Workplace: Occupational Disease and Injury – A Report to the Ford Foundation,* (The MIT Press: Cambridge, MA, 1976), sections 3.6.2 and 3.6.3.

61. Lloyd B. Tepper, "Commentary," *A Report on Federal-State Cooperation in Improvement of Workmen's Compensation Legislation and Proceedings of a Workshop,* vol. 1, Studies in Workmen's Compensation and Radiation Injury, DOL-AEC (1965), p. 29.

62. *Dillow* v. *Florida Portland Cement Co.,* 258 S.2d 266 (1972).

63. Elmer H. Blair, Reference Guide, note 10.

64. *Berman* v. *Werman & Sons.* 218 N.Y.S. 2d 315 (1961).

65. For example, see May R. Mayers, *Occupational Health: Hazards of the Work Environment* (Baltimore: The Williams and Wilkins Co., 1969).

66. Woodward and Fondmiller, Inc., "A Parallel Study," pp. 14–15.

67. Personal communication from Henry Howe. John Peters has estimated that approximately 300 physicians have specific training in occupational medicine, *The Challenges of Community Medicine,* p. 266.

68. *Criteria for a Recommended Standard: Occupational Exposure to Crystalline Silica,* (Rockville, MD: NIOSH, May 1974).

69. Ibid., 21.

70. *Occupation and Disease — A Guide for Decision-Making,* p. 119.

71. Hueper, *Recent Results in Cancer Research,* p. 3.

72. *Fitch* v. *Princess Coal, Inc.,* 463 S.W. 2d 941 (1971) (Kentucky).

73. See, for example, May R. Mayers, *Occupational Health,* pp. 7-8.

74. *The Federal Coal Mine Health Program in 1972,* (Rockville, MD, NIOSH, 1973), pp. 7-8.

75. A. V. Roshchin, "Protection of the Working Environment," *International Labor Review,* 110, no. 3 (September 1974): 239.

76. *Criteria for a Recommended Standard: Occupational Exposure to Carbon Monoxide* (Rockville, MD: NIOSH, 1972).

77. The discussion is based largely on Repko, Morgan, and Nicholson, *Behavioral Effects.*

78. David P. Discher, Goldy Kleinman, and F. James Foster, *Pilot Study for Development of an Occupational Disease Surveillance Method,* HEW publication no. (NIOSH) 75-162 (Rockville, MD: NIOSH, May 1975).

Notes to Chapter 4

1. Arthur Larson, *Workmen's Compensation Law,* selected volumes (New York: Mathew Bender). Primarily see volume 1-A, 1973, and volume 2, 1976.

2. Elmer H. Blair, *Reference Guide to Workmen's Compensation* (St. Louis: Thomas Law Book Co., 1974).

3. Chamber of Commerce of the U.S., *Analysis of Workmen's Compensation Laws,* Selected Annual Editions, Washington, D.C.

4. *Steel* v. *Cammell, Laird & Co.* 2 K.B. 232 (1905).

5. Patrick J. Kelley, "Statutes of Limitations in the Era of Compensation Systems: Workmen's Compensation Limitations Provisions for Accidental Injury Claims," *Washington University Law Quarterly,*no. 4 (1974): 541-631.

6. National Industrial Conference Board, *Summary of Report on Workmen's Compensation Acts in the United States — The Legal Phase* (Boston: NICB, 1917) : pp. 4-5.

7. *Victory Sparkler & Specialty Co.* v. *Francks,* 128 A. 635 (1925).

8. *Goldberg* v. *954 Marcy Corporation,* 12 N.E. 2d 311, (1938).

9. Statutory language was provided through the courtesy of the staff of the Interdepartmental Task Force on Workers' Compensation.

10. *Asten Hill Mfg. Co.* v. *Bambrick,* 291 A. 2d 354 (1972).

11. *Utter* v. *Asten Hill Mfg. Co.,* 309 A. 2d 583 (1973).

12. *Hammond* v. *Hitching Post Inn,* 523 P. 2d 482 (Wyoming, 1974).

13. *Fitch* v. *Princess Coal Inc.,* 463 S.W. 2d 1941 (Kentucky, 1971).

14. *Buchanan* v. *Allen-Hay Motor Co.,* 533 P. 2d 824 (Oregon, 1975).

15. *Roettinger* v. *Great A & P Tea Co.,* 230 N.Y.S. 2d 903 (1962).

16. *Stevens* v. *Village of Driggs,* 152 P. 2d 891 (Idaho, 1944).

17. *Bess* v. *Coca Cola Bottling of St. Louis,* 469 S.W. 2d 40 (Mo. App. 1971).

18. *Feist* v. *N. Dakota Workmen's Compensation Bureau,* 42 N.W. 2d 655 (1950).

19. *Ohio Bell Telephone* v. *Krise,* 327 N.E. 2d 756 (Ohio, 1975).

20. *Phillips* v. *Ingersoll-Humphreys Division, Borg-Warner Corp.,* 291 N.E. 2d 736 (Ohio, 1972).

21. *Collins* v. *Neevel Luggage Manufacturing Co.,* 481 S.W. 2d 548 (Mo. App. D.K.C. 1972). The case and its implications are more fully described in Gary Mayes, "Workmen's Compensation — Compensation for Ordinary Diseases of Life," *Missouri Law Review* 38, no. 4 (Fall 1973): 705-710.

22. 481 S.W. 2d p. 552.

23. *Warren* v. *General Motors Corp.,* 344 A. 2d 248 (Delaware, 1975).

24. *Esposito* v. *Willowbrook State School,* 362 N.Y.S. 2d 54 (N.Y. 1974).

25. *Lothrop* v. *Hamilton Wright Organization,* 356 N.Y.S. 2d 730 (N.Y., 1974).

26. *Morrow* v. *Memorial Mission Hospital,* 204 S.E. 2d 543 (North Carolina, 1974).

27. *Strouse* v. *Village of Endicott,* 374 N.Y.S. 2d 764 (N.Y., 1975).

28. *Suarez* v. *Zampieri Bros.,* 348 N.Y.S. 2d 201 (N.Y., 1973).

29. *Weber* v. *Carhart Photo, Inc.,* 362 N.Y.S. 2d 62 (N.Y., 1974).

30. *Butler* v. *National Lead Co.,* 126 S.E. 2d 453 (1963).

31. *Barentine* v. *Gleghorn Oil Co.,* 492 S.E. 2d 242 (1973).

32. *Ridley Packing Co.* v. *Holliday,* 467 P. 2d 480 (1970).

33. *Denver Metal Finishing Co.,* v. *Williams,* 516 P. 2d 1137 (Colorado, 1973).

34. *Kraft* v. *Kolberg Mfg. Co.,* 215 N.W. 2d 844 (South Dakota, 1974).

35. Survey of state administrative practices conducted by John H. Lewis, April 1976 for the Interdepartmental Task Force on Workers' Compensation; hereafter referred to as "Administrative Survey."

36. *Knoxville Poultry & Eggs Co.,* v. *Robinson,* 477 S.W. 2d 515 (1972).

37. *Electro-Voice* v. *Hurley,* 530 S.W. 2d 78 (Tenn., 1975).

38. *New Jersey Zinc Co.* v. *Cole,* 532 S.W. 2d 246 (1975).

39. *Blue* v. *Bunge Corp.,* La. App., 225 So. 2d 145 (1969).

40. *Zerinque* v. *Fireman's Fund American Ins. Co.,* La. App., 271 So. 2d 613 (1972).

41. Howard D. Fashbaugh, "Development of North Carolina Occupational Disease Coverage," *Wake Forest Law Review* 7, 2 (March 1971): 341-353.

42. See Blair, *Reference Guide to Workmen's Compensation,* notes 22-23.

43. *Murphy* v. *Enka Corp.,* 195 S.E. 536 (1938).

44. *Perez* v. *Blumenthal Bros. Chocolate Co.,* 237 A. 2d 227 (1968).

45. This section draws even more heavily than most on Larson, *Workmen's Compensation Law,* vol. 1-A, sec. 40.

46. See his reference to *Gay* v. *Hocking Coal Co.,* 169 N.W. 360 (1918).

47. Joseph D. Messina, "Workmen's Compensation: Emergence from the Serbonian Bog," *University of Pittsburgh Law Review* 35 (1973): 382.

48. *Mason* v. *YMCA,* 68 N.Y.S. 2d 510 (1947).

49. *Paider* v. *Park E. Movers,* 280 N.Y.S. 2d 140, 227 N.E. 2d 40 (1967).

50. *Vanderbee* v. *Knape and Vogt Manufacturing Co.,* Mich. App. 210 N.W. 2d 801 (1973).

51. *Herdick* v. *New York Zoological Society,* 356 N.Y.S. 2d 706 (N.Y., 1974).

52. *Middleton* v. *Coxsackie Correctional Facility,* 357 N.Y.S. 2d 732 (N.Y., 1974).

53. *Middleton* v. *Coxsackie Correctional Facility,* 357 N.Y.S. 2d 732 (N.Y., 1975).

54. *International Harvester Company* v. *Illinois Industrial Commission,* 305 N.E. 2d 529 (1973).

55. For example, see *Hinkle* v. *Heinz,* 298 A. 2d 632 (1972).

56. Larson, *Workmen's Compensation Law,* vol. 1-A, 7–166.

57. Cited in Robert V. R. Dalenberg, "Coronary Heart Disease and the Law," *Modern Concepts of Cardiovascular Disease* XLII, no. 6 (June 1973): 29–32.

58. Ibid.

59. Arthur Larson, "The 'Heart Cases' in Workers· Compensation: An Analysis and Suggested Solution," *Michigan Law Review* 65 (1967): 441–473.

60. Richard S. Cohen and Gary S. Klein, "A Proposed Solution to the Legal Problems of Workmen's Compensation Heart Cases," *Supplemental Studies for the National Commission on State Workmen's Compensation Laws,* vol. I (Washington, D.C.: GPO, 1973), pp. 179–188.

61. George A. Hellmuth, "Medical Studies on Workmen's Compensation," *Industrial Medicine and Surgery* (September 1967): 604.

62. Robert V. R. Dalenberg, "Coronary Heart Disease and the Law."

63. George A. Hellmuth, "Medical Studies on Workmen's Compensation."

64. Cited in Cohen and Klein, *Supplemental Studies,* pp. 179–188.

65. "Report of the Committee on the Effect of Strain and Trauma on the Heart and Great Vessels," *Circulation,* 26 (October 1962): 618.

66. George A. Hellmuth, Phillip J. Hellmuth, and Walter J. Johannsen, "Attorney Attitudes on Medicolegal Criteria Proposed for Workmen's Compensation Cardiac Claim Cases," *The Journal of Occupational Medicine* 11, 9 (September 1969): 466–474.

67. Hellmuth, "Medical Studies on Workmen's Compensation," p. 604.

68. Jack E. Goshkin, "Legislative Action, The Only Reasonable Solution to the Problems of Workmen's Compensation Heart Cases," *The Forum* V, no. 4 (July 1970): 329.

69. Larson, *Workmen's Compensation Law,* vol. 1-A, 7–166.

70. Cohen and Klein, *Supplemental Studies,* pp. 179–188.

71. R. Kenneth Roberts, "Problems and Suggested Solutions to Cardiovascular Cases in the Workmen's Compensation Field," *Willamette Law Journal* 6, no. 1 (March 1970): 95–110.

72. *Warren* v. *General Motors Corp.,* 344 A. 2d 240 (1975).

73. See, for example, *Solomon* v. *Gannett Co.,* App. Div., 309 N.Y.S. 2d 470 (1970).

74. *Baudry* v. *Winchester Plywood Co.,* 469 P. 2d 25 (1970).

75. *Hammond* v. *Albina Engine & Machine Works, Inc.,* 534 P. 2d 1163 (1975).

76. *Jenkins* v. *Ogletree Farm Supply,* 290 So. 2d 550 (1974).

77. *Riddle* v. *Broad Crane Engineering Co.,* 218 N.W. 2d 845 (1974).

78. See, for example, *Johnson* v. *State Workmen's Compensation Commissioner* 186 S.E. 2d 771 (1972).

79. *Self* v. *Star Davis Co.,* 187 S.E. 2d 466 (1972).

80. DHEW, *Limitations of Activity Due to Chronic Conditions,* Vital and Health Statistics Series 10, no. 80 (April 1973): 20.

81. I. J. Selikoff, E. C. Hammond, and J. Churg, "Asbestos Exposure, Smoking and Neoplasia," *Journal of American Medical Association,* 204 (1968): 106–112.

82. Seymour Jablon, "Radiation" in *Persons at High Risk of Cancer,* ed. Joseph F. Fraumeni, Jr. (New York: Academic Press, 1975), p. 160.

83. *Dillow* v. *Florida Portland Cement Plant,* 258 S. 2d 266 (1972).

84. Larson, *Workmen's Compensation Law,* vol. 2 (1976): 10–267.

85. *Bannister* v. *State Workmen's Compensation Commissioner,* 174 S.E. 2d 605 (1970).

86. *Fuentes* v. *Workers' Compensation Appeals Board,* 547 P. 2d 449 (1976).

87. Larson, *Workmen's Compensation Law,* vol. 1-A (1973): 7–333.

88. Much of the material on the background of statutes of limitations is drawn from Kelley, *Washington University Law Quarterly,* pp. 541–631.

89. Ibid.

90. *Yocom* v. *Jones,* Kentucky Court of Appeals, March 31, 1972.

91. See, for example, *Yocom* v. *Butcher,* Kentucky Court of Appeals, April 25, 1975; *Yocom* v. *Tinker,* 514 SW. 2d 686 (1974); or *Yocom* v. *Overstreet,* 512 SW. 2d 940 (1974).

92. *Bethlehem Steel Co.* v. *Gray,* 288 A. 2d 828 (1972).

93. *Carr* v. *Homestake Mining Co.,* 215 N.W. 2d 830 (1974).

94. California allowed compensation in *Van Voorhis* v. *Workmen's Comp. App. Brd.,* 112 Cal. Rptr. 208 (1974).

95. Richard Ginnold, "Workmen's Compensation for Hearing Loss in Wisconsin," *Labor Law Journal* 25, no. 11 (1974): 682–697.

96. *Kopp* v. *Delco Products Division, General Motors Corp.,* 375 N.Y.S. 2d 42 (1975).

97. *Russell* v. *Union Forging Co.,* 247 N.E. 2d 855 (1969).

98. Larson, *Workmen's Compensation Law,* vol. 1 (1972), pp. 10, 11. See also Blair, *Reference Guide to Workmen's Compensation,* note 14, "Occupational Disease."

99. See, for example, *The Report of the National Commission on State Workmen's Compensation Laws,* p. 38.

100. David P. Discher, Goldy Kleinman, and F. James Foster, *Pilot Study for Development of an Occupational Disease Surveillance Method,* HEW publication no. (NIOSH) 75-162 (Rockville, MD: NIOSH, May 1975).

101. *Stepnowski* v. *Specific Pharmaceuticals,* 87A. 2d 546 (1952).

102. *The Washington Post,* "Working Women and Birth Defects," April 17, 1976.

103. See the case of permanent and total disability described in *American Steel Foundries* v. *Industrial Commission,* 304 N.E. 2d 604 (1973).

104. See, for example, *Adams* v. *Rochester Products Division, General Motors Corp.,* 377 N.Y.S. 2d 665 (1975).

105. Ginnold, *Labor Law Journal,* pp. 682–697. Larson also cites this case as the initiator in *Workmen's Compensation Law,* vol. 1-A, (1973). The case can be found in 81 N.E. 2d 93 (1948).

106. *Hinkle* v. *H. J. Heinz Co.,* 298 A. 2d 632 (1972).

107. *Van Voorhis* v. *Workmen's Comp. App. Board,* 112 Cal. Rptr. 208 (1974).

108. Lloyd Larsen, *Dust Diseases and Workers Compensation,* Inderdepartmental Workers' Compensation Task Force, unpublished report, June 1975, pp. 4-5.

109. Ginnold, *Labor Law Journal,* pp. 682-697.

110. John D. Stoeckle, Harriet L. Hardy, and B. Chang-Wai Ling, "The Compensation Experience of Patients with Chronic Beryllium Disease," *Journal of Occupational Medicine* 17, no. 3 (March 1975): 167-170.

111. *Dickow* v. *Workmen's Compensation Appeals Board,* 109 Cal. Rptr. 317 (1973).

112. *Langlais* v. *Superior Plating, Inc.,* 226 N.W. 2d 891 (1975).

113. *Van Voorhis* v. *Workmen's Comp. App. Board,* 112 Cal. Rptr. 208 (1974).

114. *Goodman* v. *Bay Castings Division of Gulf & Western Industries,* 212 N.W. 2d 799 (1973).

115. *Aseltine* v. *Leto Construction Co.,* 204 N.W. 2d 262 (1972).

116. *Yocum* v. *Eastern Coal Corporation,* 523 S.W. 2d 882 (1075).

117. *Aetna Casulty & Surety Co.* v. *Luker,* 511 S.W. 2d 587 (1974).

118. *Fields Plastics of Tennessee, Inc.* v. *Ownby,* 518 S.W. 2d 356 (1974).

119. *Williams* v. *Clinchfield Coal Co.,* 192 S.E. 2d 751 (1972). The case is also the subject of a note in *Virginia Law Review* 59 (1973): 1632-4.

120. This is given in more detail in *Corpus Juris Secundum, Annual Supplement,* vol. 99, (St. Paul, Minnesota: West Publishing Co., 1975), p. 1154. See also *Honeycutt* v. *Carolina Asbestos Co.,* 70 S.E. 2d 426.

121. Larson, *Workmen's Compensation Law,* vol. 1-A, p. 7-333.

Notes to Chapter 5

1. National Industrial Conference Board, *Summary of Report on Workmen's Compensation Acts in the United States—The Legal Phase* (Boston: NICB, 1917), p. 6.

2. Injuries reported for Nebraska are contained in their Annual Report for FY 1974-75. Data on cases indemnified are from material supplied by Ben Novicoff to the author.

3. California Department of Industrial Relations, *California Work Injuries: 1974* (February 1976), p. 9.

4. *Countrywide Workmen's Compensation Experience Including Certain Competitive State Funds,* National Council on Compensation Insurance (July 1975), unpublished report.

5. David P. Discher, Goldy Kleinman, and F. James Foster, *Pilot Study for Development of an Occupational Disease Surveillance Method,* HEW publication no. (NIOSH) 75-162 (Rockville, MD: NIOSH, May 1975).

6. Thomas J. O'Toole, *The Incidence, Nature and Adjudication of Workmen's Compensation Claims Involving Radiation Exposure and Delayed Injury, Studies in Workmen's Compensation and Radiation Injury,* vol. II, Atomic Energy Commission and U.S. Department of Labor (undated monograph), pp. 34-35.

7. Victoria Giammattei, "Workmen's Compensation—Diseases Arising out of Employment—A Problem of Proof," *Pacific Law Journal* 2, no. 2 (July 1971): 678-696.

8. Cooper and Co., *Report on Closed Case Survey for the Interdepartmental Workers' Compensation Task Force* (1976), draft.

Notes to Chapter 6

1. Trades Union Congress, for the Royal Commission on Civil Liability and Compensation for Personal Injury, "Injuries in the Course of Employment," unpublished report, undated, pp. 13–14.

2. Cited in "Injuries in the Course of Employment," p. 5, *Wallhead* v. *Ruston and Hornsby Ltd.,* QBD, January 15, 1973.

3. Ibid., pp. 15–16.

4. Ibid, p. 17.

5. Ibid., p. 18.

6. Ibid., p. 20.

7. Ibid., pp. 19–20.

8. From Table 20.64, "Social Security Statistics, 1975," Department of Health and Social Security, U.K., 1977.

9. Personal interview with Mr. Martin Wooley, Social Security Office, June 1976.

10. *Rapport Annuel, Exercise 1974* (Brussels: Fonds des Maladies Professionnelles), pp. 71, 72.

11. Ibid., pp. 43, 44.

12. Ibid., pp. 52, 53.

13. Ibid., p. 55.

14. All quantitative data on the Swiss system are drawn from the quinquennial report, "Résultats de la Statisque des Accidents" (Lucerne: Caisse Nationale Suisse d'Assurance en cas d'Accidents, 1974). For this item see p. 23.

15. Ibid., p. 59.

16. Ibid., p. 59.

17. Ibid., p. 20.

18. "Bericht der Expertenkommission für die Revision der Unfallversicherung vom 14 September 1973" (Berne, 1973).

19. "The Kindest Place in Europe," *The Economist,* May 29, 1976; and "Holland Gets Feeling Something is Wrong," *The Washington Post,* November 27, 1976.

20. *The Washington Post,* November 27, 1976.

Notes to Chapter 7

1. This is more fully discussed in Peter S. Barth, "The Effort to Rehabilitate Workers' Compensation," *American Journal of Public Health* 66, no. 6 (June 1976): 553–557.

2. John Stoeckle, Harriet L. Hardy, and B. Chang-Wai Ling, "The Compensation Experience of Patients with Chronic Beryllium Disease," *Journal of Occupational Medicine* 17, no. 3 (March 1975): 167–170.

3. A fuller treatment of this issue that arrives at this conclusion can be found in Nicholas A. Ashford, *Crisis in the Workplace: Occupational Disease and Injury* (Cambridge, MA: The MIT Press, 1976), especially chapter 7 and section 7.3.4.

4. Robert Stewart Smith, *The Occupational Safety and Health Act: Its Goals and Its Achievements* (Washington, D.C.: American Enterprise Institute, 1976).

5. Janet B. Schoenberg and Charles A. Mitchell, "Implementation of the Federal Asbestos Standard in Connecticut," *The Journal of Occupational Medicine* 16, no. 11 (November 1974): 781–784.

6. Personal communication from the late Henry Howe.

7. Thomas J. O'Toole, *The Incidence, Nature and Adjudication of Workmen's Compensation Claims Involving Radiation Exposure and Delayed Injury, Studies in Workmen's Compensation and Radiation Injury,* vol. II, AEC and Department of Labor (undated monograph), p. 34.

8. *McGill Mfg. Co.* v. *Dodd,* 59 N.E. 2d 889 (1945).

9. Charles F. Eason, "Workmen's Compensation for the Radiation Worker—The Role of the Atomic Energy Commission," *Proceedings of the American Bar Association, Insurance, Negligence and Compensation Section* (1970), 136–153.

10. P. Cole, "Epidemiologic Studies and Surveillance of Human Cancers Among Personnel of Virus Laboratories," eds. A. Hellman, M. N. Oxman, and R. Pollack, *Biohazards in Biological Research* (New York: Cold Spring Harbor Laboratory, 1973).

11. David P. Discher, Goldy Kleinman, and F. James Foster, *Pilot Study for Development of an Occupational Disease Surveillance Method,* HEW publication no. (NIOSH) 75–162 (Rockville, MD: NIOSH: May 1975).

12. Barth, "The Effort to Rehabilitate Workers' Compensation," pp. 553–557.

13. Peter S. Barth, "The Costs of Occupational Diseases," Conference on Workers' Compensation and Occupational Diseases, Chicago, Illinois, February 9–12, 1976, part 1.

Notes to Appendix B

1. *Aseltine* v. *Leto Construction Company,* 204 NW 2d 262 (1972).

2. W. M. Gafefer, ed., *Occupational Diseases: A Guide to Their Recognition,* Public Health Service Publication no. 1097 (Washington, D.C.: GPO, 1964).

3. Ibid.

4. Thomas F. Mancuso, "Medical Aspects of Occupational Diseases," *Ohio State Law Journal* 19, no. 4 (1958): 612–667.

5. Ibid., pp. 612–613.

6. *Occupation and Disease—A Guide for Decision-Making,* Contract 210-75-0075 (NIOSH, 1976), unpublished draft.

7. Jeanne M. Stellman and Susan M. Daum, *Work is Dangerous to Your Health* (New York: Pantheon Books, 1973), pp. 368–419.

8. Ibid., pp. 399, 410–411.

9. Gafefer, *Occupational Diseases: A Guide to Their Recognition.*

10. E. E. Pochin, "Occupational and Other Fatality Rates," *Community Health* 6, no. 2 (1974): 9.

11. Philip Cole and Marlene Goldman, "Occupation," in *Persons at High Risk of Cancer,* ed. Joseph F. Fraumeni, Jr. (New York: Academic Press, 1975), table 1.

12. National Cancer Institute, "Common Occupational Carcinogens," in *Health and Work in America—Chart Book,* American Public Health Association, November 1975, table 25.

13. Bertram D. Dinman, *The Nature of Occupational Cancer* (Springfield, IL: Charles C. Thomas, 1974), p. 34.

14. Thomas F. Mancuso, "Relation of Duration of Employment and Prior Respiratory Illness to Respiratory Cancer Among Beryllium Workers," *Environmental Research* 3, no. 3 (July 1970): 251–275.

15. U.S., Department of Labor, *Beryllium* Job Health Hazards Series, OSHA #2239, (1976), p. 2.

16. *The Carcinogenesis Program-Fiscal Year 1975,* Division of Cancer Cause and Prevention, National Cancer Institute, DHEW Publication #(NIH) 76–91 (Bethesda, MD: N.C.I., 1976).

17. See Samuel S. Epstein, "Cancer and the Environment: A Scientific Perspective," *Facts and Analysis, Occupational Safety and Health* no. 25 (IUD: February 1976), p. 9.

18. Letter from J. William Lloyd, "Background Information on Polychlorinated Biphenyls," NIOSH, 3, 1975.

19. Letter from John F. Finklea, "Background Information on 4, 4' Diaminodphenylmethane," NIOSH, 30, 1976.

20. E. R. Plunkett, "Occupational Health Service, Seven Common Problems," in *Occupational Medicine Symposia* (Washington, D.C.: GPO–NIOSH, 1975), pp. III-12–III-16.

21. Donald Hunter, *The Diseases of Occupations,* 4th and 5th eds. (London: The English Universities Press, Ltd., 1969 and 1975).

22. Mancuso, "Medical Aspects of Occupational Disease," pp. 612–667; May R. Mayers, *Occupational Health: Hazards of the Work Environment* (Baltimore: The Williams and Wilkins Co., 1969).

INDEX